GREGORY S. KEALEY is a member of the Department of History at Dalhousie University, Nova Scotia.

Toronto's Industrial Revolution of the 1850s and 1860s transformed the city's economy and created a distinct working class. This book examines the workers' role in the transition to industrial capitalism and traces the emergence of a strong trade union movement in the latter half of the nineteenth century.

Immigrant workers were already organized along ethnic lines and voluntary societies like the Orange Order played an informal but active part in the broad pattern of social change. Artisan groups were more directly instrumental in developing strategies to cope with the new pressures of industrial capitalism. In the period covered by this book Toronto's moulders and printers maintained and even strengthened the traditions of workers' control in the shop. The shoemakers and coopers were less successful, but the lessons of their defeats made them important early members of the Knights of Labor in the 1880s.

The Knights of Labor gave new direction to labour organization. They recruited all workers regardless of skill, sex, creed, or race, and spearheaded the direct involvement of Toronto workers in electoral politics. The final chapters of the book trace the tortured path of working class politics from the early activities of the Orange Order to the emergence of a vibrant minority socialist tradition.

Between 1867 and 1892 Toronto workers established a strong institutional base for the new struggles between craft unionism and monopoly capitalism in the early twentieth century and Kealey's detailed study of its development adds a new and important dimension to our understanding of Canadian labour history.

GREGORY S. KEALEY

Toronto Workers Respond to Industrial Capitalism 1867–1892

UNIVERSITY OF TORONTO PRESS
Toronto Buffalo London

© University of Toronto Press 1980
Toronto Buffalo London
Printed in Canada

FOR LINDA

Canadian Cataloguing in Publication Data

Kealey, Gregory S., 1948–
 Toronto Workers Respond to
 Industrial Capitalism 1867–1892

 Based on the author's thesis, University of
 Rochester.
 Bibliography: p.
 Includes index.

 ISBN 0-8020-5488-9 bd.   ISBN 0-8020-6393-4 pa.

 1. Labor and laboring classes – Ontario – Toronto –
 History – 19th century.   2. Toronto, Ont. – Economic
 conditions.   1. Title.

 HD8110.T62K43   330.9713'541'03   C79-094837-0

This book has been published with the help of grants from the Social Science
Federation of Canada, using funds provided by the Social Sciences and Humanities
Research Council of Canada, and from the Publications Fund of University of
Toronto Press.

Contents

Tables

Acknowledgments

For financial assistance at various stages of the research involved in producing this study, I am indebted to the Central Mortgage and Housing Corporation, the Canada Council, the Dalhousie Research and Development Fund, and the Ontario Arts Council. For bibliographic and archival assistance, I would like to thank the countless librarians and archivists who have aided me in the last ten years, and especially Nancy Stunden of the Public Archives of Canada, Moreau Chambers of the Catholic University Archives in Washington, DC, and the interlibrary loan staffs at the University of Rochester, University of Toronto, and Dalhousie University. My typist, Bette Tetreault, deserves much credit for her consistently excellent work. In the latter stages of this project, I have also benefited from research assistance from Michael Ryan, Karen Sanders, Peter Lambly, Keith Johnston, and Pamela Manley. I would also like to thank Sonia Paine, Lorraine Ourom, and R.I.K. Davidson of University of Toronto Press.

My interest in the Toronto working class as a historical subject began in the late 1960s at the University of Toronto. I would like to thank Michael Bliss and J.M.S. Careless for putting up with me, Michael Cross for his sympathetic support, and Jill Kerr Conway for opening entirely new vistas to me. This book actually began as a doctoral dissertation for the University of Rochester. I owe an immeasurable debt to my supervisors: Herbert Gutman taught me how to read all over again, and Christopher Lasch began teaching me how to write. This book also owes much to the general intellectual climate of the University of Rochester History Department in the early 1970s; although not always a happy place, it never failed to be intellectually vibrant. I thank, in addition to Gutman and Lasch, Eugene Genovese for that. I also thank my student colleagues – Florence Bartoshesky, Nick Builder, Leon Fink, Russel Jacoby, William Leach, and

David Noble – for the intellectual environment owed much to their stimulation as well. Since my coming to Dalhousie, I have been equally lucky. I would like to thank my colleagues there for their help, especially Michael Cross, Don Davis, Judy Fingard, John O'Brien, David Sutherland, and all the other participants in the Department of History's North American Seminar.

My greatest intellectual debts, however, are to my most immediate colleagues, my fellow students of the Canadian working-class experience; to David Frank, Craig Heron, Ian McKay, John Manley, Bryan Palmer, Nolan Reilly, and Wayne Roberts, I offer not only thanks but a willingness to implicate them in this book. All of them have read it and have criticized vast parts of it, thereby enriching my efforts.

I don't even know how to begin to thank Russell Hann. Over the last ten years we have been engaged in a joint intellectual process of which this book is only one small part. We have shared in so many discussions, so much research, so many projects that ultimately all of my work bears his imprint. I can only hope that it lives up to his expectations.

Finally, this book is dedicated to Linda Kealey. She knows why.

Gregory S. Kealey
Halifax, 1978

Abbreviations

AFL	American Federation of Labor
APS	Anti-Poverty Society
ASC	Amalgamated Society of Carpenters
ASE	Amalgamated Society of Engineers
BLE	Brotherhood of Locomotive Engineers
BSWIU	Boot and Shoe Workers International Union
CIU	Coopers International Union
CJ	*Coopers Journal*
CLAA	Criminal Law Amendment Act
CLR	Canadian Labor Reformer
CLU	Canadian Labor Union
CMIU	Cigarmakers International Union
DA	District Assembly (KOL)
DMW	District Master Workman (KOL)
FRL	Financial Reform League of Canada
GA	General Assembly (KOL)
IAM	International Association of Machinists
IMIU	Iron Molders International Union
IMJ	*Iron Molders Journal*
ITU	International Typographical Union
JUL	*Journal of United Labor*
KOL	Knights of Labor
KOSC	Knights of St Crispin
LA	Local Assembly (KOL)
LC	Legislative Committee
MLA	Mechanics' Lien Act
MSA	Master and Servant Act

MW	Master Workman (KOL)
NTA	National Trades Assembly
OW	*Ontario Workman*
POL	*Palladium of Labor*
STA	Single Tax Association
TLC	Trades and Labor Congress
TSR	Toronto Street Railway
TTA	Toronto Trades Assembly
TTLC	Toronto Trades and Labour Council
TTU	Toronto Typographical Union
WLCU	Workingmen's Liberal Conservative Union

Introduction

This work was first conceived in the late 1960s at the University of Toronto. Those were exciting and stimulating years in North American universities, and many accepted dogmas came under rigorous re-examination. Canadian history was one discipline which did not stand up well to the new styles of questioning then prevalent. The Canadian historiographical tradition has been extremely narrow except for a brief flowering in the 1930s when, under the leadership of Harold Innis, considerable useful work was done on the Canadian political economy. After the 1930s, however, Canadian history retreated into biography and into politics quite narrowly and traditionally defined. The new intellectual currents of the 1960s and 1970s – the 'conversion' of the social sciences to history, the brilliant new English Marxist historical writing, and the new accessibility of previously untranslated Marxist theoretical work – were only then beginning to touch Canadian historical writing. They suggested quite different approaches to the study of the Canadian past.

Class was one factor of analysis that had been almost totally ignored in Canadian historical writing; the working class, for example, had received almost no systematic study. The minor tradition of labour studies had either been tied to policy-oriented research for government and business, or stemmed from outside the academy. Practitioners outside the academy had been mainly amateur enthusiasts from the labour movement itself or from left-wing political groups. Although often of great value as a historical source, their work was somewhat antiquarian and very conservative methodologically. The only exceptions to these generalizations were a few political economists such as Harold Logan and Eugene Forsey, both of whom restricted the study of the working class to its most narrow institutional sense.*

The need for a history of the Canadian working class which was sensitive to new historical approaches and methodological innovations was quite apparent. Equally clear, however, was the lack of any historical tradition upon which to build. As Eugene Forsey pointed out in the 1960s, Canadian labour history had not even established a factually accurate institutional record. This was the task he took on, and the product of his labour is now nearing completion. A synthetic work then was not possible. In the 1960s Hebert Gutman in the United States and numerous French scholars were demonstrating the utility of community studies as a method of investigating new questions about the working class.

A community study appeared to be the place, then, to begin to reconstruct Canadian working-class experience. The city of Toronto was chosen because of its economic importance and its key role in the development of the early labour movement. Living in Ontario's leading city, Toronto workers were among the first to experience the industrial revolution, to join international unions, to create a city labour centre, and to initiate a province-wide, and later a national, labour organization. Moreover, Toronto proved to be especially rich in archival and library holdings pertinent to the proposed study. The city's nineteenth-century press was extremely vibrant and well-preserved, its trade-union records and other materials were rich and exceptionally well maintained, and the city had had a lively labour press much of which was still extant.

The period of the mid- to late-nineteenth century was chosen in order to capture the Toronto working-class at its conception. The 'making' of the class lay in industrialization and in the workers' response to that process. This is a study of the interaction of the emerging working class with the economic transformation that both shaped and was in turn shaped by the new class. The birth of trade unionism, the significant struggle for shorter hours in the 1870s, the dramatic surge of an oppositional culture based on the Knights of Labor in the 1880s, and ultimately the establishment of an institutional framework for the trade union movement lay in this period. The development of the working class created important new organiza-

---

* For a fuller discussion of Canadian labour history traditions see Greg Kealey, 'Introduction,' in *Canada Investigates Industrialism* (Toronto 1973), ix–xxvii; R.G. Hann, G. Kealey, L. Kealey, and Peter Warrian, 'Introduction,' in *Primary Sources in Canadian Working Class History, 1860–1930* (Kitchener 1973), 9–20; and G.S. Kealey, 'H.C. Pentland and Working Class Studies,' *Canadian Journal of Political and Social Theory*, 3 (1979), 79–94.

tions, but a full analysis demanded that they be placed in the context of economic transformation and cultural adaptation which institutional labour history had traditionally denied them.

Research began with a systematic reading of the 1867–92 issues of the Toronto newspaper, the *Globe*. The *Globe* was chosen because it was the only daily which published throughout the period under study. It became clear, however, that the *Globe*'s highly partisan nature demanded that Toronto's Tory press be delved into as well. Thus the *Leader*, the *Mail*, and to a lesser extent the *Telegraph*, *Telegram*, and *World* were added. It also became clear that the most valuable papers were not necessarily the staid, partisan morning papers such as the *Globe* and the *Mail*. The sensational penny evening newspapers such as the *News*, published in the 1880s, proved useful because of their stance as 'the people's press.'

This day-by-day reading of the Toronto press allowed the reconstruction of consistent data on organizational activities and strike activity on the part of Toronto workers (described in Appendix II). More important, however, was the familiarity with the total Toronto world that it provided.

The first two chapters provide an overview of Toronto's industrial development in this period. They describe Toronto's industrial revolution and argue that by 1871 Toronto had already attained a significant level of industrialization. The 1871 manuscript industrial census is analysed in depth to reconstruct the Toronto economy and to delineate its most important industrial sectors. Part one also provides a brief description of the strategies of the industrial capitalists and their successful lobbying efforts to achieve a high-tariff policy. The development of the industrial capitalist economy under the national policy is sketched. By the early 1890s capital was poised to enter its monopoly phase.

Immigrants constituted between one-half and one-third of Toronto's population throughout this period. Ethnicity, then, was of crucial importance; ethnic voluntary societies, in general, and the Orange Order, in particular, were extremely significant in the workers' lives. Chapter 7 provides an analysis of the history, ritual, functions, membership, and leadership of the Toronto Orange Order. Historians have generally focused only on the order's bigoted role in national politics, but here we see the order in a local context which shows its varied uses within the working-class community. Chapter 7 assesses the impact of the ritual religious riots that periodically erupted in Toronto between Orange and Green.

Green and Orange shoemakers joined together to create the Knights of St Crispin, which previously had been treated as the exemplary case for the Commons' school version of North American labour history. Chapter 3 provides Canadian evidence to support recent American findings that demonstrate that the old view of the Knights as a backward-looking artisan group desperately trying to retain their monopoly of skill cannot be sustained by the evidence. In Toronto, as in Lynn, the Knights of St Crispin (KOSC) organized all shoe-factory workers and even tried to organize the female shoe-operatives. Their attempt to organize their sister workers was the final straw that drew the combined efforts of the factory owners to smash their union. The KOSC managed to resist these, but what the bosses had failed to achieve, the depression of the 1870s accomplished. The lessons of the 1870s were remembered, however, and shoemakers flooded into the Knights of Labor (KOL) in the 1880s in Toronto and elsewhere. Toronto shoemakers also made use of yet older traditions and in the 1870s engaged in a flurry of machine-breaking at one Toronto factory. Their use of the artisanal heritage was evident in the name and ritual of their order.

Similarly, Toronto coopers made extensive use of their traditional trade practices in their attempt to create a strong union to protect themselves against the assaults of industrial capital. Although ultimately a failure, the Coopers International Union (CIU) pioneered numerous trade-union practices in the early 1870s and, like the shoemakers, coopers learned from their losses and were an important addition to the Knights of Labor in the 1880s.

Toronto moulders and printers had different experiences than their brother workers. Moulders came up against a vigorous combined management assault before most workers in North America. Yet their monopoly of skill and their strong union allowed them to struggle successfully with iron founders across North America. In Toronto stove foundries, the bosses repeatedly tried to break the Iron Molders International Union (IMIU), but continually failed. They won short-term battles but were unable to find suitable substitute workers when the IMIU listed their shops as unfair. These struggles usually revolved around the control over production and the work process that the moulders had created over time, both of which were rigorously enforced by their union. Bosses in foundries complained throughout the period that they did not control their own businesses.

Toronto printers employed similar techniques and actually increased their strength throughout the period. They added to their skill monopoly an extremely astute political sense which they used as the major leaders of the Toronto trade-union movement and to achieve a considerable degree of importance in local and even national politics. By the time they faced a dilution of skill caused by the invention of the linotype machine, their union was strong enough to dictate the terms on which the machines would be introduced in the industry. Thus the printers not only retained their shop control but actually extended it to include the new machines and even to establish limits of production on the new equipment.

Industrialization, then, affected different workers at different times; some trades were strong enough to maintain their unions and considerable strength. Those that did not and those that could see the writing on the wall began to establish in the 1880s a new strategy based not on the maintenance of skill, but rather on the complete organization of the working class. This strategy found its fullest organizational expression in the Knights of Labor, which grew rapidly in Toronto in the middle years of that decade. The order tried to organize all Toronto workers regardless of skill, sex, race, or ethnicity. Peaking in 1886, the Knights had by then organized over 5,000 Toronto workers, including female factory-operatives and unskilled labourers. The order's struggle with the hated Toronto Street Railway Company in summer 1886 saw the working class of the city rally to the Knights' support. The collective violence of the Toronto crowd against the company's attempt to operate cars with scabs forced the company to compromise. The next time, however, the forces of capital united, and the Knights pursued a co-operative strategy that had disastrous results. The 1886 strike failures made the Knights' leadership increasingly cautious; it abandoned its own workers in 1887 and then broke an alliance with the Brotherhood of Carpenters and Joiners and the Amalgamated Society of Carpenters. These steps led to renewed trade-union opposition to the order, and together with the public political squabbling which broke out in 1887, they hastened the demise of the order, which, nevertheless, maintained an important presence into the 1890s.

The final four chapters of the book turn to Toronto workers in politics. Much recent social history has totally eschewed the realm of politics, thus begging many important questions about class which are quite important to pursue. The necessity of devising a method of understanding working-class politics which transcends the traditional views is an important challenge. The first traditional position is that workers played no role because there was no working class politically conscious of itself. The second, which avidly pursues the rise of labour politics, manages to dismiss as unworthy of consideration all political activity that does not fit this quest. The two versions, which proceed from quite antithetical political beliefs, ironically have the identical effect of dismissing the role of the working class in the political realm before the rise of third-party traditions and then assuming that the working class is defined solely in terms of those third-party traditions. The treatment of politics in this book attempts to do justice to Tory and Grit workingmen and to show the influence they had over party policy both in government and in opposition. It also tries to broaden the definition of politics to include more than just electoral behaviour. Toronto workers throughout this period were actively engaged in politics, and the working class did influence the political and economic decisions that were taken, both in a positive and in a negative sense. After 1872, and especially in the mid-1880s, governments regarded the working class with much concern.

The final chapter of the book proper focuses on the campaign for municipal ownership of the street railway mounted by labour and its left-wing allies in 1891. Although ultimately a failure, this campaign illustrated well the important oppositional role that labour had come to play by the end of the period.

There is much in the world of Toronto workers that remains unexplored here. Family life, education, the role of women, leisure activities, sports, and religion are only a few themes that might have been included to supply a fuller picture. Moreover, more data on organizational matters were available than are presented here. Each trade in Toronto could have been profiled as was done with the shoemakers and printers. A single study, however, is a limited vehicle and here I have chosen to pursue the series of topics which seemed most important and interesting over recent years. The volume does not claim to be a definitive or complete work on the Toronto working class, but is a series of studies of the workers' direct response to the arrival of industrial capitalism. The work will have succeeded to the extent that it provides convincing evidence that the working class was not just 'made' but rather was the result of a dialectical interplay of class forces in which it was one of the actors.

PART ONE
TORONTO'S AGE OF CAPITAL

1

Toronto and a national policy

Between the late 1840s and the early 1890s Canada experienced its own
industrial revolution. Toronto, Canada's second largest city, played a
major role in this transformation. Its capitalists led the strategic drive for
protective tariffs, enabling native industries to thrive and prosper; its
working class provided the leadership for organized labour in central
Canada.

Most Canadian economic history to date has dealt mainly with the role of
staple exports in Canadian development.[1] They have been viewed as
dominating the economy until the early twentieth century, when finally
some attention is paid to industrial development.[2] Although suggestive
when first pursued in the 1930s, this approach has obscured key components of the nineteenth-century Canadian economy, especially the
emergence of industry. Attention to cod, beaver, pine, wheat, and to the
rivers, the canals, and the railroads that carried them to market has unfortunately all but excluded the study of the mills and factories which grew on
their banks and built their rails and locomotives.[3]

The few scholars who have studied early Canadian manufacturing have
all too often restricted their attention to the published census returns. The
aggregate data on industrial development disguises much that the available
manuscript returns reveal. For example, Toronto in 1871 had 9400 workers
spread throughout approximately 560 shops and factories. This suggests
that the average Toronto worker was employed in a relatively small shop
situation with about sixteen other employees. But such an 'average' totally
obscures the reality of the Toronto economy in 1870. Actually 38 per cent
of Toronto's industrial work force was employed in factories of over a
hundred workers. Another 21 per cent worked with between 50 and 99
other employees and 11 per cent worked in shops with between 30 and 49

TABLE 1.1

Toronto factories employing over 30 workers, 1871

Number of workers	Number of establishments	% of ests.	Number of workers	% of workers
100+	19	3	3,594	36
50–99	30	5	2,074	20.7
30–49	28	5	1,046	10.5
Total 30+	77	13	6,714	67.1
0–29	495	88	3,285	32.9

Source: Canada Census, 1871, Industrial Mss., Toronto
Calculations throughout this book are my own.

others. Thus, fully 70 per cent of Toronto workers in 1871 worked in shops or factories employing over 30 men and women (see Table 1.1). The old pre-industrial labour market revolving around personal contact between employer and employee in small shops no longer prevailed in Toronto. How had this new industrial-capitalist labour market been created?

Answering that question first requires a discussion of the broader development of industrial capitalism in Canada. First I shall sketch the emergence of an industrial capitalist development-strategy increasingly reliant on the use of the Canadian state. Then in chapter 2 the focus will shift to Toronto to trace the specific development of Toronto industry between 1850 and the early 1890s.

Recent Canadian economic historians,[4] especially Tom Naylor, have argued that Canadian industrial capitalism developed as a peculiar hybrid shaped by the colonial context and the Canadian bourgeoisie's inability to pursue industrial development as its primary aim. Here I shall argue that industrial capitalist development in central Canada in the period under study displays no such weaknesses. The Toronto case will provide the specific evidence, but it is important first to demonstrate the creation of a concerted and comprehensive industrial-capitalist strategy of development in central Canada.

The late 1840s and 1850s mark the crucial transition years in the evolution of the Canadian economy. In the mid-1840s the British Industrial Revolution had proceeded sufficiently far that England began to dismantle its old colonial system. The system of preferential tariffs on timber and grain that had shaped the Canadian economy was systematically removed. Its removal caused a panic in Canadian merchant circles which burgeoned with the arrival in the same year of hordes of Irish-Catholic famine migrants. The disembarking of huge numbers of impoverished, starving, and often diseased Irish threw Canadian cities into turmoil. The final blow came in 1849 when Lord Elgin signed the hated Rebellion Losses Bill which recompensed all Canadians for their losses in 1837 – possibly, opponents alleged, including even some of the rebels. This was too much for the Toronto and Montreal merchant elites who rioted a number of times in the summer of 1849 and began discussing annexation to the United States.

Yet cooler heads prevailed and out of these crises emerged the major strategies that would transform the Canadian economy: protection, railways, and Confederation. The first had been present as a potential development strategy since the early 1830s. In both 1830 and 1831 Toronto cabinet-makers, led by Thomas Wallis, had petitioned the Assembly to prevent the importation of furniture which competed with the domestic product.[5] These petitions failed, and the subject disappeared until the early 1840s when shoemakers from Montreal, Kingston, and Belleville petitioned for protection against American imports.[6] The economic crisis precipitated by British free trade greatly increased interest in protection and in home manufactures. Robert Baldwin Sullivan, a former Canadian Legislative Councillor and Provincial Secretary in the Baldwin-LaFontaine ministry of 1848, became protection's most prominent promoter. In an inaugural address to the Hamilton Mechanics' Institute in November 1847, Sullivan strongly advocated a strategy of industrial development as the only solution to the current crisis.[7] In reviewing the economic history of the young country, he revised conventional wisdom, arguing that the fur trade had been of 'no use to Canada' since the 'profits of their enterprise were realized at a distance, or were remitted thither.'[8] Moreover, the timber trade was only slightly more beneficial to Canada, but 'in proportion to its magnitude, it has been of little advantage. Finally, the operation of the current wheat and flour trade was dismissed in similar terms. The Canadian economy's historical problem was clear: 'For many, very many, years, the people of this country manufactured nothing for themselves; and up to this day articles of the coarsest and most simple fabric, and in the most common use, are brought in ready-made in vast quantities.' As a result Canada was not developing:

And these towns would have furnished a home market for a large portion of the produce of the land, and have become as they did in the early times of English History, places in which the capital of the country would have accumulated. However slow and difficult the accumulation might have been, we still should have the fruits of industry ready to be expended in new enterprise. Capital would be reproducing capital, and town and country acting and re-acting on each other, to the advantage of both.

Instead, all 'the profits of the manufactures in this Province have accumulated in England.' The remainder of the lecture polemicized in favour of home manufactures as the obvious and only solution to Canada's economic woes. Searching the province for favourable examples, Sullivan described the Marmora Iron Works, a few woollen mills, and some foundries, but the very paucity of examples helped demonstrate his thesis.[9] The solution lay in the recruitment of 'more of the artizans, and more of the manufacturing capital of England' and then, when the country finally had something to protect, high tariffs. Although put extremely tentatively, the policy implication was clear:

Instead of theorizing generally upon true or false abstract propositions, my mental constitution, a narrow education, leads me to particularize before acting – I do not know what is good or bad for England, in the way of Protection, or of free trade. But I do know that if the shoes and boots made by fifty tradesmen in Toronto, were supplanted in the market, by a like quantity of shoes and boots made in the state prison at Auburn, Toronto would lose two hundred of her citizens, who build houses, pay taxes, make money, and keep it ... and the accumulation of profit from the industry of these fifty citizens, would be lost to the long future.

In 1849 protection became a key policy of the British-American League, a mainly Tory lobbying group which, while opposing Elgin, attempted to prevent the excesses of the Annexationists by proposing alternative economic and political strategies for Canada. Perhaps the most important plank in its platform demanded: 'That it is essential to the prosperity of the country that the tariff should be so proportioned and levied as to afford just and adequate protection to the manufacturing and industrial classes of the country, and to secure to the agricultural population a home market with fair and remunerating prices for all descriptions of farm produce.'[10] Later at the league's convention at Kingston, this strategy was combined with a proposed union of all the British North American colonies. This suggestion flowed from 'the necessity which exists for extending commercial intercourse with our sister colonies, thereby creating large home markets for the consumption of agricultural products and domestic manufactures.' The league's *Address to the Inhabitants of Canada* was even more explicit:

In her promulgation of Free Trade principles, she [Great Britain] has lost sight of the interests of her colonies, with the view of obtaining from all the nations reciprocal free trade, and thereby inundating the world with her manufactures. This new policy has produced in Canada its inevitable results. Unprotected by an adequate tariff, we have continued to consume a vast amount of British manufactures, whilst our produce, the principle source upon which we rely for their payment, rarely entered the English market except at a sacrifice. The result has been a monetary pressure, extensive bankruptcy, and general distress.[11]

The solution for these problems lay in protection:

The true elements of your country's wealth – the certain indices of her prosperity – can only be developed by the adoption of measures which will fill her cities with the busy hum of industry, make her streams the outlet of that wealth which will be poured forth from the loom and the foundry, the teeming harvests of her soil, and the produce of her primeval forest. For the attainment of these results it is essential that a tariff ... should be so proportioned and levied as to afford just and adequate protection to every industrial class ... so as to create a Home Market for Home Industry, and enrich together consumer and producer.[12]

One of the major propagandists of this new protectionist sentiment and an important figure in the British-American League was John William Gamble. A Toronto Tory lawyer, he put into practice the theories of Robert Baldwin Sullivan. In the small community of Pine Grove on the Humber River, upstream from Toronto, Gamble erected a primitive industrial complex which combined a grist and flour mill with a sawmill, a distillery, and a small cotton textile manufactory.[13] At the British-American League meetings in 1849, Gamble gave the major theoretical speeches, justifying the move to protection. In an argument reminiscent of Sullivan, he showed that British colonial policy had favoured Britain at the expense of Canada and he pointed to the United States as proof of what could be accomplished with protection. Adam Smith had been his intellectual companion since his youth, 'but practical experience had of late forced upon him the conviction, that the beautiful theory was not borne out by corresponding benefits.' Thus he had come to adopt 'the views of the American Protectionists as those most consonant with sound reason and common sense.' The solution followed: 'The proper remedy was to protect our native industry, to protect it from the surplus products of the industry of other countries ... Where the raw material produced in any country is worked up in that country, the difference between the value of the material and the finished article is retained in the country.'[14]

In a late fall meeting in Toronto, British-American League delegates degenerated into wrangling over the question of constitutional change. Compact Tory elements opposed a proposal for an elected legislative council. Unanimity remained, however, on the questions of union of the British-American provinces and the need for a protective tariff. Orange leaders Ogle Gowan and George Benjamin gave their support to J.W. Gamble who again led the fight for protection.[15]

The tariff was increased from $7\frac{1}{2}$ to $12\frac{1}{2}$ per cent in 1849, but this was not enough to satisfy the advocates of protection. Gamble continued his agitation in the legislature and introduced unsuccessful motions in 1852 and 1853 in favour of increased tariff protection.[16] He did manage, however, to have tariffs lowered on some raw materials, which were needed for home manufactures and could never be produced in Canada.

The campaign for higher tariffs gained strength in the 1850s with the rapid growth of Canadian industry which accompanied that decade's railroad boom. During this period the Canadian state pursued a systematic and vigorous policy of encouraging railroad building, for which two major pieces of legislation provided the necessary guarantees of government financial support. Francis Hincks' Guarantee Act of 1849 allowed the government to guarantee the interest on half the bonds of any railway over 75 miles in length, provided that half the railway had already been built. Three years later, Hincks' Municipal Loan Fund Act created a government fund to back municipal debentures, since the Canadian government was more highly regarded in international capital markets than local towns.[17] The railway boom that followed these government policies was an orgy of corruption and excess, but at the end of the decade the Canadas had over 2,000 miles of railway compared with only 66 in 1850. The railroad boom was of crucial importance to Canadian industrial development. It also demonstrates the important role the Canadian state played in augmenting domestic capital formation. There are various estimates of capital importation into the Canadas in the 1850s, but none are lower than a minimum of $100,000,000. This represented an inflow of foreign capital of at least four times the magnitude of any previous capital importation. Pentland has pointed out the importance of the 'unintended effects':

They represented, first, a commitment of fixed capital, overhead costs, and permanent staffs, that are the essence of metropolitan economies. By integrating the Canadian market, they opened the way for Canadian manufacturers to conquer it.

Most important, the overflow of foreign capital into Canada made it possible at the second and third remove for Canadians to amass funds which could be invested in new enterprises. The water-power sites created by the canals, the metal industries necessarily introduced by the railroads, and the mass of labour with urban preferences drawn by the construction of work, all had the same result.[18]

Capital was certainly accumulated in Canada, especially by contractors hired to build North-American railroads in the nineteenth century, and by Canadian politicians and their close friends and colleagues involved in countless shady deals in Canadian business. It is worth pointing out at this point that the Canadian state and business were, and remain, intertwined in ways that appear to extend beyond the interlocking in other capitalist societies.[19] The capital accumulated in railroads quickly was transformed into industrial development as a producer-goods industry sprang up to feed the new railways. Locomotive manufacturing, rolling mills for rails, rolling stock construction, and other secondary metal manufacturing rose to meet the voracious appetite of the new transportation system. This new rail network also integrated the Canadian market and brought new areas into the exchange economy. Consumer goods industries centred in the rapidly growing cities, such as boots and shoes, and clothing grew to service their immediate populace and an increasingly extensive hinterland. The railroads had an extensive impact on the Canadian economy, encouraging a rapid expansion in the 1850s which developed both a logic and a dynamic of its own.

Toronto entrepreneurs played major roles in this boom and the city benefited greatly. By 1853 the Northern Railway connected Toronto to Barrie and by 1855 was completed to Collingwood on Georgian Bay. One year later the Grand Trunk opened from Montreal to Toronto and the Great Western joined Toronto to Hamilton and points west.[20] The railway boom of the 1850s committed the Canadian state to a policy of industrial development. By the late 1850s Canadian capitalists, facing the depression conditions that spread rapidly after 1857, again began to agitate strenuously for protection. Montreal merchant William Weir arrived in Toronto in 1856 and began publishing the *Canadian Merchants' Magazine and Commercial Review* the following year,[21] which from its inception took the lead in advocating the development of 'Home Industry.'[22]

For three years Weir toured the Canadas, writing vivid descriptions of industrial successes.[23] To these he added initially didactic editorials explaining the benefits of home manufactures.[24] As the economic crisis of the late 1850s deepened, however, his pen became increasingly polemical.

Among the protectionists, he was perhaps most persuasive in articulating what were to become the major themes:

Canada is not in the same position as England, nor even as the United States. It has but few manufactures, and they are yet in their infancy. If, therefore, they do not receive here the benefit of that encouragement which was afforded to them ... in those countries, and which the laws of the United States still accord to them, they will perish in their infancy, our resources will become of no avail, capital will be banished from our country, and the energies of our countrymen will be paralyzed by the want of that occupation which they need. Thus we drive them to a foreign land in search of what our foresight might have found for them at home; that labour which is a condition of their subsistence.[25]

This reasoning led him to call for 'reciprocity in duties as well as free trade' with the United States, since the Canadian tariff should 'ensure to the manufacturers such Protection as other Governments have accorded, and still accord.'[26]

By April 1858 the sentiments for tariff reform had increased to the point that Weir described it as a 'movement' and the august Montreal Board of Trade, which he had earlier identified as the major bastion of opposition to protection, agreed to co-operate with a committee founded to propose 'legislative measures as may foster Native Industry.'[27] In that same month Weir joined forces with Hamilton merchant Isaac Buchanan to create the Association for the Protection of Canadian Industry (APCI), which held a public meeting in Toronto's St Lawrence Hall to commence its campaign.[28] This body lobbied systematically for a new tariff. The APCI's rationale restated the earlier arguments of Gamble, Sullivan, and Weir, blaming the new economic distress of the late 1850s on

the present tariff being based on erroneous principles, admitting as it does, at low rates of duty, the manufactures of other countries, that can be made by a class of labour now in Canada, unfitted for agricultural pursuits, and charging high rates on articles that cannot be produced in the country, thereby preventing the development of the natural resources of the colony, as well as injuring Canada as a field of immigration.[29]

The APCI proposed an alternative plan for: raw materials to enter at very low rates or even free; articles of consumption such as sugar, tea, coffee, molasses also to enter at very low rates; an intermediate list of goods not produced in Canada and only semi-processed to be charged at a medium rate of about 15 per cent; and finally that 'all manufactures in Wood, Iron, Tin, Brass, Copper, Leather, India Rubber, &c., competing with our industrial products ... [to] be charged a duty of about 25%.'[30]

Prominent among the members of the APCI were leading Toronto industrialists such as Robert Hay and William Lyman. Future Toronto manufacturer Hart Massey, then still manufacturing agricultural implements in Newcastle, was also active.[31] Buchanan's agitation for a concerted and consistent policy of protection increased over the next few years. An active propagandist, he published a series of books, pamphlets, broadsheets, and letters throughout the early 1860s.[32] In all of these writings, he lay the basis for the alliance of Tory and producer that figured so prominently in the politics of the 1870s and 1880s. On many occasions he cited as evidence for the need to produce an alliance of industrial capitalists and workers to save the economy of the nation the statement of a British labour radical in Hyde Park: 'if political economy is against us then we are against political economy.'[33] The pervasive influence of protectionist sentiments and, of course, the growth of industry can also be seen in the Toronto Board of Trade's gradual shift from a policy of free trade to one of protection. By the 1860s its enthusiastic reports on industrial development in Toronto marked its final conversion.[34]

William Weir continued his activities as well, as secretary of the APCI and editor of the *Merchants' Magazine*. In the fall of 1858 he published a comprehensive essay on 'The Manufactures of Upper Canada' which, after surveying the state of local industry, argued for a three-pronged government policy to aid manufacturers. In addition to a 'sound commercial policy' which would admit needed raw materials free, raise the necessary government revenues by taxing luxury imports heavily, and strongly protect home manufactures, he also called for direct assistance to manufacturers through bounties and for active government promotion of Upper Canadian prospects abroad to help recruit British and American capital.[35]

These campaigns – the propaganda work of Weir and Buchanan and the lobbying activities of the APCI – were eminently successful. The Galt-Cayley tariff of 1858 and the Galt tariff of 1859 met the demands of Canadian manufacturers. There has been considerable debate recently as to whether these tariffs were actually protectionist. A recent rigorous econometric analysis has proved conclusively that they did represent an advanced example of tariff-building, employing a three-tier system of tariff levels to promote industrial development.[36]

Debate about these tariffs has centred on Galt's description of them as only 'incidental protection.' Historians who argue they were not protective on this basis ignore the fact that Galt made this argument while in Great Britain to offset the complaints of British manufacturers about the new Canadian policy of protection. His special pleading on that occasion was clear to the British manufacturers who were not satisfied by his explanations. He admitted that there was in Canada a large and influential party that advocated a protective policy, but claimed that the policy had not been adopted. He admitted, however, that 'the necessity of increased taxation for the purposes of revenue has, to a certain extent, compelled action in partial unison with their views, and has caused more attention to be given to the proper adjustment of the duties, so as neither unduly to stimulate nor depress the few branches of manufacture which exist in Canada.' Although denying that the tariff increase would lead to any considerable development of manufacturing industry, he did note that the government would be gratified if 'the duties ... should incidentally benefit and encourage the production of many of those articles which we now import.'[37]

Despite recent arguments, then, the 1859 tariff was protective. Nineteenth-century commentators certainly had no doubts. In his autobiography, William Weir concluded that 'for the first time was the principle of protection applied to Canadian manufactures.'[38] Throughout the 1870s speakers in Dominion Board of Trade debates on protection identified the Galt tariff as protective.[39] And in 1880, John MacLean, a leading protectionist, described the 1859 tariff 'as the first ever framed in this country for the avowed purpose of developing home manufactures, and in obedience to a popular demand.'[40]

Moreover, the Upper Canadian protection advocates were delighted. Weir, for example, observed that 'our tariff is constructed upon principles, which, if not ultra-protective, yet afford a fair advantage to the home manufacturer against the foreigner ... the consequence is that the manufacturers of Canada ... may be safely regarded as the most successful and promising class that the country possesses at the present moment.'[41] The next step, Weir felt, was to recruit immigrants who possessed capital and manufacturing experience.

Alexander Somerville, 'The Whistler at the Plough' of Chartist fame, advanced this theme in the pages of the *Canadian Illustrated News* in the early 1860s. Frequently he argued that Canada needed a selective immigration policy, that British immigrants without capital or agricultural experience were of little use to the Canadian economy, and that what Canada needed was men of moderate capital. 'We want more manufacturers in textile fabrics, iron work, pottery, glassware, leather, etc. We have abundance of raw material for all of these, and an extensive market as well, and only require the capital in order to commence their manufacture on a large scale. Let us secure that and labourers will follow it in abundance without any spasmodic efforts on our part to increase them.'[42] He combined this interest with a fascination for the development of Canadian industry; the pages of the *Illustrated News* were crowded with engravings and descriptions of Canada's fledgling factories.

Both Somerville and Weir continually called for an active state role in industrial development. One response to these demands was the Board of Arts and Manufactures of Upper Canada. The board established and supervised mechanics' institutes and industrial exhibits, organized Canada's participation in overseas trade exhibitions, published the *Journal*, and in general promoted Canadian industrial development. Under the editorship of Henry Youle Hind, Toronto engineer, explorer, and scientist, and later of William Edwards, the major force behind the Toronto Mechanics' Institute, the *Journal* from 1861 to 1867 published educational, scientific, and descriptive materials for Canadian manufacturers. Predictably Edwards advocated protection, since without it 'no new country could succeed in establishing extensive manufactures.'[43] Because of its status as a government publication, the *Journal* did not engage in an extensive commentary on the economic significance of confederation, but the old Hamilton politico, Isaac Buchanan, did.

On retiring from active politics, Buchanan issued a strong call for confederation in 1865, which he and many other central Canadian proponents of industrial capitalism saw as the natural option after the abrogation of the Reciprocity Treaty in natural products with the United States. He argued that it was vital to both the Maritimes and central Canada to have each other as markets to substitute for the loss of the United States. It was self-evident, he added, 'that now we must either be drifted by industrial necessity into Annexation, ... or must find markets for our industry and an outlet for our trade through an intimate and indissoluble union of all the provinces of British North America.'[44]

Unlike other promoters of confederation, Buchanan opposed the 1866 reduction in the Canadian tariff. This reduction was intended as a conciliatory gesture to the eastern provinces where there was little interest in protection, and where anti-confederate forces focused considerable attention on the dangers of protection for the Maritime economy. Buchanan reorganized the Association for the Promotion of Canadian Industry in September 1866, noting that 'the immediate objects of this society [the old APCI] having been triumphantly arrived at, it was allowed to die out, after leaving to the country that tariff which we now seek to have restored.'[45]

Most of the province's important industrial capitalists gathered together in Toronto to protest the new tariff. Toronto representatives included Robert Hay, W. Gooderham, William Hamilton, J.J. Taylor; representatives from shoe firms such as W. Hamilton and Sessions, Carpenter and Co.; tobacco manufacturers such as A. Dredge and A. Schack; and woolens producer Joseph Simpson. At least 22 Toronto firms were represented at this meeting and joined the new association.

The declaration of the new APCI evidenced the increasing self-consciousness of the new industrial capitalist class. They complained bitterly that 'we hear much of the shipping interest, also of the railroad interest; it is now full time that the manufacturers' interest should assume that place in public affairs, to which its importance fully entitles it.' Their aims were simply 'to obtain protection to a moderate extent, to endeavour to secure a permanency in our tariffs, to use every possible means to effect a return to the tariff list discarded at the last session of Parliament, and to avail ourselves ... of all opportunities for enlightening the public mind [of] ... the truth regarding the importance of manufacturers to this country.' Unfortunately for them, the exigencies of creating the new nation were more immediate than their arguments and the tariffs were not readjusted in 1866.

The APCI re-emerged in the early 1870s as the Manufacturers Association of Ontario, which in turn transformed itself in the 1880s into the Canadian Manufacturers' Association, still the chief lobbyist for industrial interests in Canada.[46] In the 1870s the manufacturers also carried their fight for higher tariffs to the Dominion Board of Trade where Toronto delegates led an annual battle against free-trade advocates. In 1871 William Elliott recommended a tariff increase on manufactured goods to 20 per cent in order to promote Canadian industry. In supporting the motion, Toronto Board of Trade colleague and textile manufacturer John Gordon pointed out that 'there had been, in 1859, an intention to inaugurate a policy that would encourage manufacturers.' This policy had met with considerable success, 'but on the abrogation of that tariff, that capital languished and languishes still.'[47] Elliott's motion failed, but Toronto provided three of the six favourable votes.

The onslaught of a depression in 1873 gave protectionist efforts more credibility, and in 1874 Toronto clothing manufacturer John Gillespie again moved for a tariff increase to 20 per cent.[48] This motion gained strong support in two position papers. The first by Dr L.S. Olle of St Catharines promoted 'a generous policy of protection' and 'liberal subventions in the shape of bonuses, bounties, grants of public land, etc.' in order to develop a

Canadian iron and steel industry. The second paper, titled 'Buchanan's Postulates and Remedies,' denounced 'the imposition on Canada on the *Free Trade and Hard Money Heresies of England*, which simply amount to an ignoring, or abnegation, of practical patriotism.' Instead, Isaac Buchanan called for 'a *Patriotic Industrial Policy*' – either free trade with the u.s. or reciprocal duties (emphasis in original). Other Toronto delegates spoke in favour of Elliott's resolution, reminding those present that his nearly identical 1871 motion had been 'in a considerable minority then.' After a lengthy debate the board, by a vote of 42 to 12, accepted Thomas White's more moderate proposal which requested that 'the principle of protection to the manufacturing industries of the country be embodied in such revision of the tariff, so far as the same can be carried out consistently with the commerce and revenue requirements of the country.'[49]

The failure of the Mackenzie government to respond favourably to this proposal, and the deepening depression led to a more vigorous expression of protectionist positions at the 1876 meeting. There Hamilton's Adam Brown, seconded by Toronto paper manufacturer Hugh Staunton, called for legislation to protect 'the capital already invested in manufactures' against the effects of the depression which was 'mainly owing to the competition of American manufacturers, who make of Canada a slaughter market for their surplus products.' Since 'this system of unfair and unequal competition will ... increase in intensity in the future,' he resolved, 'that in the opinion of this Board the true and patriotic policy for the Canadian Government would be to adopt a thoroughly national commercial policy, and with that view that in any readjustment of the tariff, reciprocal duties with the United States be adopted.'[50] Citing Horace Greeley favourably, Brown argued 'squarely for a national policy, ... the only true policy for a new country to build itself up.' Toronto's W.H. Howland supported the motion, stressing the severe difficulties of Ontario manufacturers; moreover, confederation was failing, he argued, since old north-south trade patterns persisted and the provinces were little 'more than a bundle of sticks loosely tied together.' For these reasons, Howland also demanded a national policy. This strongly protectionist motion carried 22 to 14, with all Toronto delegates supporting it.

The 1877 meeting passed a similar motion after hearing lengthy descriptions of industrial distress throughout the nation, which included W.H. Howland's version of the near collapse of the Toronto furniture factory of Robert Hay.[51] Similar motions were endorsed in 1878 with the addition of a more specific call for aid to the nascent iron and steel industry. Finally, in 1879 Montreal's Thomas White Jr smugly summed up the experience of the

1870s: 'It must be a matter for very great congratulation that this subject which has occupied our attention at this Board during the last five years, is now being discussed not as a controversial question at all, but as to the manner in which our views are to be carried into effect.'[52] The lonely position held by Toronto Board of Trade delegates in 1871 not only had become the accepted orthodoxy of the Dominion Board of Trade but also was about to be enacted as part of the national policy by the triumphant Macdonald government.

The difficulty of winning control of the Dominion Board of Trade had also led to the formation of the Manufacturers' Association of Ontario in 1875. Leading roles in that association were played by Toronto manufacturers Lyman (drugs), Staunton (paper), Gurney (stoves), Hay (furniture), W. Hamilton (machinery), and W.B. Hamilton (boot and shoe).[53] At their meeting in November 1875 they complained bitterly of the impact of U.S. goods being dumped on the Canadian market and called for increased protection. Significantly this call for higher tariffs, at least back to the level of the Galt 1859 tariff, came from both Liberal and Tory manufacturers.[53] This economic stance led to the creation of purportedly non-partisan associations, such as the Dominion National League which threw its support behind the Tories in the crucial national policy election of 1878. William Fraser, the secretary and major force in the league, held the same position in the Manufacturers' Association of Ontario, and was a vociferous delegate at Dominion Board of Trade meetings.[54]

The 1878 Tory election triumph led to the closer ties between manufacturers and the Canadian state that were to anger western farmers and maritime nationalists for the following century. Manufacturers met in Toronto and Montreal in 1879 and decided upon tariff levels.[55] Delegations made their wishes known to the new Tory government, and a complicated process of trade-offs then commenced. Critics were certain that the famous 'Red Parlour' meetings in Toronto's Queen's Hotel between Macdonald and the industrialists revolved more around campaign funds for the Tories than the good of the country.[56] Be that as it may, by 1879 Canadian industrial capitalists had come to dominate the state and were able to dictate their self-interested policies in the name of the common good. John A. Macdonald had pledged himself to this policy in a speech in 1878 when he announced, 'I cannot tell what protection you require. But let each manufacturer tell us what he wants, and we will try to give him what he needs.'[57]

Toronto industrial capitalists played prominent roles in all these developments. Besides creating the strong and important lobbying bodies such as the APCI, the Manufacturers' Association of Ontario, and later the Canadian Manufacturers' Association, they were also active in the Dominion Board of Trade. In addition, in 1878 because of the importance of the national policy election, one of their leaders, furniture manufacturer Robert Hay, formerly a Liberal, ran for office in support of protection and sat as one of Toronto's members of parliament for two terms.

The national policy was modified only slightly in the 1880s. All tariff adjustments were in aid of home industry and the only major change came in 1887 when iron and steel interests received substantially increased protection. Thus from 1850 to the early 1890s, the period in which industrial capitalism transformed Canadian society, the Canadian bourgeoisie played an active role in using the state to further capitalist accumulation. This period of considerable economic growth, but most importantly of qualitative transformations, has been too long ignored by the staples interpretation of Canadian economic history and by the nationalist focus on Confederation. The four decades which followed the crisis of 1849 lay the foundations for the twentieth-century Canadian economy, and without an understanding of the development of industrial capitalism in Canada it would be impossible to understand the present situation.[58]

Let us now turn to a specific analysis of the transformation and growth of the Toronto economy.

2

Toronto's industrial revolution

The triumphant march of industrial capitalism is apparent in any analysis of the Toronto economy in the years 1850 to 1890. By the 1840s capitalist handicraft production had firmly established itself in the city. The 1850s witnessed a consolidation of handicrafts into manufactories either through uniting various different craftsmen as in carriage-making (wheelwrights, blacksmiths, carpenters, painters, and others), or through an ever-increasing division of labour, as in shoemaking (cutters, fitters, makers, and so on). Although much larger than the artisan's shop and displaying an increased division of labour, the manufactory was still largely dependent on hand production. From the 1860s to the 1880s the modern factory emerged with the introduction of machinery.

This process of economic transformation underlay the strategies of Toronto capitalists that we analysed in the preceding chapter. If Toronto capitalists with a strategy of industrial development had not spoken for the nation in 1849, by 1879 there could be little question that their views reigned triumphant under the guise of the national policy.

Data on the Toronto economy in the 1840s are slight but it is clear that production was centred in small shops and perhaps a few manufactories.[1] The 1846 *Canadian Gazeteer* listed numerous artisans, such as 37 black-smiths, 49 shoemakers, and 25 cabinet-makers but no businesses of a substantial size.[2] The sketchy 1848 census listed 75 'factories' in Toronto but the more detailed census of 1851 found only 55.[3] Most of these were probably artisan shops employing a few journeymen and apprentices. A closer look at four Toronto industries – cabinet-making, metallurgy, shoe manufacturing, and tobacco manufacturing – will illustrate the shift to manufactories and finally to modern industry.

Cabinet-makers were present in Toronto quite early. Perhaps the key development in the industry was the unheralded arrival in 1831 of two British journeymen cabinet-makers, Robert Hay and John Jacques.[4] Hay, born in Scotland in 1808, apprenticed as a cabinet-maker at the age of 14; Jacques, born in England in 1804, began learning the trade at six. On their arrival in York, both went to work as journeymen, and in 1835 they joined forces to buy the shop of William Maxwell, Jacques' boss. Besides themselves they employed only two apprentices, and were so successful that by the 1840s they had accumulated sufficient capital to build their first manufactory. There were two other relatively large cabinet-making shops in Toronto in the 1840s: the City Chair Factory, which employed between 8 and 10 men, and the cabinet works of the O'Neill Brothers, which employed 15 to 20 men. Jacques' and Hay's factory outdid their rivals', however; by the early 1850s it employed between 90 and 100 men and had its first steam engine to power substantial new machinery. In 1853 they expanded once again into a new factory employing 200 men and bought a bigger engine. A disastrous fire destroyed the plant in 1854, but with a generous loan from the city of Toronto, they rebuilt it. After a second fire and rebuilding, in 1857 the company diversified by buying forests north of Toronto and erecting a sawmill and rough factory in New Lowell to process wood for the Toronto plant. In 1861 they reported a total capitalization of $200,000, and employed 200 men and 50 women in Toronto and 30 men in New Lowell.

By 1865 the Jacques and Hay factory complex in Toronto included a building housing the boiler and 35 hp steam engine, the factory proper, a warehouse, and a retail store and office. In the factory the operation was divided by floors: on the first was the heavy machinery and the turning department where for much 'the hand still guided the tool'; the second was the location of chair production from which came most of the chairs and desks for the expanding Upper Canadian school system; the third was another 'place of comparative quiet' where the finer cabinet-making was done, some of the best of which reached export markets in Scotland and England; the top floor was reserved for design and repair. Thus, although there were still pools of handicraft labour left in the factory, the basic organization was industrial with a highly developed division of labour, separate management and design functions, and extensive mechanization. Employee lists demonstrate both the advanced division of labour and the maintenance of skill in the factory. Along with the many labourers and managers (including a timekeeper) typical of the factory were found cabinet-makers, chair-makers, carvers, turners, carpenters, finishers, sawyers, and upholsterers.[5]

Although a few small shops remained in the 1850s and 1860s, by the early 1870s Jacques and Hay dominated the furniture market in Toronto. The industrial revolution had transformed the Toronto furniture industry.

The foundry and iron business in Toronto developed steadily if less spectacularly. There were a number of small foundries in the 1830s and 1840s, some substantial enough to build large steam engines.[6] The new railway age gave the industry its major impetus. The foundry of James Good, for example, which had previously specialized in stoves, manufactured the second locomotive for the Northern Railway.[7] Money made in railway contracting by entrepreneurs such as Casimir Gzowski and D.L. Macpherson was wisely reinvested in producer-goods industries that could supply the growing railway network of Ontario. These two men set up the Toronto Locomotive Works in the 1850s and in 1860 the Toronto Rolling Mills, which by 1866 employed over 300 men. Although primarily involved in rerolling old rails, the Rolling Mill also puddled new iron for the head of the new rails. Powered by a 500 hp engine, the mill was the most spectacular of Toronto's mid-century industries.[8] The unusual painting of the mill by William Armstrong suggests how far industrialization had proceeded by 1864 and how far it had to go, especially in terms of labour management.[9]

The Toronto economy in this period developed the producer goods that are essential for a strong industrial base. Most of the machinery which powered the new Toronto factories was built at home. Important producer-goods manufacturers were the Toronto Car Wheel Co., Currie Boilers, the Soho Foundry, and Dickey, Neill and Co. – the makers of engines for Jacques and Hay and 25 other Toronto factories. Currie employed around 40 workers and Dickey over 100 by the mid-1860s.[10] Millwright and machinist Francis Metcalf opened his Don Foundry in the late 1840s and specialized in steam engines and heavy castings for grist and saw mills.[11] Perhaps the most important of these early manufacturers was William Hamilton, a Scottish born, English-trained machinist. He arrived in Toronto in 1850 and found work at James Good's foundry because of his knowledge of steam-driven machine tools. In 1852 he established the St Lawrence Foundry, Engine Works and Machine Shop. Although work there in the 1850s was primarily restricted to castings of various kinds, he still employed over 400 men by 1861.[12]

The American Civil War provided a major impetus to the Canadian machine industry as manufacturers there turned to war production. The St Lawrence Foundry especially benefited and expanded swiftly in the early 1860s. It constructed a complete machine system for the new Toronto

Rolling Mill, machinery for Joseph Simpson's Toronto Knitting Co., and, most importantly, nearly all the power presses for the rapidly expanding Toronto tobacco industry.[13] The foundry also pioneered new processes:

Hamilton's production techniques differed markedly from those then most current in Toronto. Good, for example, had been producing what were virtually handmade machines since the 1830s. Hamilton used a larger number of machine tools while retaining numerous well-trained artisans; his techniques attracted machinists, inventors, and moulders of high calibre.[14]

A more specialized secondary-metal manufacturer was the J.J. Taylor Safe Works. An American immigrant, Taylor arrived in Toronto in 1855, and exported safes to the United States until the outbreak of the Civil War. Even after that trade failed, his company continued to grow and by the mid-1860s employed 50 workers. One enthusiastic observer noted that they had 'reduced their business to a system' and used 'machinery made on the most approved principles.' These included turning-lathes, drilling machines, pinching and shearing machines, and a 'powerful' steam-engine. In addition they had their own cabinet shop (for the interior woodwork) and separate paint and blacksmith shops, as well as a filing and engine room.[15]

Other metal consumer goods production included a large number of foundries specializing in stoves. The largest of these, the Phoenix Foundry, employed over 100 men. Other large foundries were the Beard Brothers, James Armstrong, and after 1868 E.C. Gurney and Co.

With the exception of the Toronto Rolling Mill, all the producers we have described so far grew from small shops into increasingly larger enterprises. Jacques and Hay, for example, had begun production as artisans, as had most of the Toronto founders and machine builders. This was of course Marx's 'revolutionary path' to the factory, but other industries developed differently.

The industrial development of Toronto's shoe industry, for example, although displaying the transformation from shop to manufactory to factory, also shows that that transformation was not always linear for the artisans involved. In 1846 one investigator discovered 49 shoemaker shops in Toronto.[16] The 1851 census reported two shoe 'factories' in the city.[17] In the early 1850s the introduction of sewing machines revolutionized the structure of the industry. A Montreal firm, Brown and Childs, which had pioneered machine production in Montreal, introduced sewing machines to Toronto as well.[18] Their Toronto branch, Childs and Brown, originally established as a retail shop for Montreal goods, began to manufacture for the growing western market and by 1858 employed 100 workers. By 1856 two other companies had also commenced manufacturing shoes in Toronto: Gilyat, Robinson, and Hall; and E.K. Paul and Co.[19] They were quickly followed by Sessions, Carpenter and Co.[20] All of these firms had previously 'imported most of their goods, but the high tariff had induced them to turn their attention to manufacturing at home.'[21]

The introduction of the sewing machine was the first step in bringing the factory to shoe production. Steps leading to the emergence of the central shop, a 'manufactory' in our terms, included an ever-increasing division of labour, the development of pegged shoes, and standardization of the product. These three developments, however, had gone on within the general framework of craft production. The sewing machine of the early 1850s, the pegging machines of the later 1850s, and finally the McKay machine of the early 1860s ended craft production as the major method of manufacturing shoes.[22]

A rapid increase in Toronto shoe production occurred in the late 1850s and early 1860s. The major impetus came from the growth of the Canadian market. Agricultural specialization and the improved transportation network allowed the new urban interests to triumph over former rural production.[23] The tariff also played an important role in the development of the shoe industry. In the 1850s, when the tariff stood at $12\frac{1}{2}$ per cent, New England goods apparently competed successfully, but the 25 per cent tariff of 1859 combined with the dislocations of the Civil War to close off American shoes to the Canadian market.[24] The tariff was lowered in 1866 but was subsequently raised to $17\frac{1}{2}$ per cent in 1874 and to 25 per cent in 1879 to meet manufacturers' self-interested demands.[25]

By 1860 Childs and Brown, which had become Hamilton and Childs in Toronto, employed 40 men and 15 women in its four-storey establishment on Wellington Street East. These workers 'were kept constantly employed in cutting, fitting and stitching, besides a number – generally over a hundred – who work in their own homes at what is termed bottoming – so that upwards of 150 hands are engaged.' The company owned ten sewing machines and utilized all the other 'latest appliances in labour-saving machinery.' The factory occupied only the top two flats; the other two were given over to sales and storage.[26] The coming of the McKay machine in the early 1860s ended the 'putting-out' of bottoming for the large factories like Hamilton and Childs. As we shall see, however, not all Toronto shoe companies transformed their production so totally.

The 1861 census reported a total of seven shoe factories, but directories identified only four competitors of Childs and Hamilton in the wholesale trade. Nevertheless, the rapid growth of shoe manufacturing was proudly described in the Toronto Board of Trade reports, and in 1860 Erastus Wiman wrote of the 'decrease of the manufactures of small towns over the country,' speculating that these shops would slowly become little more than cobblers' shops for the repair of city manufactures. The following year he stated that 'the large shoe shops in each village where from five to ten men were wont to be employed' were a thing of the past.[27] Two years later he reached a new eloquence in describing the industry's transformation:

Eight years ago there was only one regular traveller from Montreal and one from Toronto who solicited orders from the country trade, and these seldom left the line of the railroad. Now it is no uncommon thing to meet from fifteen to eighteen in a single season – all keenly alive to business, and pushing into all sections of the country, remote or otherwise ... business formerly distributed over a thousand workshops in the country districts ... [had become] the eighteen or twenty establishments of the five cities of the provinces.[28]

Major Toronto manufacturers quickly implemented the latest changes in production. J.M. Trout enthusiastically described the wonders of these new devices that reduced all to a system: 'Childs and Hamilton's establishment is a perfect beehive of activity, and the admirable order and arrangement of the whole is as perfect as long experience and the best business tact can make it.'[29]

Other manufacturers grew rapidly in the mid-1860s. Sessions, Carpenter and Company doubled its production in 1865 and hoped to redouble it again in 1866. Employing 250 hands in 1867, it expanded to 400 in 1868 and then to 510 in 1870, when the firm, now Sessions, Turner and Cooper, opened its new Front Street factory. This 1870 factory demonstrated the complete transition to machine production. Built at a cost of $30,000, the new three-storey building 'utilized machinery to an extraordinary extent.' The basement was used for storage, the ground floor for offices and shipping, and the first floor for cutting and finishing. This floor also housed the channelling machine, which shaved and cut the sole, removed strips, and left the leather ready for the sewing machine. The 78 sewing machines were located on the second floor; they were operated by 119 women who had their own separate entrance and were completely segregated from the male employees on the other floors. The men's work was done on the third floor and involved the heavier sewing, peg work, and the larger McKay machines used in bottoming.[30]

Taylor Safe Works (Special Collections, Hamilton Public Library)

Stone-cutting Yard, Toronto, 1887 (Ontario Archives)

Toronto *Telegram* Linotype Operators, c.1905 (Metropolitan Toronto Library)

Toronto Rolling Mills (Metropolitan Toronto Library)

The development of the tobacco industry reveals a somewhat different experience. Insignificant before 1862, it enjoyed a rapid growth due to the dislocation caused by the American Civil War. By 1863, Wiman reported four separate companies in Toronto, each employing more than 100 workers and using 'the latest and best machinery.' This industry, with its more than 500 workers, rose in response to the U.S. war tax; two of the companies in Toronto were American firms trying to retain their control of the Canadian market.[31] The extent of mechanization was impressive:

A steam engine of ten horse power, complete steam warming and drying apparatus keep the temperature to the requisite height throughout the building ... Two immense hydraulic presses and nine smaller ones from the St. Lawrence Foundry, together with a hydraulic pump, compresses, packing apparatus, etc. are all of the best and most complete kind, quite as good, if not superior to anything that could be got in St. Louis or Louisville, where the manufactory of this class of machinery is a long established trade.[32]

The above description of S.S. Preston and Co., which employed 125 men, applied also to competitors, J.D. King and Co. (150 to 160 men), Withers and Wright (125), Rossin and Brothers (95), and Lewis and Thompson.[33]

The rapid expansion of the tobacco industry, however, quickly created a situation that reoccurred frequently in Canada's early industrial history: over-production. With the end of the Civil War and the re-entry of U.S. products, the industry faltered. In 1865 the Board of Trade noted that both Rossin Brothers and S.S. Preston and Co. were under new management, and that J.E. Withers and Co. had suspended production in May because of the glutted market. By 1871 the industry had levelled off, but it was never to be as large as it had been in the Civil War boom years. One of the major tobacco manufacturers, J.D. King, who had employed 160 workers in 1862, transferred his accumulated capital into the manufacture of boots and shoes. King's decision demonstrated both the demise of tobacco as an important Toronto industry as well as the emergence of the type of industrialist who invests only capital and general management skills and does not possess a detailed knowledge of production.

Thus by the 1870s modern industry had come to Toronto, albeit unevenly. In furniture, shoes, machinery, and tobacco, factory production had to some degree displaced the craftsman. The factory was not limited to these industries, but these are the sectors of the Toronto economy which are most fully described in the extant sources. An analysis of Schedule Six of the 1871 census provides us with a summary of the total Toronto industrial

TABLE 2.1

Annual production, Toronto factories, 1871

No. of employees	No. of factories	Value of product in $000s	% of Toronto product	Value added in $000s	% of Toronto value added
100+	19	5,320	39	2,083	54
50–99	30	2,507	18	562	15
30–49	28	1,499	11	443	12
0–29	495	4,360	32	738	19
Total	572	13,686	100	3,826	100

Source: Unless otherwise specified the source for the tables in chapter 2 is Canada, Census, 1871, Industrial Mss.

picture and allows us to analyse the sectors for which other sources are slight. This reconstruction is not possible for either the previous period or the following decades because of the inadequacies of earlier censuses and the statutory closing to researchers of the later returns.

We have already summarized the growing concentration in employment in Table 1.1. Table 2.1 shows how dominant the largest factories were in terms of total Toronto production and especially in terms of value added. Factories with over 50 workers accounted for 57 per cent of Toronto's value produced and 69 per cent of her value added. Size and production levels of a work force employed in a given factory are of course only two of many measures of the arrival of industrial capitalism. Sources of power and the extent of mechanization are other important indicators.

If we analyse the use of steam power in Toronto, many interesting patterns emerge. Table 2.2 shows how very uneven the spread of steam power was in Toronto. As one would expect, the machinery, foundries, and metal-working industries were the largest users. But perhaps surprising is how little it was used in the clothing and shoe industries – Toronto's largest employers in 1871. Also surprising is the evidence of Table 2.3 which suggests that the size of the work force was not totally able to predict whether a firm would utilize steam power. Table 2.4, however, which sets the clothing and shoe industries off, demonstrates that when they are excluded, the predictive value of number of employees rises dramatically. Indeed, only six other factories employing more than thirty workers did not avail themselves of steam power.

TABLE 2.2
Steam power by industry, 1871

Industry	0–19 employees		20+ employees		Total horsepower	% of total
	No. of factories	Horsepower	No. of factories	Horsepower		
Metal	8	79	16	608	687	31
Woodworking	12	119	7	267	386	17.4
Brewing and distilling	9	134	1	116	250	11.3
Flour	2	130	1	50	180	8.1
Pork packing	2	17	2	95	112	5.1
Publishing	0	0	6	84	84	3.8
Chemicals	5	52	1	20	72	3.2
Furniture	4	23	1	40	63	2.8
Clothing	0	0	3	43	43	1.9
Baking and confectry	3	17	1	25	42	1.9
Musical instr.	0	0	2	40	40	1.8
Tobacco	0	0	3	36	36	1.6
Boot and shoe	0	0	2	30	30	1.4
Brass, tin, etc.	4	22	1	8	30	1.4
Carriage	0	0	1	12	12	.5
Other	12	66	4	87	153	6.9
Total	61	659	52	1,561	2,220	100.1

TABLE 2.3

Toronto industries using steam power, 1871

No. of workers	No. of factories using steam	No. of factories not using steam	Total no. of factories	% using steam
Over 100	13	6	19	68.4
50–99	15*	12	27	55.6
30–49	13	15	28	46.4
20–29	11	26	37	29.7
0–19	61	388	449	13.6
Total	113	447	560†	20.2

* One unit (Globe Printing Co.) has been added. The census was clearly in error here.
† Two factories which utilized water power not counted.

TABLE 2.4

Toronto industries without steam power,
employing more than 20 workers, 1871

No. of employees	Clothing	Boot and shoe	Other	Total
100+	3	2	1	6
50–90	5	4	3	12
30–49	11	2	2	15
20–29	13	0	13	26
Total	32	8	19	59

Our initial surprise at these findings should be allayed considerably by consideration of the mid-Victorian industrial context in both the United States and England. In a recent article Raphael Samuels warns: 'Steam power and hand technology may represent different principles of industrial organization, and to the historian they may well appear as belonging to different epochs, the one innovatory, the other "traditional" and unchanging in its ways. But from the point of view of 19th century capitalist development they were two sides of the same coin.'[34] Samuels contrasts England's maintenance of hand technology with the relatively more rapid acceptance of mechanized production in the United States; recent studies of the maintenance of craft traditions and workers' successful resistance to machinery in the United States, at least for a time, should enlighten our analysis of the Toronto industrial structure. A more specific sector-by-sector survey of the 1871 Toronto industrial setting will allow us to consider the nature of 'combined and uneven development.'

The series of tables in Appendix 1 provides a comprehensive breakdown of the leading sectors of the Toronto industrial economy in 1871. The clothing industry (Table 1.1) led the city in number of workers employed, in value of product, and in the number of women employed. Factory production was less dominant here because of the industry's continued dependence on outwork and subcontracting. The two straw works and Joseph Simpson's knitting factory were definitely modern factories with steam-powered engines. The clothing, tailoring, and millinery firms are more difficult to classify; little descriptive information is available for these firms in the 1860s and 1870s but their dependence on child and female labour is quite apparent: In the firms employing more than 50 workers, 81.6 per cent of the work force consisted of women and children. For the clothing industry as a whole, this figure fell only slightly to 74.6 per cent. It employed 17 per cent of all child workers and 63 per cent of all women workers in Toronto (see Table 1.2).

Boot and shoe (Table 1.3) exemplifies 'combined and uneven development' within one industry. On the one hand, there were modern factories such as Sessions and Turner, and Damer, King, that used the most advanced machinery and fully centralized operations; Childs and Hamilton certainly, and probably many of the other large producers, had McKay machines and channelling machines as well as the ever-present sewing machines. On the other hand, some of them (including Childs and Hamilton) continued to put out some of their bottoming work. In addition to this putting-out, there still existed a market for custom-made shoes, and some of the manufacturers (Dack, for example) specialized in this line. This uneven development accounts for the large differences in the shoe industry in which ten producers employed 90 per cent of the workers and produced 86 per cent of the value added, whereas the other 39 shops (80 per cent) employed only 11 per cent and produced only 14 per cent of the value added. The failure of all the largest producers to mechanize fully, as indicated by their lack of steam power, might also suggest the competitive problems the Toronto industry would have to face in the following decade.

Metal works in Toronto, primarily focused on the engineering industry and stove foundries, dominated the industrial scene (Table 1.4). Although it trailed the clothing and shoe industries in size of work force, metallurgy led in value of product and value added. It was also the most consistently mechanized with nearly all producers, large and small, employing steam power and machine tools. Yet, as we shall see, its workers, especially machinists and moulders, maintained both their skills and their customary work habits throughout the period covered by this study. Thus, even here, at the very heart of the industrial revolution with huge boilers, fiery furnaces, and powerful trip-hammers, metallurgy also displayed the characteristic mix of old and new which typified Victorian industry everywhere.

Other large Toronto industries in 1871 included publishing, furniture and tobacco. The city's many newspapers were complemented by an emerging publishing industry which employed extensive numbers of women in bookbinding (Table 1.5). The furniture industry showed the dominance of Robert Hay and Co., (Table 1.6), the development of which we have described earlier. The demise of the tobacco industry is made clear in table 1.7. The unusual reversal that shows the smallest tobacco employers showing the greatest value added is due to the fact that the four small producers employing under 30 workers were all profitable cigar manufacturers. In 1871, cigar-making was not yet mechanized.

Brewing and distilling showed an extremely high value added for the number of workers involved (Table 1.8). The industry was dominated by Gooderham and Worts which employed 63.6 per cent of the industry's workers and accounted for 82.6 per cent of the value added. Emigrating from England in the early 1830s, Gooderham and Worts gradually transformed their tiny mill and distillery into one of Toronto's major industries and one of the city's most important fortunes. Their activities diversified to include a linen mill in Streetsville as well as other mills at Meadowvale and Pine Grove.[35] Their only competition in Toronto, by 1871, was a small distillery employing only seven workers.

Data on the brewing industry are obscured by its classification with distilling. All nine Toronto breweries had under 20 workers in 1871. Together they accounted for a value added of nearly $160,000. In the next decades this industry grew in importance, with the advent of refrigeration.

The major sectors of the Toronto economy in 1871 then were highly industrialized with large concentrations of workers, extensive mechanization, and an elaborate division of labour. Industrialization did not extend to all production in Toronto, however. Numerous artisanal pursuits remained, in which production was still centred in small shops with very few employees and a minimal level of mechanization. As we have seen, even within the most industrialized trades, such as boot and shoe, there were still many small shops producing custom-made goods for the luxury consumer market. Examples of crafts in which mechanization had made little impact included baking, carriage-making, harness-making, and brass, tin, and sheet-iron work (see Tables 1.9–1.12). Small production was also the rule for Toronto coopers. The unevenness of industrial development had major repercussions for the emerging working-class movement. A city that just 20 years before had possessed only artisan shops and a few manufactories now saw 71 per cent of its industrial work force employed in units larger than 30 workers, and its major factories – boot and shoe, engineering, furniture – making extensive use of the most advanced machines. By 1871, Toronto had experienced its industrial revolution and the following two decades would see the continued growth of the city's manufacturing.

The years immediately following 1871 were quite prosperous for Toronto industrial capitalists and the future looked bright. Then disaster struck. The world-wide depression of the mid-1870s began to affect Toronto seriously in 1874, and business failures throughout Canada soared to almost double their previous rate.[36] Especially hard hit by the depression was the Canadian boot and shoe industry in which over-production and American dumping led to numerous failures.[37] The depression also caused failures in Toronto's basic metal production. Gzowski's Rolling Mill, the St Lawrence Foundry's expansion into railroad car manufacturing, Hugh Allan's Canada Bolt and Nut Co., and the Toronto Car Wheel Co. all failed.

The decline in boot and shoes never reversed itself. The depression caused a further decline in the already-troubled tobacco industry. In both of these industries, Toronto producers succumbed before the flood of cheaper Quebec goods into the Ontario market. Montreal and Quebec producers, perhaps because of the availability of cheaper labour, won the bulk of the Ontario tobacco and shoe markets. In the 1880s significant Toronto factories in boots and shoes, such as Hamiltons' and Charlesworth, shut their doors for good.[38] A slight decline in production in the 1870s in other industries such as furniture and distilling, however, was quickly offset by rapid growth in the 1880s.

Tactics for dealing with the depression did not reflect a retreat from a strategy of industrial development. Indeed, as has already been seen, Canadian manufacturers, in general, and Toronto industrialists, in particular, sought a solution to the troubled 1870s in a policy of high protective tariffs. This, they argued, was the key to restoring prosperity.[39] Similar tactics were reflected in the increased number of schemes to recruit more industrial capital to Toronto. Substantial civic bonuses were offered in 1876 (between $100,000 and $200,000) for any entrepreneur willing to undertake the smelting of iron in Toronto.[40] This scheme found no takers,

TABLE 2.5

Major Toronto factories, 1878 and 1884

	No. of factories	No. of hands	Wages in $000s	Value of annual product in $000s	Capital invested in $000s
1878	55	3,195	1,045.5	4,109.0	2,430.5
1884	91	6,852	2,378.2	9,715.3	4,761.5
Increase 1878–84	36	3,657	1,332.7	5,606.3	2,331.0

Source: Canada, Parliament, *Sessional Papers*, 1885, no. 37, 9–10, 17

but the city was successful in wooing the Massey Agricultural Implements Works away from Newcastle in 1879.[41] Additional recruitment brought the Abell Agricultural Implements Works from Woodbridge in 1880 but failed to find an industrialist willing to start a locomotive works in the east end of the city in return for a ten-year tax waiver.[42] The whole strategy of bonuses to foster industrial growth became very controversial in the 1880s. In 1888, for example, a controversy broke out in city council over the Masseys' offer to build a malleable iron works in return for ten taxless years.[43] The Toronto labour movement in the late 1880s opposed all bonus schemes, arguing that they were simply a method of taxing the general public to increase the profits of industrial capitalists.[44]

The impact of the national policy tariff on the development of Toronto manufacturing was substantial. A comparison of the industrial sector of the Toronto economy before and after the national policy conducted in 1885 showed significant growth between 1878 and 1884 (see Table 2.5). Toronto benefited, for example, from the significant growth in the musical instrument industry, a growth which Alfred Blackeby attributed solely to the impact of the national policy tariff. Blackeby, the commissioner entrusted with the investigation of Canadian manufacturing in 1884, argued:

Prior to the change in tariff, [the musical instrument industry] was very insignificant ... but as soon as efficient protection was afforded against outside competitors the trade increased surprisingly ... Prior to the change in fiscal policy, the Canadian trade was almost entirely in the hands of the United States manufacturers, now at least 70% of the trade of Ontario and 50% of the trade of Quebec is done by Canadian makers.[45]

TABLE 2.6

Toronto industrial growth, 1871–91

Year	No. of estabs.	No. of employees	Capital in $000s	Raw materials in $000s	Wages in $000s	Annual product in $000s	Value added in $000s
1871	561	9,400	4,036	7,169	2,691	13,686	3,826
1881	870	12,708	11,502	9,761	3,721	19,100	5,617
1891	2,109	24,470	29,261	21,228	9,042	42,489	12,219

Source: Canada, Census, 1871, 1881, 1891

Another clear case of the utility of the new protection was the foundry and engineering industry, which recovered rapidly in the 1880s.[46] Yet the national policy tariff only reinforced the industry already in existence in Toronto; it did not create an industrial revolution in any sense but only augmented the one which had already taken place. Moreover, the national policy was further evidence of industrial capitalists' power; their interests now were identified as those of the Canadian state.

Aggregate data, all that are available, from the 1881 and 1891 published censuses allow further analysis of the growth of Toronto industry in these years. By 1881, prosperity had returned and the census showed an increase in manufacturing in the 1870s despite the dislocations of the depression. The following decade saw even greater growth (see Table 2.6). A closer look at the data shows that the various segments of the garment industry together continued to make clothing the largest industry in number of workers employed, in value produced, and perhaps most importantly in value added (see Table 1.13–1.15). The two other major growing sectors were engineering and publishing. Engineering growth slowed greatly in the depression of the 1870s but recovered rapidly in the 1880s. Publishing grew steadily throughout the two decades. Agricultural implements rocketed to prominence; by 1891 the Massey plant alone accounted for 3 per cent of Toronto's annual product and 5.3 per cent of her value added. No other single company played so large a role, although, as we have seen, in 1871 Gooderham and Worts had. Furniture and musical instruments showed steady growth with major increases in the 1880s. Meat packing in 1891, although growing in employment and value produced, actually fell beneath its 1871 value-added total.[47] Distilling decreased somewhat but brewing grew rapidly in the 1880s, with the new possibilities for concentration that refrigeration brought; Toronto brewers were quick to innovate.[48] Tobacco, after a slight recovery in 1881, continued its precipitous decline. Meanwhile the boot and shoe industry, increasingly monopolized by J.D. King and Co., declined in employment and value produced but managed to increase its value added.

Although we cannot reproduce, from the aggregate returns, as detailed a breakdown of the Toronto economy for the 1880s, the pattern of continued overall growth is still apparent. Increasing specialization into relatively skilled and well-paid industries is also evident with the significant growth of publishing, machinery, musical instruments, and agricultural implements. (The garment industries represented an important exception to this pattern.) Tables 1.13–1.15 show the healthy diversity of Toronto's industrial growth; the major industries did not dominate the economy in 1891 to the same extent as they had in 1871. This can best be seen in their decreased contribution to Toronto's annual product and value added.

Piano manufacturing, was often cited, along with agricultural implements, as an example of Toronto's pre-eminent position in Ontario. Heintzman and R.S. Williams were joined by the new firm of Mason and Risch where, the *Globe* noted, 'every department is organized under a perfect system [according to] thoroughly scientific principles and methods.' Such firms transformed the Canadian market: whereas in 1876 90 per cent of pianos were imported, by 1891 95 per cent were produced at home.[49]

Other sources make clear that increased concentration of capital of two kinds was taking place in Toronto between 1871 and 1891. Toronto workers continued to be gathered into larger production units (see Table 1.27); and in addition, Toronto became the centre for the production of many commodities that had been previously manufactured throughout Ontario. Economic geographers working with historical data have provided us with considerable evidence of this process, and it was well illustrated by moves such as those undertaken by the Massey and Abell firms in the early 1880s.[50]

In the 1880s the enlargement of production units began to take place in segments of the economy that were run on a small scale in 1871. For example, the confectionery industry was transformed by the introduction of factory production (although baking remained a small-shop operation in 1891) (see Tables 1.24 and 1.27). Small shops still remained, but the number of workers employed in them as a proportion of the total Toronto work force became less and less significant as the century passed.

The increased concentration of capital led to considerable concern about the evils of monopoly. Although cartelization had not emerged as a significant force in the Canadian economy in the 1880s, both industrialists and anti-monopoly forces began to anticipate its arrival. Cotton manufacturers attempted to create a price-fixing arrangement in the mid-1880s which anticipated their mergers of the 1890s. In 1881 the Masseys bought out their major Toronto competitor, the Toronto Reaper and Mower Co. Ten years later they merged with the Harris Company of Brantford to create the Massey-Harris Co. Ltd., which was to dominate the agricultural implements field in Canada. Six months after that merger, their two major remaining competitors, Patterson and Brothers of Woodstock and J.O. Wisner Son and Co., realizing they could not compete, sold out.[51] Anti-monopoly sentiment in the 1880s and early 1890s was sufficiently strong that a Tory MP from the Toronto area, Clarke Wallace, instituted a select committee in 1887 to investigate combines. The following year he introduced legislation which, in its original intent at least, attempted to prevent the growth of combinations in Canada.[52]

By the late 1880s and early 1890s, Toronto had experienced her industrial revolution, and a new set of economic forces and political responses were emerging. As the centralization and concentration of capital increased, Toronto stood poised on the brink of the next stage of economic development – monopoly capitalism. That phase of development lies beyond the scope of this study.

PART TWO

TORONTO WORKERS AND THE
INDUSTRIAL AGE

3

Shoemakers, shoe factories, and
the Knights of St Crispin

Toronto workers experienced the transformation to industrial capitalism in different ways and at different times. By the 1860s they all shared a life in an industrial capitalist society, but the ways in which it affected them at their place of work varied dramatically from craft to craft. Toronto shoemakers, for example, were among the first to face a serious assault on their craft by the new factories, which were well established by 1871. In response, shoemakers created, in the late 1860s and early 1870s, one of the strongest and most important of the first wave of international unions in North America. This chapter examines this union in its Toronto milieu and relates its advent to the economic transformation that was destroying an old mode of production and replacing it with industrial capitalism.

Cordwainers, shoemakers, Crispins – by whatever name they were known – these 'most persistent of working class intellectuals'[1] were ever-present figures in the struggle for a freer and more egalitarian world. In rural England these village radicals acted as spokesmen, organizers, and ideologues in the struggles of the agricultural labourers.[2] In urban Paris they joined their brother, *sans culottes*, in the streets at the Bastille.[3] In London they were the main carriers of the Jacobin tradition.[4] In the United States they helped create a radical tradition of Republicanism which figured again and again in nineteenth-century labour struggles.[5] In the 1837 Mackenzie Rebellion in Upper Canada, no artisan group played a more prominent role.[6] What elements in the shoemakers' craft prepared them for such prominence?

One old nineteenth-century Massachusetts shoemaker, reflecting on the recently lost traditions of his trade, suggested one answer:

The peculiar nature of his business requiring of the workingman little mental concentration, allowed him to take part in discussions, or fix his attention upon any question that might engage his thoughts. His work went on mechanically, as it seemed, without needing any of that nice care which is indisposable in many of the mechanic arts. This circumstance made every workshop a school and an incipient debating club; and from this doubtless has arisen the general intelligence which is said to characterize the sons of Crispin.[7]

Shoemakers were 'given to deep thinking' in New England and their shops were often visited by ministers desirous of testing their sermons before delivery. These centres of popular theological debate were considered unequipped if they did not contain a Bible, a dictionary, a grammar, and a weekly newspaper. Also part of every shop's standard equipment were 'one or more extra seats or boxes for the accomodation of visitors' who would drop by either to read to the working journeymen, or to join in listening and debating as 'the best reader in the crew ... read the news.'[8] Only the pub challenged the shoe shop as a centre of popular culture and often shoemakers or other artisans ran these. Frank Foster, a printer and leader of the Knights of Labor in the United States, referred to every shoemaker's shop as a lyceum and credited the craft with 'the old time front rank of comparative intelligence.'[9]

Shoemakers had, in addition, a particularly vibrant craft tradition. Stories of St Hugh, of Saints Crispin and Crispianus, and other types of lore provided a set of familiar and well-defined customs that instilled the craftsmen with pride and solidarity.[10] On 25 October, the feast of St Crispin, cordwainers the world over marched beneath banners depicting their patron saints and engaged in drunken frolics. Shoemakers in Canada built on these traditions. This craft lore was undoubtedly brought to Canada by emigrating crispins, who later took a prominent role in organizing unions. Toronto shoemakers struck for higher wages and better conditions as early as 1830 and again in the 1850s. Other early shoemakers' societies were reported in Montreal, Halifax, and St John.[11] Generally, in British North America wherever shoemakers gathered in sufficient numbers, they organized.

Any understanding of the life of shoemakers in this period must start at their workplace. There can be little doubt that in the pre-industrial city the artisan's relation to work was central to his identity. As we have seen in chapter 2, shoemaking in Toronto experienced its industrial revolution in the 1850s and 1860s with the introduction of the sewing machine first and of the McKay machine later. Handicraft production disappeared under the onslaught of machinery and factory production, conversion to which was well advanced by 1871.[12] This process was, of course, uneven and some small shops remained, some custom work was still done in the old ways, and some bottoming was still done at home. By the 1880s, all but custom work had disappeared.

How did the shoemaker respond to the arrival of the factory system? Formerly he had worked in a small shop; now he found himself in a factory with hundreds of other workers. Whereas before he alone had made an entire shoe by hand, now he worked only on parts of it with the aid of machines. In the old shops he had control over his time, his discussions, his visitors, and his work; now he was subject to factory discipline like any other worker. The separation of the journeyman from his master, at one time relatively undefined, had been growing for some years, but under the shop system a certain familiarity remained. The factory created massive barriers of social distance between owner and worker. Most important, industrial capitalism stripped the shoemaker of his most valuable possession – pride in his craft and in his product. That the memory of both old and new was a tangible part of each shoemaker's life in this period can be seen in a newspaper description of one Montreal factory as late as 1885: 'Indeed, there were several employees of both sexes, some of whom came to the firm as children, whose experience compasses nearly all of the improvements in boot and shoe machinery ... One old man, named Dennis Barron, who had been in their employ 43 years, remembered helping to put up the first sewing machine used on boots and shoes ...'[13]

Shoemakers did not wait long to register their opinions about industrialization. As early as the 1850s, A.J. Bray reported that in Montreal the changes initiated by the firm of Brown and Childs were 'violently opposed by the shoemakers, but progress triumphed over prejudice.'[14] In England the Northampton shoemakers fought a series of strikes in the years 1857 to 1859 in an attempt to resist the introduction of the sewing machine.[15] In Lynn, Massachusetts artisan resistance culminated in the Great Strike of 1860.[16] In Quebec City, in the 1860s 'nos bons cordonniers ... se ligüerent contre les petits americains, ainsi qu'ils appelaient Messieurs Coté et Bresse et voulurent les chasser de la place.'[17] These early manifestations were local in nature.

In Toronto opposition to the sewing machine was begun by the journeymen tailors, not the shoemakers. In 1852 the tailors struck successfully against the introduction of sewing machines by merchant tailor Thomas Hutchinson, celebrating their triumph with a procession down King Street, Toronto's major business thoroughfare. The parade featured a sewing machine, carried by the tailors 'after the fashion of a corpse on its way to the burial grounds.'[18] The victory was short-lived, however, and in 1854

Hutchinson defeated his tailors – but only after a lengthy strike and criminal proceedings against pickets for intimidation.[19]

Toronto shoemakers did not resist the sewing machine directly but used their organization to maintain wage rates. In September 1857, they successfully dictated a new scale to their employers; in January 1858, however, they were forced to strike when their employers lowered the wages. This strike gained considerable attention when a strikebreaker pressed charges of conspiracy and riot against eight union leaders, on whose house 'the marks of shot and shoemakers' sprigs [awls] were found about the windows and shutters.'[20] The city's police magistrate referred those charged to the coming assize and held the defendants on the large sum of £50 bail each. The shoemakers were acquitted of all seven charges of conspiracy, assault, riot, and the common law transgressions of molesting, intimidating, and threatening when they appeared at the winter assizes. The decision was met with sustained applause in the courtroom, but the rather unclear grounds for acquittal did nothing to prevent Toronto employers from invoking similar charges later.[21]

Toronto shoemakers demonstrated their strength and solidarity in the late 1850s and displayed all the signs of the skilled worker's defence of his craft control. They set wages and withdrew their labour if their demands were not met. Journeymen who transgressed their fellows' dictates were dealt with harshly and regarded as totally beyond the pale of manliness.[22]

The introduction of the McKay machine in the mid-1860s changed the nature of unionism in the shoe industry. The local unions quickly perceived that the new factory system, made possible by the McKay machine, demanded a more widespread form of organization than they had previously evolved. Therefore, a meeting of Ontario shoemakers was called in Toronto in 1867 and the Boot and Shoe Makers Union of the Province of Ontario was formed – only five months after the founding of the Knights of St Crispin in Milwaukee and before that body spread beyond Wisconsin. Representatives from eight Ontario towns were present and in three days of meetings they created a provincial structure that provided the basis for the expansion of the Knights of St Crispin into Ontario in 1869 and 1870.[23] Toronto shoemakers provided the leadership in these developments.

Newell Daniels, who had worked in the shoe industry in his native Massachusetts, founded the KOSC in Milwaukee in March 1867. By April 1870 the order included 327 locals and by April 1872 there were about 400 lodges. In 1868 the Knights entered Canada, organizing a lodge in Montreal (Lodge 122), following in 1869 with lodges in Quebec, St John (Lodge 171), Toronto (Lodge 159), Guelph (Lodge 202), Hamilton (Lodge 212), and

Windsor. The next year two more lodges (315, 356) were organized in Toronto as well as in Halifax, Chatham (326), Georgetown, London (242), St Catharines (34), Stratford (233), and Barrie (353). In 1871 lodges were added in Galt (371) and Orillia (372).[24]

An analysis of the Crispin experience in Toronto demonstrates the inadequacies of much of the previous literature on the subject. The old view of the order as a pre-industrial anachronism, or the later view of it as a harbinger of industrial unionism, has not proved particularly useful.[25] The order merged the old traditions of the shoemaker with the new realities of factory production. As Alan Dawley has pointed out, the same workers 'bridged the world of the artisan and the world of the factory worker.'[26] The Crispin society in Toronto was always more than an economic institution. It organized excursions, balls, dinners, and even a quadrille club.[27] These social functions played important roles in maintaining craft solidarity in the early years of the factory.

The order also provided a funeral benefit; perhaps even more important than the financial aid supplied was the solemnity and dignity the attendance of one's brother Crispins lent to such an event.[28] Funeral attendance was stipulated in the by-laws of the lodges and fifty-cent fine was levied for absenteeism. Moreover, if next-of-kin were not available to arrange a funeral, the dead member's lodge would undertake to do so.[29] The order had a special funeral rite, which in itself demonstrated ritual and actual solidarity,[30] showing outsiders as well the strength of the order by the large number of Knights in attendance.[31]

Processions were also an important way of maintaining solidarity. As 'festivals of the old artisan way of life presented in the context of the new system of industrial capitalism,'[32] they symbolized for the participants (and now for the historian) the meeting place of the two worlds. In a confederation parade in Hamilton, 'The shoemakers with King Crispin and his champion and sundry other worthies grotesquely habited were a decided attraction. The King was dressed in robes of pink with a crown of gold upon his head, while the champion looked decidedly like a warrior of olden times.'[33] Five years later, when marching for the nine-hour day, Hamilton Knights of St Crispin were 'headed by their marshall in uniform on horseback and their officers wearing the uniform of the Order. They carried a very handsome banner bearing the portrait of St. Crispin and having the motto "Union is Strength."'[34] Toronto shoemakers marched in similar celebrations carrying symbols of St Crispin, an organic link with a past artisanal world.

Ritual ran throughout the workings of the order in the form of oaths *adaptation not opposition*

secret work, and ceremony – all showing the adaptation of old artisan traditions to the unprecedented situation shoemakers faced. For example, the KOSC initiation ode used the legend of St Crispin in similar ways to the traditional *Histories of the Gentle Craft* which had been given to each new shoemaker at the end of his apprenticeship in England:

> St. Crispin is the name we take;
>   May we now be inclined
> His virtues all to imitate,
>   In him a pattern find.[35]

The names and roles of the order's officers share much in the tradition of Masonry, and in discussions about changes in the constitution in 1872, this debt was made explicit by the International Grand Secretary, S.G. Cummings: 'In all other orders, such as the Masons, Odd Fellows, Good Templars, and others, digests are used, and many a trouble has been amicably settled that threatened to become serious. Why should we not have one? An Order like ours, composed of such diverse elements, liable at any moment to come into collision with each other, makes a digest an imperative necessity.'[36] Cummings' second point tells us much of the role of ritual in creating solidarity.

Other parts of the Knights of St Crispin Ritual illustrated awareness of the new reality facing shoemakers:

You well know our trade has become unreliable and fluctuating, that our wages are reduced on the slightest pretexts and that at no season of the year do we receive fair compensation for our toil; therefore we have banded ourselves togeither [sic] for the purpose of securing identity of interest, and unity of action among those of us employed on the various parts of boots and shoes.[37]

Here we see a recognition of the new division of labour, that the craft mode of production was gone. The merging of the old and new was best described in Sir Knight's charge which immediately preceded the initiate's solemn oath of obligation: 'Brother ... you have wisely resolved to join this order of ours, and thus aid us in the work of rescuing our labor from its present depressed condition, and secure, through organization that degree of independence that justly belongs to us.'[38] The emphasis on ritual in the KOSC, and later in the Knights of Labor, has not received sufficient attention from historians. E.J. Hobsbawm's discussion of ritual in *Primitive Rebels*, for example, raises many questions about the longevity of ritual in the North

American labour scene. Employing a perhaps overly schematic distinction between 'form' and 'content,' Hobsbawm writes of the triumph of content by the 1830s and 1840s. The tenacity of complex ritual in North American labour and its utility in new struggles have perhaps been underrated by historians who have not understood the importance of pre-industrial culture to the emerging working class.

At the heart of the entire Crispin effort was an attempt to regain the control that shoemakers had previously exercised over their lives. Their loss went beyond their workplace, for they also sacrificed the pride and self-respect they had enjoyed in their communities. While visiting Toronto in April 1870, Newell Daniels repeatedly touched on this theme, ending one speech with a poem that reiterated the traditional understanding of the labour theory of value:

Whom shall we honour as heroes?
　To whom our praises sing?
The pampered child of fortune?
　The titled lord or king?
They live by others labour,
　Take all and nothing give.
The noblest types of mankind
　Are they that work to live.

Who spans the earth with iron?
　Who rears the palace dome?
Who creates for the rich man
　The comforts of his home?
It is the patient toiler
　All honour to him then ·
The true wealth of a nation
　Is in her workingmen![40]

In Toronto, the Crispins were successful in organizing the entire male factory labour force. At first, they accepted as members all workers employed in the factory and attempted to police hiring policies only later. Membership was open to any male over eighteen years of age 'who has worked an aggregate of two years at boot or shoe making ..., and shall at the time be engaged at his trade.'[41] The timing of their organizing success is difficult to pinpoint but from the 60 members in the one lodge with which they began in January 1869, they reached an estimated peak of 600 in three or four lodges by December 1870.[42] Not satisfied with organizing only the men, they also made serious efforts to help create a Daughters of St Crispin lodge in Toronto but were stymied by the manufacturers' intransigence on that issue.[43] The Knights' unsuccessful attempt to organize the women operatives toughened employer opposition to the order in general. Toronto employers' flexibility in meeting the Knights' demands would have been dramatically limited if they had had to face an organized group of women workers as well. Yet the order had considerable success organizing women in the United States and the Daughters of St Crispin took their place beside Susan B. Anthony's female printers at National Labor Union meetings.[44]

The personal histories of the approximately 80 members of the KOSC identified by name in the daily and labour press and in the minutes of the Toronto Trades Assembly (TTA) and the Canadian Labour Union (CLU) reveals much about the composition of the order.[45] It consisted solely of working shoemakers. No bosses, foremen, or even independent shoemakers or cobblers were ever mentioned as belonging to the order. The constitution specifically excluded 'agents and foremen ... with the power to fix the rate of wages paid, or to discharge those employed' from membership.[46] The subsequent careers of these men showed how narrow were their options under industrial capitalism. The overwhelming majority of them remained shoemakers. A few became proprietors of small grocery stores or saloons, traditional sanctuaries for former working-class leaders of the nineteenth century. One even became a labourer during the depression of the 1870s but he returned to shoemaking after a few years. The only other noticeable change was that another four or five became the proprietors of small cobbler shops where they repaired factory shoes and perhaps did a little custom work on the side. None became a leader in the industry. It should be noted again that many of the pioneer industrial capitalists in this field were not practising shoemakers but simply entrepreneurs with available capital.

These workers provided considerable stability and experience to the trade union movement of the 1880s. Perhaps the outstanding example among Toronto shoemakers was Michael Derham, whose career spanned the establishment of the Ontario-wide body of 1867, the KOSC, Knights of Labour Local Assembly (LA) 2211, and the Boot and Shoe Workers International Union. Two other Crispins of the 1870s, James Draisey and G. Duncan, also served later in the Knights of Labor (LA 6250).

The Toronto manufacturers' counter-attack against the Crispins started in late fall 1870. When the 1869 contract came up for renewal, the Crispins sought price increases on certain types of work.[47] All the manufacturers agreed to pay the increase and peace seemed assured for another year until W.B. Hamilton refused to sign the contract, insisting that his word should suffice. In the end the Knights forced him to sign by means of a short turnout at his factory. This is a good example of the transformed nature of trade unionism under factory conditions. Whereas before shoemakers had declared their price and withdrawn their labour if it was not met, now they demanded signed bills of wages – a clear indication of their understanding of the effects of skill diminution on their ability to control the labour market.[48] The Knights struck against Hamilton again in late December or early January, after he broke the agreement by reducing the wages of some of the men. This time, however, solidarity broke down, and 27 Crispins tendered their resignations from the union and indicated they would return to work. Their resignations were refused and, when they returned to work and broke their oaths by revealing lodge proceedings, they were expelled from the order. The strike continued. In January 1871 both Childs and Hamilton, and Henry Cobley and Co. published a circular attacking Crispin tyranny and closing their shops to members of the order. They accused the Crispins of limiting their lines of manufacture, of coercing other workers to join the union, and in general of 'arrogant and overbearing conduct.' The rhetoric of this struggle ran through most strikes during this period. Although often involving wages, strikes were also usually viewed as a struggle for control of how production should be organized. Were the old, skilled workers in the new factories to retain a significant part of the control they had exercised over pre-factory production and over their own time, or were they simply to become wage labour, totally subject to the clock and to the manager? The Knights generally demanded to 'exercise the right to control our labor and to be consulted in determining the price paid for it.'[49] The Toronto Crispins specifically perceived the employers' attack on their control as an attempt to destroy the union: 'Their object is of course very apparent. If they could break up the organization of the men, they would be enabled to dictate terms, cut down wages to the lowest niche, make whatever objectionable rules they please, and harass their employees perpetually.'[50] They vowed to fight the companies and commended the other Toronto manufacturers who continued to run union shops.

This strike continued into the spring, with the companies enjoying some success in recruiting scabs, but they were not able to return production to its normal level. The employers actively searched for replacements from as far away as England, where Canadian emigration agents sought 400 shoemakers for Toronto, Hamilton, and London, all centres of active Crispin organization. There was even some discussion of following the example of one New England manufacturer and importing Chinese labour.[51] The emerging anti-emigration policy of the Canadian labour movement must be studied in the context of such blatant anti-working-class efforts.

The situation in Toronto took an ominous turn for the worse when the order called a strike at a second large factory. In early April, the shoemakers at the firm of Damer and King turned out. The immediate issue was the firm's refusal to fire a number of young boys who had been hired without permission of the KOSC. There were a series of other issues, however, which had been aggravating the shoemakers for some time. One of these was the company's refusal to recognize a female operatives' union that the Knights had helped to organize. Another complaint concerned the inferior nature of the shoes being produced, which not only upset the Crispins' pride but also cost them money since the uppers were so defective they took longer to work. The final blow, however, was management's 'heaping indignities upon us, such as causing us to enter and retire from the shop by a back lane so full of dirt and slush that we could not help but wet our feet.'[52] The shoemakers' pride was clearly not something to be tampered with.

The Crispins held a demonstration on 4 April, when 50 of the strikers left to seek jobs in Chicago and other points west. From 400 to 500 shoemakers marched through Toronto streets, headed by the band of the Tenth Royals, a local militia company, and carrying the flags of the United States and Great Britain. On their arrival at the Great Western Depot, they were addressed by H.L. Beebe, a Crispin leader, who assured them they had the support of all Toronto workers in their resistance to the bosses' unjust oppression. Tension, already high as a result of the two strikes involving the city's largest union, was increased when *The Leader* launched a hysterical attack on the order as a seditious and Yankee-controlled threat to all things Canadian; the evidence produced was that the Stars and Stripes had been carried in the procession to the station. *The Leader* even argued that 'the Mayor would have acted properly had he prevented the flag of a foreign nation being flaunted in the faces of our citizens on the public thoroughfares on such an occasion.'[53] Not surprisingly, the first report of violence came only one day after *The Leader*'s shrill attack. Shoemakers reportedly assaulted a man at work in a Yonge Street workshop. Two men were arrested, but the details were not revealed. Late on Thursday night, or in the early hours of Friday morning, 6 and 7 April, the factory of Childs and Hamilton was the scene of, what the *Globe* termed, 'a dastardly outrage.' A person or persons entered the factory through a door on a back lane and proceeded to selectively destroy machines, work in progress, shoemakers' kits, and the foremen's outwork records. The damaged machines included a McKay machine, battered with a sledge-hammer, a channelling machine, and a rounding machine. The only areas of the factories damaged were those where the scabs worked; the leather storage areas and the female operatives' workroom were untouched.

Immediately the manufacturers and the press blamed the KOSC. W.B. Hamilton told the press of his certainty that the Crispins were responsible. *The Telegraph* argued in an editorial that 'under the circumstances the Knights of St. Crispin must be held responsible.'[54] The *Globe*, more cautiously, suggested that 'the appearances point strongly to members of the Society as the perpetrators of this outrage.' Even the staid *Monetary Times* felt called upon to indict the Crispins as a 'belligerent organization.'[55] The order predictably 'repudiated any connection with it whatever,' adding that the act was 'not tolerated by the officers nor by the rules of the society.'[56] Initially the order offered a fifty-dollar reward but withdrew the offer when it detected discrepancies in Hamilton's story. The owner claimed not to have discovered the outrage until late morning, but the order claimed to have a witness who swore that he had seen Hamilton's son there earlier. The order then argued that the act had been committed to damage the society's reputation and went so far as to suggest that Hamilton should seek the perpetrator among his 'independent' men.

Although police investigated, the case was never solved. The manufacturer's allegations against the Crispins remained unproved. Whether the Knights as a body were responsible will never be known, but the evidence certainly suggested that the act was performed either by members or by sympathizers of the order. The attack was selective with regard to its targets, as in most traditional examples of 'collective bargaining by riot.'[57] This selectivity indicated the premises of the attack: damage to the machines would limit production and the destruction of shop records and workmen's kits stood as stark warnings to strikebreakers to reconsider the magnitude of their decision. Nevertheless, in this case it was an act performed in weakness, not in strength, and represented the failure of the order to impose its will through the new methods and techniques of collective bargaining. This recourse to violent tactics to enforce workers' power was destined to fail against a manufacturer as large as Childs and Hamilton who had access to far more support than did the small textile manufacturers assaulted earlier by Ned Ludd and his followers. Again we should be cautious, however, for too much should not be made of the traditional in this assault. Workers have continued to respond to the power of industry (reinforced, when necessary, by armed state power) with violence throughout the twentieth century. Also, these were quite unusual acts in Crispin history. John Hall found no examples of machine breaking in Massachusetts.[58] Nevertheless, many of the assumptions of Crispin organization that we have already discussed lent themselves well to these actions. Rituals, oaths, and secrecy were the constant companions of earlier occasions of property damage in working-class history. The very inability of the Toronto police to break the case was indicative of the shoemaker's collective refusal to cooperate with the investigation. Only solidarity could have protected the proponents of direct action, for the community of shoemakers was small enough that absolute secrecy within the craft seemed unlikely, if not impossible.

There were other incidents in this strike. Only one week after the machine breaking, a striking shoemaker, who either indicated his intent to scab or was too vociferous in his criticism of the strike, discovered that his kit had been destroyed by fellow workmen who then jeered his invective over the damage. In mid-May, the picket captain at Damer and King's factory was arrested and convicted of using threatening and abusive language to strikebreakers. A twenty-dollar fine or a two-month imprisonment was demanded for his freedom with the word 'scab.' Although the two strikes continued throughout the summer, they failed. In the fall the newly organized Toronto Trades Assembly took up the shoemakers' cause and attempted to arbitrate between the order and three non-union factories. Although the minutes record some initial success, the final outcome was never recorded.[59] It is possible, however, that the industry-wide 10 per cent increase of prices on 1 January 1872 indicated a compromise with the Toronto Crispins.[60]

Crispin activity remained quite visible in Toronto and throughout Ontario despite the setbacks of 1871.[61] In December 1872 Toronto lodge 159 absorbed lodge 356 leaving Toronto with two lodges.[62] The following year the Ontario Grand Lodge broke away from the International Grand Lodge and reverted to its earlier independent provincial association. Active organizing went on, and new lodges were chartered under a new numerical system which followed the Crispin pattern. Toronto Lodge 159 became the new number 1, and Toronto Lodge 315 became Lodge 6. The new lodges organized in 1873 and 1874 were: Peterborough (Lodge 12), Brantford (Lodge 13), Belleville (Lodge 14), Thorold (Lodge 15), Ingersoll (Lodge 16), and Preston (Lodge 17). In 1873 strikes were fought in Orillia and Guelph. The province-wide nature of the organization was reinforced by celebrations such as the 1873 St Catharines' excursion picnic. In late August approximately 300 Crispins and friends sailed from Toronto to St

Catharines where they joined 200 of their Hamilton and St Catharines brothers. After marching with bands and banners through the main streets of the city, they arrived at Montebello Gardens for games, speeches, and refreshments. In early 1875 Toronto Lodge 1 had 200 members and Lodge 6, 55; by the end of that year, however, Lodge 1 dropped to 50 members under the impact of the deepening depression.[63]

In 1876 the Canadian Grand Lodge met for the last time in Hamilton, where it was noted that 'although the depressed conditions of trade had thrown many of the lodges back in point of numbers, the order on the whole was in a flourishing condition.'[64] This last convention again sought international affiliation with the revived Knights of St Crispin. For this purpose they named a delegate to the next meeting of the International Grand Lodge of Crispins, who was 'to strike a basis of union.' Probably nothing came of this initiative. The lodge's disappearance at the provincial level was undoubtedly due to the severe dislocations of the depression. The boot and shoe industry was particularly heavily hit:

During 1875, the manufacturing of boots and shoes received a severe check by frequent failure and because of a grossly overdone state of business. Again in subsequent years, the industry was plunged into a fearful condition of doubt and uncertainty ... It was not until the spring of 1880 that it could be said to have before it a future which promised sound conditions.[65]

After the demise of the Provincial Grand Lodge, local chapters in several shoe towns retained their organization. This was certainly true in Toronto where the KOSC remained on the scene until 1886, when they entered the Knights of Labor as Crispin Local Assembly 6250.[66] The tenacity of the Crispins in Toronto was not unique. A Crispin-led lasters' strike occurred in Montreal in 1882[67] and St John Crispins marched in a labour parade in 1883.[68]

The Toronto Crispins had a continuous existence until they joined the Knights of Labor, but after 1877 they ceased to be the only organization of shoemakers in Toronto. In that year a group of factory operatives, some of whom had previously belonged to the Crispins, organized the Wholesale Boot and Shoemakers' Union.[69] The KOSC from this point on included only custom shoemakers. This group of skilled shoemakers fought strikes in 1881, 1885, and 1887. In 1881 and 1887 they won pay increases and in 1885 they successfully resisted Dack and Sons' attempt to introduce team production in the custom trade. The proposed teams would have consisted of five shoemakers, all working by hand, thus dividing the functions involved in custom shoemaking which previously had been managed by one worker.[70]

The Wholesale Boot and Shoemakers' Union was successful in negotiating contracts without recourse to strikes in 1879, 1881, 1882, and 1883.[71] The first major strike of female workers in Toronto occurred in April 1882 when the operatives of five major factories demanded union recognition, a uniform bill of wages, and a wage advance.[72] Toronto unionists provided massive support for the female strikers. The Wholesale Boot and Shoemakers' Union lent advice, financial aid, and in the end went out on a sympathy strike with their sister shoe workers. The KOSC also supplied financial aid, and Crispin leaders often appeared at strike meetings to proffer support and solidarity. These daily meetings were high in spirit and militancy throughout the three-week strike. Many of the operatives were not happy with the final settlement which won them a uniform bill in the future, but no guarantee of an advance, although this remained a cloudy issue with many claiming that there had been such a promise. One-third of the women voted to remain on strike. The women who had sung the following song in April struck again in December of the same year and again in November 1883:

We won't sew on a button,
  Nor make a buttonhole;
We won't stitch up a shoetop,
  All ready for the sole,
Until the price is raised a peg,
  On all the shops' pay-roll.[73]

The uniform bill that the bosses had promised was finally delivered in February 1884, almost two years after the first strike. Although there was much discontent with the new bill, no collective action was taken against its provisions. The union of female boot and shoe workers was also the first women's union to join the Toronto Trades and Labor Council.

In September 1882 the Wholesale Boot and Shoemakers' Union joined the Knights of Labor as a body. The new organization, Pioneer Assembly (LA 2211), existed until 1890, when it left the Knights of Labor to join the new Boot and Shoe Workers International Union as local 77. The new union was a break-away from the Knights of Labor and had been created out of National Trades Assembly 216, the national organization of Knights of Labor shoemakers. National Trades Assembly 216 was founded with an invocation to Crispin traditions which 'put the shoemaker in the very vanguard of the labor movement.'[74] The Knights of Labor had built on Crispin experience in Canada as they had in the United States.[75] In Hamilton, as well as in Toronto, shoemakers were among the first workers to join the new organization. Pioneer LA 2211 carried on many Crispin practices. It took as its major objectives 'benevolence and mutual protection, to secure to each other just remuneration of our labour, and the burial of deceased members.'[76] A forty-dollar funeral benefit was paid to a member's widow or next-of-kin. In addition, a well-attended funeral was almost guaranteed by a stiff fine for members who failed to attend.

The ever-increasing division of labour in shoe factories necessitated a more complicated shop-committee structure than the Knights of St Crispin had had. Shop committees were elected every six months and were composed of at least one member from each branch of the trade represented in the shop. No individual was allowed to talk to the boss or foreman regarding a grievance; instead it would be taken up by the shop committee, which had the 'power to settle all disputes between employer and employee in their respective shops,' but did not have the power to call a work stoppage without consultation with the entire local assembly. As we shall see later, limitations such as these caused considerable discontent among workers in the Toronto shoe industry.

The relative quiet in the boot and shoe industry in Toronto after 1882 was at least partially related to its declining economic status. Two of the largest Toronto factories failed in the mid-1880s: Damer in 1883 and Charlesworth in 1886.[77] The new Boot and Shoe Workers International Union fought and won its first strike in February 1890 against J.D. King and Co. Nevertheless, leverage against management was decreasing as the industry declined in Toronto.[78]

Ontario workers had been aware of this danger as early as 1882 when they had rallied to the support of striking Montreal lasters. The recording secretary of Hamilton shoemakers' assembly (LA 2132) had written to T.V. Powderly that 'we believe that a cut in their wages is the first step towards a reduction in ours, as the competition is so keen in our business, between Montreal, Toronto, and Hamilton.'[79] The ever-increasing centralization and concentration in the industry was apparent in 1888 when, of the 18 remaining Ontario shoe factories, 11 were located in Toronto. By then Montreal had 34 and Quebec City 25.[80] The situation deteriorated rapidly, from a Toronto point of view, and by the 1890s J.D. King and Co. was the only major remaining Ontario producer. By 1894 the *Monetary Times* bemoaned the fact that Toronto had become little more than 'a distributing centre for Quebec-made shoes.' Even J.D. King had been forced to open a factory in Levis, Quebec, because of the lower wages paid there.[81] Three years later the *Times* noted even more emphatically that 'the shoe trade of Ontario has passed to the province of Quebec.' 'The five or six busy shoe factories' of Toronto had given way to only 'two firms who manufacture shoes by factory methods.'[82] Later that year when workers struck against J.D. King, the paper blamed the Toronto industry's decline totally on trade unionism.[83]

The history of the shoemakers' response to industrial capitalism consists of much more than strikes and trade-union organization. Indeed, it is a history of the cultural adaptation of old forms to counter the new pressures of factory production. In 1887 Frank Foster celebrated the old role of the shoemaker in early labour organization and looked forward to the new:

The 'blazoned banner' of St. Crispin has ever been flung out at the head of the labor column. The organization may come and the organization may go; but we may have faith that the love of right and liberty underlying all social reforms will in the future, as in the past, give inspiration to the workmen in the gentle craft of leather. Crispin, Unionist, Knight of Labor, have all had for their ideal a better livelihood and larger possibilities for their members, and in this broadening sweep and loftier tread of labor organization lies the high hope of the days to come and children yet unborn.[84]

The transitional roles of the Crispins and Knights of Labor can also be seen in John Hall's encounter with an old Massachusetts shoemaker:

I even found an aged laster in Lynn who claimed to have been a Crispin, though it seems clear he was confusing the Crispins with the Knights of Labor. The way he spoke of the Crispins made it unmistakable that to have been a Crispin was a proud and a glorious thing. If the craftsman had to surrender his pride in his individual skills, he was no less a man of spirit. His pride henceforth would be in his loyalty to his fellow workmen and to the standards of mutual help necessary to deal with socialized and mechanized production.[85]

Never anachronistic in their response to industrial capitalism, the shoemakers demanded their share in the manifold gains that latter-day Whigs constantly heralded as companions of the new order.

4

Coopers encounter machines: the struggle for shorter hours

The experience of coopers in Toronto and throughout Ontario in the late 1860s and early 1870s provides another example of artisan response to industrial capitalism. Although their reaction was less dramatic than the Crispins' Luddism, the coopers shared with the shoemakers the unfortunate fate of watching the destruction of their craft by a combination of mechanization, the rise of factory production, the depression of the 1870s, and an all-out employer offensive.

The making of barrels was a very old handicraft steeped in tradition. In England, the United States, and the Canadas coopers enjoyed all the prerogatives of the skilled artisan. Bob Gilding, an old cooper and trade union militant, described the old traditions of his craft: 'The cooper who worked at the block was very much his own master. He was on piecework, paid for the work he produced, not for the hours he kept. He had his own allotted space, his "berth", upon which the uninvited stranger trespassed at his peril. He had his own set of tools which could run to as many as fifty.'[1] The trade had strong rituals and habitual methods of work, which in England were maintained well on into the twentieth century. The historian of the American craft described vividly the old-time cooper's life style:

Early on Saturday morning, the big brewery wagon would drive up to the shop. Several of the coopers would club together, each paying his proper share, and one of them would call out the window to the driver, 'Bring me a goose egg', meaning a half-barrel of beer. Then others would buy 'Goose Eggs' and there would be a merry time all around ... Saturday night was a big night for the old time cooper. It meant going out, strolling around town, meeting friends usually at a local saloon, and having a good time generally after a hard week's work. Usually the good time continued over Sunday, so that on the following day he usually was not in the best condition to settle down to the regular day's work. Many coopers used to spend this day sharpening up their tools, carrying in stock, discussing current events and in getting things in shape for the big day of work on the morrow. Thus Blue Monday was something of a tradition with the coopers, and the day was also more or less lost as far as production was concerned. 'Can't do much today, but I'll give her hell tomorrow,' seemed to be the Monday slogan. But bright and early Tuesday morning 'Give her hell' they would, banging away lustily for the rest of the week until Saturday, which was pay day again, and new thoughts of the 'Goose Eggs.'[2]

At mid-century, however, these traditions were coming under attack from trade unionists as well as efficiency-minded manufacturers. A St Louis cooper's letter of 1871 depicted both the tenacity of the old tradition and the new critical attitudes of some skilled workers:

The shops are paid off every two weeks, on which occasion one of these shops is sure to celebrate that time-honoured festival, Blue Monday. When Blue Monday falls it usually lasts for three days. And the man who succeeds in working during the continuance of this carnival is a man of strong nerve and indomitable will. Mr. Editor, did you ever year of Black Monday? Perhaps not. But I tell you wherever Blue Monday is kept, there also is kept Black Monday. The only difference is, Blue Monday is celebrated at the shop, while Black Monday is observed at the cooper's home. The man celebrates Blue Monday, but the wife and family observe Black Monday.[3]

In 1870 craftsmen created the Coopers International Union (CIU) in order, as the Chicago *Workingman's Advocate* so aptly put it, to avoid the fate of the ship caulkers and ship carpenters, artisanal victims of the new age of iron and steam.[4] The new union, with head offices in Cleveland, was 'in many ways the model of a successful organization of skilled mid-nineteenth century American craftsmen.'[5] Its leaders were devoted to labour reform, which found its organizational expression through the U.S. National Labour Union. In Canada, John Hewitt of the Cooper's International Union played an active role in organizing the Toronto Trades Assembly and the Canadian Labour Union, and was one of the major theorists of the nine-hour movement of 1872. The CIU created a union structure which provided sick and death benefits, an international strike fund, and a card system for tramping members. The incentives to organization were depicted clearly in the CIU's extensive ritual: 'You are coopers and come here to unite with us for the mutual benefit and protection of our trade, ourselves and families, and that we may have steady work, and that we receive for our labour fair and uniform remuneration, throughout the year ...'[6] The attack on older artisanal traditions demanded a new tactic: 'Therefore for our own protection and benefit we have decided to keep our business transactions within these walls strictly to ourselves and allow no one outide our circle to be any the wiser for our organization.'[7]

As with the Knights of St Crispin, secrecy and ritual played an important role in coopers' unionism. In his report to the 1871 international convention, President Martin Foran re-emphasized this: 'Especially would I recommend a more stringent and binding obligation and the adoption of a more imposing, solemn and impressive ceremony. The experience of the past year has more than ever confirmed me in the belief that the more secret you make the order the more you increase its power.'[8] Toronto coopers' leader John Hewitt made his position clear on this question that same year:

Among these excrescences upon society, might be mentioned that king scab and covenant breaker, Thomas Galloway. This wretch that by some accident claims affinity to that class of the animal creation known as human, but having all the instincts of the lower class of creation without one redeeming or ennobling quality that would entitle to manhood ... For this thing the men of Guelph want a name ... He made it a matter of sport to expose our unwritten work, and thereby set at naught those solemn covenants that can only test man's honor and truthfulness.[9]

Coopers did not take their ritual lightly! Again at the 1873 convention the subject came up, and they decided to maintain the old grip, the countersign, and signals but to change the sign of recognition, the passwords, and the testword.[10]

Entering Canada in 1870, the union organized 24 branches in the first two years of its existence.[11] On a visit to Chicago in early 1872, John Hewitt announced that 'the coopers in Canada were alive and active and increasing their organization rapidly.'[12] Their decline was to be just as precipitous as their rise. But let us first examine the basis of their strength.

Coopers, like most skilled workers in the late nineteenth century, can best be described as 'autonomous workmen,' defined by Benson Soffer as workers possessing: 'some significant degree of control over the quantity and quality of the product; the choice and maintenance of equipment; the methods of wage payment and the determination of individual wages and hours; the scheduling and assignment of work; recruitment, hiring, lay-off and transfer; training and promotion of personnel; and other related conditions of work.'[13] A reading of *The Coopers' Journal*, the excellent magazine of the CIU, provides considerable evidence that Canadian coopers enjoyed most of these prerogatives.

As was true for most unions of skilled workers in the nineteenth century, wages were not arrived at by collective bargaining. The union members met together, arrived at the price of their labour, informed management of their decision, and either accepted the new rate with gratitude or struck if the boss refused. Local unions had no trouble dictating terms in prosperous times, as can be seen in the August 1871 report of the Brantford local which simply stated that they had imposed a new price list and expected no trouble.[14] In January 1872, representatives from seven of the fifteen existing Ontario CIU locals met in Toronto to arrive at a province-wide price list.[15] This document not only imposed prices but also called for a maximum ten-hour day province-wide. It dictated prices for 37 different categories of piece work and added a day rate of $1.75 for work not included on the list.

In addition to assuming control of hours and wages, coopers also restricted production, especially when work was short. In their *Ritual* was an attack on 'working nearly two days in one [which] inevitably [produced] an excess in supply above demand and competition and a general tumbling down of prices.'[16] As we shall see, this problem also led them towards a strong advocacy of shorter hours. By restricting production they could spread the work around, and also prevent speed-ups or other infringements on their shop-floor control. In the Ontario reports, stints are mentioned by locals in St Catharines, Seaforth, Oshawa, and London.[17] This union-dictated restriction of output was, of course, the greatest evil in the eyes of the manufacturer. Coopers also struggled to control the methods of production, as in this Brantford case:

H.W. Read, a boss cooper of this place, has shown his dirty, mean spirit by discharging three flour bbl. [barrel] makers from his shop; they were making bbls. at nine cts. jointed staves and circled heading. The boss took the jointer boy away, so that the hands had to join their own staves, which they did until noon, when they refused to make any more barrels, unless the staves were jointed for them or they were paid extra. For thus demanding their rights, Boss Read discharged them ... But we fear him not, for no respectable cooper will take a berth in his shop under the circumstances.

The union also enforced personnel decisions in the shop. The monitor of each shop made sure that new members' union cards were clear, and that non-members ('nons') would abide by the shop rules. 'Nons' who refused often found themselves moving on to the next town sooner than anticipated. In Brantford in 1871 for example: 'A scab in one of our shops, by the name of David Clawson, made himself very obnoxious to our men by his persistent abuse of the Union. At our last meeting it was ordered that the shop should strike against him, which was accordingly done, the consequence of which was that the mean tool of a man tramped and our men were out but half a day.' One year later in Seaforth:

J. Carter [who was suspended in January 1872] got a berth at Ament's shop ... The monitor of the shop immediately went to him and asked him to pay up his dues ... And also that if he did not pay up, either he or they should not work there. [After he refused] the monitor of the shop went to the boss and told him that he must either sack Carter or they would take their tools out of the shop ... [When he refused] they did instantly.

The coopers controlled admission to the craft and their ritual pledged them to 'allow no one to teach a new hand [in order] to control the supply of help.'[18] Use of helpers and apprenticeship rules were tightly supervised by the union.[19] For example, when Hamilton cooper Joseph Gleeson arrived in Toronto with his brother, an apprentice, Hewitt objected and appealed successfully to the CIU against the importation of apprentices.[20]

In each of the examples cited the ultimate enforcement resided in the coopers' willingness to withdraw their labour. Undoubtedly many other shop disagreements were settled without recourse to anything other than the threat of a strike. The English shop tradition allowed any two coopers in a shop to request a 'roll-up' at any time during working hours to discuss problems with the price list, with shop conditions, or with the quality of materials, or any other grievance. When a roll-up was called, the boss was excluded from the discussion until the men decided on a collective position, which was then communicated to the boss by the 'collector' (shop steward). No one returned to work until the issue was resolved. If the boss refused to meet their demands or if a satisfactory compromise was not arranged, a strike would result.[21] North American coopers appear to have engaged in similar practices when their union was sufficiently strong.

But perhaps even more striking than the recourse to immediate shop action was the pervasiveness of appeals to manliness, which David Montgomery has argued was a crucial component of 'the craftsmen's ethical code.'[22] Skilled workers carried themselves with pride and felt themselves to be the equal of their boss. CIU President Martin Foran's novel, *The Other Side*,[23] illustrated this theme well. The hero was a proud, respectable workman surrounded by unscrupulous capitalists and unmanly workers who had surrendered their self-respect in order to carry out the evil tasks of the monopolistic bosses. In discussing his didactic novel, Foran claimed:

The main incidents of this story are founded upon 'notorious fact', so notorious that anyone wishing it can be furnished with irrefragable, incontestable proofs in sup-port of all the charges made against the typical employer, Revalson; that working men have been – because being trade unionists – discharged, photographed on street corners, driven from their homes, hounded like convicted felons, prevented from obtaining work elsewhere, arrested at the beck of employers, thrown into loathesome prisons on ex parte evidence, or held to bail in sums beyond their reach by subsidized, prejudiced, bigoted dispensers of injustice, & in every mean dishon-ourable manner imaginable, inhumanly victimized and made to feel that public opinion, law & justice were Utopian 'unreal mockeries' except to men of position and money.[24]

Canadian coopers saw manliness as the keystone of their struggle and for them honour and pride were sacrosanct. 'Owls' or 'nons' who broke pledges or violated oaths were less than men:

At our last monthly meeting, the name of George Morrow was erased from our books, it having been proven beyond a shadow of doubt that he had violated his obligation by making known the business of our meetings to his boss. This thing Morrow, for I cannot call him a man, has never been of any use to us, he has not only betrayed us, but degraded himself in the estimation of every good man in our community.[25]

The Hamilton corresponding secretary went on to describe Morrow as a 'compromise between man and beast.'

The tradition of autonomy in work and the culture which grew from it made the coopers men to be reckoned with. Yet, if the rise of the CIU was rapid, its decline was even more precipitous. By late 1873 only seventeen locals remained and by 1875 this number had plummeted to approximately five.[26] The Canadian case was in no way unique; from a peak membership of over 8,000 in 1872, the union's total declined to 1,500 by 1876. In that year *The Coopers' Journal* suspended publication.

This disastrous decline was related both to the depression of the mid-1870s and to a concerted employers' assault on the trade. The best account of the coopers' demise describes the displacement of the hand cooper by machines in the Standard Oil works in New York and Cleveland. These cities, which contained the largest concentrations of coopers in North America, saw an epic struggle as Standard Oil moved to crush the CIU, the one remaining obstacle in its path to modernization and total monopoly.[27]

A similar, although less dramatic, process took place in Ontario. Coopering began to crack its purely artisanal mould in the 1860s when the need for well-made, tight oil barrels in western Ontario led the Woodstock (later London) firm of R.W. and A. Burrows to introduce stave-making and dressing machinery.[28] Their Eastwood Barrel Factory also possessed Canada's first jointing machine. That factory's 40 hands were able to produce 150 barrels a day with machinery doing all – 'setting up' and hooping excepted.[29] These innovations were adopted by larger cooperages in the province, such as those at distilleries in Windsor and Toronto, where the three shops, Burrows, Walker, and Gooderham, also differed from the old-time cooper's shop in size: they resembled small manufactories far more than artisans' shops. Walker, the Windsor distiller, broke his coopers' strength over a four-year period. Up until 1868 all barrels were 'made from the rough'; that is, the craft mode of production still prevailed. For a barrel made in this way the cooper received 80 cents. That year, Walker bought machinery to dress the staves and heads, cutting the price to 60 cents. In the following years the price was reduced twice, first to 50 and finally to 40 cents a barrel. Hewitt sarcastically commented, 'Seeing the men before me happy and contented that their lot was such a good one, I bade them adieu, and left them alone in their glory.'[30] Similarly, in Toronto Gooderham employed 40 coopers, whereas the next biggest shop in 1871 had only seven.[31] Here once again, then, we see a process of combined and uneven development wherein the small producers maintain a craft mode of production while the larger producers move into a manufactory stage. Gooderham's two shops do not even figure in the census data because of their integration into the distillery statistics (see Tables 4.1 and 4.2).

These small producers were hardly cut off from their employees at all. Samuel Thompson, for example, was described by the secretary of the Toronto union as 'a good friend to our trade,' when he subscribed to the *Coopers' Journal*.[32] Later he, Thomas Delaney, and Michael O'Brien – all small bosses in 1871 – subscribed to a coopers' union benefit fund.

Although creating some problems for the CIU, the early machines of the 1860s did not abolish the need for skilled workers. Skill and knowledge were still important components of barrel-making, and as late as 1871 Martin Foran still found consolation in the cooper's skill:

[margin handwritten note: labour became more simple thus cheapened]

Many of our members place far too much significance on machinery as a substitute for their labour. I have given the subject much thought and consideration, and am unable to see any serious cause for apprehension in barrel machinery ... Ours is a trade that cannot be reduced to the thumbrule of unfailing uniformity. To make a general marketable piece of work, of any kind particular to our trade, it requires tact, judgement and discrimination on the part of the maker ... when the friends of barrel machinery succeed in inventing a thinking machine they will succeed in making a success.[33]

Within two years of this statement, however, Standard Oil's version of a thinking machine was a success.

The process was less revolutionary in Ontario, but the effects of increased mechanization can be seen in the reports of the Toronto local.[34] Gooderham's distillery was controlled by the union in 1870 when hours and wages were dictated by the workers. CIU President Martin Foran acclaimed 'Gooderman's [sic] shop as without exception the finest cooper shop [he had] ever seen,' in 1871. At its peak strength in March 1872, the Toronto local had complete control over the trade with 96 members and the membership still increasing. The next month, however, trouble became evident when a meeting was held to discuss scabs at Gooderham's shop. It was decided to do nothing since 'so many unions were getting into strikes' as part of the nine-hour movement. Later that summer Hewitt complained of the existence of bad feeling and still later explained that the union had experienced 'a reduction on beer work, owing to some of our men working in the largest shop in the city, going on that class of work at reduced rates.' Hewitt promised that this would be corrected as they were 'fully determined to sustain the Ontario price-list to the letter.' By December, however, the union suffered a severe setback and Hewitt inveighed that Gooderham's 'contained the most inveterate set of owls to be found on this continent and the few good men we have there, not being able to control the shop, I fear have concluded to sacrifice their principles and work for whatever price the great Gooderham chooses to pay rather than demand the bill of prices and run the risk of losing their berths.'

The ability of the coopers to dictate terms, however, was seriously undermined elsewhere in Ontario by the advent of machinery. In 1874 the Seaforth local noted that the installation of two barrel machines would throw a great number of coopers out of work. Six months later they reported their failure to control the machines because non-union coopers took their jobs at low rates. By the 1880s the struggle was over; the cooper's craft was dead. In 1887 a cooper in Windsor argued before the Labour

TABLE 4.1

Cooperages in Toronto, 1851–91

	1851	1861	1871‡	1881	1891
No. of establishments		5	6	5	10
No. of workers*			28	27	43
Wages in $000s			9.6	9.4	16.8
Raw material in $000s			9.6	13.4	17.8
Value of product in $000s		10.4	24.1	28.1	45.7
Value added in $000s			4.9	5.3	11.1
No. of coopers†	43	45	71	81	NA

* As recorded in Industrial Census.
† As recorded in census occupational listing.
‡ Aggregate, not manuscript returns.
Source: Canada, Census, 1851–91

TABLE 4.2

Cooperages in Toronto, 1871

	Capital in $000s	No. of workers	Motive force	Wages in $000s	Raw materials in $000s	Value of product in $000s	Value added in $000s
M. O'Brien	1.8	4		1.0	4.5	6.5	1.0
J. O'Brien	0.9	3		1.3	0.4	1.6	−0.1
T. Delaney	1.0	5		2.1	0.8	3.5	0.6
R. Charmichael	4.0	6		2.6	1.8	5.0	0.6
S. Thompson	3.0	7		2.7	1.8	7.2	2.7
C. Brown	1.4	3		0.5	0.2	1.9	1.2
Total	11.1	28		10.2	9.5	25.7	6.0

Source: Canada, Census, Industrial Mss., 1871

Commission that machinery had 'killed the trade,' and that there was no longer 'a man in the world who would send his son to be a cooper.'[35]

The power that coopers had possessed as artisans they tried to adapt to the industrial age. The former trade practices of independent craftsmen were transformed into union rules and struggled over with new style bosses. One base of their power disappeared rapidly in the 1870s, however, as technological innovation stripped them of 'their monopoly of particular technical and managerial skills.'[36]

Yet, we should always be careful in positing technological change as the crucial factor, for other workers, as we shall see, were more successful in their resistance than the coopers. 'Klinkhammer,' a cooper in Seaforth, recognized this only too clearly: 'The men here have much to say about the barrel machine. The machine is not to blame. If the union men had been supported by the nons last fall and the latter had not taken the berths vacated by the union men and worked at 4 cents the machine would not be making barrels now.'[37] Their one real hope was to ally with other workers, as 'Klinkhammer' suggested. The CIU recognized this principle and in 1871 Foran had 'strongly recommended or even directed that our unions in the various cities of the country take active measures toward the formation of district and state trade assemblies ... to compel the several state legislatures to grant all reasonable demands emanating from the great body of workingmen.'[38] Coopers' leader John Hewitt played an instrumental role in the creation of the Toronto Trades Assembly (TTA), the nine-hours movement, and the Canadian Labor Union (CLU) which grew out of the 'shorter hours' agitation. When Martin Foran visited Toronto, he praised the new TTA highly as being 'so perfect in all its parts that many older bodies might well envy their effectiveness.' He especially delighted in Hewitt's role as first president.[39]

Hewitt, as we shall see later, was the major ideologue of the early TTA. His experiences as a cooper witnessing the destruction of his craft deeply influenced his reflections on class and conflict. He argued that trade unions and strikes were 'a necessity in the present condition of society [for] there exists and will exist while the world is cursed with the wages system "an irrepressible conflict" between capitalists, not capital, and labor ... there is an irrepressible desire on the part of capital to cheapen labor and an irrepressible desire and determination on the part of labor to prevent such an unholy consummation.' Unions were necessary, then, 'as simply a barrier to the rapacity of the more powerful class (more powerful because it was better organized).' Hewitt viewed mechanization as part of the capitalists' struggle to cheapen labour. He saw machines as responsible for

bringing into existence large, non-productive, influential, speculative classes, – middlemen, amassing princely fortunes in amazingly short spaces of time, so that the blessings that have made production within a century fifty per cent greater upon the same amount of physical outlay, has done nothing but create a vast amount of rings, all vultures hovering about the prostrate carcass of labor until their greed has become almost intolerable.

Machinery then was an 'unmitigated evil to the great mass of humanity' because it created surplus labour and thus allowed wages to be reduced. The solution for this impasse was shorter hours for workers. In that way labour would still be required and workers would benefit from increased leisure time. This, Hewitt argued, was the worker's right. Moreover, 'the general cry of the working classes was "give us more time that we may acquire more knowledge."' In addition, workers needed more leisure because work had intensified greatly, placing 'a new strain on man's physical nature.' Finally, with more time workers could enjoy more fully 'the associations and endearments of the enlightened and intelligent home circle.'[40] The shorter-hours movement thus grew directly from the workplace experiences of individuals such as Hewitt and of crafts such as coopering.

As we have already seen, the depression of the 1870s and progressive mechanization brought an end to the CIU but workers' organization did not disappear totally from the barrel factory. Like the shoemakers, the coopers learned from their experience. Toronto coopers retained an independent union after the demise of the CIU, and were successful in raising their rates in spring 1882.[41] The next year they participated in the creation of a new international union, and P. Edgar of the Toronto union was elected second vice-president.[42] In 1886 the Toronto union joined the Knights of Labor as Energy Assembly, LA 5742.[43] This path was followed by many other coopers' locals throughout Canada and the United States. In 1889 Energy Assembly conducted a successful strike against the few Toronto shops which had not accepted a new scale of prices.[44]

The experiences of shoemakers and coopers illustrate well the first wave of concerted working-class resistance to industrial capitalism. The first generation of factory workers incorporated older artisan traditions into their struggles with the new industrial capitalists. Although the Knights of St Crispin and the CIU were broken in these initial struggles with their employers, only the institutional forms disappeared. Out of their experience, the men who had built these organizations created the newer organizations of the 1880s. The heritage of the KOSC and the CIU was clearly expressed in the Knights of Labor, which arrived in Toronto in 1882.

Other Toronto workers were not confronted by the destruction of their craft as early as the shoemakers and coopers. We now direct our attention to them.

5

Toronto metal-trades workers
and shop-floor control

Skilled workers in the nineteenth century exercised far more power than is generally realized. Well into the industrial period craftsmen, through their trade unions, played important roles in community affairs, in politics, and especially on the job. As we have already seen, in Toronto work places, some craftsmen used their monopoly on skill and experience to dictate terms to their employers in a wide array of areas which gave to these late-nineteenth-century craftsmen a high degree of control over production. This chapter will describe two groups of Toronto metal-trades workers from the early 1860s to the 1890s to illustrate further the extent of this power. The two unions under discussion are the Iron Molders International Union (IMIU) No. 28, and the National Union of Machinists and Blacksmiths, Ontario Local No. 1, whose workers were employed in Toronto's heavily capitalized stove, machinery, and agricultural implements industries.

So far our discussion of artisan resistance to the arrival of industrial capitalism has focused on the maintenance of pre-industrial work habits, the tenacious hold of cultural ties with the 'old country,' and the deep suspicion craft workers felt for 'the new rules of the game' demanded by the advent of industrial capitalism.[1] These particular factors help account for the Crispins' and Coopers' early experience; in studying the history of Toronto moulders and machinists, we shall discover additional devices for resisting industrialists' incursions on the power of skilled workers.

David Montgomery has suggested that we must look beyond pre-industrial cultural forms if we are to understand the behaviour of skilled workers in late-nineteenth-century America. These workers often were 'veterans of industrial life [who] had internalized the industrial sense of time, were highly disciplined in both individual and collective behaviour, and regarded both an extensive division of labour and machine production as their natural environment.'[2] This statement certainly describes the world of Toronto machinists and moulders. They depended on old craft traditions but also went beyond them; although drawing on 'residual' cultural categories, there was much about their world that was 'emergent,' if we can borrow the important theoretical distinction drawn by Raymond Williams.[3]

Montgomery also discerns different stages in the workers' struggle for control of production in the late nineteenth century. Following the stage of the 'autonomous workman,' well described by Benson Soffer, came the necessity for workmen to codify their traditions into strict and well-defined union rules.[4] The autonomous workman's control over the quantity and quality of his product, his tools, his wages and hours, and his co-workers ceased to be customary as it met with ever-increasing hostility from the employers, and therefore had to be legitimized in union rules which were backed by the collective strength of all the craftsmen.[5]

In the late nineteenth century, Toronto metal workers came to terms with the new industrial society, but only through constant resistance and struggle. The successes that they and other skilled workers achieved forced management and government to devise entirely new strategies which have commonly become known as 'scientific management' and 'progressivism.' These innovations, however, lie beyond the period of this study. Here we shall limit ourselves to an analysis of how the metal workers struggled for shop-floor control.[6]

I

Mid-nineteenth-century moulders displayed all the characteristics that Montgomery and Soffer identify as typical of 'autonomous workmen.' From its inception, the IMIU fought to legitimize these traditions in work rules. Two facts distinguished them from the coopers: first was their impressive success in tenaciously maintaining these traditions into the twentieth century; second was their presence, from the start of this period, at the centre of the industrial capitalist world.[7] Moulders were not artisans working in small shops such as those of pre-industrial times. In Toronto, Hamilton, and throughout Ontario, moulders worked in the important stove, machinery, and agricultural implements industries, whose firms, among the largest in nineteenth-century Ontario, led Canadian industry in attempting to fix prices and later to create multi-plant firms.

Not surprisingly, these companies were also continually in the forefront of managerial innovations regarding labour. In 1865, for example, the National Association of Iron Founders of the United States and Canada declared war on the IMIU. The organization sought to 'emancipate the workingman from those arbitrary restrictions upon his manhood to which he is subjected by the Molders' Union.' The now familiar rhetoric was twisted here to serve the interests of the employer. Moreover, the founders continued, the employers combined only to regain 'the right to direct and control our own businesses as our discretion may dictate, and the right to make our own contracts with labor, and with whomsoever we deem proper.'[8] The following year Canadian founders established their own association with identical purposes, including 'the power to control their own shops.'[9] They also blacklisted active union militants.[10] Twenty-five years later Edward Gurney recalled that his father had played the major role in creating the Founders' Association. He also admitted that the secret association fixed prices and fined members who broke the agreement by underselling their fellow founders.[11]

Moulders in Toronto organized their first union in 1857.[12] Some time in 1860 this local joined the IMIU, organized in 1859.[13] The IMIU made clear its position on questions of shop-floor control from its inception. The original constitution claimed the power 'to determine the customs and usages in regard to all matters pertaining to the craft.'[14] This gave the union control over the price of the moulders' labour. In stove shops, the union shop-committee would meet and discuss the price to charge for moulding new patterns as the boss brought them in. The committee would meet with the boss or foreman and arrive at a mutually acceptable overall price for the whole stove, but, as there were always a number of pieces involved in the assembly of any stove, the committee would then decide how to split this price among its members working on the different castings. This 'board price,' once established, was considered to be almost non-negotiable, and these prices quickly became recognized as part of the established customs and usages that were the union's sole prerogative. This price was not the only source of the moulders' wages for there was a second element, termed the 'percentage,' which was a supplement to the piece rate. This percentage was negotiable and wage conflicts in the industry generally revolved around it, since very few bosses made the mistake of trying to challenge the board price. Any subsequent change in price had to go through the shop committee.[15]

This was one considerable area of strength for the union. But there were others. The shop committee also dictated the 'set' or 'set day's work,' which was the number of pieces that a member was allowed to produce in

one day. Thus production control was also taken out of the bosses' hands.
It was, of course, in the union's self-interest to set a reasonable amount of
work which an average craftsman could perform. Craft pride would dictate
against 'setting' too low, but equally craft strength could prevent any
attempt at a speed-up.[16] Peterborough moulders enforced the set and
brought charges against members who rushed up work.[17] Generally part of
each local's rules, the set was made part of the international constitution at
the 1886 convention in London: 'Resolved that all molders working at piece
work be not allowed to make over $3.50 a day.' In 1888 this was struck from
the constitution and was again left to the discretion of each local. The
following came to be considered a 'standard' clause in locals' rules: 'No
member shall be allowed to increase a set day's work unless authorized to
do so by the shop comm. Any member glty of such offense shall be fined $5
on rept of the comm to the union. Any member persisting in rushing his job
after being warned by shop comm shall be held liable to censure, fine, or
suspension as the union may determine.'[18] Canadian locals continued to
enforce this control over production; in Peterborough, in June 1891,
'Brother Burns brought a charge against Brother Donovan for earning over
$3 a day.'[19]

Another area in which the union dictated terms was hiring. Members
who made the mistake of applying to the foreman instead of to the shop
committee were often fined.[20] In one such case in Toronto, moulders
directly recruited by the owner were casually turned away by the shop
committee to whom the potential recruits had been directed by the workers
after asking for the foreman.[21] An equally striking case was in Hamilton
where union moulders were instructed to apply for work at the Clyde Hotel
whose proprietor was an honorary member of the IMIU.[22]

The number of apprentices allowed in a shop was also set by the union.
The Peterborough local, in 1889, refused to allow 'Mr. Brooks to bring in
any more apprentices,' and in 1891 reasserted that the union would 'allow
no more than the regular number of apprentices, one for every shop and one
to any eight moulders.'[23] This formula prevailed in Toronto also.[24]

The most controversial area of workers' control in the foundry business
involved the question of helpers. It had been customary, before the founding of the IMIU, for a moulder to employ one, and often two or even three
helpers. These 'bucks' or 'berkshires' traditionally were paid directly by
the moulder out of his own wages and thus were employed by the
craftsman, not by the employer. The IMIU moved strongly against this
system, arguing that it led to the disintegration and overcrowding of their
trade. An 1873 description illustrates the problem well: 'Let us pay a visit to

a carwheel shop. What do we find? Two men working together: one is a molder, the other is a helper. Between them they do two days' work. The helper prepares the chill, inserts the pattern, does all the ramming, and the molder finishes the mold: but if it is Blue Monday, the molder lays back on his dignity, and the helper becomes both molder and helper for the day.'[25] In 1876 the IMIU allowed its members to employ a helper 'to skim, shake out, and to cut sand, but for no other purposes.'[26] In the same year it also forbade its members, who were working by the piece, to pay a helper directly out of their own wages.[27] Employers fought the IMIU strongly on this question. One historian has noted that 'For almost a half century there was a continuous struggle between the union and the employers on the berkshire question.'[28] This was true in Toronto where the major strikes of the period revolved around the issue of helpers.[29]

Finally the union also struggled to impose a closed shop on its employers, members often refusing to work with non-union moulders. Thus in the moulding industry, the setting of price, productivity, and hiring were controlled by the union.

The extent of this control was neither won nor maintained without constant struggle, for manufacturers used every device in their power to break it. In 1866 the newly founded employers' association in the industry passed a resolution to 'proceed at once to introduce into our shops all the apprentices or helpers we deem advisable and that we will not allow any union committees in our shops, and that we will in every way possible free our shops of all dictation or interference on the part of our employees.'[30] The 'Great Lock-out of 1866,' which followed the employers' posting of the above 'obnoxious notice,' extended into Canada, culminating in a costly victory for the union.[31] Canadian stove manufacturers also organized, as we have seen, and were active in the 1870s in fixing prices, advocating increased protection, and most significantly, in pressing a concerted effort to deal the union ('one of our greatest troubles') a smashing defeat.[32] In this they too failed.

In the Toronto moulding industry, the union's claim to control was the central issue. There were at least fifteen strikes in the years between the founding of Local No. 28 and 1895 (see Table 5.1). The moulders engaged in major strikes to resist demands by the manufacturers that the customs and usages of the craft be sacrificed. In 1863 Toronto moulders were unable to attend the international convention because of a shortage of funds. A strike had forced them 'to pay considerable sums to the strikers to take them where they could find work.'[33] James O'Neal assured the convention, however, that 'our union is now as sound as it has ever been, and we mean

TABLE 5.1

Toronto moulder's strikes, 1860–95

Year	Shop	Cause	Duration	Outcome
1863				
1864	McGee	No. of apprentices		
1867	McGee	No. of apprentices, wages	3 months	Victory
1870	Gurney	Demand work with bucks	4 months	Loss
1871	Beards	Wages, closed shop		Victory
1872	Dickey	9-hour day		
1872		Wages	1 day	Victory
1874	Armstrong			Victory
1875	Hart & McKillop		1 month	Victory
1880	Hamilton	Wages		Victory
1887	Gurney	Wages		Victory
1890	Gurney	Bucks, wages	15 months	Loss
1890	Massey	Bucks, wages	10 months	Loss
1892	Gurney	Sympathy with Hamilton		Loss
1895	Tor. Hardware	Wages		

Sources: Toronto *Globe* 1867, 1892; IMIU, *Proceedings*, 1859–95; IMIU, *Journal*, 1864–92

to have it remain so, so long as there is a principle that elevates a man above a brute.'[34] These principles were tested less than a year later when John McGee of the Phoenix Foundry tried to force union moulders to work with more than the approved number of boys. His shop was closed to union moulders and tramps were warned away since 'employers like to see an overplus of men about.'[35] McGee tried again in 1867, insisting on his right to hire as many apprentices as he pleased. The union again triumphed.[36]

In 1870 Gurney tried to force his moulders to work with 'bucks.'[37] Twenty years later both Gurney and Massey offered their moulders a choice between a substantive cut in the previously unchallenged board price or accepting bucks.[38] In 1892 Gurney demanded that his moulders not only accept a reduction on the percentage rate but also commit themselves to this rate for a year, a new scheme to prevent their raising the percentage as soon as the economic climate changed.[39] The same battles were to be fought yet again in 1903–04.[40]

The strikes were not minor struggles in the history of the Toronto working class. The boss moulders were leaders of the general employers' offensive of the late 1860s and early 1870s formed to counter the emergence of a strong and self-confident working-class movement. They pioneered various techniques in their attempt to defeat the union: when coercion failed, they fell back on outmoded statutes and the power of the law. The well-known case of George Brown's 1872 prosecution of Toronto printers for conspiracy was preceded by numerous court uses on the part of stove manufacturers. In 1867 McGee had six moulders from Buffalo charged with deserting his employment. Recruited by his foreman for a one-year term, they quit work when they discovered that they were being used as scabs. The magistrate claimed that he was being lenient because of the implicit deception used and fined them only $6.00 each.[41] Two apprentices who left McGee's before their terms were up because of the union blacklist of the shop were not so lucky: they received fifteen days in jail for deserting his employment.[42] Three years later, Gurney, a large Toronto and Hamilton stove manufacturer, made use of the courts to fight the union in a slightly different way. He had two union members charged with conspiracy and assault for trying to prevent scabs from filling his shop after he turned out the union men for refusing to work with 'bucks' and a large number of apprentices. After the men were found guilty, the Toronto Grand Jury commented:

It is with sincere regret that the Grand Jury have had before them ... two persons charged with assault and conspiracy acting under the regulations of an association known as the Molders Union and they feel it their duty to mark in the most emphatic terms their disapproval of such societies being introduced into our new country calculated as they are to interfere with capital and labour, cramp our infant manufactures and deprive the subject of his civil liberty.[43]

Not surprisingly the moulders viewed this use of the state's legal apparatus quite differently. Toronto's correspondent for the *Iron Molders Journal* (IMJ) complained bitterly that 'the rigours of an old English statute, that was, perhaps, enacted, when all labourers were serfs, had been brought to bear against them.' Moreover, 'this statute as interpreted by a subsidized judge, placed them at the mercy of their oppressors.'[44] The following month the same correspondent noted that 'all the powers of the law had been invoked in behalf of the employers,' and despite fines and prison sentences, he asserted, 'the men "don't scare worth a cent." ' That same spring the Beard Brothers' stove foundry charged ten of their apprentices with 'unlawfully confederating to desert his service with the intent to injure the firm in their business.' Their real offence had been to seek a wage increase, and then using the traditional moulder's weapon of restricting their output to enforce their demand. On their last day on the job, they all did the same limited amount of work. They were found guilty.[45] Nevertheless, the founders' tactics failed. The victory that the moulders won here was especially sweet given the force brought to bear against them. This victory was clearly contingent on their monopoly of skill and their ability to control the labour market. Thus the *Globe* reported that Gurney was forced to resort to employing moulders such as 'John Cowie who quit one job to go scabbing in Gurney's shop where he had never worked before, simply because he was of so little account they would never hire him – circumstances sometimes make strange companions.'[46] The union 'defied anyone to produce such a lot of molders as were in Gurney.' But, if the victory over Gurney was pleasing, that over Beard was valued even more highly:

It appears that for a year or two past, Beard and Co. of Toronto, have been running an independent scab shop refusing to be 'dictated to by the Union as they felt competent to conduct their business in their own way.' ... They found that reliable men were all union men, they found that the sober men were all union men, and what was of more importance, they found that all the good molders were union men and they were obliged to take the off-scourings of creation, all the drunken scallaways and botch workmen, that found their way to Toronto ... Their scab foreman was not equal to the situation and they found that their trade was fast leaving them and to save themselves from utter ruin the nauseous dose had to be swallowed.

In the fall of 1871, after his tour of all the Canadian locals, International President Saffin assessed No. 28 as 'one of the most flourishing organizations in the I.M.I.U., comprising as it does nearly all the moulders in Toronto, in fact all who they are willing to take in.'

Labour relations were relatively quiet during the depression of the 1870s with the exception of one minor union victory in 1875. This success was immortalized in doggerel by enthusiastic Toronto moulder, John Nolan.

McKillop to Buffalo went, to get scabs was his intent. Nine scabs from Buffalo came, with McKillop on the train; but a telegram ahead of them came, from Martin: 'Nolan watch the train.' The boys posted right and left, and did the business you may bet. At 7:00 the train arrived and McKillop was overjoyed. The party left the depot very soon, and were rapidly driven to King's saloon.

We had a man, his name was Smitt, who acted his part in German wit. McKillop did not know what he said, and he soon with the scabs a bargain made. The foreman went out to see if he could get the scabs boarding free; the landlord insisted on cash pay, and to borrow the money the foreman went away. He had hardly made his first

tack, before the scabs were in two hacks, and being driven to Western Row to take the train back to Buffalo. O was it not a – shame for Union men to spoil such a scabby game!
THE END.

The rest of the decade, however, did not go so well for the IMIU.

The 1880s saw the maturing of the industrial relations system that emerged out of the 1860s and 1870s. Toronto foundrymen mounted no challenges to the basic rights of the union in the 1880s, and only the percentage came under consideration. In 1880 moulders sought and gained a 10 per cent increase but, when the economy turned in late 1883, they were forced to accept a 20 per cent reduction. In 1886 they won a 12.5 per cent increase, but in 1887 their request for a further 10 per cent increase was resisted by Gurney. After a nine-week strike, a compromise 5 per cent was accepted. In early 1887 the Ontario branches of the IMIU came together to form a district union. The thirteen Ontario locals, with over 1000 members, were brought together to organize more efficiently and to run joint strikes more effectively.[47] In 1887, for example, the Hamilton moulders' strike against Gurney spread to Toronto, when Gurney locked out his moulders there. In 1890 moulders at Masseys' Hamilton plant refused to work while their Toronto brothers were locked out.

But perhaps the best example of these cross-industry strikes was a strike in the United States in 1887. In March moulders struck the Bridge and Beach Manufacturing Co. in St Louis with the sanction of the international union. Immediately the new Stove Founders National Defense Association attempted to manufacture the required patterns for the company. Their moulders responded by refusing to work on the patterns from that company. This process spread until almost 5,000 moulders were locked out in fifteen centres. Finally in June, the Defense Association called the patterns in and supplied the St Louis company with a force of non-union moulders, and work resumed as before at the other shops. Both sides claimed victory but most important was that each side had demonstrated to the other its respective strength and staying power. Almost immediately after the end of this strike, negotiations were commenced which were to lead to the establishment of national conciliation in the industry through conferences of the contending parties.[48]

The Canadian industry did not take part in these conferences, not did conciliation apply to the machinery-moulding branches of the trade. Until these industry-wide agreements in stove foundries had occurred, the strength of the moulders depended entirely on their skill and control of the work process, and their ability, through their union, to maintain these as well as to exercise some degree of control over the labour market. Even Gurney candidly admitted this when testifying before the Royal Commission on the Relations of Labor and Capital in 1887: 'One trouble has been, where strikes have occurred, a shop full of half moulders has been created; the boss has insisted on their being kept on and they have been taken into the union, and so a lot of inferior workmen has resulted.'[49] This was, of course, precisely the union's argument and also its greatest strength.

Labour market control then was of the greatest importance and has been admirably discussed by C.B. Williams with reference to the moulders.[50] Moreover, the importance of the union card to the individual moulder cannot be overestimated: 'within the jurisdiction of his own local a union card was man's citizenship paper; in the jurisdiction of other locals it was his passport.'[51]

The early 1890s saw a new employer offensive in Hamilton and Toronto as Gurney and Massey both attempted to smash the moulders' continuing power in their plants. The Gurney strike which commenced in February 1890 lasted an amazing sixteen months before local 28 ended it. The Massey strike covered ten months from October 1890 to July 1891.[52] In both cases the companies pursued a similar strategy. They shut down their moulding shops, ostensibly for repairs, and after a considerable lapse of time, called in the shop committees and asked them to accept either a sizeable reduction in the piece rate or work with 'bucks.'[53] In both cases the moulders refused for 'union rules did not permit "bucks" and the men thought they saw in it their eventual displacement by these labourers and a menace to their trade.'[54] Both Gurney and Massey claimed that they could no longer afford union rates and compete successfully, but the moulders suspected 'a long conceived plan in the attempt at a reduction.'[55] In each case management and labour settled down for a protracted struggle. Five months after a strike began David Black, the secretary of local 28, wrote: 'Our fight with Gurney still continues and bids fair to last quite a while longer, we succeed very well in relieving him of his good men, but he has plenty of money and it will take hard fighting and time to beat him.'[56] The Toronto local spared no expense or risk in this struggle and a number of their members were arrested and tried for intimidating scabs.[57] In September the local issued an appeal 'To the Canadian Public' which explained that the workers had been locked out 'because they refused to make their work cheaper than for any other employer in the same line in the city; and thus assist them to destroy their competitors and monopolize the Canadian market at our expense.' The public was called on to buy only union-made goods, since 'by this means our victory over monopoly will be assured; our right to organize and obtain fair wages for our labour will be vindicated; while the superior quality of our purchase will amply repay your preference.'[58]

The union eventually lost both these struggles, but it did not sacrifice its pride. When IMIU President Martin Fox visited Toronto in January 1891, the union proudly and defiantly asserted that, although temporarily defeated, it had not been disgraced. Gurney and Massey had driven 173 moulders out of Toronto, 'but they had gone away as union men' with their manhood intact. The union took great pride in the fact that there had been but 'one recreant' in the lengthy struggle.[59]

The cost to capital was also high. Gurney, in early 1891, when his victory seemed sure, brayed triumphantly that 'the only change resulting from the strike is that he now controlled his shop.' However, faced with the open incredulity of the union representatives present at the meeting, Gurney modified his statement somewhat, adding that 'of course the whole year had not been as smooth.' As capital entered the stage when it recognized the necessity of supervising more closely the process of production, it had to confront and defeat workers' control through their union rules. This gives Gurney's parting chortle added significance: 'The men must work for someone else until they come to one of my proposals. I do not think (with a smile) that there is any likelihood of my going to local union 28 and asking them to come and take control of my foundry.'[60]

Gurney's last laugh was a little early, however, for the IMIU recovered quickly in Toronto in the late 1890s, and a new wave of conflict erupted in the foundry business in 1902–04.[61] That struggle lies beyond the scope of this book but it is important to emphasize that the moulders' power was not broken permanently in 1890–92. Gurney and Massey delivered only a partial defeat and the moulders came back strong. J.H. Barnett, Toronto IMIU secretary, described one struggle in 1903: 'Just after adjourning the meeting this afternoon the foreman of the Inglis shop, R. Goods, came to the hall and informed us that he had discharged all the scabs in his shop and that he wanted the union men in on Monday, that the firm was tired of the scabs and was willing to give the nine hours.'[62] One year later, in yet another struggle with Toronto foundrymen, then supported by the National Foundry Association, Barnett wrote again of the continued monopoly on skill that the moulders enjoyed:

They are having greater losses in the foundry now than when they first started.

They have been trying to make a big condenser and can't make it. They have started the old St. Lawrence shop with some of the old country moulders who refused to work with Ersig, the NFA foreman up in the new shop. Jas Gillmore and Fred McGill is instruction [sic] them but ain't doing any better.[63]

Iron moulders then, unlike coopers, maintained a high degree of shop control into the twentieth century. This was primarily due to their strong organization and partially to the slowness with which technology replaced their skill. Machines for moulding were experimented with in the mid-1880s but were an extremely expensive failure.[64] Massey imported its first moulding machines in 1889.[65] Thus, unlike coopers and shoemakers, moulders had time to perfect their organization before their major contest with machinery.

Moulders also developed an early understanding of the need for solidarity with their unskilled co-workers. Thus, when the Knights of Labor struck against the huge Massey works in Toronto in 1886, moulders left their jobs in support. Peterborough IMIU local no. 191 also co-operated closely with the Lindsay Knights of Labor.[66]

Moulders, interestingly enough, did not challenge their bosses in one area of workshop practice: conditions in the foundries were dreadful, but moulders accepted them as part of the trade. Although some complained that some of the local shops were 'not fit for a horse to stop in,' most moulders did not think about health questions.[67] As one moulder put it, 'they think about it just as much as I think about being President of the United States.' Gurney learned this lesson – to his own chagrin:

When I built the present foundry, I built a room (against the opinion of my father who had more knowledge of such things than I), so that the men might have a place to wash in ... The men would not go there; they washed in the pots in the foundry, as they had always done, and as their fathers did before them. I got well laughed at and by none more so than the men.

Tradition ruled here as it did in so much else. Moulders' conditions were especially bad in summer, when 'a man comes out of the foundry more dead than alive, in fact he does not look like a man, and does not feel like one.' One established method of dealing with the heat was by drinking on the job: 'I have worked in a shop where every man was a union man and we did not allow others to come in, and yet except myself and one other, everyone has been drunk every chance he could get.'

A moulder-poet of Albany's IMIU no. 8 captured much of the skilled worker's pride and the rhythm of the sand artist's work in his 'A Day in the Foundry':

Seven o'clock, the whistle's blowing,
    Ev'ry man his riddle grasps,
Now his shovel seeks the sandheap,
    Then he his trusty rammer clasps.

Thump, thump, thump, is now the music
    To a ceaseless flow of talk;
All the problems of the nation
    Now are solved without a balk.

See that workman rap his pattern
    And deftly draw it from the sand?
The mold's indeed a thing of beauty
    Showing plain the practiced hand. ...

Who is that man coming up the gangway
    With eyes so keen and face so brown?
Mark the independent swagger
    'Tis a ho-bo molder just struck town.

With an old-time pard he soon is chatting –
    And how is Jim? What don't you know?
On the road – fell off the bumpers,
    And ground to pieces near St. Joe.

The foreman soon he interviews,
    Floors are filled? Well, pard, good day,
Our tourist friend now seeks his 'Pullman'
    He's next week a thousand miles away.

Blast is on, you hear it murmur,
    Soon o'er the spout bright sparks gleam,
Now belches out the fiery sputter,
    Now issues forth the molten stream.

Rich, brawny molder grasps his ladle,
  Broad chest bared, and sleeves uprolled,
He 'catches in' – to his floor he hastens,
  And with glowing metal fills each mold.

There's a commotion in yon corner,
  What's the trouble with Joe West?
O, flask 'run out,' Joe's shoe was broken,
  Joe is good for six weeks' rest.

Toiling on the sturdy workmen
  Fill the molds, floor after floor,
Panting, with the perspiration
  Streaming forth from ev'ry pore.

The cast is over, now the melter
  Cries a warming, strikes the props –
With a rush and roar, a cloud of dust
  And a blinding glare, the bottom drops.[68]

II

Machinists, unlike the moulders, had a rather spotty organizational history throughout North America; in Toronto in 1858 they joined a branch of the British Amalgamated Society of Engineers;[69] this branch existed until 1902, but was described by one Toronto machinist as little more than a benefit society;[70] this union was joined by a branch of the International Machinists and Blacksmiths Union on 4 May 1871;[71] after its demise Toronto machinists joined the Knights of Labor in large numbers in the 1880s – especially Maple Leaf (LA 2622), and George Stephenson (LA 9005), named after the inventor of the locomotive (see chapter 10). After the decline of the Knights they joined the International Association of Machinists.

The machinists' pride equalled the moulders', however, and from its inception Toronto Machinists and Blacksmiths Union, Ontario No. 1 accepted only the best craftsmen: 'One machinist was rejected on account of inability as a workman. Our Union is progressing slowly, but surely, as we intend to admit none but first-class men.' Technological expertise was often displayed in the pages of the *Machinists and Blacksmiths Journal*.

For example, Toronto machinist Charles E. Tutton sent a formula for gearing lathes which he avowed 'had stood many tests.' Like the moulders, machinists also believed that they should control their work since labour, not capital, possessed the knowledge of the craft. Thus, after union members were victimized at the Soho Foundry in November 1871 they founded a co-operative shop. This was a common step for skilled workers and suggests that the gap between journeyman and small master continued to diminish.

Again, like members of the IMIU and other skilled workers, machinists placed a high premium on manliness. In 1872 Toronto's Dickey, Neal and Co. posted in their shop a notice that any 'workman known to either agitate or support the agitation for reducing the number of hours now constituting a day's work' would be fired. The *Journal* sarcastically noted that 'all mechanics who are willing to doff their manhood, can find employment in a number of the machine shops of Toronto, by simply subscribing to the above rule.'

Because of the relative weakness of their various unions during this period, machinists did not establish as complete a set of shop rules as moulders. There were, however, 'unwritten rules of the trade, enforced by a common sentiment or a feeling, that a man was a black sheep who would operate more than one machine.'[72] These customary practices became written rules with the establishment in the early 1890s, of the International Association of Machinists.[73]

III

What ramifications did shop-floor power have in terms of how workers thought about their society, how it was changing, and of their own role in it? David Montgomery has argued that the major consequence was the skilled workers' growing belief that the key institution for the transformation of society was the trade union.[74] From their understanding that they, through their union, controlled production, it was a relatively easy step to the belief that all capitalists brought to the process was capital. Thus, an alternative source of capital would transform the society, end the iniquities of capitalist production, and create the producers' society that they all dreamed of. This ideology looked to co-operative effort through trade unions as the major agent of change. All the unions we have discussed so far favoured co-operation.

John Monteith, President of Toronto's IMIU Local 28, wrote *Fincher's Trades Review* in 1863 to describe the work of Canadian members in discussing and investigating co-operation. A union moulders' committee had contacted Rochdale and now recommended both producers and consumers co-ops to their local unions. The committee sought co-operation because 'our present organization does not accomplish what we want. That is to take us from under the hand of our employers and place us on an equal footing.'[75] Co-operation, of course, would accomplish this very end. Five years later another Toronto moulder complained: 'We are but little better off than our forefathers who were serfs to the feudal barons. We are serfs to the capitalists of the present day.' His solution:

Let the next convention create a co-op fund to be devoted entirely to co-operation ... We have been co-operating all our lives, but it has been to make someone else rich. We have been the busy bees in the hives while the drones have run away with the honey and left us to slave in the day of adversity ... Day after day the wealth of the land is concentrating in the hands of a few persons. The little streams of wealth created and put in motion by the hard hands of labour gravitate into one vast reservoir, out of which but a few individuals drink from golden cups; while labour, poor, degraded and despised labour, must live in unhealthy hovels and feed upon scanty, unhealthy foods from rusty dishes.[76]

The IMIU founded as many as twenty co-operative foundries in the 1860s.[77]

Toronto printers started three co-operative newspapers. At the height of the nine-hour struggle in 1872, the *Ontario Workman* was started as a co-operative venture, as was D.J. O'Donoghue's *Labor Record* of 1886. In 1892 during the strike at the *News*, a group of printers banded together and founded the *Star*.[78] The *Ontario Workman* operated as a co-op paper for only six months, and the *Labor Record* and the *Star* each lasted about a year. Capital for the *Star* was raised from the Toronto Typographical Union (TTU) and the Toronto Trades and Labour Council (TTLC). It initially was printed on the presses of the *World* since W.F. Maclean offered his facilities in return for 51 per cent of the operation. This 'Paper for the People' enjoyed quick success in winning the readership of the *News*, which from its inception in 1882 had posed as the paper for Toronto workers.[79] Riordan, the owner of the *News*, attempted to buy the operation, and Maclean tried to merge it with the *World*, but the printers refused both offers and instead bought a press. However, they failed to make a go of it and the paper suspended publication in June 1893. Later, it resumed publication as a pro-labour paper, but by then control had passed out of the printers' hands.[80]

As mentioned earlier, machinists and blacksmiths in Toronto organized a co-operative foundry early in 1872 after losing a nine-hour strike at the Soho works.[81] Six years later Toronto cigar-makers established the Toronto Co-operative Cigar Manufactory Association. As with the moulders in the 1860s, the push for co-operation came as a logical extension of their knowledge of the trade and their refusal to accept management's reduction of wages. Alf Jury, a Toronto tailor and labour reformer, denounced 'the wage system as a modified form of slavery,' and demonstrated at a cigar-makers' strike meeting that year that there could be 'no fraternal feeling between capital and labour.' Jury then cited production statistics to repudiate the employers' claims that the reduction was necessary. A number of bosses who had agreed to pay union rates supported this assertion. Jury's logical solution was the great aim of the working-class struggle: 'to do away with the capitalists while using the capital ourselves' – the establishment of a co-operative factory.[82] An association was founded, shares were issued, a charter was obtained, and the factory opened for business in March 1879. About a year later the Toronto local of the Cigarmakers International Union (CMIU) reported that the co-operative was progressing finely and doing a good trade.[83] Cigar-makers in Stratford also founded a co-operative factory in 1886, owned by the Knights of Labor and run according to CMIU rules. It employed between 20 and 30 men, and produced a brand of cigar known as 'The Little Knight.'[84]

Toronto Wheatsheaf LA 3499, set up a co-operative bakery which lasted about two years in the mid-1880s.[85] Toronto workers' major experiment with co-operation came in 1886 after the virulent street railway struggles of the spring and summer. Here again the Knights of Labor leadership, acting on their notions, tried to beat capital by displacing it (see chapter 10 for details).

The successes or failures of these co-operative ventures are of less importance than the ideological assumptions on which they were based. Often inspired by crisis situations, they nevertheless flowed directly from the shop-floor experience of skilled workers and the practices of their unions in struggling to control production. It was a relatively easy step to envision a system that was free of the boss who did so little. A moulder from Chatham wrote in 1864:

This then shows both classes in their just relations towards each other – the capitalist and the mechanic; the one, the mechanic is the moving power – the capitalist bearing about the same relation to him that the cart does to the horse which draws it – differing in this respect, that the mechanic makes the capitalist and the horse does not make the cart; the capitalist without the mechanic being about as useful as the cart without the horse. The capitalist no doubt at times increases the sphere of usefulness of the mechanic; so does the cart that of the horse, and enables him to do more for his owner than otherwise he could do; but deprive him of it, and there is little that he can do with it that he could not accomplish without it. In short the workingman is the cause the capitalist the effect.[86]

The syntax may be confused but the moulder's meaning comes through clearly. In 1882, at the time of a carpenters' strike in Toronto, a reporter asked union leader Thomas Moor during a discussion about a co-operative planing mill if the carpenters had the requisite skills. Moor's response was simple but profound: 'If the men can manage a mill and make it a success for their employers, surely they can do the same thing for an institution in which they have an interest.'[87] During the carpenters' strike of 1887, they again began to raise capital to start a Working Carpenters Co-operative Association.[88]

If co-operation was the obvious extension of workers' control for nineteenth-century craftsmen, then socialism would become the similar response for many of their twentieth-century comrades.[89] Capital, however, also began to respond to the challenges raised by the growing tradition of workers' control. F.W. Taylor, capital's main ideologue of the workplace, understood very well the power of the 'autonomous workman':

Now, in the best of the ordinary types of management, the managers recognize the fact that the 500 or 1000 workmen, included in the 20 or 30 trades, who are under them, possess this mass of traditional knowledge, a large part of which is not in the possession of management ... The foreman and superintendents know, better than anyone else, that their own knowledge and personal skill falls far short of the combined knowledge and dexterity of all the workingmen under them.[90]

Taylor also reminisced about his first job experience in a machine shop at the Midvale Steel Company in the late 1870s:

As was usual then, and in fact as is still usual in most of the shops in this country [1912], the shop was really run by the workmen, and not by the bosses. The workmen together had carefully planned just how fast each job should be done, and they had set a pace for each machine throughout the shop, which was limited to about one-third of a good day's work. Every new workman who came into the shop was told at once by the other men exactly how much of each kind of work he was to do, and unless he obeyed these instructions he was sure before long to be driven out of the place by the men.[91]

After his appointment as foreman, Taylor set out to increase production. He fired some of the men, lowered others' wages, hired green hands, lowered the piece rate – in general engaged in what he described as a 'war.' He attributed his limited success in this 'bitter struggle' to not being of working-class origin. His middle-class status enabled him to convince management that worker sabotage, not the speed-up, was responsible for a sudden rash of machine breakdowns.[92]

The new popularity of Taylor and other proponents of scientific management in the early twentieth century was indicative of capital's new attempt to rationalize production.[93] This, combined with the rise of the large corporation, the rapid growth of multi-plant firms, and the ever-increasing extension of labour-saving machinery challenged directly not only workers' traditional control, but also the very existence of the labour movement.

Toronto workers, who had struggled throughout the late nineteenth century for shop-floor control, were about to face new, more virulent battles. Workers' control, widely regarded as a right, had become deeply embedded in the ethos of the working class. The fight, initially to maintain and later to extend this control, became the major locus of class struggle in the opening decades of the twentieth century.

Thus, even in the cases where craft unions eventually abandoned the traditional practices of the autonomous workman in return for concessions, or out of weakness, the leadership could not always assure management that the membership would follow union dictates. As one investigator noted about the foundry business:

The customs of the trade ... do not always vanish with the omission of any recognition of 'the standard day's work' in wage agreements. Nor can it be expected that the entire membership of an organization will at once respond to the removal of limitations on output by a national convention of that organization. Trade customs, shop practices, grow; they become as much a part of the man as his skill as a molder.[94]

Written in 1904, these cautions were as true of other skilled workers as they were of moulders. It is important to remember that 'working class control of production, however, was not a condition or a state of affairs which existed at any point in time, but a struggle, a chronic battle in industrial life which assumed a variety of forms.'[95] Customs of control, established by struggle, would not vanish; they had to be vanquished by persistent assault by management.

6

Printers and mechanization

Publishing, as we have seen earlier, was one of Toronto's major industries. The printers who worked in Toronto's newspaper and job shops played an important role in the history of trade unionism. Toronto's first union, established in 1832, lapsed in late 1836, but it was refounded in early 1844 and has had a continuous existence since then.[1] The Toronto Typographical Society, after considerable debate, joined the National Typographical Union in May 1866, becoming Toronto Typographical (TTU) Union, No. 91.[2] With the subsequent addition of other Canadian locals, the National became the International Typographical Union (ITU) in 1869.[3]

In addition to being active in their own unions, Toronto printers played leading roles in organizing other Toronto workers. They also provided an excellent model of trade-union practices. For the historian they present a unique opportunity to trace 'the gradual transformation of sentiments into customs and the evolution of trade interests into "union principles."'[4] The availability of complete documentation allows us to reconstruct the industrial experience which shaped, and was in turn shaped by, the printers' responses. For as Ethelbert Stewart pointed out in 1905 'the "fundamental principles of trade unionism" are often the codified experiences of former generations under industrial conditions that no longer exist, and cannot now be understood by a mind not inheriting an intuitive perception of them.'[5]

Toronto printers occupied a position somewhere between the industrial experience of the cooper and that of the moulder. The printers' craft was divided by the new technology of the mid- to late-nineteenth century, for large, steam-powered presses resulted in a new division of labour in the craft by creating pressmen. Printers traditionally had set the type and operated the presses; after mid-century they became increasingly divided

into compositors and pressmen. Compositors remained relatively untouched by machinery until the early 1890s; pressmen, however, were
products of the machine age. Printers and pressmen tended to work in
shop-like situations, although many of the newspapers or publishers for
whom they worked were large companies with many employees and were
highly capitalized. Nevertheless, the composing room and the pressroom
were intimate environments resembling shops far more than modern factories.

The control enjoyed by Toronto metal-trades workers, and their struggle
to retain it, were more than equalled by the experiences of Toronto
printers. In the 1890s the president of the Toronto local of the ITU insisted
that 'The work of the composing room is our business. To no one else can
we depute it. It is absolutely ours. The talk of running another man's
business will not hold. It is ours; we learned it and must control it.'[6]

Unionism among the Toronto printers owed much to the customs and
traditions of the craft. Organized first as the Toronto Typographical
Society in 1832, it explained its existence to the public:

Owing to the many innovations which have been made upon the long established
wages of the professors of the art of printing, and those of a kind highly detrimental
to their interests, it was deemed expedient by the Journeymen Printers of York, that
they should form themselves into a body, similar to societies in other parts of the
world, in order to maintain that honourable station and respectability that belongs
to the profession.[7]

This first union demanded a standard rate, limitation of hours, limitations
of apprentices, and a closed shop.[8] In 1836 it tried to achieve wage parity
with New York printers and failed.[9] The failure, combined with the political uncertainties of the pre-rebellion period, caused the society to lapse.[10]

The society was refounded in 1844 to resist a new employer's departure
from the 'settled usages of the trade.'[11] In 1845, when forced again to fight
the initiatives taken by newspaper publisher George Brown, the printers
issued a circular to the public demanding 'to maintain that which is considered by all the respectable proprietors as a fair and just reward, for our
labour and toil – "the labourer is worthy of his hire." '[12] Here the tenacity
of pre-industrial notions of traditional wages can be seen. Customary usage
dictated wages – not any abstract notion of what the market might bear.
Employers, as well as workers, had to learn the new rules of a market
economy, and the disruptions caused by the Browns' arrival in the trade in

moral economy

the 1840s suggest that until then wages had been 'largely a customary and not a market calculation.'[13]

The printers possessed a strong tradition of pride in, and identity with, their craft. In their 1845 statement to the Toronto public, they resolved 'to maintain by all legitimate means in their power their just rights and privileges as one of the most important and useful groups in the industrious community.'[14] Members of the 'art preservative,' they thought of themselves as the main carriers of rationalism and enlightenment. No trade dinner or ball (and these were frequent) was complete without toasts to the printers' patron, Benjamin Franklin, to Gutenberg, and to other famous printers. Franklin replaced the older European tradition of saints and his rationalism fitted well with the printers' disdain for other societies that resorted to secret signs and fiery oaths. The printers prided themselves on the fact that: 'initiation ceremonies, melo-dramatic oaths, passwords, signs, grips, etc., though advocated by many worthy representatives, and repeatedly considered by the national union, never found a place in the national or subordinate constitutions.'[15] The printers saw themselves as crucial agents in the maintenance of all that was best in the western literary tradition. 'To the art of printing – under whose powerful influence the mind of fallen and degraded man is raised from nature up to nature's God,' toasted one printer at a dinner in 1849. The shop committees were 'chapels' and the shop steward was 'the father of the chapel.'[16]

The Toronto printers had a strong sense of the history of their craft and their union. They were particularly proud of being the oldest Toronto union, a fact which was stressed at their frequent fetes. The 1888 picnic program, for example, contained original histories of both the art of printing and the Toronto Typographical Union.[17] And in 1889 a committee was formed 'to raise subscriptions to buy the very finest and best silk banner for union that money can purchase.'[18] All these traditions were put to use by the printers in stirring addresses invoking custom in the struggle against oppression:

Fellow-workingmen, knights of the stick and rule, preservers of "the art preservative", – ye whose honourable calling is to make forever imperishable the noblest, truest, and most sublime thoughts of the statesman, the philosopher, and the poet, – to you is committed the mightiest agent for good or ill which has yet been pressed into the service of humanity. The printing press, the power mightier than kings, more powerful than armies, armaments, or navies, which shall yet overthrow ignorance and oppression and emancipate labour, is your slave. Without your consent, without the untiring labour of your skillful fingers and busy brain, this mighty giant, with his million tongued voices speeding on wings of steam all over this broad earth of ours, would be dumb. Shorn of his strength which your skill imparts, his throbbing sides and iron sinews might pant and strain in vain; no voice or cry of his or your oppressors could ever reach or be heard among men. Realizing this my friends it is easy to determine our proper station in the grand struggle that is now in progress all over the civilized world, the effort of the masses to throw off oppression's yoke ... We belong in the front rank, at the head of this column. Since the discovery of printing, humanity has made great progress and already we see the dawn of the coming day when light and knowledge shall illuminate all lands and man shall no longer oppress his fellow-man.[19]

the privileged advanced section

Central to the power of the ITU was the extent to which each local maintained its control over production.[20] The composing room was the preserve of the printer. Management's only representative there, the foreman, was a union member and subject to the discipline of his brothers.[21] It was thus in Toronto from the inception of the TTU, and in 1858 the NTU convention ruled that, 'The foreman of an office is the proper person to whom application should be made for employment; and it is enjoined upon subordinate unions that they disapprove of any other mode of application.'[22] The new ITU constitution of 1867 fined members who applied for jobs to anyone other than the foreman. Four years later this control was reasserted, but the foremen were also warned 'that the foreman of an office belongs to the union under which he works and the union does not belong to the foreman ... and that no foreman has the right to discharge a regular hand ... on any other ground than that of shortness of work or willful neglect of duty.'[23] Moreover, chapels could fine a foreman for breaking union rules.[24] In an extraordinary case, the ITU ruled that the Ottawa local was correct to strike against J.C. Boyce, the proprietor of *The Citizen*, when he took over the operation of his own composing room. Only if Boyce submitted a clear card from the London (England) Trades Society would he 'be allowed to work under the jurisdiction of the Ottawa Union.'[25]

The effective union control of this hiring practice was augmented by the foreman's role in enforcing the printer's right to divide work. In newspaper offices each regular employee had a 'sit,' and with this place came the right to choose a replacement any time the regular wanted time off. Although the replacement was not technically employed by the regular printer, that was actually what the practice amounted to. In Toronto, the *Mail* paid the regular who then paid the 'sub' from his salary.[26] When bosses tried to regulate this custom by compiling lists of substitutes from whom regulars were to choose, the ITU roundly condemned the practice and refused to allow locals to co-operate with it.[27] This 'elaborate system of sharing work' flowed from a fraternal regard for fellow craftsmen, and from the well-learned lesson that total control of the labour market by the union was crucial for strength. The right to divide work was carried to the extreme that, in times of depression, it was the practice for unmarried regulars to give the larger part of their work to [married] subs.

The ITU claimed ever more interest in the hiring process. In 1888 a resolution was introduced 'that would have placed the hiring and discharging of employees entirely in the hands of the local unions.' In 1890 'the priority law' was passed by which the grounds upon which foremen could discharge were even more tightly circumscribed. Only incompetency, violation of rules, neglect of duty, or decrease of labour force were acceptable causes for firing, and on discharge a member was entitled to a written statement of cause. In addition, subs in an office had priority when positions became available.[28] The power of the union in controlling the selection of printers was almost total; in Toronto the foreman did all the hiring.[29] One should note here again the progression from customary practice to union rules as the century passed. The legitimation of custom was necessitated as employers increased their interference.

The union also retained a strong position in bargaining. After arriving at an approved scale of prices unilaterally, they would then approach the employers.[30] Some negotiation was possible but much of the scale was regarded as non-negotiable. For example, after striking for a nine-hour day in 1872, the union considered the subject closed to further discussion.[31] (For a summary of strike activity see Table 6.1.) The scale was a complex document divided into three major sections: 1) time work; 2) piece work, news and magazines; and 3) piece work, books. Time work was not the traditional method of payment in the printing industry, but throughout the late nineteenth century more and more job shops adopted it. The time rate, however, was closely tied to the piece rate.[32] In Toronto, where the piece rate was $33\frac{1}{3}$ cents per 1,000 ems,[33] the time rate was $33\frac{1}{3}$ cents an hour – the general assumption being that a hand compositor averaged 1,000 ems an hour. In newspaper offices the usual method of payment was by the piece, which in the compositor's case was measured by the area of type composed, expressed in ems. Printers were thus paid per 1,000 ems of matter.

There were a number of areas of conflict implicit in this type of payment. Rates were set for the newspaper as a whole, but special rates were set for material classified as difficult, such as for foreign languages, tables, or even

TABLE 6.1

Toronto printers' strikes, 1832–92

Year	Shop	Cause
1836	All	Wages
1845	*Globe*	Wages
1853	*Globe*	Wages
1854	*Globe*	
1872	All	Hours, wages
1877	*Globe*	
1878	Bell-Hawkins	Hours
1883	*Telegram*	
1884	*Globe, Mail*	Resist reduction
1887 (pressmen)		Wages
1888	*World*	Shop procedures
1889		
1892	*News*	Machinery

Sources: Toronto Press; ITU, *Proceedings*; TTU, *Minutes*;
    Toronto, Printing Pressmen's Union, *Minutes*.

illegible copy.[34] As the century progressed, more and more newspaper work consisted of printing advertisements, which contained far more blank space than regular material. This copy became known as 'fat' matter and was the most lucrative for the printer.[35] The printers insisted that rates were set for the paper as a whole, thus retaining the higher rate for fat matter as well. The traditional way to distribute the material was to hang all copy on the 'hook' as it arrived in the composing room; the compositors then picked it up in the order it arrived, thus ensuring an even distribution of the fat. Bosses began to object to this practice and tried to create departments in which specific printers did the special composing. This the union resisted strenuously and forbade locals from accepting departments. As a compromise, it allowed members to bid for the fat matter. The successful bidder would pay back to the union the amount of his bid, usually a percentage of his earnings, which would then be used to buy things in common for all the printers or to hire a person to clean everybody's type, or it was distributed equally among the members.[36]

The Toronto local, however, resisted most employer incursions in this area. Toronto employers certainly tried. In 1882 the *Mail* offered its printers a raise and in return demanded the return of the ads. The union, however, reiterated that 'where weekly and piece hands are employed the piece hands shall have their proportionate share of "fat" matter.'[37] When the labour commission interviewed Toronto printer Stewart Dunlop in 1887, he assured the commissioners that the work was given out more fairly in union shops and that the fat was 'equally divided; whatever may be first on the hook is given to the first man calling for it.'[38] Three years later, another new scale insisted that 'compositors on newspapers were entitled to equal distribution of any "phat."'[39] The complexity of the Toronto printer's scale is suggested by the 39 sections of the 1883 contract and 35 sections of the 1890 contract.[40] All this led one managerial strategist named DeVinne, who was later to play a major role in the employers' association, the United Typothetae, to bemoan that 'It is the composition room that is the great sink-hole. It is in type and the wages of compositors that the profits of the house are lost.'[41]

So far we have spoken only of compositors. Until the mid-1800s in the cities and until much later in small shops, a printer was both the pressman and the compositor. With the rise of power presses, the pressman's role became more complex, and increasingly the old-time printer who did both jobs disappeared. By 1869 the Toronto local had special piece rates for pressmen and it defined the compositor's job so as to prevent him from performing press work. The pressmen's new consciousness led the ITU to begin to charter pressmen's locals separately in 1873, and ten years later the Toronto pressmen set up their own local. Disputes with ITU Local 91, however, led them to join the new International Printing Pressmen's Union in 1889.

The disputes stemmed from the new division of labour. In effect, pressmen ceased to be handicraft workers with the coming of steam-powered cylinder presses, and later rotary presses. Compositors, in contrast, continued to set type as they had since the sixteenth century. The literacy and traditions of the compositors made theirs the parent craft and they behaved accordingly, controlling the ITU. The new mechanical skill required to run advanced machines, however, subtly began to change the pressmen's view of themselves and of the old hierarchy. Moreover, it was to them that management increasingly looked for their profits, still not being able to break the compositors' control of typesetting.[42] Both their knowledge of machines and management's dependence tended to increase the pressmen's estrangement from the compositors.

The final split came when New York's 'Big 6' settled an 1888 strike by ignoring the interests of the pressmen.[43] The Toronto local was more than anxious to heed the New York local's call for secession, since it had had a similar experience in 1887 when the ITU printers' local did not support its strike to gain higher wages.[44] Thus tensions had been building up for a number of years and the creation of the International Printing Pressmen's Union came as no surprise.

Although the major focus of this chapter is the printers' power on the job, one cannot discuss the Toronto printers without alluding also to their political strength in the city, and in provincial and even national politics. They provided the Toronto working-class movement with important leadership. It was natural for these literate, working-class intellectuals to play key political roles, but the extent of their dominance is striking nevertheless. Although not the initiators of the Toronto Trades Assembly (this honour belongs to John Hewitt of the Coopers International Union), they did play an important part in the Toronto Trades Assenbly and in the Canadian Labour Union. In the 1880s they helped found the Toronto Trades and Labor Council after the 1881 Toronto meeting of the ITU, and they later were active in the meetings of the Trades and Labor Congress. Of the six labour papers published in Toronto between 1872 and 1892, three of them were published and edited by printers: *The Ontario Workman* under J.S. Williams, J.C. McMillan, and David Sleeth, all prominent members of Local 91; Eugene Donavon's *The Trade Union Advocate/Wage Worker*; and D.J. O'Donoghue's *Labor Record*.

Other members of Local 91 were prominent leaders in labour reform. John Armstrong, a former international president of the ITU (1878–79), was appointed to Macdonald's Royal Commission on the Relations of Labor and Capital in 1886; D.J. O'Donoghue was a labour member of the Ontario Legislature (MPP), leading Canadian Knight of Labor, and later collector of labour statistics for the Ontario Bureau of Industries; E.F. Clarke was mayor of Toronto, an MPP and an MP; and W.B. Prescott was International President of the ITU from 1891 to 1898. These men were from just one generation of Local 91's membership; the next was to include two other mayors of Toronto and a senator.[45]

The political role of Local 91 stemmed in part from its union activities. Toronto printers, for example, had little use for George Brown's brand of liberalism. As early as 1845, they had noted the irony implicit in his labour relations policies: 'A person from the neighbouring Republic commenced business here and has ever since been unremitting in his Liberal endeavour to reduce as low as possible that justly considered fair and equitable rate of remuneration due to the humble operatives.'[46] His 'Liberal' endeavours were to lead him into continual conflict with the printers, culminating in a strike for a nine-hour day in 1872. In this, the most famous of nineteenth-century Canadian labour struggles, the newly created Master Printers'

Association challenged only a few of the well-established prerogatives of the TTU. They guaranteed, for example, that 'each man should be left as free as practicable to determine the duration of his labour [and that they would] leave compositors unfettered as to the number of hours they shall work so long as intended absence is intimated.'[47] What they refused to grant was the nine-hour day for job shop printers. Brown's use of antiquated British laws against combination to arrest the leaders of the TTU was turned against him by Macdonald's passage of the Trade Unions Act. The Tories controlled Toronto working-class politics for a number of years following, until D.J. O'Donoghue, the Knights of Labor, and the legislative responsiveness of the Mowat Ontario government started a swing towards the Liberals.[48]

The political expertise of the printers had grown throughout their various struggles, and the perfected tactics of 1872 were used again in the 1880s. Thus, when John Ross Robertson's *Telegram* came under union attack in 1882, the union first turned to the boycott to bring pressure on the owner. They decided that in this way they could expose 'the treatment which union printers have received at the hands of J.R.R. for many years past, and the manner in which that gentleman (?) invariably casts aspersions upon the union mechanics of this city generally through the columns of his vasculating [sic] paper.'[49] John Armstrong and O'Donoghue were appointed to visit the merchants who advertised in the *Telegram* and convince them to place their ads elsewhere. The next year, when ITU No. 91 passed a new scale of prices, they struck against the *Telegram*, pulling most of the compositors out on strike. They then received the endorsement of the whole Toronto Trades and Labor Council for the boycott, and late in March held a mass meeting at which speeches by most of the prominent labour leaders pledged support for Local 91.[50] Although resembling their earlier tactic against Brown in 1845 and 1853 (in that they appealed to the public for support), the boycott, nevertheless, was new to the labour movement as a formal tactic. Inspired by Irish rural experience and popularized by the Irish Land League and the Knights of Labor,[51] It was a weapon especially well suited to the printers' battles with newspapers which depended, in the nineteenth century at least, on their readership.[52] Toronto printers, then, were very quick to adapt new forms of struggle in the 1880s. The step from the boycott to politics was a short one, as evidenced by the ITU's denunciation of the Republican party in the 1884 American presidential election because of the labour policies of Whitelaw Reid's New York *Tribune*.[53]

In Toronto the 1884 strikes against the *Mail* and the *Globe* displayed the same political acumen. The papers united with other Toronto publishers and print shops to demand a 10 per cent reduction in the printers' wages, giving only a week for consideration. The printers refused and struck. The union was successful in forcing job offices and smaller papers to withdraw the reduction, but the *Globe* and the *Mail* held out. The *Globe* insisted that it had never become a union shop for the reason that 'the boss needed absolute control in a newspaper office.'[54] The *Mail's* publisher, Christopher Bunting, refused a TTLC arbitration offer by commenting that 'as he was the sole control of his office he should assert his right to do as he liked.'[55] After a hard fight, the morning papers won the reduction to 30 cents per 1,000 ems down from 33⅓ cents, but their victory was short-lived. In 1885 the *Globe* reversed its position of a year before and the political game of the 1870s by becoming an open shop for the first time. This left only the Tory *Mail* holding out against the typesetters. The *Mail* succumbed in February 1886 and became a union shop, withdrawing the iron-clad contract that it had adopted after the troubles in 1884. The *Globe* followed quickly in March.

What tactics had the ITU used to win these long-range victories after their apparent defeat in 1884? The printers had employed their usual measures against the papers. They first withdrew all their members from the shops, and, when they failed to prevent the shops from filling up with the much despised 'country mice,' ('They come and go like swallows,' was one printer's description of these non-union small-town workers),[56] they then turned to boycotts and mass demonstrations.[57] They, like many other skilled trade-unionists in other struggles, noted with great pride that of the 300 printers who had struck, only three or four had surrendered 'their manhood' and broken ranks.[58] Building on 'the strong feeling of unanimity in resisting the tyranny of the capitalists among the wage workers of Toronto,' the ITU turned to political action.[59] They requested all workingmen to boycott any candidates supported by the *Mail* in the municipal election campaigns of the winter of 1885–86.[60] Local 91 passed a resolution: 'That this union will oppose to its utmost any candidate for municipal honours who may be supported by the *Mail* newspaper.'[61] The following weeks saw union after union endorse the ITU motion, as well as a number of Tory ward heelers running for cover and abandoning the *Mail*. The union issued a circular exposing its dealings with the *Mail* since 1872, and then placed advertisements in the Toronto papers in January 1886 that strongly attacked Manning, the *Mail's* candidate for Mayor:

Resolved that this union consider Mr. Manning a nominee of the Mail, he having advertised in that paper ... and having been editorially supported by it, particularly so on Saturday morning January 2; and therefore we call on all workingmen and those in sympathy with organized labour to VOTE AGAINST MANNING, THE NOMINEE OF THE MAIL.

The same Local 91 meeting also decided to blacklist alderman candidates who had not broken with the *Mail* and to issue 10,000 circulars denouncing Manning and these candidates. After Howland's stunning election as mayor, widely regarded as a working-class victory, the ITU issued this statement:

To the Trades and Labour organizations of Toronto – Fellow unionists: Toronto Typographical Union No. 91 takes this opportunity of thanking the labour organizations of this city and their friends who so nobly supported us at the polls in our effort to defeat the Mail. To the workingmen of Toronto who have had the honour and manhood to rise above party ties in the cause of labour, the heartiest thanks of the 300 members of the TTU are due ... At a time when we needed your assistance you have shown that the motto of our union 'United to support not combined to injure' is the guiding stone of the honest toiler everywhere ...

This electoral defeat led to the *Mail's* total reversal in February 1886 when it surrendered to the union. Thus the seeming defeat of summer 1884 had been translated by political means into a significant victory for Local 91. Neither the *Globe* nor the *Mail* was to cause the union difficulty again in the late nineteenth century.

Similar tactics were employed successfully against Maclean's *World* in 1888, when he tried to defeat the union's control of fat matter. The struggle was precipitated by a fight over the price of an advertisement that was inserted twice. The union rule was that if the advertisement was run in an identical manner, then the compositor was paid only once, but that if any changes were made, the compositor was paid again for the whole advertisement. The foreman supported the printers' case but Maclean, after paying the money owed, locked out the union.

The ITU then reiterated its position on fat matter: 'Only by the getting of the advertisements and other "fat" matter are the men able to make anything like living wages, and this fact is recognized by all fair-minded employers as well as the men.' In late July, after filling his shop with country-mice, Maclean sought an injunction against the ITU's boycott of the *World*. It was granted on an interim basis and then made permanent in mid-August.[62] The injunction did not solve Maclean's problems: 'The *World* is in sore straights as a result of the law compelling union men not to

TABLE 6.2
Membership, Toronto Typographical Union, No. 91, 1867–89

Year	Initiated	Admitted by card	Rejected	Withdrawn by card	Suspended	Expelled	Reinstated	Died	Total members
1867	36	9		16					92
1868	27	11		13	10		12		90
1869	53	20		24					144
1870	47	27		38	17		1		160
1871	33	32		33	6		1		190
1872	No report								
1873	11	34		82	6	37	1	5	135
1874	24	52		51	2	12	2	1	160
1875	33	63	5	70	6	1			178
1876	32	64		105	6				185
1877	22	60		59		1		1	165
1878	10	40		54	26	16		2	160
1879	20	18		33	13	16			168
1880	18	29		43	5	5	3	1	160
1881	26	25		36	2	4	1	2	189
1882	53	66	1	64	2		3	2	243
1883	56	45	1	54		7	6	4	270
1884	29	48	1	63	7	5	6	4	313
1885	23	49		80	6	25	5	3	256
1886	41	47		54					289
1887	81	65		68	5	6	19	7	367
1888	58	105		68		2		6	439
1889	45	79	2	93	6	2	3	6	446

Source: International Typographical Union, *Proceedings*, 1867–89

buy it or patronize merchants who advertise therein. Internal storms are of such common occurrence that a couple of weeks ago the vermin employed there went out on strike even but returned to the nest again.'[63] The 'vermin's strike' occurred because even non-union printers apparently carried some of the old craft traditions. They struck because the foreman refused to give cause for firing one of their colleagues, an interesting assertion of the printers' traditional control. In a list of ten grievances that they issued on striking, they also included the method of work in the office and the victimization of their chosen leader, who, despite their non-union status, was referred to as the 'chairman of the chapel.'[64] Later in 1890 Maclean again sought to make his paper a union shop.[65] Again the political dimensions of the settlement are clear. W.B. Prescott, the president of Local 91, wrote John A. Macdonald and sought his intervention with Maclean to ensure that the *World* came around. Prescott pointed out that 'the cheap labour policies of the *World* antagonized organized labour.'[66] Perhaps one reason that Maclean and the *World* felt the pressure was because the local had quickly found a way to circumvent the injunction by promoting union papers rather than naming those boycotted.

They continued to use this technique, especially in a political context. In the municipal campaigns of 1891–92, for example, they issued the following circular:

Having been informed that you are seeking municipal honours, we desire to call your attention to the fact that there are a few printing and publishing houses in this city who do not employ union labour, and we, believing it would be to your advantage to patronize only those who do employ such, request you to place your patronage and advertising in union offices only, as we can assure you that from past experience, your chances of election are greater by so doing.[67]

The circular then listed the dailies that were union shops; by 1891 they included all but the *Telegram*, which was shortly to enter the fold. In March 1892 the TTU also began the use of the union label.[69] Thus the power of the Toronto printers continued to grow throughout the late nineteenth century, and more Toronto printers were unionized in the early 1890s than at any previous date.[69] (For TTU membership data see Table 6.2.)

The initial encounter with mechanization had served to strengthen the printers' position. Until the invention of linotype and monotype machines in the late 1880s, typesetting had remained unchanged from the sixteenth century.[70] In Toronto, the *News* introduced the Rogers typograph machine in 1892 and offered the operators 14 cents per 1,000 ems. The ITU recommended in 1888 'that subordinate unions ... take speedy action looking to their [linotype machines] recognition and regulation, endeavouring everywhere to secure their operation by union men upon a scale of wages which shall secure compensation equal to that paid hand compositors.'[71] This recommendation was amended in 1889[72] to demand that in all union offices, only practical printers could run the machines and that the rates on the machines would be governed by the local unions.[73] Moreover, with the arrival of the linotype machine, the time-honoured dependence on piece rates was replaced by a demand that compositors be paid a time rate on the machines because of 'the newness of the work and the consequent difficulty of estimating the average output to be expected.'[74] The ITU even entered into informal negotiations with the Mergenthaler Company, the major manufacturer of the linotype machines. In return for an agreement that the ITU encourage its locals to control rather than to oppose the new machine, the company guaranteed that it would not cooperate with any management attempts to utilize the machine to smash the union's power.[75] This agreement was kept, and the union itself actually broke the one strike against the introduction of the machine that took place in Zanesville, Ohio.[76]

In Toronto, the union's right to control the operation of the machine was not challenged initially and in March 1892 its *Typographical Journal* correspondent reported 'that so far we have not suffered from their use.' However, that summer the *News*, appealing to the craft custom of piece rates, refused to pay operators by the day. After a seven-week strike the union won its demand that the printers be paid by time. They were to receive $12.00 a week for six weeks while learning the machine operation and then $14.00 after they demonstrated their competency, which was set at 2,000 ems per hour or 100,000 ems per week. This settlement not only brought the union control of the machine and the wage style it sought; it also implicitly recognized the printers' right to limit production, since the rate of competency set was far below the speed of the machine, estimated to be anywhere from three to eight times as fast as hand composition.[77] The ITU was also concerned to prevent any proliferation of speed-ups with the new machine, and ruled that 'no member shall be allowed to accept work ... where a task, stint, or deadline is imposed by the employer on operators of typesetting devices.'[78] Members were forbidden, from 1896 on, to participate in speed contests of any kind involving the machines. The attainment of high speeds would only result in higher expectations on the part of management and thus lead to pushes for increased production, reasoned the ITU[79] Indeed this occurred later but the ITU successfully resisted the attempts by employers to speed up work totals. The victory over the *News* and the union's previous success with Robertson's *Telegram* also brought Local 91 control of all Toronto newspapers for the first time in its history.[80] The printers had learned their lessons well. They would leave the century not only with their traditions intact but also with their power actually augmented. They had met the machine and triumphed.[81]

Thus former ITU president Samuel Connelly, in testimony before the U.S. Industrial Commission, argued that 'the introduction of the machines had not injured the compositors, but had benefitted the craft.'[82] Equally George Barnett's detailed study of the union's encounter with the linotype concluded that 'the introduction of the machine has been a great advantage to the printer in several directions,' although he also noted that the resulting intensification of labour was somewhat of a drawback.[83] But it was American Federation of Labor (AFL) president Samuel Gompers who summed up the experience best:

The printers have had a most remarkable history, particularly within the last five years. The machine ... was introduced, and it is one of the cases where a new machine, revolutionizing a whole trade, was introduced that did not involve a wholesale disaster even for a time; and it is due to the fact that the I.T.U. has grown to be an organized factor and recognized by those employing printers as a factor to be considered.[84]

The success of the ITU stemmed from the strength of the union and from the traditions of control which were so much a part of the printers' history in Toronto and elsewhere. For, as Ethelbert Stewart noted in 1905:

... the history of the typographical union is marked by the gradual elimination of general propositions from its councils; the progressively emphatic tightening of the lines on strictly trade matters. Its strength lies largely in its experience, and the long line of precedents established, which enable it to know the best thing to do and to do that quickly and with firmness. It is organized not vaguely at the top by the International alone; but in every union printing office there is a chapel, or office organization, and its discipline and control, as well as its attempts to adjust grievances, settle troubles, or make agreements begins at the chapel.[85]

Power flowed from the shop floor up. This was the printers' great strength in the nineteenth century; it was also to prove a limitation later – as Stewart hints in the above quotation.[86]

7

The Orange Order in Toronto:
religious riot and the working class

Toronto, like other North American cities, received part of the massive emigration from the British Isles in the nineteenth century. On arrival these immigrants immediately created institutions to alleviate the dislocating effects of the transatlantic voyage, and in Toronto the predominance of Protestant immigrants made the Orange Order one of the largest ethnic voluntary associations there. The city even became known as 'The Belfast of Canada.'[1]

The order's importance in the political sphere and the Orangemen's propensity to engage in riot and other forms of collective violence have gained them some historical attention. Unfortunately most Canadian historians, in their haste to deplore such illiberal behaviour, have failed to explore seriously the culture that generated these collective actions; instead, they focused concern on the vagaries of Orange leadership in national politics, ignoring the order's social composition, its constellation of ideas, its roots in traditional Irish society, and its important local functions. More specifically, historians of the Canadian working-class experience have been satisfied with an easy dismissal of ethnic and religious associations as being detrimental to the emergence of some ill-defined notion of class-consciousness.[2] Yet, closer study demonstrates that Orangeism offered Toronto workers a profoundly ambiguous heritage – a set of traditions which, on the one hand, aided Protestant workers in their struggle to exist in the industrializing city but which, on the other hand, led them, on occasion, to riot against their Catholic fellow workers.

The Orange Order's most perceptive student, H.C. Pentland, has argued that until 1870: 'Orangeism and the moderate political conservatism which it built represented the artisan well at a time when capitalism had not advanced enough to subordinate all other divisions to the one between

TABLE 7.1
Toronto population, 1848–91

| Year | Population | Increase by decade | |
		Number	Percentage
1848	23,503		
1851	30,775	7,272	31
1861	44,821	14,046	46
1871	56,092	11,271	25
1881	85,415	30,323	54
1891	144,023	57,608	67

Source: Canada, Census, 1848–91

religion: a significant factor in city politics

capitalist and proletarian.'[3] This chapter will explore the implications of that assertion by analysing the cultural roots and developing beliefs of the Orange Order generally, and then turn to a specific analysis of the order in industrial Toronto – its class composition and collective behaviour. An examination of its political impact on the Toronto working class will be left for later analysis.

A few demographic characteristics of the Toronto population will aid our consideration of Orangeism. The rapid economic development that we have described earlier led to significant population growth. The city grew steadily each decade but leaped ahead in the 1850s (see Table 7.1). The population was notably homogeneous throughout these years, Irish Catholics being the only significantly 'foreign' group in the city. Inadequacies in published census data do not permit a total reconstruction of the population by birthplace; however the trends, as shown in Table 7.2, indicate that the number of Canadian-born persons increased significantly over the four decades. The slight decline in Canadian-born persons between 1848 and 1851 was probably caused by the influx of Irish famine migrants. By 1891 65 per cent of the population were native-born and 24 per cent were of American, English, or Scottish origin.

The city's religious pattern demonstrated a similar homogeneity, being overwhelmingly Protestant and, throughout these years becoming increasingly so (see Table 7.3). The Catholic population declined from a high of 27 per cent in 1861 to only 15 per cent in 1891. Of the Protestant churches, the Methodist grew the most, although the Baptist and Presbyterian also increased their membership. The percentage of Anglicans declined slightly

TABLE 7.2

Ethnic structure of Toronto, 1848–91

Birthplace	1848 No.	%	1851* No.	%	1861* No.	%	1871 No.	%	1881 No.	%	1891 No.	%
England	3,789	16	4,958	16	7,112	16	11,089	20	14,674	17	22,801	16
Ireland	1,695	7	11,305	37	12,441	28	10,336	18	10,781	13	13,252	9
Scotland	9,044	39	2,169	7	2,961	7	3,263	6	4,431	5	6,347	4
France			113	0.4	66	0.1	61	0.1	67	0.1		
Germany	59	0.3			336	0.7	336	0.5	492	0.6	799	0.6
Canada	8,119	35	10,433	34	19,490	44	28,578	51	51,489	60	93,162	65
United States	753	3	1,407	5	2,031	5	1,997	4	3,357	4	5,086	4
Other	44	0.2	402	1	854	2	209	0.4	1,124	0.1	2,576	2
Total	23,503		30,775		44,821		56,092		86,415		144,023	

* Data available only on ethnicity by origin, not by birth.

Source: Canada, Census, 1848–91

TABLE 7.3
Religious affiliation in Toronto, 1848–91

	1848		1851		1861		1871		1881		1891	
	No.	%	No.	%	No.	%	No.	%	No.	%	No.	%
Anglican	8,315	35	11,557	38	14,125	32	20,668	37	30,913	36	46,804	33
Presbyterian	3,655	16	4,544	15	6,604	15	8,982	16	14,612	17	27,449	19
Methodist	2,965	13	4,123	13	6,976	16	9,596	17	16,357	19	32,505	23
Baptist	528	2	948	3	1,288	3	1,953	4	3,667	4	6,909	5
Congregationalist	575	3	646	2	826	2	1,186	2	2,018	2	3,102	2
Lutheran	22	0.1					343	0.6	494	0.6		
Roman Catholic	5,903	25	7,940	26	12,135	27	11,881	21	15,716	18	21,830	15
Jewish	27	0.1	57	0.2	153	0.3	157	0.3	534	0.6	1,425	1
Other and not given	1,513	6	178	0.6	1,834	4	594	1	255	0.3	4,739	3
Total	23,503		30,775		44,821		56,092		86,415		144,023	

Source: Canada, Census, 1848–91

but they remained by far the largest group, claiming almost a third of the city's souls in 1891.

This ethnic and religious homogeneity made Toronto quite different from other major North American cities such as Montreal, with its large French-Canadian population, or New York, with its much higher proportions of foreign-born. Despite the relative homogeneity, however, significant ethnic and religious conflict between the various elements of the working class did occur in this period.

The Orange Order in Toronto provides us with a particularly successful example of the adaptation of an old-world culture to the contingencies of a new society. This chapter suggests some reasons for the order's success and demonstrates not only its adaptation to the new world, but also its transition from rural, pre-industrial roots to a society based in an urban industrial world. The internal tensions engendered by the changes were great. The ever-shifting, but successful, resolution of these tensions allowed Orangeism to remain an important factor in Toronto working-class life throughout the nineteenth century despite the changing nature of the city and its working class.

An analysis of Orangeism in Toronto must begin with the origins of the order in Ireland. The Irish countryside was permeated with agrarian secret societies as early as the mid-eighteenth century. The original groups – the Steelboys, Whiteboys, Rightboys, and Oakboys – were primarily economically motivated in that they sought to protect the interests of agricultural labourers and small cottiers against farmers and landlords, regardless of religious affiliation. These movements existed in both the north and the south and were successful in achieving limited aims:

Although the agrarian secret societies failed to achieve tithe reform in the years before the Union, they may have prevented the type of wholesale eviction which took place in Scotland in the last half of the eighteenth century ... secret societies succeeded to some extent in enforcing tenant rights and other regulations which they believed necessary for their protection.[4]

Nevertheless, the existence of deep hatred between Protestants and Catholics made it relatively easy for the landlords to transform these economic struggles into sectarian strife. In addition, the success of the American and French revolutions transformed the nature of rebellion in Ireland, as well as in the rest of the world. The ability of Jacobin agitators, such as Wolfe Tone, to unite the Defenders, a Catholic agrarian secret society, with his United Irishmen, an urban revolutionary grouping, led to a similar union among Protestant peasant groupings. The Peep o'Day Boys evolved into the Orange Order and took on an avowedly sectarian, anti-Catholic, and anti-revolutionary cast. The revolt of 1798 further reinforced these tendencies. Although agrarian secret societies re-emerged in pre-famine Ireland, their potential for linking the Protestant and Catholic lower classes was gone. Sectarian warfare had gained primacy, and ruling-class interests now possessed the co-operation of societies such as the Orange Order which provided 'an invaluable link between ascendancy power in terms of land on the one hand and the Protestant farming and working classes in Ulster on the other.'[5] Although the order served this function in periods when Ireland's British connection was in question, it continued to be troublesome to the established authorities at all other times.

A movement of lower-class forces which never could be quite trusted, Orangemen found their society outlawed on numerous occasions throughout the nineteenth century. Thus, even in Ireland the Orange Order arose from a curious conjunction of peasant revolt and patriotic reaction. This legacy could only grow more ambiguous when transferred to a country where the economic underpinnings of sectarian strife were far less prominent.[6] For, in Ireland 'religion had determined the side on which a man stood, but the struggle had been one for land and power, and religion had been the badge of difference rather than the main bone in the dispute.'[7] In Canada, land would not be an issue, but power was quite a different question.

Orangeism came to Canada with British troops and with Irish Protestant immigrants in the first years of the nineteenth century. Initially the lodges among soldiers were founded on the authority of the Irish Grand Lodge and the rituals, songs, degrees, and forms of organization were totally imitative of Irish practices. The formal history of a separate Canadian Orangeism begins in 1830 when Brockville's Ogle Gowan, an Irish immigrant with Orange leadership experience, called together representatives from central Canada's scattered pioneer lodges and knit them into a new Grand Lodge of British North America.[8]

In these early years, Gowan did much to separate Canadian Orangeism from pure Irish models. After the proscription of the Orange Order in Ireland, Gowan had been a major force in creating the new Orange Patriotic and Benevolent Society, wherein the militaristic and sectarian sides of Orangeism were de-emphasized, and instead, fraternal and benevolent functions were developed. Although unsuccessful in Ireland, this emphasis was well-suited to Canadian conditions. Partially because of his personal political aspirations, Gowan moved toward a broader definition of

Orangeism as a type of immigrant-aid society which might at times even ignore religious differences. This interest was evident in his alliance with Catholic Bishop Macdonnell before the Rebellion of 1837, at which time the threat of republicanism united both Orange and Green. The early growth of the order was largely due to Gowan's ability to implement these benevolent aims and thus adapt successfully the old institution to its new home.[9]

This is not to deny the order's militant Protestant British identification or its sizeable representation in the Canadian militia. A Canadian tradition of patriotic armed struggle was being created alongside the glorious Irish past. Thus, for Canadian Orangemen the 1837 Rebellion came to be almost as celebrated in song and verse as the Battle of the Boyne. Violent encounters with Irish Catholics in Canada, such as the 1849 Slabtown affair, were juxtaposed with famous Irish encounters such as the Diamond.[10] Thus a Canadian heroic mythology emerged to replace the Irish past – no doubt a prerequisite for the order's successful adaptation to Canadian soil.

Although updated and revised throughout the century, the basic aims of Canadian Orangeism were formulated quite early. Certainly by the mid-forties the standard *Laws, Rules and Regulations* had been devised. Members were committed to four duties: 1/ to uphold the principles of the Christian religion; 2/ to maintain the laws and constitution of the country; 3/ to assist distressed members of the order; and 4/ to promote other 'laudable and benevolent purposes' consistent with Christianity and constitutional freedom. The latter two duties demonstrate how integral the social welfare function was to the Canadian order, unlike its Irish parent. Nevertheless, that Orangemen were quite capable of ignoring these principles will be seen later in their willingness to engage in various illegal collective actions.[11]

Ritual played a crucial role. All Orange candidates swore a sacred oath before entrance into the order. Allegiance to the monarch was part of the oath, but on the condition that the crown uphold the Protestant religion and constitutional rights. This surprising qualification from a proudly loyal organization demonstrates again the ambiguities in the Orange tradition, and shows the depth of Orange suspicion for constituted authority. The oath also committed the initiate to uphold the Empire, to fight for justice for all brother Orangemen, to hold sacred the name of William, to celebrate William's victory every July 12th, to refrain from becoming a papist, never to disclose or reveal the secret work of the order, and lastly, to support and maintain the Loyal Orange Institution.[12]

The solemn oath formed part of the ritual of most nineteenth-century secret societies. In societies involved in transgressions of the law, these oaths represented a potent method of allying and binding the initiate to his new brothers. Even in Canada, where much of the necessity for absolute secrecy was lacking, these oaths continued to be important. In the Orange Order the oath was only the initiation part of an elaborate ritual inspired by Masonic forms. For example, the order had five degrees to which one graduated in a hierarchical order through faithful service: the Orange, the Purple, the Royal Blue, the Royal Arch Purple, and the Royal Scarlet. Initiation into each of these involved a unique ceremony with a ritual introduction, a prayer by the chaplain, an obligation or oath on the part of the candidate, a ritual investiture, and finally a charge to the recipient by the Grand Master of the lodge, or by a more important official in the case of the highest degrees. The oaths and charges depict an interesting symbolic ascent with degree representing greater responsibilities and duties: the Orange simply emphasized faithful personal performance; the Purple called upon the member to scrutinize his brothers and proffer criticism and advice where necessary; the Blue reiterated that charge and called for yet greater diligence; the ritual for the Royal Arch Purple cautioned that 'The mysteries and solemnity of this degree require that the utmost respect, order and decorum be observed by all the brothers. No one shall be admitted into the lodge room in a slovenly or unbecoming dress, nor without a sash appertaining to the order ... No brother shall engage in any levity.' The charge of the degree demanded that the new holder take an increased interest in the well-being of his brothers. The final and most solemn degree was the Royal Scarlet. Its ceremony was full of blood imagery drawing on biblical accounts of the Passover. After being invested with a sword, spurs, a scarlet mantle, and a cord and tassel, the candidate was charged to use his sword 'in defense of our glorious institution' and 'to war against the enemies of destitute widows, helpless orphans, and the Protestant faith.'

The function of this hierarchy of degrees was undoubtedly to provide additional interest and incentive to persevere and to obey Orange strictures in order to attain the reward of a higher degree. An Orangeman's achievements were visible to the entire community in each July 12th parade, for each degree and office carried with it a distinctive regalia.[13]

Special rituals accompanied other important events, such as the dedication of a new Orange Hall and funerals. Funerals had played a crucial role in traditional Irish society. A Harvard anthropologist, reporting on the Irish countryside in the 1930s, was so impressed with the vibrancy of funeral custom that he argued: 'The most important secular ceremony of rural life is the wake and funeral ... Every man in death can command a multitude. To stay away, to make no recognition of the day, is to give deadly af-

TABLE 7.4

Orange lodges in Toronto, 1860–90

Year	Number	Year	Number
1860	20 (21*)	1884	32
1865	20	1885	36*
1870	17*	1886	36
1875	26*	1888	39
1879	31	1890	45 (50*)
1880	31*	1895	56*

* Figures from Houston and Smyth, 'Toronto, the Belfast of Canada,' Fig. 1.

Sources: Saunders, *The Story of Orangeism*; Grand Lodge, *Annual Reports*; *Globe*; Toronto City Directories

front.'[14] The Orange ceremony involved a eulogistic review of the deceased brother's achievements, a renewal of the solemn oaths of the remaining Orangemen over the grave of their late brother, 'sealed' by dropping the rosette of each member's degree into the open grave. These Orange rituals must have been very powerful for members of the lodges.[15]

Toronto, the Belfast of Canada, was the acknowledged centre of nineteenth-century Canadian Orangeism. The tenacity of Orange traditions in rural areas of Ontario has misled some modern observers into assuming that the order was weaker in the cities. A closer look at the Orange Order in Toronto should correct this error.[16]

Data on the early organization in Toronto are limited,[17] but it is known that lodges were already in existence before Gowan's 1830 reorganization (they are not important for our purposes). Subsequently approximately 12 lodges were founded in Toronto in the 1830s, 17 in the 1840s, and 15 in the 1850s; however, by 1860 only 20 of these still functioned.[18] The 1860s was a period of organizational quiescence and by 1871 attrition had reduced the number of lodges to seventeen, totalling 1,494 members. The next five years saw the order grow quite rapidly and in 1876 there were 26 lodges with 2,215 Orangemen. By 1880 the number of lodges had grown to 30 but membership had fallen off to 1,724 and by 1883 there was a further decline to 1,632. Membership continued to decline slightly until the late 1880s. Those years saw the order grow in Toronto at an unprecedented rate. From 32 lodges in 1884, the order grew to 36 by 1886, 39 by 1888, added 7 lodges in 1889 and by the end of 1891 had grown to over 50 lodges (see Tables 7.4 and 7.5). Although statistics of individual membership are not available for the

TABLE 7.5

Orange lodges founded or reorganized in Toronto, 1860–90

Year	Number	Year	Number
1860–64	0	1880–84	2
1865–69*	0	1885–89*	14
1870–74	9	1890–91	7
1875–79	8		

* Houston and Smyth, in 'The Orange Order in Nineteenth-Century Ontario,' p. 43, claim one new lodge in the 1860s, 15 as opposed to my 17 in the 1870s, and 13 as opposed to my 16 in the 1880s. Their sources are varied but seem to come from GOLBNA, *Register of Warrants*, 4 vols, where the status of 'reorganized' lodges might account for the variations.
Source: Saunders, *The Story of Orangeism*

late eighties, a conservative projection based on the lowest average number of members per lodge from the previous years would suggest that by 1892 Toronto Orangemen numbered well over 2,500. Houston and Smyth's detailed study of Orange membership in Toronto in 1894 argues that by that year there were approximately 4,000 followers of King William in the city, and that because of the volatility of lodge membership, there were probably as many ex-Orangemen as current members at any one time.[19] Thus the political and social importance of the order always transcended its official membership.

The Orange Order in Toronto was overwhelmingly working-class in composition (see Table 7.6). Contrary to earlier impressions, however, membership was not limited to successful artisans, since the lodges were filled with labourers, street railway workers, grooms, teamsters, and others from the lower levels of Toronto's working class. No imaginative flights can transform Toronto Orangemen into a labour aristocracy.[20]

An analysis of lodge records reveals much about membership patterns. Four lodges were studied: Armstrong Lodge 137 and Virgin Lodge 328, both of Toronto Centre and founded in the 1840s; Boyne Lodge 173, also of Toronto Centre, founded in 1878; and Enniskillen Purple Star Lodge 711 of Toronto East, founded in 1872.[21] Each had a distinctive social character and all show a majority of working-class members, except Virgin Lodge whose unique emphasis on social control and intent to cater to middle-class sojourners in the city made this lodge unattractive to workers: 'This lodge was originally opened, for the purpose of giving unmarried young men,

TABLE 7.6 Membership of selected lodges by trade, 1872–92

	Virgin Lodge 328 1872	Enniskillen Lodge 711 1872–74	Boyne Lodge 173 1878	Boyne Lodge 173 1885	Armstrong Lodge 137 1885–91	Enniskillen Lodge 711 1887	Enniskillen Lodge 711 1890–92*
Professionals	2	0	0	1	2	1	1
Government employees	2	0	0	0	0	1	0
Manufacturers	0	1	1	0	1	1	0
Merchants	4	3	1	9	5	3	4
Master craftsmen	2	1	4	0	2	4	1
Clerks	5	1	4	5	8	4	2
Non-working-class total	15	6	10	15	18	14	8
Artisans	8	7	17	21	9	35	16
Unskilled	6	15	32	56	19	33	12
Working-class total	14	22	49	77	28	68	28
Percentage	48.3	78.6	83.1	83.7	60.9	82.9	77.8
Total number with occupations	29	28	59	92	46	82	36
Total number listed	48	72	94	121	90	152	80
% with occupations of total listed	60	39	63	76	51	54	45

* New members only.
Sources: Manuscript Lodge Records, Metropolitan Toronto Central Library

students, or mercantile men, etc., a lodge where they could assemble together ... and also of improving on the working and discipline of the Order, as carried out at that time, which was very lax in many lodges.'[22] Its transformation, in 1869, into a benevolent and temperance lodge did not augment its attractiveness for working-class Orangemen. Armstrong Lodge had a less-pronounced majority of working-class members, with a number of socially prominent honourary members who played no role in lodge life. They attended no meetings and paid no dues.[23]

Boyne Lodge 173 had a large number of street-railway employees from its inception. It grew from nine drivers and a conductor in 1878 to six conductors, six drivers, and twelve grooms in 1885. The lodge also contained seven teamsters and three coachmen in the latter year to round out the picture of a concentration of workers in horse transport. Enniskillen Purple Star, founded by Toronto brewer Thomas Allen, in contrast, had from its beginning a large number of brewery labourers and teamsters. Fifteen years later the lodge contained five machinists from one shop, a number of teamsters and building trades workers employed by the same contractor, and several labourers from the Toronto Gas Works. Most of the members of this lodge lived in a neighbourhood bounded by Parliament St., Queen East, River St., and Spruce St.

Each Orange lodge, then, possessed its own history, and some articulated specific idiosyncratic aims. The splitting of the city into three Orange districts in 1876 provided a further rationale for choosing which lodge to belong to. The split was intended 'to foster a friendly rivalry that will induce to the benefit of our order.' (No doubt the new districts, which conformed to Toronto's federal electoral divisions, were also intended to be politically efficient.) A prospective member chose a lodge (and was chosen) on the basis of job-associated friendships and neighbourhood ties. The concentration of workers from single workplaces implies that the lodges were perhaps used as forums for job-related controversies. Lodges in the new working-class suburbs showed higher concentrations of working-class members and probably provided ample time for issues of community concern. This framework, where job, neighbourhood, and leisure came together, contrasts sharply with more modern patterns in which the three are separated.

Recent work by Houston and Smyth confirms these findings. In their sample of 325 Toronto Orangemen in 1894, they found almost 67 per cent to be working-class. In three Toronto lodges examined, they found each to range from 43 per cent to 50 per cent in working-class membership. They also found similar patterns of workplace-related membership. Finally, and perhaps most important, they point out that 'financiers and large industrial capitalists' were not represented in the order.[24] Admittedly, their emphasis throughout is on the social mix of the order, being more impressed by its cross-class profile than by its working-class majority. The middle-class elements they point to, however, tend to be professionals and small-shop owners. The former, who often depended on the order for their business, and the latter, who shared that dependence, were often upwardly mobile, graduating from the working class on only the most tenuous basis. In my opinion, rather than middle-class members dictating Orange standards, it is more likely that it was the working class that exercised control, especially at the lodge level.[25]

If the membership of the lodges was predominantly working-class, then what was the class background of the leaders? Did middle- and upper-class Orangemen exercise a pervasive control over lodge office? An analysis of the occupations of Orange leaders in Toronto suggests not. A survey of lodge masters from 1871 to 1888 indicates that although middle-class members held the majority of masterships in the 1870s, this was reversed in the 1880s (see Table 7.7). Further, when one extends the analysis to include all lodge offices, the role of working-class members increases strikingly (see Table 7.8). Although the middle class supplied a disproportionate number of Orange leaders, their control was far less pervasive than has been previously claimed. Tables 7.7 and 7.8 probably exaggerate the non-working-class role, for three of the categories are open to further investigation. Both the government-employee and clerk categories include a number of patronage appointees who, though working-class in origin, earned jobs as Orange leaders, not the reverse. Similarly, the merchant category includes many small publicans and grocers, traditional avenues of limited social mobility for a select few workers. Again Houston and Smyth's analysis confirms my own. The proportion of leaders who were working-class in the three lodges they examined was as follows: 50 per cent, 100 per cent, and 88 per cent.[26]

Final conclusions concerning the class affiliation of Orange leaders must await further study of individual leaders. In Toronto working-class individuals not only became lodge officers but also filled more eminent positions. For example, the editors of *The Orange Sentinel*, the order's most influential organ, were prominent trade unionists; E.F. Clarke had been a leader in the printer's strike of 1872 and his co-editor, John Hewitt, perhaps the most important theorist of the nine-hour movement, had been international vice-president of the coopers union. Two other prominent Toronto

TABLE 7.7

Lodge masters by trade, 1871–88

	1871	1876	1878	1880	1886	1888
Professionals	1	0	2	3	4	1
Government Employees	1	1	0	3	1	2
Manufacturers	1	1	0	0	0	2
Merchants	1	4	7	4	5	5
Master craftsmen	2	2	2	1	3	0
Clerks	1	1	2	2	1	2
Non-working-class total	7	9	13	13	14	12
Artisans	3	5	3	3	15	9
Labourers and unskilled	0	4	1	4	5	7
Working-class total	3	9	4	7	20	16
Working-class percentage	30	50	24	35	59	57
Number identified	10	18	17	20	34	28
Total number	17	27	29	30	35	39
Percentage identified	59	66	58	66	97	71

Source: See note 27

Orange leaders who played important trade-union roles were J.S. Williams, a printer and editor of the *Ontario Workman*, and Robert Glockling, a bookbinder and District Master Workman of the Knights of Labor. Orange bands were always prominent features at labour demonstrations throughout this period. Clearly, the ties between organized labour and Orangemen suggest that easy assertions about the order's preference for 'leaders with social prestige' should be regarded with considerable scepticism.[29]

The rapid growth of Orangeism in Toronto may have been precipitated by a combination of national and local issues of sectarian strife, but what kept men in the order when the tides of religious struggle retreated? What was the basis for the continued success of an institution, which, as writers

TABLE 7.8

All Orange lodge officers, 1871–86

	1871	1878	1886
Professionals	3	9	8
Government employees	4	8	9
Manufacturers	2	0	4
Merchants	9	21	14
Master craftsmen	4	3	11
Clerks	8	11	23
Non-working-class total	30	52	69
Artisans	51	42	91
Labourers and other unskilled	19	10	47
Working-class total	70	52	138
Working-class percentage	70	50	67
Number identified	100	104	207
Total number	190	197	315
Percentage identified	53	52	66

Source: See note 28

and pundits constantly asserted, had no reason for existence in a country with freedom of religion and no great land question? What motivated Toronto workers to maintain their Orange identities?

The answers to these questions lead one to an appreciation of the breadth and the strength of Orangeism. The order offered much to many quite different people. For some, there was the obvious patriotic and Protestant-defender appeal. For others, there was the confidence that came from belonging to a society which would help carry them through the difficulties of working-class life: if you were unemployed, you could depend on your lodge brothers for aid; if you were sick, the lodge would provide a doctor free and pay any additional medical expenses; or, if you died, the lodge would pay your funeral costs and pave your path into the next world with an impressive ritual, as well as providing financial aid to your widow and orphans. These benevolent functions tended to be informal until the 1880s when, faced with the competition of a whole series of fraternal societies specializing in insurance and other types of aid, the Orange Order formalized their systems into the Orange Mutual Benefit Society.[30]

There was, in addition to these practical advantages, the camaraderie and fraternity of the lodge. Here one found a male society away from women and the pervasive influence of the middle-class-inspired cult of domesticity. Faced with the increased size of their workplaces and their city, these men turned to institutions such as the Orange lodge to recreate the old familiar intimacies of smaller communities. Others probably joined in the expectation of personal gain or, at least, increased security. It was clear that in Toronto there was a whole series of corporation jobs which served as retainers for an Orangeman's faithful service. Although never as formalized as Tammany, the Orange Order served similar uses in machine politics. Orange-controlled jobs included the post office and the customs house at the federal level, and the gasworks, waterworks, police and fire departments at the corporation level. Houston and Smyth point out, for example, that in 1894 LOL No. 207 had four members who gave their address as the Parkdale fire station and LOL No. 781 had eleven firemen as members.[31] *The Irish Canadian*, no friend of Toronto Orangemen, complained in 1876 that the city had employed only two Catholics, who were subsequently fired. In the 1880s, *The Irish Canadian* ran a series of editorials exposing Orange jobbery in the civic corporation.[32] In 1885, for example, the paper systematically analysed the civic list and found only 21 (6 per cent) Catholics in a total of 327 city positions. This included 4 Catholics in the 73-member fire department and 14 in the 159-member police force.[33]

For those who were more ambitous the possibility existed of making a larger mark and receiving the sinecures that came from higher political intrigue. And for the most ambitious there was the political route itself. For a generation of Conservative politicians, the order represented a method of breaking the stranglehold of Compact Tories on nominations. It should be noted, however, that this route was open to few Orangemen and probably played a minor motivational role. At the local level the merchant, undertaker, or tavern keeper living in a working-class neighbourhood found lodge membership a prerequisite for attracting clients. Each candidate for Orange membership probably mixed these motives in distinctive ways.[34]

The Orange Order's role in political life was especially important in Toronto, where politicians built or demolished their careers in proportion to lodge support. The order did not provide an easy path to prominence in public life, for the politician was caught between the Orangeman's continuing need and love for the traditional marches, songs, rituals, and informal riots and the emerging industrial society's demand for order and control. Ogle Gowan's own political career demonstrates the snares upon the path to political success and respectability. His first electoral success was entirely contingent on Orange poll violence – behaviour that he was later instrumental in attempting to suppress.

The conflict between Orange tradition and new societal demands continued throughout the 1850s, 1860s, and 1870s. Whereas Orange workers identified with the old ways and happier days before the alienating onslaught of industrialism, Orange leaders found themselves under ever-increasing social pressure to control their compatriots' excesses. Thus Gowan encouraged the inception of Temperance lodges in the 1850s, which constituted a major break with Orange tradition with its heavy emphasis on the social role of drink. Recognizing the implications of such a step, he argued: 'Our institution is not confined, wholly, or even chiefly, to the uneducated classes of the community, but includes large masses of intelligent and educated men. Remove from them the mirth and hilarity of the festive bowl, and some other source of enjoyment must be provided.'[35] As a solution, he suggested that 'every lodge have its own library and reading room.' After 1859, Orange lodges were forbidden to meet in hotels, taverns, or saloons. Throughout the 1850s Gowan also proposed that lodges set up saving banks, and that Orange bands be required to study music – until then an unheard of proposition.[36]

Virgin Lodge was avowedly organized to stiffen Orange discipline and to socialize younger Orangemen to new models of Orange behaviour. Originally, the name Virgin, which they later adopted officially, was hurled at them as an insult by their more senior and less 'controlled' brothers in the order. The various attempts to assert a new discipline over the membership were not totally successful in the 1850s. The conflict continued into the 1870s and 1880s and heated discussions of whether to drink or not to drink became as much a part of July 12th as King Billy and his white horse.[37]

Another example of the order's increasing concern for respectability was the creation, in 1875, of a Grand Lodge committee on regalia. This committee reported in favour of formalizing and regularizing the old traditional modes of dress: 'The time has come when this Grand Lodge should adopt a uniform regalia; wanting this, our processions fail to favourably impress the public, and the grotesque and ridiculous things often worn as regalia make a laughing stock not only of those who wear them, but of the Association.' The committee went on to specify the different robes for every degree and office in the order, the elaborateness of which was so great that it encouraged the emergence of firms that specialized in manufacturing Orange regalia at exorbitant rates.[38]

The events of July 12th always created great problems for Orange leaders in Canada. The day was so deeply entrenched in the Orange calendar that each member had to swear to celebrate annually the Battle of the Boyne. In periods of great tension, civic authorities often exerted considerable pressure to prevent Orangemen from marching. Orange leaders co-operated with such injunctions only in the most extreme cases, and even then were often unable to prevent their members from marching. It was bad enough that Orangemen demanded to march, but, what was worse, they usually insisted on fighting also. July 12th, March 17th, and November 5th were days when riot became ritual.

These riots, at least in mid- to late-nineteenth-century Toronto, were controlled and not particularly violent. Only extraordinary happenings transformed them into serious outbreaks of collective violence in which severe damage or injury occurred. One historian of Orangeism has noted: 'Even in Ireland the disorders caused by the July 12th processions were relatively minor irritations, the real evil being the nightly raids on Catholic dwellings and the reprisals which grew out of a land question that had no counterpart in Canada.'[39] In Toronto the riots maintained a 'territorial' basis but they also took on an increasingly ritualistic aspect.[40]

Orangemen and Irish Catholics clashed 22 times in the 25 years between 1867 and 1892. On only two of these occasions did serious violence occur to fracture the pattern of restrained ritual riot. Before discussing these two events and what transformed them into bloody occasions, let us describe the calendar of sectarian conflict in Toronto.[41]

Twelve of the riots quite predictably took place on July 12th and March 17th (eight and four respectively). One coincided with the Orange celebration of the discovery of the Gunpowder Plot in November and four others occurred at Orange and Green picnics in August. Thus 17 of the 22 riots accompanied celebrations of import in the annual Orange and Green calendars. The pattern should not surprise us, for collective violence of this kind is neither random nor spontaneous but is most often 'given some structure by the situation of worship or the procession that was the occasion for the disturbance.'

Parades, then, were at the centre of violence in Toronto. This parallels the Irish experience, for 'where you could "walk" you were dominant and the other things followed.' In Toronto, however, this testing of territory took on a ritualistic aspect, seldom progressing to the Belfast model of house-wrecking. A more careful study of the events of July 12th and March 17th will clarify the ritualistic nature of this violence.[42]

The July riots were of three types: those prompted by Green aggression toward the Orange celebration, those prompted by Orange challenges to Green neighbourhoods, and finally Green retaliation post 12 July. The first type was quite rare in Toronto because of the predominance of Orangemen, but in cities which were demographically more balanced or more Catholic, as in Montreal, it became more prominent. This type did occur in 1870 when a foolhardy Green drove his cart, bedecked with green ribbons, through the July 12th procession. It should be noted that although a risky business at best, he did attempt this disruption in the heart of a Catholic neighbourhood. An earlier example of Green interference occurred in 1833, when Irish Catholics imitated the Orangemen by marching with green flags, with one of their members astride a white horse obscenely mimicking King Billy. Not surprisingly, a riot ensued.[43]

Riots of the second type were the most frequent in Toronto. In 1870, 1876, 1877, and again in 1888, riots were caused by Irish Catholics who attacked Orange fife and drum bands as they marched through the heart of a Green residential area playing tunes such as 'Croppies Lie Down,' 'Protestant Boys,' and 'The Boyne Water.' In 1877 an Orange fife and drum band chose Cosgrove's Hotel, a centre of Irish Catholic activity, as a likely spot to serenade. When their lusty performance of 'Protestant Boys' was greeted with stones and jeers, they fought back. A crowd then gathered and proceeded to stone Cosgrove's Hotel, successfully smashing all the windows. This same hotel was attacked and wrecked successively in 1870, 1875, and 1878 – the one example of the Irish model of wrecking in sectarian strife. Cosgrove was a prominent Green leader and, on occasion, served as marshal in the St Patrick's Day procession. His tavern was reputed to be a meeting place for Toronto Fenians.[44]

The third type of riot, Green aggression after the 12th, was infrequent and occurred only in 1873 and 1874.[45]

Riots that took place on March 17th, St Patrick's Day, were usually instigated by Orangemen challenging Green marchers, as in 1871 when an Orange carter drove his horse through a Catholic procession, or when Orange bands marched in Catholic neighbourhoods playing their favourite party tunes, as they did in 1872 and 1889. (The fourth incident of a March 17th riot will be discussed later.)[46]

Most of these riots, then, were highly ritualized and specific. They focused around the major fetes of the Orange and Green calendar but, unlike that in Belfast, the violence was usually quite localized and slight.

The milder form of celebration had been true of an earlier period in Ireland, where 'The marching around the countryside of large bands had about it something of the holiday spirit. Parties usually met by mutual agreement and exchanged shots and insults outside of effective range until the magistrates arrived.'[47] In Toronto, the riots seldom involved shooting; sometimes the parties came close enough to exchange blows, but they showed more bravado than blood.

Some riots did occur outside of the fetes. A number of them involved the Orange Young Britons and the Young Irishmen, their Catholic counterparts, in altercations at dances and over female attention. These adolescent wings of the Orange and Green closely resembled modern street gangs. They were certainly among the most militant on either side and, when arrests occurred, it usually involved these youthful sectarians. The events of September 1870 suggest the street-gang analogy. A fight broke out between a number of Orange Young Britons, who had come to a 'low' (no doubt, Irish Catholic) dancehall to avenge some slight that one of their more daring members had received there. The fight that followed set off a wave of riots that led one leading Orangeman, John Ross Robertson, to editorialize in his *Daily Telegraph* against these 'Young Rowdies,' who were motivated by nothing more than 'a spirit of braggadocio and rowdyism.' Orange leaders sprang to the defence of the Young Britons. At a protest meeting held after the conviction of some of their colleagues for riotous and disorderly conduct, one Orange leader proposed a motion condemning Robertson after denying that any of those arrested were Young Britons.

The Orange and the Green have at all times lived in this city in peace and harmony, each pursuing tenets, religious and political, playing their own favoured music, religious and national, and celebrating their own peculiar anniversaries and fete days without offense, molestation, or interruption and that this joyous and happy state of society it has now for the first time been attempted to be interrupted by the foul and atrocious articles which have recently been printed in certain newspapers in this city.

The same speaker went on to condemn the actions of the police in intervening in the altercation. This is the clue to Orange fury in this case, for the convictions following these events were among the first brought down against these ritual riots. Young Britons previously arrested had escaped with nothing more than a reprimand from the police magistrate. Orange leadership rallied behind their members on this occasion for the last time.

Orange Procession in Toronto (*Canadian Illustrated News*)

O'Donovan Rossa Riot (*Canadian Illustrated News*)

The willingness of civic authorities to suppress Orange riots, and the support that Robertson lent them, symbolize the fact that Orange riots were on their way to becoming as much a memory as the Battle of the Boyne itself. This change, like others in the Orange Order, was bitterly resisted and was not accomplished overnight. Robertson's experience in attacking the Young Britons in 1870 was instructive: 'The *Daily Telegraph* office was threatened with destruction: letters similar to those laid on the tables of obnoxious Irish landlords were received by the editor and reporters; and those taverns and shebeens in which the Young Britons concoct their fearful fights echoed with howls of vengeance against the *Daily Telegraph*.' If that was the case, Robertson must have taken great satisfaction when Gowan, in 1873, made a motion that:

Whereas a number of societies or orders such as the Orange Young Britons ... have been introduced into Canada, or have been organized in the last few years. And whereas such societies have been allowed in some places to walk in public processions and otherwise identify themselves with the Orange Institution, without being under the control, or owing any direct responsibility to the Grand Lodge of the Order for their acts, words or proceedings; and it has become highly desirable and necessary that if such bodies are to be continued, they should be placed under the direct control of proper officers, responsible to the Grand Lodge.

This motion was carried in 1874, but the Young Britons chafed under the authority of the Grand Lodge and a number of them split from the order in the early 1880s. But conflict over the old Orange models and the new Orange design was present. One young leader argued for the new control:

I would recommend the cultivation of the young mind ... how much time do young men generally spend in frivolity or idleness; how much in what is worse – vicious indulgences: smoking, gaming, riotous and ribald conversation, or indolent lounging which ought to be devoted to the pursuit of knowledge and the attainment of business habits ... This is not as it ought to be. Every hour should be appropriated to some useful purpose. We should be as niggardly of time as is the miser of his hoarded treasure.

Following on that appropriate simile, he went on to propose that they should become 'valuable members of society, efficient businessmen, and active moral agents.' Things had moved a long way from the earlier 'festive bowl.'[48]

The conscious efforts of some Orange leaders to instil tougher discipline and to enforce a rigid control over their membership came to fruition in the 1870s. The slow disappearance of the social base for pre-industrial Orange behaviour played as large a part as the conscious efforts of Orange leaders. But whatever the cause, of the 22 riots between 1867 and 1892 only four took place after 1878, and these were all clustered in the three-year period 1887–90. Perhaps even more persuasive was the changed nature of the descriptions of July 12th events in the Toronto press in the 1880s: reminiscence prevailed as writers reflected on how July 12th *used to be*. It was even noted that some of the traditional ritual dress had been dropped. 'The striking white trousers have practically become a thing of history,' wrote one journalist with a tinge of regret. *The Irish Canadian*, a Green paper, noted gleefully throughout the mid-1880s that the numbers were falling off at Twelfth celebrations and that the celebrations were now 'quiet,' 'tame and flat.' It also described the decline of the 'broils that in years gone by disgraced the Orange anniversary,' and emphasized the decline of the old traditions:

And then the traditional grey horse is not as prominent and ubiquitous as was his wont – a circumstance not without significance as indicative of that fatal indifference which preceded the final collapse ... We refer to these trifles merely to show that the discipline of the Twelfth is not as rigid as it used to be, and it looks as if a horse of any colour will now serve where formerly it was treason to hint at anything but the sleekest grey.

The two exceptional riots of the 1870s and the O'Brien riot of 1887[49] provide further indications of changes in Orangeism in that period. The Jubilee Riots of 1875 were undoubtedly the bloodiest sectarian struggles in Toronto's history. The second most violent was the riot which greeted the Fenian leader, O'Donavon Rossa, when he lectured at a March 17th Hibernian celebration in 1878. In both cases the Orange crowds were aroused by the transgression of the informal limits set upon sectarian display by years of ritual riot. In both cases, Toronto Catholics seemed to be extending their territory beyond previous definition. March 17th marches were acceptable, but the importation of an Irish revolutionary to speak in Toronto was an affront that could not go unchallenged. Equally, processions with green ribbons and Hibernian slogans were acceptable, but a pilgrimage through quiet Toronto streets on the Sabbath, with symbols of Popery and apparently on the bidding of the Vatican, could not be allowed to pass unchallenged.[50]

The response of Toronto community leaders is instructive. They decided that they must defend the Catholics' right to religious procession. The entire police force and three companies of militia were utilized to assure Roman Catholics their right to march in 1875. In 1878, however, they did little to protect Rossa. The police took a severe beating on both occasions, but the copious arrests of 1875 contrast noticeably with the record of no arrests in 1878.

The use of Orange militia companies by an Orange mayor against an Orange crowd must have made it very clear to rioting Orangemen that their conduct no longer received tacit approval. It was, of course, partially this armed intervention that transformed the Jubilee Riots into a serious affray. A look at the 29 men arrested reveals eleven identifiable Orangemen. The occupations of the arrested men represent a cross-section of Toronto's working class.[51]

The extraordinary nature of these Roman Catholic marches aroused Orange ire and, when combined with the aggressive attempt by the authorities to suppress the riot, changed the general form of Toronto ritual riot into a full-scale sectarian struggle. There was an important national context as well. The Guibord Affair was still working its way to a macabre close, and only weeks before the Toronto riots, a crowd of Roman Catholics had prevented the burial of Guibord's body in a Montreal Catholic cemetery, despite a court order to the contrary. Meanwhile, only a month before, the Catholic community had hosted an unprecedented August O'Connell Centenary for Hibernians from all over the province.[52] This was probably the largest Catholic demonstration ever held in Toronto. Local Orangemen thus had much on their mind when later they heard of plans for a procession to be held for Catholic bishops visiting the city. In addition, the Catholics planned to march on church visitations to gain indulgences which were connected with the Pope's declaration of 1875 as a Jubilee Year. All of this parading seemed as if Catholics were trailing coats, and the Orangemen requested that Archbishop Lynch cancel these affairs. He refused, and the processionists were met with a small riot on Sunday, 26 September. After these events, Orange leaders called a special public meeting. There, after speeches attacking Ultramontanism, they moved that both sides refrain from marching on the coming Sunday. Lynch again refused and instead demanded from the mayor that, if he forbade his laity to resist, they would be assured of police protection. To this the mayor reluctantly agreed.

The riot that ensued involved as many as 6,000 to 8,000 people, and the entire city core was out of control for a number of hours. Given the crowd's immense size, one is struck by its self-control. The pilgrims were attacked but there were few reported injuries, and the only property damage was incurred by every Orangeman's favourite Toronto target, Owen Cosgrove's Hotel. One scene, reported in the press, vividly portrays the irony of the situation. A fervid anti-processionist appealed to the crowd to attack a Catholic church by reminding them of the old days 'when they walked eight deep' on July 12th. The crowd did not sack any churches that day. Although they might continue to walk eight deep on the Twelfth, the years of ritualized riot were all but over.

The events of 1878 were limited to one night of riot. Insulted by the Catholics' very attempt to bring Rossa to Toronto, Orangemen gathered to prevent the lecture from taking place. In this they failed and, when Rossa managed to elude them after the speech, they proceeded to stone the hall and later to attack Cosgrove's. After 1878 Toronto was to enjoy relative quiet until the late 1880s. Those years saw a few half-hearted attempts at religious riot but the times had changed. The re-emergence of anti-Catholic sentiments in various third-party movements, and the creation in the 1890s of the Protestant Protective Association, modelled on the nativist American Protective Association, suggest the breakdown of the old Orangeism and hint at one of its uses.[53]

The ritualized violence of Toronto Orangemen, which seldom exceeded a set of informal limits, was far less menacing than the nativist movements which replaced it in the 1890s. This restricted violence also prevailed in the 1850s, when the Brown wing of the Grit party exceeded the order in pushing anti-Catholic positions. Orangeism was never racist; its replacements were. The relative mildness of Canadian sectarian strife, when compared with events in the United States, suggests that the Orange institution, which was never strong in the United States, may have played a major role in tempering sectarian strife by institutionalizing elements of it. Shows of strife more often resembled rugged games than vicious riot.

The Orange Order played an ambiguous role in the life of the Toronto working class. Although clearly dividing the working-class community in two, it nevertheless provided some of its Protestant members with a number of strengths that were usefully carried into the realm of unionism. The Orange lodges trained their members in parliamentary procedure and taught them how to conduct and lead meetings. The order also provided leadership for the labour movement. Perhaps of more import, however, was the reinforcement that the order gave to old themes of working-class life. The virtues of mutuality, fraternity, and benevolence had roots deep in the pre-industrial community, and institutions such as the Orange lodges succeeded in transferring them to the increasingly fragmented world of the industrial city. Rowland Berthoff has argued that similar, but less traditional, societies in the United States 'stood in reaction against the social, cultural, and spiritual inadequacies of the nineteenth century. Ineffectual or insubstantial though they might be, they had at least begun the evolution of new institutions and a new community capable of satisfying eternal human needs in forms suited to modern society.'[54]

The other aspect of the Orange tradition with a positive heritage for working-class achievement was its activism. The Orangemen carried with them an Irish dislike of constitutional authority and a willingness to impose their own justice. As one scholar has argued of their Green brothers, but which applies equally well to Orangemen:

Rioting to secure ... political recognition, or religious liberty as popularly construed can be explained by reference to Irish tradition and social organization. It was simply a continuation in Canada of all the devices, including oath-bound secret societies, developed extra-legally in response to legal, civil and religious deprivation ... The violence indicates not massive social disorganization but the persistence of a social order.

These traditions were carried on, he continues, in 'early trade unionism and the political machine.' Even in the extreme case of religious riot, 'the violence is explained not in terms of how crazy, hungry, or sexually frustrated the violent people are, but in terms of the goals of their actions and in terms of the roles and patterns of behaviour allowed by their culture.'[55]

The Irish background and the Toronto working-class experience then explain much about Orange actions, but explanations are not, of course, apologies.[56] The divisive influence of the Orange Order in Toronto's working-class community did exist, albeit mainly in the realm of politics. D.J. O'Donoghue and Alf Jury, two working-class leaders with Liberal party ties, often inveighed against the reactionary Orangemen, but one should treat the evidence of these political losers with extreme caution. For they were just as committed political partisans – all that differed was the party. E.F. Clarke's and John Hewitt's toryism must be weighed on the same ideological scale, not on one that registers only Orangemen. Irish Catholic liberalism was as disruptive to the emergence of a working-class party as Orange toryism.

A distinction must also be made here between the sectarian strife of religious riot and economic discrimination and that of partisan politics. Religious riot had all but disappeared by the 1880s, and riots to keep

Catholics out of jobs did not occur in Toronto in this period. No examples of ethnic or religious riot at the workplace have been found. Partisan political strife, on the other hand, continued. Nevertheless, by the 1880s, common class issues emerged to unite Irish Catholic Liberal trade-unionists like O'Donoghue, Orangemen like Hewitt and Glockling, and even secularist Alf Jury and theosophist Phillips Thompson. In arriving at this point, many rival and mutually exclusive cultural traditions played a role, and Orangeism was by no means the least important.

Thus, by the 1880s, although the Orange Order was still a vibrant part of working-class life, in the economic sphere at least class had triumphed over ethnicity. In the political sphere, as we shall see later, class emerged as only a momentary victor in 1886 but was submerged again thereafter in a tide of ethnic, religious, and partisan political strife.

8

The Toronto working class enters politics: the nine-hours movement and the Toronto junta

In this book I have examined so far the transformation of the Toronto economy and the immediate and direct response of the working class to change through an analysis of trade unions, strikes, and other workplace activities. The working-class world, however, neither began nor ended at the factory gate. Although this book cannot study all the aspects of Toronto workers' lives, their politics demand attention. A history of their response to industrial capitalism must consider their ideology and political behaviour as they developed in this period. In this chapter I shall analyse workers' politics in Toronto from 1867 to 1878, but the discussion will range far beyond parliamentary campaigns. Elections are, after all, only one form of political activity; voting statistics and election campaigns tell us much about workers but so do their lobbying activities, their demonstrations, their acts of collective violence, the speeches they attended on Sundays in Queen's Park, and the myriad of political organizations they formed. These ranged from the Workingmen's Liberal Conservative Union to the Free Thought Society, from the Income Franchise Association of the 1870s to the Bellamyite Nationalist Clubs of the 1890s, and from Fenianism and the Irish Land League to the Loyal Orange Lodge.[1]

A simple survey of Toronto election campaigns between Confederation and the death of Macdonald provides considerable evidence of the importance of working-class votes. Although attempts at overt manipulation were the accepted political practice of the day, there is little evidence to suggest that Toronto workers were fooled by the Machiavellian methods of either the Tory or Grit tacticians; indeed there is ample material to demonstrate that workers cast their ballots in support of the party that convinced them that it would best serve their class interests while in power. When neither party satisfactorily answered these needs, independent labour politics emerged. However, as Brian Harrison and Patricia Hollis have pointed out in the English context, the assumption of many labour historians that all roads must lead to the creation of the labour party has led to 'depreciating the mid-Victorian Liberal working man,' totally neglecting 'the working class Tory.'[2] This chapter will place these workers in the historical context in which they operated.

An analysis of late-nineteenth-century Toronto politics must capture the fluidity of these decades in Canadian history. The period was typified by extremely rapid economic and social change which saw the political parties jockey for position in a race where no one could envision the home stretch, let alone identify the finish line. Moreover, the development of the industrial capitalist economy, although in the long run solidifying the class nature of the society, initially confused far more than it clarified. The transitional nature of this period lent it a dynamism present only in societies in rapid flux. Both new classes – the industrial capitalists and the workers – had to learn the economic rules of a new order. This complex process was further complicated by the new political arrangements of a just-born nation. The creation of a new country from the quite disparate relics of British Imperialism in America raised the possibility of significant political realignments. The new constitutional arrangements also added an entirely new political arena – the province – which had considerable jurisdictional importance for working-class legislative concerns. The national project of the Montreal and Toronto business communities had culminated successfully on 1 July 1867, but the question of the new nation's political and economic direction remained. The working class played a significant role in the resolution of these new problems.

The discussion of working-class politics in Toronto begins with the years 1867 to 1881, the period of clear Tory hegemony. Later chapters will examine the labour upsurge of 1881–87, when workers challenged both the new order and its Tory spokesmen; the return to normalcy which accompanied the decline of the Knights of Labor; and finally the campaign for municipal ownership of the street railway. In this chapter we shall first examine the roots of Tory hegemony in the class conflict of the early 1870s, and then discuss the important legislative victories of the Toronto 'junta.'

I

Toryism had deep roots in the Toronto working-class world. The Loyal Orange Lodge, as seen in chapter 7, enjoyed vast success as the city's most powerful working-class voluntary organization. Although the relationship between the order and the party was frequently stormy and often a source of deep embarrassment to genteel Conservatives, Orangeism successfully harnessed Toronto working-class voters to the Tory machine. The Orange Order offered much to Toronto workers, and its relationship to the Tory party was one of its major assets. The reciprocity of these arrangements was always apparent; in return for their votes Orangemen gained political appointments, patronage jobs, an aura of respectability, and the power that alone could induce equal treatment from men who pretended to be their social betters. The party in turn gained the votes which helped maintain it in power.

The Conservative party promised workers more than just loyalty, the empire, and glorious British traditions. A significant group of Tories offered an ideology that was profoundly attractive to working-class political economists and to the trade-unionists whom they led and influenced. Tory producer ideology, which argued for a reciprocity of interest between small manufacturers and workers, appealed to workers because of its roots in an older society. Moreover, some Tories' emphasis on protection for the encouragement of native industry, their belief in the primacy of labour, their willing acceptance of the labour theory of wealth, their belief in monetary reform, and their empathy and sincere concern for the conditions of workers added to this appeal. In many ways Tory ideology demanded little or no modification in early working-class beliefs about political economy. Unlike Manchester Liberalism and the increasingly popular laissez-faire attitudes, Canadian Toryism retained a flexibility that allowed working-class identification without any sacrifice of principle or apparent ideological concession. This strain of Toryism was most apparent in Hamilton where it was led by Isaac Buchanan, the pioneer Canadian protectionist. But it was present among the ranks of Toronto Tories as well, especially in the 1870s when its major journalistic advocates, *The Peoples' Journal* and later *The National*, were published there.

There were other ideological traditions struggling for working-class support in the Toronto context. The Orange-Tory alliance, for obvious reasons, held little attraction for Irish Catholics, who constituted a significant segment of Toronto workers; nor did the party of George Brown fare much better. Brown's rabid anti-Catholicism in the 1850s estranged him from the Catholics as well. Deeply scarred by their Irish experience, these men and women were extremely hostile to their traditional Orange enemies and to the Scottish nativism of Brown; but in the 1860s and 1870s they were hampered politically by the Hibernian Society's lack of legitimacy because of the fears and hostility associated with the recent Fenian Raids on

Canada. Moreover, the *Irish Canadian*, the major spokesman for Irish Catholic oppositional currents in the city, was still struggling to recover from the blow of editor Patrick Boyle's arrest and imprisonment resulting from his suspected allegiance to the Fenians.[3] The currents of Irish Catholic radicalism, however, grew stronger in Toronto and surfaced in the Knights of Labor and the Irish Land League.

A second major partisan tradition available to Toronto's non-Tory workers was reform. However, the party of William Lyon Mackenzie, the leader of the 1837 Rebellion, still laboured under the heavy weight of this tradition. The major contribution of Reform leader George Brown to his party had been to give it a new legitimacy by downplaying much of this older tradition. But in doing so he managed to alienate many of his Clear Grit and former Chartist immigrant allies, who had previously aligned themselves ideologically with Reform. This loss and the alienation of Roman Catholics were perhaps less serious than Brown's rigid Manchester liberalism. Brown's party held closely to the tenets of classical political economy, and the Liberal leader, an employer of labour himself, was an entrenched opponent of trade unionism. If this had not been evident to all before 1872, the nine-hours-movement and the Toronto printers' strike made it abundantly clear to Canadian workers. These events left a legacy of ill feeling with which the new Reform leaders, Oliver Mowat and Edward Blake, had to cope in the following decades. Of the two major parties, then, the Tories had a considerable edge in the quest for working-class electoral support. The party left's commitment to economic growth through industrial development led it to seek an open cross-class alliance with the working class. Perhaps as important was the party mainstream's willingness to play the game of class politics. Meanwhile the Liberals, severely limited by the ideological rigidity of George Brown, found themselves trying desperately to maintain the fiction of a classless society.

Toronto workers first went to the polls under the new Confederation scheme in the dual elections of September 1867.[4] True to their Tory heritage they returned four Conservatives: James Beaty and Robert Harrison to the House of Commons in Ottawa and Matthew Cameron and John Wallis to the Provincial Legislature in Toronto.[5] Although workers did not figure prominently in this campaign, this proved to be the exception, for the candidates in subsequent elections heatedly contested for their vote. Moreover, this quest for workers' votes met with receptive audiences in the taverns, streets, and halls of Toronto. The struggles of 1872 thrust class conflict into the centre of the political arena, where it remained.

The year 1872 started on a rather dismal note for the Conservative party as Edward Blake and his Ontario Liberals took power after defeating John Sandfield Macdonald's Tory government. The 1871 election had seen the Liberals win one Toronto seat when Adam Crooks, later Blake's first attorney general, defeated John Wallis in Toronto West.[6] But if the Liberals were elated by these events, their enthusiasm was to prove short-lived.

The trade-union movement had grown rapidly in the 1860s and an entirely new spirit emerged from a combination of increased numbers, British and American influences, and the dynamics of industrial capitalist expansion. Industrial growth was transforming the world of the artisans through mechanization, many of whom stepped forward to become the leaders of trade unionism. As has been argued in other national contexts, the leadership of the early working class came from the ranks of respected, skilled workers.[7] This fact was as true in Toronto where the first executive of the Toronto Trades Assembly (TTA), founded in 1871, reflected its artisan roots; the president was John Hewitt of the Coopers International Union, the recording secretary was J.S. Williams of the Toronto Typographical Union, and the corresponding secretary and treasurer were H.L. Beebe and James Dean, respectively, of the Knights of St Crispin. Also represented on the executive were the local branches of the Cigarmakers and the Iron Moulders Unions.

The establishment of the TTA led to an active organizing drive. It also played a prominent educational role in bringing to Toronto Martin Foran of the Coopers International Union, John Fehrenbatch of the Machinists and Blacksmiths, and Richard Trevellick of the National Labor Union to speak in 1871 and 1872. An active correspondence was carried on with American trade-unionists, especially with William Jessupp of New York, a personal acquaintance of Hewitt's from his sojourn in that city. These American connections were all of great importance in the emergence of the nine-hours movement in winter 1872.[8]

The nine-hours movement is undoubtedly the most discussed event in nineteenth-century Canadian working-class history. (A complete narrative of the events of spring 1872 is not necessary here.[9]) The movement was a significant benchmark both in the evolution of Canadian working-class consciousness and in the development of mature organizational forms. The focus here will be on the legal status of trade-unionism and the impact of the 1872 events on working-class politics for the remainder of the decade.

The Toronto Music Hall was packed to the doors on the evening of 14 February. J.S. Williams took the chair in front of a row of platform guests representing nearly all the Toronto unions. When Williams announced they had met to seek the best method of agitating for the nine-hour day, the crowd cheered enthusiastically. The audience then settled back to hear the four main motions of the evening, prepared earlier by the Toronto Trades Assembly. Cooper John Hewitt rose first to make the motion:

Whereas the progress of the present age has brought into existence many useful labour-saving appliances, that have greatly increased the production of manual labour and whereas the producing classes have not received any benefit commensurate with the increase of production, be it resolved by the working men of the city of Toronto in mass meeting assembled that we demand a nine hour system of labour as a right and shall use all honourable means to secure this.

In support of his motion Hewitt endorsed the American eight-hour movement: the symmetry of eight hours each for work, for improving one's mental faculties, and for sleep. At that time, however, he sought only the nine-hour day. He also alluded to the need to have supporters in the Legislative Assembly. This led him to call for franchise extension and the secret ballot. As we have seen earlier, all these suggestions flowed from the coopers' industrial experience.

Andrew Scott of the Amalgamated Society of Engineers followed with the evening's second motion: 'Whereas, the increase of intelligence among the masses of the people has opened up a new appetite that must be fed, it is resolved, that we deem it absolutely necessary to supply the rapidly developing mentality of the present age, we consider it expedient to secure a reduction in the present protracted hours of labour.' Scott and his seconder, printer John Armstrong, both spoke of the workingman's need for time to cultivate his intelligence, which they viewed as an integral part of the spirit of the age. The third resolution was moved by John Collins of the Hay & Co. cabinet works:

Whereas the wonderful increase of knowledge and power and mind hitherto unknown in the producers of all wealth, which is fast raising them to an equal with their fellow men, so that they are in reality productive and mental labourers, be it resolved, that the physical exhaustion resulting from the double task can only be remedied by a great moral and physical reform.

Crispin James Dean endorsed this motion with an assurance that workers would produce as much in nine hours as in ten. Employers would not be losers but rather gainers by the change. Workers, finally realizing they were not slaves but freemen, should 'not grasp the sword as communists' but rather reason with their bosses. John Walker of the Coach Builders Union presented the final resolution of the evening:

Whereas, the association and endearments of an enlightened and intelligent home circle, demand more time from him, to whom they look not only for support, but for much of his presence, to add pleasure and happiness to their mutual social intercourse, be it resolved that in view of the God-imposed duties we owe to those nearest and dearest to us, that we must obtain the time requisite to devote to those important responsibilities.[10]

These speeches at the first nine-hours meeting present the workers' arguments for shortening the working day. They reveal a unique world view. Note, in the first resolution, for example, the underlying assumption of the labour theory of wealth. As Grant of the Stonemasons had said in support of Hewitt's motion, 'What could capital do without labour?' The demand for nine hours was not requested as a favour but rather demanded as a right. 'Labour is both superior and prior to capital and alone produces capital,' asserted *The Ontario Workman*, the official organ of the nine-hours movement and the Toronto Trades Assembly.[11] Or, as Montreal's *Northern Journal* put it, the old servant class is 'asserting the right of every man to the entire proceeding of his own labour.'[12]

The second set of beliefs that runs through these motions is the pride and self-respect of artisans and skilled workers. These men fully believed, as their newspaper argued, that 'there has never been any considerable social advancement, wherein the artizan as a class has not first or last played a prominent part.'[13] The rhetoric about 'a new appetite that must be fed' and 'an enlightened and intelligent home circle' encompassed artisan ideals. This was how they viewed themselves as a class and how they expected the rest of society to view them.

A third theme – more evident in the speeches than in the actual motions – was the sense of internationalism that shaped this working-class mentality. When they alluded to events in England and the United States, they identified their own struggles with their fellow workingmen there. They clearly rejected their opponents' constant refrain that Canada, as a new country, was an exception to old-world experiences. This internationalism was very much in evidence in their 'Memorial to Trade Unionists in Great Britain':

inasmuch as your expressions of sympathy and moral support will be the means of showing the employers of this country that, though seas divide they do not separate us, and though locally apart, we are actively allied, and that any attempt in one part of the British Dominion to violate the principles of freedom we have so long been taught to possess will only have the effect of calling forth a scathing rebuke from all the rest.[14]

This appeal did not fall on deaf ears. Financial support later came from the Scottish and English bookbinders unions.[15]

Internationalism was also a major theme of National Labor Union leader Richard Trevellick's address to Toronto workers at the height of the nine-hour struggle: workingmen knew no country, he argued echoing Marx, but the time would come 'when they would join hands around the world and if kings and emperors and presidents wanted to fight, let them fight it out by themselves.'[16] This internationalism also gave them access to radical theorists such as Ira Steward and Karl Marx.[17] Steward, the American theorist of the eight-hours movement, formulated a critique of classical political economy which touched on Marx's in many places. His complete break with the wage-fund theory was echoed in the literature of the Canadian nine-hour movement, and excerpts from his work were published in *The Ontario Workman*.[18] Internationalism was also evident in the response of the TTA to a letter from the International Workingmen's Association in London in December 1871 when it was decided that Hewitt, as secretary, should correspond with that body.[19]

Toronto employers' response to the nine-hours movement also tells us much about the ideological dimensions of the period. Initial response was cautious and paternalistic. John Ross Robertson's *Daily Telegraph* advised sagely:

The present is not a safe time for the workingmen of Canada to put the manufacturing interests of the country in jeopardy, by any action threatening a diminution of our power to meet foreign competition. And when we speak of manufacturing interests, we beg to state most emphatically, that we include under that term the interests of the employed as well as the employers.

Instead workingmen had to wait until the unfortunate tariff compromise of 1866 was replaced by a protective tariff in the tradition of 1859. With that added security for Canadian infant manufactures, workers could press for more.[20] George Brown's first editorial in the *Globe* reluctantly granted the men their right to formulate such a demand, but reminded them that employers had an equal right to refuse and that the sentiments of moral philosophy should not be confused with the laws of political economy. Supply and demand dictated wages, and trade-union actions could not affect this process.[21] Brown's biographer concluded that this rigid Manchester liberalism led the *Globe* editor 'to acknowledge a union's right to exist – but very little more. It might function as a benevolent society; yet he would scarcely concede it the power it needed to ensure effective bargaining.'[22]

As the nine-hours movement gained strength, the situation grew far more tense, and the March demands of the Toronto printers for shorter hours and for a simultaneous wage advance led to virulent editorial denunciations and to a stiff anti-union stance by the Master Printers' Association (MPA), founded by George Brown. Only one paper, James Beaty's *Leader*, acceded to the union's demands. Earlier, the *Leader* had been only lukewarm to the movement; it acknowledged the workers' right to shorter hours but argued that the price of leisure and consequent self-improvement was lower wages: 'if they wanted a holiday, they must pay for it.' The *Leader* also attacked Richard Trevellick's major speech as illogical and full of 'clap-trap.'[23] Thus, the emergence of the *Leader* as the major pro-labour voice after the printers struck against Brown and the master printers was certainly ironic, if not totally opportunistic.

Meanwhile, the tone of Brown's attacks on the workers became ever more shrill. The workers were trying to place Canadian employers under the U.S. National Labor Union and its leader Trevellick, a 'professional agitator.'[24] Brown found other enemies as well: first were 'the agents of the English trade unions who make money out of labour agitation and are trying to transfer to this city;' second was 'another class, perhaps even more dangerous – men of dreamy, imaginative character who form exaggerrated notions of the evils of manual labour and vague aspirations after a different, and what they consider, a much higher life.'[25] Most important, he believed that 'the assault' on the press was but a forerunner of the coming assault on employers and employed in all branches of industry, and the necessity of firmly resisting it could hardly be overestimated.[26] Brown did more than spread rhetoric against the nine-hour movement; he also organized the stiff employer resistance by means of the MPA. (Brown's role in devising the association's hard line was exposed by other master printers when they later defected from the alliance during the strike.) Indeed, Brown orchestrated the collective response of capital across Ontario. A petition, refusing to grant the nine-hour day, appeared in the *Globe* on 8 April. Signed by hundreds of employers, it included many small Toronto businesses along with the owners of major Ontario industries. This statement refuted the notion of shorter hours by asserting the normality of ten hours, by claiming that anything else would weaken the young nation irreparably, and by denouncing the nine-hours movement as a 'communistic system of levelling.'[27]

Brown's pre-eminent role flowed directly from his history of conflict with the Typographical Union, which, as we have seen earlier, involved major struggles in the 1840s and 1850s. At one point he claimed that 'The proprietors have suffered for years from intolerable and increasing oppression and the effort they are now making is to free themselves from it and gain control of their own business.'[28] These sentiments reinforced his belief in a liberal political economy that dictated that society 'must allow supply and demand free action.'[29] But his social vision involved more than those adages. He attacked those who sought shorter hours as 'being too lazy to earn their bread' and concluded 'laziness is detestable.' In denouncing Trevellick, he asserted that all Canadians were workers. Canada had 'no such class as those styled capitalists in other countries. The whole people are the capitalists of Canada.' Moreover, the politicians 'come from the people, and are of the people still.'[30] Because Canada knew 'no class distinctions ... labour agitation had been utterly without reason.'[31]

Brown used the law to reinforce capital's position. The use of the courts was not as unusual in this period, as indicated by much of the literature on the printers' strike. Toronto employers, as we have seen, resorted to the Master and Servant Act frequently in the 1850s, 1860s, and 1870s.[32] Brown himself, at the time of the previous printers' strike in 1854, had the union prosecuted successfully for conspiracy to combine.[33] Thus the furor that resulted from this procedure in 1872 is a testimony to the new militancy and organized strength of Toronto workers. The working-class response in 1872 led to an immediate critique of the legal system and to ongoing demands for legislative remedy.

Quite early in the strike, Brown warned of possible legal action against the strikers.[34] The MPA commissioned a legal opinion from Robert Harrison, QC, which, as quoted in the *Globe*, said 'that no member of the Typographical Society may be able to plead ignorance to the law of Canada in regard to trade combination, and the coercion of workmen.'[35] Harrison insisted correctly that the English statutory protections of trade unions had no standing in Canadian law. English common law therefore remained in effect, so that any combination to interfere with a man's decision to work or any collective attempt to raise wages was an indictable conspiracy. Harrison found a precedent in a Canadian court decision in the 1858 shoemakers' conspiracy trial.[36] Combinations of workingmen were illegal if they tried to affect hours, wages, the amount of work, or the behaviour of other employees.[37] With Harrison's mandate Brown simply bided his time. On 3 April he noted that evidence of criminal acts had been submitted to counsel for a decision regarding prosecution. That day John Ross Robertson of *The Daily Telegraph* successfully prosecuted John Auld, one of his striking printers, for deserting his job. Auld was fined $30 or given 30 days, a harsh punishment for such an offence against the Master and Servant Act.[38] Two weeks later, thirteen TTU members were arrested and charged with 'unlawfully conspiring ... to induct and persuade workingmen who had contracted with the Master Printers to serve them ... unlawfully to absent themselves from the said service, without the consent of the said employers.'[39]

The court proceedings proved less conclusive than Brown might have hoped. Acting under the influence of Harrison's opinion, Police Magistrate McNabb cared only if a combination existed, and evidence of other coercive activities was viewed as superfluous to the charge.[40] Thus Brown's successful conviction of the printers for combination was a Pyrrhic victory at best, for Ottawa trade-union leaders D.J. O'Donoghue and Donald Robertson met with Macdonald immediately and demanded a Canadian statute to legalize trade unions.[41] The result – the 1872 Trade Unions Act – although a far more ambiguous piece of legislation than was at first apparent, nevertheless won for Macdonald labour's gratitude, and for Brown, their enmity.

Although intriguing, the details of the legal struggle are less important than the political situation they created. On one side, a militant trade-union movement confronted an anachronistic legal structure, and on the other unreconstructed Manchester liberalism contested a combination of Tory political opportunism and producer ideology. The former conflict was to shape much of labour's program for the rest of the 1870s; the latter contest was to leave Toronto Reformers striving desperately to overcome the immense impediment created by Brown's refusal to countenance class politics. In leading the capitalist cause in 1872, Brown prescribed a classical model for political-economic development that proved far less attractive to Canadian workers than the Tory road. This latter path eschewed the conventional myths of political economy, but in actuality it imitated the American process of industrial development which employed an active state and high protective tariffs.

For the remainder of the decade, politics centred on labour's successful strugggle to force the state to legalize trade unions, to guard workers' wages against unscrupulous capitalists, especially in the building trades, and to equalize the contractual relationship that ensued from the sale of labour to capital. Hardly revolutionary, these demands nevertheless assured the ongoing existence of the workers' main defensive institution. Interestingly, these gains were wrested from Brown's Reform successors, who clearly had learned the lesson of 1872: workers were to be assaulted only at great cost.

This lesson had been driven home to the Reformers in the 1872 election campaign in which trade-unionists played key roles on platforms across Ontario in support of Macdonald. The role played by the *Leader*, owned by Tory MP James Beaty, throughout the nine-hours struggle made it relatively easy for the Tories to use this whole episode as the major thrust of their campaign in the cities. As early as June, Macdonald himself realized that protection, which would appeal to both manufacturers and workers, combined with the defence of trade-union rights (as evidenced by his Trade Unions Act) would be an unassailable urban package. Writing to his Hamilton lieutenants, Macdonald indicated that the Trade Unions Act and 'the arbitrary and oppressive action taken by George Brown with respect to his printers' assured them of mechanics' support. 'This,' he added, 'may be utilized at the next election.'[42] An earlier letter to the new editor of the *Mail*, T.C. Patteson, suggests the political sagacity with which Macdonald was playing this game: 'You must take great care not to offend the employers of labour in this nine hours movement. When the present excitement is over you must look to them and not to the employed for support. At the same time there is, of course, no necessity for your head against the navvies in the way that the *Globe* is doing.'[43]

Usually viewed as little more than a prelude to the excitement of the Pacific scandal, the 1872 election was an important landmark. In this campaign the Tories took their first tentative steps towards an avowedly protectionist tariff to encourage manufacturing. The campaign also saw the initial use of the phrase 'National Policy.' Most important, the 1872 election was the first in which workers affected national politics in a major way. With good reason, *The Ontario Workman* crowed proudly after the election that the campaign had brought 'a new era in the annals of the political world.'[44]

True to form, Brown helped the Tory cause greatly by his own vituperation. When he heard that Toronto workingmen had planned a demonstration for Macdonald to thank him for the Trade Unions Act, he retreated to his earlier argument that Canada knew no classes.[45] Moreover, the working classes of Canada had 'no grievance of a legal character.' For the Tories 'to bring into Canadian politics, class distinctions and class jealousies, in order to introduce class legislation, would be worse than a fault, it would be a crime.'[46] His fulminations against the printers continued; however, he now pretended that he had never intended prosecution for combination, but only for intimidation, which was still illegal both in Britain and in Canada under the terms of the Criminal Law Amendment Act which had accompanied the Trade Unions Act in each country.[47] The strikebreakers, he charged, 'were watched, they were dogged, they were threatened with personal violence, and in two cases they were beaten.' Moreover, 'bricks were thrown in through the windows of the offices ... plots were laid to destroy machinery, pistols were fired, and bribery was employed' – all of this sanctioned by the printers' union.[48]

The *Globe*'s campaign to expose the Tory's pretence of being friends of the worker was aided by the arrival of Terry Clarke. A member of the bricklayers union, Clarke published letters in the *Globe* charging that the TTA's presentation to Macdonald was a Tory plot. A stream of malicious attacks followed on the Toronto nine-hours movement leaders, then campaigning openly for Macdonald: Hewitt could 'scarcely be called a workingman. He is a professional agitator ... continually moving about now in Hamilton, now in Cleveland, now in New York ... always dabbling in agitation of one kind or another';[49] the coopers' leader lived 'by his wits and not be the sweat of his brow'; McCormack and Williams were simply 'puppets and tools of Sir John A. Macdonald'; and under Williams *The Ontario Workman* was 'flaming, full fledged [and] Tory' from its inception.[50]

How are we to assess Clarke's charges? His accusations in the *Globe* caused the TTA to expel him as a man 'no longer entitled to the confidence of honest men.'[51] That action, together with the Tory courtship of the labour leaders, did not make these men tools of Macdonald, as Clarke claimed and as later historians have accepted. In the debate on the Macdonald presentation, John Hewitt answered the charge that the TTA had been transformed into a political engine. 'If these men were going to make political engines of the workingmen,' he said, 'we in turn can use them to gain our ends.' In addition, avoidance of politics was impossible 'for political questions arise from time to time of the greatest moment to the working class.'[52] This debate behind the closed doors of the Trades Assembly Hall illuminates the emerging strategy that Toronto trade-union leaders pursued in summer 1872. The failure of direct militant action in the nine-hours campaign caused them to turn their attention to politics and the possibilities of legislative change. The Tories' Trade Unions Act, their interest in working-class issues, and their developing political economy were attractive to Toronto trade-union leaders. Brown's aggressive anti-labour stance made labour's decision far easier.

In embracing Macdonald, they never suspended their critical judgments, however. That was well illustrated in their response to the Trade Unions Act. *The Ontario Workman* greeted news of the proposed legislation with little enthusiasm: passage of the bill without any change from its English model 'would be a fatal mistake,' since that bill had proved 'in very many respects unsatisfactory to the operative classes of the mother country, and will undoubtedly be materially changed by amendments ere long.'[53] One week later the paper urged passage of the new legislation to 'give the protection we require, and to which we are justly entitled.' The printers' hazardous legal situation made little else possible, but the editorial also criticized the Criminal Law Amendment Act as redundant, harsh, and oppressive.[54] The Toronto Trades Assembly followed the same strategy. Its first response of cautious congratulations for Macdonald's prompt and considerate action was coupled with a request for more details on the proposed bill. Simultaneously they asked the trade unions in London (England) for copies of the British Act and 'details regarding the arguments which the unions purposed making thereon.'[55] A month later, after the bill had been introduced in the House, a TTA Special Committee recommended critical support, since it was too late to do much else. The TTA concluded, however, 'that there were many deficiencies of great importance.'[56] A motion to thank Macdonald was defeated; it was decided to allow the bill to pass quietly and push for amendments later.

Support for the Tories in 1872, as indicated in *The Workman*, resulted from the party's awareness of the need for legislation to ameliorate labour's legal situation. Brown, *The Workman* said, believed workers had 'all the rights they are entitled to [and] legislation in their behalf would be class legislation.'[57] The Tories, moreover, reinforced the labour alliance with a brilliant strategy devised by Isaac Buchanan. Rejecting Macdonald's choice for Tory candidates in Hamilton, he nominated H.B. Witton as Canada's first workingman's candidate.[58] Following closely on the heels of the nine-hour struggle and the Trade Unions Act, this formal excursion into Tory-Labour politics helped to strengthen further the nascent relationship.

In the summer campaign of 1872, the outstanding leaders of the nine-hours-movement graced Tory platforms. John Pryke of Hamilton, James Buchanan of Brantford, and Toronto's Williams, Hewitt, Scott, and McCormack appeared regularly in support of Witton and other Tory candidates.[59] Brown's accusations cost his party dearly in Toronto and in other urban centres. The Tories carried two of the three Toronto seats, losing the new central Toronto seat to the Liberal Robert Wilkes who had held a workingmen's meeting to dissociate himself from Brown. He also endorsed the right of workers to combine to protect themselves against the huge corporations, and urged that 'obsolete laws be swept away.'[60]

Brown, however, was unmoved by these losses. After the election, he addressed in an editorial 'Plain Words to Workingmen:'

In Canada there is no idle class, for those who do not labour with their hands, work with their brains, or with their capital, and are equally useful and essential members of the community ... There is nothing in a new country to bind any man to a particular sphere if he has but the ambition and the energy to strive for a higher position ... Let the working class so-called repudiate a distinctive appellation so manifestly inappropriate in a country where all are workers and labour is deemed honourable, asserting their just claim to be regarded as unpatronized citizens of a free community.[61]

Brown's continued intransigence, and the successes of summer 1872 thus furthered the growing intimacy between Tories and labour leaders.

II

After the campaign, Macdonald secretly loaned J.S. Williams and his new partners, J.C. McMillan and David Sleeth, all prominent members of the Toronto Typographical Union, the necessary funds to purchase *The Ontario Workman* from the original co-operative.[62] He also granted it a share of the available government patronage, a much needed aid for any newspaper of the day.[63] In the first issue under these new arrangements, *The Workman* noted its pleasure with the recent election but found the Tory government far from perfect. Labour had 'to work as indefatigably in organizing and consolidating our forces as ... in the past, prepared to go forward in the grand social reform ... so well inaugurated.'[64]

How 'indefatigable' were *The Workman* and its Toronto labour colleagues in pursuing class interests over the narrow gains of sectarian politics? This is the key issue in the analysis of working-class politics in the years after the 1872 election. On the surface Macdonald's secret backing of *The Workman*,[65] the patronage appointment of J.S. Williams as one of the Canadian commissioners to the Vienna Exhibition,[66] and the newspaper's increasingly shrill pro-Tory stance all indicate a narrowing of (indeed, even a loss of) class perspective. Nevertheless, tangible legislative gains were won in these years – legal gains often dismissed by historians preoccupied by Macdonald's Machiavellian intrigues.[67] Despite the emergence, in the pages of *The Ontario Workman*, of partisan attitudes, the Toronto 'junta' performed stalwart service in the interests of the Canadian working class. The appellation 'Junta' is appropriate because, by late 1873, this group of Toronto leaders, who had risen to prominence in the nine-hour struggle and who had increased their reputations by gracing Tory platforms in the 1872 election, exercised almost total control of the central-Canadian working-class movement.[68] Their influence over *The Ontario Workman*, their leadership of the TTA, and their prominence in the new Canadian Labour Union, which they organized in 1873, gave them a near monopoly of visible positions of power in the new movement.

Their dominance in the TTA extended to official positions. Hewitt was the TTA's first president and then served as corresponding secretary for four terms until he resigned to take a patronage job at the Toronto Water Works and to become E.F. Clarke's assistant editor at *The Sentinel*, Toronto's Orange weekly. Williams served two terms as recording secretary, becoming the third president of the TTA, and then succeeded Hewitt in the crucial position of corresponding secretary. He filled that position for the remainder of the TTA's existence, a total of nine terms. Other junta members, such as J.C. McMillan, Joseph Levesley, Andrew Scott, and Andrew McCormack, also filled key executive positions.[69] Within the corridors of power in Toronto and Ottawa, junta members enjoyed access to political leaders and were the acknowledged voices of the labour movement. Between 1873 and 1878, they succeeded in winning legal status and a fair degree of political influence for the trade-union movement.

How did the junta build this political power? After the 1872 election its position in Toronto was temporarily shaken by the accusations of Terry Clarke and the *Globe*. A crisis came in early September. Distressed by Clarke's verbal assaults, Hewitt demanded a public meeting to clear the air. Cooler heads prevailed, and Scott and Williams opposed Hewitt's plan, claiming that a meeting would only provide a new platform for Clarke and Brown. The latter were now limited to the *Globe's* columns, and the spring events had shown that the *Globe* had a declining influence. Such a meeting 'open to public debate would be attended by an element entirely hostile to trade unionism and whose object would be to sow dissension among the ranks of workingmen.'[70] After a lengthy debate, it was resolved that McCormack should name the donor of the gift to be presented to Macdonald. McCormack agreed to consult that mysterious gentleman and report back. If he ever did, it went unrecorded in the TTA minutes.

With this issue resolved, the junta continued to move toward 'grand social reforms,[71] turning first to the legislative program of the Mowat Ontario government. Its initial assault was levied against convict labour at the Toronto Central Prison. A TTA committee, featuring Hewitt, Williams, and Levesley, twice interviewed Mowat's attorney general, Adam Crooks, and after failing to get a satisfactory response, they planned a mass protest meeting.[72] The junta contacted the Ottawa Trades Council, which was dominated by building trades' workers who were upset with the limited Mechanics' Lien Act,[73] transforming the protest into a broader meeting 'to discuss questions of moment now before workingmen.'[74] Crooks was also asked for copies of his new Lien Law and of his Act designed 'to facilitate the adjustment of disputes between masters and workmen.'[75]

Publicity for the planned demonstration included a full-out assault on the Mowat government by Hewitt in *The Ontario Workman*. Crooks' Mechanics Lien Act was of no use to workers because it applied only to debts over $50, much more than the usual amount due workers involved in a contractor's bankruptcy. 'The operative,' Hewitt said, 'seems to have been intentionally excluded from its provisions.' The proposed arbitration bill, furthermore, was attacked as 'a very loose measure,' of no real use to the worker since it gave the potential boards no authority regarding wages.[76] Hewitt's early critique of these boards is supported by the fact that none was ever formed under the authority of this act.[77]

Toronto's St Lawrence Hall was filled for the protest meeting. The Mechanics Lien Act was condemned as utterly failing 'in its provision to protect skilled and other labourers.' A bill was required that 'protects all classes of labour, collecting from one day's wages and upwards.' The workers asked that the lien be extended to include the structure under construction and not just the contractor, and that the $50 minimum be dropped from the bill. Printer D.J. O'Donoghue, the new labour MPP from Ottawa, in seconding the meeting's motion, referred to the bill as a sugar-coated pill – sweet on the outside but very bitter on the inside. All they sought was justice, and perhaps the only way to gain it was by electing more workingmen to the legislature. The rest of the evening proceeded according to the junta's plan; the government's amendments to the Master and Servant Act, its new Trades Arbitration Act, and its act 'to facilitate agreements between masters and workmen for participating in profits' were all severely criticized. Mowat's policy of employing convict labour received outright condemnation. The limited extension of the franchise was commended, but a further extension was urged. The government's attempts to end the direct election of mayors, and to extend the term for aldermen to three years were both opposed. The evening's work must have left the junta well satisfied.[78]

Opposition, however, emerged at a Hamilton meeting the following month,[79] setting off an interesting year-long controversy on the *Ontario Workman* politics, the labour movement, and the respective merits and demerits of the Grits and Tories.[80] One Hamilton worker called for a party 'which will not look to the great *Globe* or the black *Mail* for its tuition, but will seek apart from there to build up a political faith of its own.'[81] To the brewing dissension, Hewitt responded that 'party differences have long been the bane of labour progress'; he asked 'workingmen to remember that neither of the existing parties are parties of labour and that neither will give the reforms we need except in compliance with the demands of a well-directed and united agitation.' Then he launched one of the harshest attacks on Macdonald ever to appear in *The Workman*. He demanded that the Tory federal government repeal the Criminal Law Amendment Act, and condemned their Election Act as 'unworthy of a party whose eyes ought to be open to the needs of this progressive age.' The act did nothing to extend the franchise or grant the secret ballot, and Hewitt objected strenuously 'to man's franchise being based on any other basis than honor and manhood.'[82]

This harsh attack on the Macdonald government was the beginning of the junta's newest campaign – full repeal of the Criminal Law Amendment Act, the piece of legislation which had accompanied the Trade Unions Act in both England and Canada and had brought into question the legality of strikes.[83] At a special TTA meeting to debate how best to commence this lobbying activity, the delegates decided to circulate a petition among Toronto trade-unionists.[84] As usual, the committee entrusted with the wording of this memorial consisted of junta members Scott, Hewitt, and Williams.[85] In May the TTA recognized the increased regularity of its lobbying role by appointing a three-member parliamentary committee, to which Williams and Hewitt were named.[86]

Early in summer 1873, the junta launched an ambitious scheme which had important repercussions.[87] Hewitt had waxed eloquent the previous May about the first meeting of the Canadian Labour Protective and Mutual Improvement Association and had immediately formulated plans for a meeting the following January.[88] For unexplained reasons, it had been delayed, but the plans now re-emerged. A series of meetings lay the groundwork for the first convention of the Canadian Labour Union (CLU), held in Toronto in September 1873.[89] The 45 delegates included representatives from Toronto, Hamilton, Ottawa, St Catharines, London, Cobourg, Bowmanville, Seaforth, Kingston, and Oshawa. But 26 of the 45 delegates hailed from Toronto and the junta was very much in evidence. Although not an official delegate, Williams attended as editor of *The*

Workman.[90] Late in the convention, Hewitt was elected CLU secretary and McMillan, treasurer.[91]

The dominance that the Toronto junta enjoyed in the TTA replicated itself in the CLU. From 1873 to its demise in 1878, the executive always had at least one junta member,[92] and during the years that a parliamentary committee was appointed, the junta placed two of its inner circle on it.[93] The CLU, then, was largely an extension of the TTA, allowing the junta to make broader claims of representing labour opinion for the entire province. For the first two years of the CLU's existence, this claim had some basis in reality, but the last two conventions consisted almost exclusively of Toronto delegates.[94]

By 1874 the TTA and CLU wre solidly established. The CLU was quite avowedly a political organization of the labour movement: 'Its objects shall be to agitate such questions as may be for the benefit of the working classes, in order that we may obtain the enactment of such measures by the Dominion and local legislatures as will be beneficial to us, and the repeal of all oppressive laws which now exist.'[95] The junta's lobbying successes in this period therefore deserve careful study.

These years basically saw the continuation of the 1873 patterns. Pressure was exerted on the Mowat government for extension of the suffrage, for a more restrictive immigration policy, and for improved Mechanics Lien legislation. The federal government was petitioned for the repeal of the Criminal Law Amendment Act (CLAA) and for substantial amendments to the Master and Servant Act to render it equitable. In each of these activities, the labour movement of the 1870s met with legislative success – a remarkable achievement; in many cases the measures secured were not totally acceptable, but most of them went a considerable way toward meeting labour demands. A closer examination of the measures further emphasizes the junta's impact.

The federal legislation was especially important. Macdonald's 1872 Trade Unions Act, although formally recognizing the legality of trade unions, was accompanied by the CLAA which took away with one hand what had been granted with the other. Writing of identical British legislation, one historian has argued:

This Act was, it is true, on the main only a restatement of various judicial decisions of the '50s and '60s. Nevertheless it gave a wider meaning than any previous statute had done since the days of the old Anti-Combination Laws to the offences of coercion, molestation, etc.; and its effect was to make almost all the traditional forms of action necessary for a successful strike (such as peaceful picketing) a crime and, if done by several men in concert, a criminal conspiracy.[96]

Calling for repeal of this Act, *The Ontario Workman* pointed out that the argument that 'the law in Canada has never been used is not the point.'[97] An event in late March 1873 prompted a campaign for the repeal; an Orillia shoe manufacturer charged four leaders of the Knights of St Crispin for conspiracy under the terms of the CLAA. Although the charges were eventually dropped against two shoemakers and the others were acquitted, this case represented a stark reminder of the legal problems faced by Canadian trade unions. *The Ontario Workman* noted:

It is high time that it should be out of the power of any man ... to take men from their occupations into a court of law, and bring a charge of 'conspiracy' against them, without the slightest evidence to substantiate the charge beyond the fact that the Amendment Act declares it a criminal act to 'coerce' ... and a statute so confused and so undefined, entrusted to the definitions of unprofessional magistrates, renders it quite possible, and more than probable, that innocent men, besides being placed at the mercy of vindictive employers, may be punished for a crime they never even contemplated.[98]

At its first convention, the CLU joined the TTA call for total repeal 'of that obnoxious appendage to a measure in itself good, the Trade Unions Act.'[99] The following spring, the TTA wrote a hurried letter to the Ottawa Trades Council, asserting that nothing but total repeal would satisfy Toronto trade-unionists. The Commons had instituted a special committee to investigate the matter, and the TTA was warning its Ottawa comrades not to concede anything too easily.[100] The TTA also set up a committee to write to unions in other cities to petition Parliament for total repeal.[101] All this agitation enjoyed some success and Thomas Moss, Reform MP for Toronto West, wrote the TTA that he would investigate the problem and would probably support Aemilius Irving's (Hamilton Reform MP) effort to amend the Act in labour's interest.[102] The TTA also corresponded in late May with the House Special Investigatory Committee[103] and the Ottawa 1874 CLU convention continued the pressure for repeal.[104] In November Irving submitted his draft amendments to the TTA for comment, an act which showed his recognition of their new political importance.[105] After consideration, the TTA endorsed his amendments and set up a new committee to consider their implementation.[106]

On 11 February 1875, Irving introduced his bill to the House of Commons, noting that 'the law was considered obnoxious by numbers of his own constituents, and also to constituents of his honourable friend from West Toronto [Moss], who fearing that the matter might be shelved in England, desired that the matter should be brought before the House this session.'[107] On 26 February, in conjunction with the CLU, the TTA called a mass meeting in Toronto to aid the repeal bill.[108] Termed a success by both the daily papers and the TTA, the meeting passed resolutions endorsing the 'Irving Bill'. Copies went to the government and to Irving.[109]

Before the bill's second reading, the TTA received correspondence from Moss and Irving. The latter wavered as the Government considered their own legislation on the matter. The TTA demanded that Irving press for a division of the House 'to known who are our friends and who are our enemies.'[110] When the bill came up for second reading, Irving gave a substantive speech in support of his bill, noted its 'great interest to a very large class of persons,' and argued the trade union position on the bill. The original legislation had been passed as favourable to trade unionism, but the CLAA had 'laid on workingmen heavy liabilities, against which they since had grounds for serious complaint.' Moreover, the House Investigating Committee had agreed at the last session that judicial construction 'had not operated fairly to the working classes' and had recommended 'further and more remedial legislation.' Irving hoped that a Reform Government would not disappoint the labour movement.[111] Thomas Moss seconded Irving's motion with a learned exposition of the legal status of trade unions worthy of a future chief justice of Ontario. He too noted the irony of the legislation of 1872 which 'in one breath gave them [workingmen] rights and struck a blow at their liberties.' Moss condemned the imprecision of the wording of the statute. This openness to judicial construction was especially danger-ous because of the fact that the judgments were left to untrained 'magis-trates who may have intimate relations with the employers.' After enumerating a few of the vicious constructions that had been given the law in England, Moss closed by criticizing the provisions of Irving's Bill which he thought inadequate, although worthy of support since it was vastly preferable to the present statute which 'was unfair, unjust, and altogether uncalled for.'

This searing attack by two Liberal MPs forced the government's hand. The Minister of Justice, Telesphore Fournier, admitted that the law 'was of too harsh a character for the circumstance of this country, [that] the offences were not sufficiently defined, [and that] too much was left to the magistrate.' He suggested, however, that it was too late to introduce corrective legislation in the session. Irving rejected this as an excuse but offered to withdraw his motion if the government guaranteed action in the spirit of his proposal. Fournier refused, and Irving asked for a second reading. Blake, however, sought and gained an adjournment.

Three days later Fournier introduced the government's bill to amend the

CLAA. On 1 April the bill received second reading with little comment. Moss congratulated the government, while John A. Macdonald argued that the act was only a half-measure and pledged the Tories to full repeal. The act was passed before the end of the session.

The significance of this debate lay both in this initial success of the new trade-union lobby and in the pattern of political support that emerged. Irving and Moss both sat for urban, industrial seats and, as that eminent politician John A. Macdonald noted, they could ill afford to ignore the mass meetings and agitation of their constituents.

Trade-unionists were not entirely satisfied with these gains, however.[112] Their concern was greatly accentuated by yet another case of the dangers of judicial construction. A prosecution against two (and subsequently four more) members of the Toronto Stonecutters Union provided a tangible test for the new CLAA provisions. The case was clear cut. Stonecutter John Wilson had been employed on 6 April as a strikebreaker by J. Esson at the rate of $2.75 a day. He was fired two days later when the union returned and refused to work with him. Wilson, formerly a member of the union, had been suspended earlier for working under the standard $3 daily rate. On the evening of 6 April, he had been warned by the first two defendants that he was scabbing and working under rate. On 7 April, fourteen stonecutters employed by Esson told him that they would not return unless he dismissed Wilson and two other men working under rate. Esson confirmed Wilson's testimony and complained that he had also paid a $20 fine to the union for hiring under price.[113] When the case continued the following week, the prosecuting attorney argued that the new CLAA changed very little. Defence attorney McGregor contended that the new Act was substantially different as attention to the intent of its framers would make clear. Police Magistrate McNabb kept insisting, as he had in 1872 in the case of the printers, that the question did not revolve around the defendants' acts but simply around their union membership. McGregor concluded his argument by claiming that the events of the case did not constitute 'molesting' or 'intimidation' as defined by the new statute. McNabb was not convinced, and the case was adjourned for three days.[114]

When the case was renewed, the defence shifted its ground to meet the hostile position of the police magistrate. Union president Alex Gibbs testified that the union had not made Wilson's dismissal a prerequisite before the men returned to work; all the union did was to tell Esson to do as he wished. He also pointed out that Murchie, one of the defendants, although a good union man, was not even a member at the time, since he was working in Toronto on a foreign union card.[115]

As a result of a clear alibi, defendant Smith was discharged, but his co-defendant, Murchie, was remanded.[116] Murchie's case was adjourned on two further occasions to allow the police magistrate time to give it serious study.[117] In early June it was joined to a similar case,[118] in which four additional members of the union were charged with coercion for refusing to work with the same Wilson on the Toronto Customs House, a different job. In this case, Wilson had been hired on 31 May and worked until he was fired, after all the other stonecutters had quit. This time the defence attorney argued that the new CLAA demanded proof of overt intimidation, molestation, or threatening, whereas in the present case, all the defendants had done was refuse to work with the accused. Since there had been no overt acts, there could be no coercion. The prosecuting attorney countered that the hounding of his client from building site to building site was sufficient evidence of coercion.[119] McNabb found the five defendants guilty as charged and sentenced them to fifteen-day jail terms.[120] This decision, greeted with howls of indignation from organized labour, once again effectively took away their right to strike despite their earlier legislative victory. The TTA then resolved to:

express its strong disapprobabation of the recent decision of the Police Magistrate being in our opinion both unlawful and unjust and at the same time to accord to the convicted stonecutters our sincere sympathy in this their hour of trial and pledge itself to use its legitimate efforts to obtain their release from prison and the punishment of the man who has so unjustly incarcerated them.[121]

The TTA and the stonecutters indignantly organized a protest meeting. Chairman McMillan denounced McNabb's 'illegal decision,' and if it was actually legal, then it was 'time for the people of the Dominion to rise and rectify the law.' Stonecutter Alfred Oakley angrily denounced McNabb as an imbecile and the law as a disgrace to the country. O'Donnell, a Knight of St Crispin, drew from the law the lesson that 'those who have money and influence with the government get such laws passed to make workingmen submit to them.' Political action by labour was thus a necessity. In a formal motion condemning McNabb, Alfred Jury pointed out that the police magistrate had 'acted in the case more as a counsel for the prosecution than as a magistrate.' But as usual, the immediate political implications were drawn by the junta. Williams' motion, seconded by McCormack, called for total repeal of the CLAA. He reviewed the history of the CLAA and condemned the recent amendment as insufficient. A good law was known by its fruits and with this case before them, it was now clear that the new Act was 'a miserable abortion.' Since there could be no room for judicial interpretation, labour's demand had to be total repeal.[122]

The case was subsequently appealed, and the conviction quashed as illegal under the Act. The appeals court judge ruled without even allowing the prosecution or McNabb's lawyer to speak. Nevertheless, a lesson had been learned by the trade-union movement.[123] All the ambiguities in the law had to be overcome, and only total repeal would be satisfactory.

In its campaign for total repeal, the TTA met again with Moss and Irving. Irving tried to convince the assembly that the amended bill was satisfactory, and that they need not push for repeal. The TTA begrudgingly conceded, after his explanations, that his bill was 'more satisfactory than heretofore thought' but continued to press for total repeal.[125] Its position was strengthened by British legislation passed that year by the Disraeli government.[126] In May the TTA corresponded with George Potter of the London *Bee-Hive* regarding this legislation, and in August John Carter, who carried TTA credentials on his trip to England, returned with copies of the new legislation and 'an interesting account of the position of trade unions, the state of the labour question, and recent legislation relating thereto.'[127]

The CLU meeting held in 1875 in St Catharines provided further evidence of labour's discontent with the spring amendments. In his opening remarks, President Carter commended Irving and Moss for their efforts but regretted their refusal to press for a second reading of their bill despite the strong urgings of the trade-union movement. He attacked Fournier's amendments as leaving workingmen 'as much open to abuse as they were before.' The committee on laws affecting trade unions reported similarly and called upon Irving and Moss to 'persevere in the matter until all obnoxious clauses are repealed.' Later in the session, J.S. Williams read a long paper clarifying the legal issues which reinforced the delegates' commitment to total repeal.[128]

A Toronto West by-election, necessitated by Moss's appointment to the Ontario Supreme Court, provided labour with an occasion to lobby for repeal. The TTA named a committee to attend candidates' meetings in order to question them about the CLAA.[129] When Edward Blake, the minister of justice, appeared in Toronto to support the Liberal candidate, he pledged his support for further change.[130] Blake fulfilled his promises by introducing a new bill on 17 February 1876 to amend the criminal law relating to violence, threats, and molestations. New legislation was needed because of the changes made in England and because it was necessary to clarify the 1875 law.[131] The TTA approved Blake's bill and thanked him for his prompt action. A mass meeting gave it public support.[132] Second reading took place on 7 March, and Blake used the occasion to explain the slight variations from the British bill. A tighter definition of 'intimidating' in the proposed legislation provided some additional protection to trade unions.[133] Tory MPs Hector Cameron and John A. Macdonald raised objections to the bill on the grounds that it was overly generous to trade-unionists by defining intimidation as only violence. Macdonald argued that intimidation often could be nothing more than a threat to injure a man's reputation.[134] Macdonald's definition of course allowed wide judicial construction, exactly what the legislation meant to end. Blake promised to consider these objections, and said extreme care was needed to avoid 'the charge of class legislation.' These attacks upset the TTA, and its mass meeting not only supported the Blake measure but also condemned 'the obnoxious suggestions made on second reading.'[135] The Tories subsequently withdrew their objections, perhaps with this meeting in mind, and the bill was passed on 14 March.[136]

The CLU meeting held in August initially congratulated itself on its success in winning further changes but later again noted severe hesitations about the need for legislation.[137] Although 'he felt on safer and sounder ground than heretofore,' John Carter saw no reason for the CLAA at all. J.S. Williams echoed this sentiment but lent his support for a motion to approve the amendments and to thank Blake.[138]

Thus ended one chapter in the junta's lobbying activities. They had used the TTA, the CLU, and mass meetings effectively, and in the process had forced the government itself, through members of parliament, to respond to their demands. The right to strike, the very basis of trade-unionism, had been endangered, and the junta had forced legislative changes to restore the rights that they and their British comrades had established through direct action over the course of the century. Here again it was the reality of class conflict in Toronto, as evidenced by the stonecutters, which underlay the lobbying activities. In addition, one should note the important rank-and-file support at the various mass meetings.

The second major legislative campaign undertaken by the junta focused on the legal inequalities of the Master and Servant Act (MSA). Although the Act, even in its name, had a curiously anachronistic ring, Toronto employers made frequent use of the power that it bestowed upon them (see Table 8.1). Prosecutions against workers were heaviest in the years of high trade-union militancy (1870–73), and the greatest number occurred in the trades where class conflict was most overt, especially in the Toronto foundries.[139] The economically advanced sectors of the Toronto industrial

TABLE 8.1

Toronto arrests under the Master and Servant Act, 1867–78

Year	Disobedience and desertion of employment			Non-payment of wages			Total
	Men	Women	Total	Men	Women	Total	
1867	27	1	28	21	3	24	52
1868	15	2	17	44	1	45	62
1869	17	4	21	49	5	54	75
1870	37	9	46	40	3	43	89
1871	46	9	55	36	2	38	93
1872	39	9	48	34	1	35	83
1873	26	8	34	17	2	19	53
1874	18	4	22	12	4	16	38
1875	12	7	19	34	3	37	56
1876	18	2	20	56	7	63	83
1877	3	1	4	40	7	47	51
1878	6	0	6	47	6	53	59

Source: Toronto, City Council Minutes, *Report of Police Chief, 1868–1878*, City of Toronto Archives

capitalist economy used the Act effectively to enforce industrial discipline and to combat worker militancy and trade-union strength. The Act's utility in enforcing discipline was most clearly revealed in successful prosecutions for disobedience. Its use in more overt struggles included prosecutions during the 1871 moulders' and cigar-makers' strikes and the 1872 printers' strike.[140] Like the CLAA, it directly threatened trade unionists; the struggle to change this Act was of crucial importance to the future of the trade-union movement.

The junta's campaign to amend the MSA began more slowly than the drive to repeal the CLAA, probably because unionists regarded the latter as more important, but also because there was considerable confusion regarding jurisdiction. An amendment to the MSA was initially included in demands made upon the provincial government, when in late March 1874, Williams requested changes from Mowat.[141] When action was not forthcoming, the TTA called on all Ontario unions to petition the Mowat government.[142] At the CLU convention in August, John Carter's call for thorough discussion of the MSA was accepted and the legislative committee's report demanding substantial amendments was endorsed. The following year the MSA received more attention from the CLU. The legislative committee called the

MSA 'a piece of class legislation of the most despicable character.' The report recommended that breach of contract be made a civil offence for both employer and employee and suggested that the 1875 English Act be adopted.[143] Meetings were held the following spring with Mowat but again were unsuccessful.[144]

Labour's success with the CLAA, however, provided an additional impetus, and in August 1876 the CLU convention pushed for amendments more strongly than previously. Toronto tailor Alfred Jury argued successfully for a tough committee report since 'every day poor people were being charged before the Police Magistrate for desertion of employment.' The original report, which had simply recommended another visit to Mowat, was revised to condemn the extant MSA and to call for equality before the law. The executive was instructed to act promptly on this matter.[145]

Shortly after the CLU meeting ended, a delegation, including Williams, McMillan, Carter, and Jury, visited Mowat to protest the law, pointing out its inequality and complaining especially about the propensity of Magistrate McNabb to jail workers for as long as a month for breaches of one-week contracts. Mowat again indicated that he would consider their request.[146] Following this meeting, Williams was called upon to defend the CLU's parliamentary committee against the editorial snipings of the *Globe*. The newspaper felt that it detected an inconsistency in the CLU's request for equality before the law in the MSA case, and preferential treatment in requesting advantageous status under the Mechanics Lien Act.[147]

The *Globe* still had not absorbed the political lessons of the decade. Fortunately for the Liberal party, its new leaders, especially Mowat and Blake, showed a more subtle appreciation of the trade-union movement's new political importance.[148] In responding to the *Globe*, Williams noted that legislation favouring the working class was not 'class legislation' because the relationship between buyer and seller of labour differed from other relationships in the community in that it was intrinsically a contract between the weak and poor, the strong and the rich. Moreover, he added, the worker did not accumulate capital by expending his only capital, that is his labour, whereas the owner's capital increased in proportion to the worker's labour.[149] Williams later denied the *Globe*'s continued assumption that labour was equal before the law, and in contradicting the claim that trade unions did not aid workers, he cited Brown's hero, John Stuart Mill, asking Brown to open his eyes and look around him.[150] Finally, he suggested that the *Globe* argument, that most capitalists started life as workers, was a myth. If George Brown was not keeping up with the most recent developments in English political economy, the same could not be said about Canadian labour leaders.

This newspaper exchange was little more than a sideshow to the serious business of amending the MSA. A delegation to Mowat in February 1877 learned that the government had decided that the requested changes were *ultra vires* of the Ontario Legislature.[151] The TTA immediately redirected its attention to Ottawa, where the sympathetic Blake introduced a Breaches of Contract Bill in early March,[152] explaining that several provinces had antiquated labour laws modelled on a law recently repealed in England. Since 'the modern spirit of the law' treated these matters as civil rather than criminal law, the federal government must act to amend its criminal law. At the same tine, however, the government would retain as criminal offences those that caused bodily harm or loss of property, that deprived a town of its gas or water supply, or that prevented the progress of a train with mail or passengers.[153]

The bill ran into tough opposition on second reading.[154] Blake again explained that the bill's aim was only to replicate the British measure and to recognize that breach of contract was a civil matter. In defence of the possible objection that the retention of the three criminal exceptions maintained a measure of class legislation, he carefully explained that this measure would apply equally to employer and employee. The major debate revolved around Blake's two special clauses. Aemilius Irving, Hamilton workingman's friend, attacked the need for the two special clauses, arguing that this most 'inopportune' law was motivated only by the panic which followed the recent Grant Trunk strike.[155] He claimed that reports of violence had been badly exaggerated, and eloquently defended the railroad engineers' respectability and importance to the community. Blake's bill was a flagrant piece of 'class legislation,' and since parliament must 'protect the labourer against the capitalist as well as the capitalist versus the labourer,' he moved the three-month hoist, assuring the bill's failure.

David Blain (Liberal, York West), crediting the Brotherhood of Locomotive Engineers with aid in formulating his views, argued that this 'Bill was a direct attempt to break up the B.L.E.' These two speeches and one by John Beverly Robinson (Conservative, Toronto West) infuriated the House of Commons, and ten MPS rose to defend the Grand Trunk, attack the BLE, and condemn their fellow MPS for countenancing violence and supporting illegality. Mackenzie Bowell (Conservative, North Hastings) and Charles Tupper (Conservative, Cumberland) were both especially hard on the pro-labour MPS and attacked the government for mismanagement of the Grand Trunk strike. Never before had a debate in the House revolved so clearly around class polarization. Equally striking, however, was the MPS inability to recognize the issue at stake in these revisions of the MSA. Only two MPS focused on the first and major clause which ended class discrimination by making nearly all breaches of contract civil offences. Both of these men expressed concern that labour discipline might be detrimentally affected by these changes. Blake, in his summation before the division of the House on the three month's hoist, emphasized the bill's original intentions: 'In general terms, save under special circumstances, breach of service was not a crime,' he explained. To put Irving and Blain at ease, he asserted that the bill was not an 'attempt to interfere with the rights of employees to combine,' and showed again that 'employers and employees should stand equal before the law' with regard to his special clauses.

The division of the House on the subject was interesting as the hoist was defeated 125 to 46. Five Liberals, including Irving and Blain, crossed party lines to support the hoist, but a total of 41 Tories supported the government on the grounds, if the debate is indicative, that the special clauses seemed to be tough measures aimed at events such as the recent Grand Trunk strike.[156]

The TTA response to Blake's new bill was ambivalent. It demanded that 'the railroad and other companies be liable to criminal prosecution for breach of contract when such breaches will have the tendency of stopping trains, the supply of gas, etc., etc., so as to place them upon the same footing as employees in regard to breaches of contract.'[157] Blake pressed on, and in Committee of the Whole many familiar arguments arose.[158] Many MPs still believed that it was a bill against strikes, despite Blake's constant denials. MPs from both sides of the House used the opportunity to inveigh against the evils of trade-unionism and to call for even harsher jail terms under the special clauses. Blake assured John A. Macdonald that the trade-union movement felt in general that the 'measure was based on just and equitable principles,' but he also demonstrated a keen awareness of the TTA objections. In introducing the final clause of the bill, he noted that the only punitive measure against employers was a fine, not imprisonment as faced by employees under the special clause, since a corporation could not be imprisoned. This half-hearted reply to trade-union criticism was exposed by a Tory MP who suggested that company officials could easily be made responsible. Blake responded that this was a 'very serious step [that] would not do at all.'

The bill passed third reading two nights later without a division.[159] The TTA, after reviewing the legislation in April, 'regretted that the Minister of Justice could not see his way clear to place railroad and municipal companies in the same position as the workmen or other persons committing breaches of contract.' However, they also thanked Blake since the bill was a 'great boon to the working classes of Canada, as it tends to place employer and employee on the footing of equality before the law in reference to such breaches.'[160]

Thus the junta's second major lobbying campaign came to a relatively successful conclusion. The clauses maintaining certain breaches as criminal offences, which Blake added to the bill, certainly weakened the general thrust of the legislation. Court construction of these clauses could have caused considerable problems, but fortunately for the trade-union movement, they apparently were never tested. Blake's unwillingness to withdraw these clauses, when combined with the level of hostility evidenced to trade-unionism in the House debates, suggests that the balance of class forces in Canada was shifting significantly in the late 1870s. The CLU had failed the previous year, the TTA was on its last legs, and the depression had made serious inroads into trade-union locals all across the province. This new weakness and the highly visible Grand Trunk strike placed trade-unionism in an extremely defensive position.[161]

Perhaps the most eloquent testimony to the junta-led trade-union movement's political successes of the 1870s came in the Ontario legislature in 1877 and 1878. In the debates on franchise extension, Toronto lawyer James Bethune (Liberal, Stormont) launched a vicious counter-attack on the emerging political power of the working class.[162] He proposed a new municipal franchise which would grant freeholders extra votes for each $1000 of the assessed value of their real property.[163] His rationale was 'the prevalent corruption' in civic government; but when the trade union movement responded with hostility, his real aim became clear:

The mass meeting of workingmen recently held with regard to this Bill was the best reason in the world for its adoption. It was a common thing for appeals for support to be made on the cry that one workingman should help another; and the result was that many of the best men in the community – those who had the largest interests in the municipality – were altogether shut out from their proper share in the management of its affairs.[164]

The TTA, led by the junta, succeeded in defeating this anti-democratic thrust aimed at destroying labour's recently established power,[165] but then quietly retired from the field as the depression deepened. The unheralded demise of the CLU and the TTA set off another round of hectic political contestation.

9

The national policy and the Toronto working class

There can be no question that the economic downswing and the decline of trade-union militancy played a significant role in the resurgence of working-class partyism. The junta had fought hard for Canadian workers and had won some extremely important legislative victories that represented 'the first stage in the creation of the legal prerequisites for freedom of association in Canada.'[1] From the very first moments of intra-city and inter-city trade-union organization, questions emerged regarding the role of the working class in politics. The campaign for shorter hours and the subsequent prosecution of the Toronto printers had made perfectly clear the necessity of trade-union involvement in the political arena. Both the TTA and the CLU had recognized the need for working-class representation in Parliament. Junta forces at the first CLU meeting had argued that it was 'essential to the recognition and establishment of the just and equitable rights of the workingmen of this country that they should have their own representatives in the Dominion Parliament.' To further this aim, they had called for 'a workingmen's platform to be put before the industrial classes of the country.'[2] Toronto printer William Joyce had indicated that the greatest question of the day was how to accomplish 'the social and moral elevation of the working classes.'[3] To unite the working classes, 'the people must have thorough training.' The CLU must take the responsibility to 'drill their army to fight manfully at the great battleground – the polls – and teach the enemy that election funds are of no avail against men determined not to sell their birthright for dollars.'[4]

The necessity of 'drilling their army' was only a partial answer, however, for once disciplined, the troops still needed a battle plan. Two major strategies were available to this new labour army. The first was independent labour politics, an electoral strategy free of party and all entangling alliances – a path frequently discussed but seldom acted upon in the 1870s. A derivative, which maintained independence but sacrificed initiative, was labour support for the candidate who promised to act in labour's best interests. This tactic was endorsed by the TTA in the 1875 West Toronto by-election, when candidates were interviewed regarding their stand on the CLAA and other issues of great interest to labour.[5]

The second major strategy was to work within the two old parties and to push labour issues. Partyism was the more popular working-class strategy in the 1870s and, not surprisingly, the Tories were its major beneficiary. Attempts at a Lib-Lab alliance were rare in the 1870s because of the role of George Brown and his wing of the party. The committed Manchester liberalism of the old Reformers had little to offer Toronto workers. The younger Mowat-Blake wing of the party, however, was far more sympathetic to labour. In the 1870s this was most evident in the parliamentary activities of Thomas Moss, in the legislation introduced by Blake as Minister of Justice, and in the editorial opinions of John Cameron's *Liberal*.[6] It was also apparent in the Ontario legislature, where Mowat acted on numerous labour demands and in the process attracted to the Liberal party D.J. O'Donoghue, the independent workingman's MPP from Ottawa.[7] Nevertheless, this nascent Lib-Labism was not to come to full fruition until the 1880s, although it had some allies among recent English skilled immigrants in Toronto, such as tailor Alf Jury, painter John Carter, and stonecutter Alf Oakley. The obstacles erected by Brown, and the bitterness and hostility of 1872, were too fresh to be overcome easily.

The remaining alternative was a Tory-Labour alliance, a strategy of labour politics in the 1870s that initially grew out of the Nine-Hour Movement and then focused around *The Ontario Workman*. The evident eagerness of the Tories to play the game of class politics was a major factor.[8] John A. Macdonald, 'cabinet maker' and workingman's friend, was willing to dirty his hands with an overt cross-class political alliance which the hardworking and upwardly mobile Reform leaders, George Brown and Alexander Mackenzie, rejected as ideologically repugnant. But Macdonald's paternalism was probably less important than the careful cultivation of the working class as fellow-producers by the populist wing of the Tory party which perceived this alliance as a crucial component of its major strategy. This protectionist and soft-money wing of the party, led by Isaac Buchanan, played a crucial role in cementing the Tory-Labour alliance. Buchanan, from the 1850s on, had argued for a high-tariff policy to protect Canadian manufacturers and to create jobs for Canadian workers. A group of younger men – William Weir, A.W. Wright, John Maclean, R.W. Phipps,

G.B. Brooks, Phillips Thompson, to name a few – rallied around Buchanan's powerful ideas. Mainly journalists and propagandists, they were deeply influenced by Buchanan and his American allies, who were active in the influential National Labor Union and in Greenback politics.[9]

Labour leaders, such as junta members John Hewitt and J.S. Williams, were attracted by these ideas. Hewitt especially took up currency reform. As the most intellectual of the junta members, he was also in closest contact with the American labour movement through his sojourn in New York and through his role as vice-president of the Coopers Interational Union. Currency reform was an extremely important influence on the American labour movement of the late 1860s and 1870s.[10] Hewitt, not surprisingly, became the first labour leader to embrace wholeheartedly the high-tariff argument of the Tory Populists. In his report to the 1874 CLU convention, Hewitt condemned the proposed Reciprocity Treaty with the United States:

It is high time that this Dominion was laying aside its swaddling clothes and becoming self-sustaining, and we can only become so by a fair and liberal protection. The U.S. did not build up her iron, woolen, and other industrial interests under free trade. Nor did England ... we do not ask too much when we claim the right to get a foothold upon our own soil without being pushed down by foreigners.[11]

As the Depression of the 1870s deepened, protection as a solution to bad times and to unemployment started to look increasingly better to Toronto workers.

The concerted nature of the campaign to win the Tory party itself over to protection has not been previously appreciated. Nor has the class character of the 1878 election debates been sufficiently analysed.[12] The 1878 campaign in Toronto was fought almost entirely on the issue of protection and its effect on the working class. The yeoman service, performed by the Tory populists in the 1860s and 1870s, was immensely important in preparing the way for the breakthrough of the election. For two decades, Buchanan and his disciples had been agitating on platforms for a higher tariff in newspapers and in pamphlets. *The People's Journal*, under John Maclean, was one important organ of the movement in the late 1860s and early 1870s. Published initially in Hamilton and later in Toronto, it pushed for a protective tariff and industrial development. In late 1871, after the paper's demise, Buchanan congratulated his protégé Maclean: 'You however have the satisfaction that you have done an almost incalculable amount of good in having educated the people your Journal reached on the subject of the

National Policy which is becoming a necessity for Canada.'[13] Maclean then became secretary of the Ontario Industrial Association, the first of many successors to the old Association for the Protection of Canadian Industry. Here, among other tasks, he prepared propaganda material for the Commons Select Committee on the extent and condition of the manufacturing interests of the dominion.[14] Again Buchanan urged him on:

The adoption of a National Policy is of vital importance to Canada as the only means of preventing Canadians having something to envy in looking across the Frontier. And patriotic exertions to bring out the truth of our position is [sic] the more imperatively called for, as the most obnoxious efforts are being made by the press, and other parties representative of English public opinion utterly ignorant of our circumstances, to make it appear a mere selfish or manufacturers' movement.[15]

The necessity of combatting free-trade rhetoric in the press led Maclean to the *Mail*, the Tory successor to Beaty's *Leader*. Again he coordinated his efforts with the aging Buchanan:

You may have observed that I am writing up the cause in the Mail, over the signature of 'Argus,' and I have got in also an editorial or two that practically commit the paper, and in a certain sense the Government, to 'my policy,' as Andy Johnson used to say. Our side is gaining in the 'Mail' and will certainly carry the day.

Moreover, urged Maclean, Buchanan should pen 'a few lines [to] Sir John on the subject, [since it] is at his instance that I am allowed what rope I have been allowed in the columns of the Mail.'[16] In the late 1880s, when T.C. Patteson, the *Mail*'s first editor, was asked about the paternity of the National Policy, he gave the following version:

Meantime you may be surprised to hear that I have always thought the chief parent of the National Policy, for it had many fathers and more sponsors after a time, was W.H. Howland, a man for whose personal character and avowed professions I have no liking. His instrument was John Maclean. His vehicle the *Mail* under my management. The campaign was started very surreptitiously in 1874 and conducted more openly in 1876 – attaining the grandeur of a party platform plank in 1877.[17]

It is obvious from Maclean's letter to Buchanan that the campaign started before Patteson realized. W.H. Howland, as we have previously seen, was an active proponent of protection in the Dominion Board of Trade and in the Ontario Manufacturers' Association.[18] We shall meet him again as a labour-endorsed mayor of Toronto.

Another important propaganda piece for the national policy was *The National*, edited initially by Phillips Thompson and later by A.W. Wright. This paper was a brilliant, independent Toronto organ that provided a new group of popular intellectuals with space to explore their hopes and aspirations for the new country in ways that the constricting formal party newspapers did not allow. It was here that R.W. Phipps,[19] George Brooks, Watson Griffin, and others published the articles they identified with, as opposed to those they ground out as the hired pens of party rags.[20] Buchanan congratulated Thompson warmly in 1875 on the paper's line and supported *The National*'s searing critique of the aristocratic pretensions of the Canada First movement.[21] Wright too was closely connected to Buchanan and readily 'acknowledged that to your [Buchanan's] writings I largely owe my opinion on the matter [the National Policy].'[22]

A less successful paper was David Edward's *Beehive*, named after Beesley's London paper. The paper would 'represent the interests of all workers [and] aim chiefly at the social and national welfare of the people.' Here popular political economy, written directly for Toronto workers, appeared. In the first issue John Hewitt attacked reciprocity and urged that protection would benefit workers by creating jobs.[23] The mid-1870s were not an auspicious time for a labour-oriented paper to make its debut but, although short-lived, the *Beehive*'s economic analysis did indicate labour's political direction for the rest of the decade.

The Tories badly needed the new and attractive policies of their populist wing after the humiliating defeat that followed the Pacific scandal. Even Tory Toronto elected four Liberals while the scandals were uppermost in the public's mind. The first Liberal victory had come in a by-election in Toronto West in December 1873 when Thomas Moss, a new Liberal and a close friend of Edward Blake, scored a commanding upset victory over his Tory opponent, Bickford. Moss, who later played an important role in the CLAA amendments, represented a significant break with the Brown-dominated Reform party. Nevertheless, junta leaders and *The Ontario Workman* supported Bickford. They had hoped for 'a *bona fide* workingman' candidate, since workers needed their own class representatives in Ottawa because 'every class fights for its own interests.'[24] When their hope failed to materialize, they established a committee to interview the candidates.[25] The results of these interviews were never published, but the paper endorsed Bickford because the Tories had promised to nominate a workingman at the next provincial election.[26] Despite junta and *Ontario Workman* support, Bickford went down in defeat.[27]

The populist wing of the Tory party was extremely unhappy with the result in Toronto West, and E.K. Dodd's *Sun* bitterly blamed 'the contemptible snobbishness' of a large number of old Tory leaders for the defeat.[28] On the other hand, the victorious Moss credited the labour vote for his triumph and made clear that in his parliamentary activities he would remember his working-class support.[29]

The Liberals swept all three Toronto seats in the 1874 general election. Contested decisions in the courts and Moss's promotion to the Ontario Supreme Court, however, allowed the Tories to regain two of the three seats in by-elections within the next year. The special pleading of *The Ontario Workman* in the 1874 campaign had not been enough to compensate for the Pacific scandal. The paper had endorsed wealthy Tory Emerson Coatsworth as 'a veritable workingman,' a statement which strained everyone's credulity. Moreover, it had condemned Liberal candidate John O'Donohue because one of his committee men had signed Brown's anti-nine-hour manifesto in 1872. Finally, it had welcomed the candidacies of the two other Tories, blue-blooded John Beverly Robinson and former Toronto mayor Angus Morrison, with little justification. All three Tories lost. Robinson learned well the lesson that Dodds had attempted to teach the Tory scions earlier. When he ran the next year in a West Toronto by-election, he kept a significant eye on the working-class vote. Jimuel Briggs, the *nom-de-plume* and alter ego of Phillips Thompson, satirized Robinson's campaign by advising him 'as a friend of the workingman' to don seedy clothes, spit on the floor, return home by back alleys, and blow his nose on his fingers. Jimuel suggested the following speech for this Toronto aristocrat:

You began life at the foot of the ladder. Your parents were poor but honest. You were a carpenter or blacksmith, or any other trade you like, and used to carry a tin dinner pail to your work containing your frugal meal. You worked hard and studied Greek or Geometry and things in the evenings. By dint of industry and economy you became a self-made man.[30]

Toronto aristocrats did more, however, than just pose in campaigns, for Robinson actively defended the Brotherhood of Locomotive Engineers in the debate following the 1877 Grand Trunk strike. The new political strength of the working class led it to embrace strange bed-fellows.

The most important campaign of the 1870s was undoubtedly that of 1878.

The campaign actually started almost two years before. In the summer of 1876, Macdonald hit the picnic trail with his new national policy proposals.[31] The following year the Tories added a new strategy for winning the working-class vote. They organized the Workingmen's Liberal Conservative Union of Canada (WCLU), which had a grand lodge and a series of local lodges organized on a constituency basis.[32] The inspiration for the WLCU undoubtedly came from England, where the Tories had quickly adjusted to suffrage extension by creating the National Union and Conservative Workingmen's Associations.[33] The Canadian rationale for this organizational innovation is not entirely clear, but it would seem that the Tories were less than completely confident of depending on either legitimate trade-union elements or the Orange Order to capture the working-class vote. The junta's independence, and especially its success in lobbying with Blake for the CLAA changes and the new Breaches of Contract Act, led the Tories to seek alternative methods of harnessing the workingman's vote. They proceeded to organize WLCU chapters in the Toronto constituencies, an act which created considerable alarm in the rapidly declining TTA. It passed a motion in December 1877 that 'if proof can be produced to show that the TTA is in any way compromised by the Workingmen's Association that the Secretary call a special meeting to consider the matter at once.'[34] Approximately two weeks later, the TTA met 'to consider whether the Trades Assembly should take any action in regard to statements implicating the Assembly in [an approaching] John A. Macdonald testimonial.' After considerable discussion involving the two remaining junta members, McMillan and Williams, it was decided that 'the Corresponding Secretary be instructed to notify all the unions that the Trades Assembly had nothing whatever to do with the John A. Macdonald testimonial and that the trade unions be at liberty to use this letter.'[35] The unions did not blow the whistle on the Tory organizers, but the remaining junta leaders were conspicuously absent from the platform on the evening of the testimonial. John Hewitt and Andrew McCormack, both then outside the trade-union movement, were visible participants, but Williams and McMillan were not present.

This episode was part of a growing disenchantment with partyism as a solution to the question of labour in politics. The Tories had clearly offended the TTA, but that body and the CLU were equally dissatisfied with the behaviour of D.J. O'Donoghue, the Ottawa workingmen's MPP, in moving very close to the Liberal caucus in Ontario. At the last CLU meeting in 1877, Alf Jury had commented derisively that 'the labouring classes had only one man and they had only half of him.' William Ternent of the TTA (and more importantly of the WLCU) was even more hostile: 'O'Donoghue was no longer a representative of the labour party, and he held that until they could get a labour man who would faithfully attend to the interests of his class, there was no good in sending a man to parliament.'[36] In the spring of 1878 the TTA found itself criticizing O'Donoghue for accepting a compromise Mechanics Lien Act which the trade-union movement did not regard as adequate.[37] But, given the increasing weakness of the labour movement, there was little that they could do in 1878. In May the CLU's parliamentary committee announced that there would be no congress in 1878, no labour candidates in the expected federal election in the fall, and offered only a dim hope of labour candidates in the next provincial election.[38] This announcement evidenced the movement's growing frailty.

In this political vacuum, the WLCU and Tory populist types had plenty of room to manoeuvre. The Liberals recognized what was happening and moved to match the Tories by establishing a Toronto Workingman's Reform Association.[39] Coming a full eight months after the Tory WLCU initiative, it was destined to fail, especially given the state of the economy, which was blamed on the party in power. Nevertheless, the votes of Toronto workingmen were being avidly cultivated by both parties.

The WLCU was not the only special group operating within the framework of the Tory campaign. After failing to convince Howland and the Ontario Manufacturers Association (OMA) that what the country needed was 'a national patriotic union rather than an association of manufacturers to compel the adoption of a wise commercial policy.'[40] Isaac Buchanan helped organize the Dominion National League in late 1877. Ever consistent in his claim that protection was in the interests of all classes in Canada, Buchanan was quite critical of OMA's strategy:

As you are aware I have always seen it to be a false step of manufacturers to come out as a separate or *class interest* instead of continuing the broad organization of 1858 – 'The Association for the Promotion of Canadian Industry' – the resuscitation of which as the Dominion League was no doubt a wise measure ... If present therefore at your meeting I would strongly have recommended that your only business at it should be to fix up your class organization of *manufacturers* and to become as individuals members of the Dominion League.

He emphasized that this strategy was crucial to create 'confidence ... in the Public Mind, and especially among working men.'[41] The OMA did not take this advice totally, although many members provided financial support to the National League. It organized lectures across Ontario for its two major propagandists, W.H. Fraser and A.W. Wright. These 'peripatetic apostles of the National Policy,' as the *Globe* sarcastically dubbed them, enjoyed perhaps their greatest success in Toronto, where they cooperated with the WLCU in constructing the amphitheatre. This open-air stadium on James Street was to be the scene of most campaign activity that summer, and provided the Tories with an important edge in the fight for the working-class vote. Although ostensibly set up as a non-partisan place to debate the benefits and detriments of the national policy, its initiation put the Liberals in a difficult position. Invitations were proffered to Liberal politicians to appear beside their Tory competitors at the bi-weekly meetings, but no Liberal MP accepted the challenge. Instead, Alf Jury and his fellow trade-unionists from the Workingman's Reform Association were left to do polemical battle with the Tory promoters of the national policy. This campaign launched both Alf Jury and Wright into a prominence that continued long after 1878. The frequent meetings attracted crowds of up to 5,000 and allowed for significant debate on the issues of protection, free trade, and their effects on the working class.

Tory speakers followed the high-tariff guidelines laid down long before by Buchanan and cited his favourite political economists as authorities. Thus Carey, Greeley, and even Alexander Hamilton were strutted out before the working-class audiences as the major proponents of the protectionist tradition. So was the apparent common-sense appeal that protection brought more home manufactures, which in turn equalled jobs and prosperity. Jury's major argument that protection did not extend to the labour market and therefore wages would be low because of an ever-expanding labour pool, while prices would be high to consumers because of protection, convinced few in deeply depressed Toronto.

The campaign led to a smashing Tory victory across the country. In Toronto, the party swept all three seats.[42] But the auspicious beginnings of the new Macdonald ministry's relations with the Toronto working class became problematic quite quickly. The unlikely alliance of WLCU Tory Populists and elements of trade-union leadership with the Conservative party broke down almost immediately under the pressures of office. The first defections came shortly after the government assumed office, when the Tory populists became disenchanted with the policies of their party in power. R.W. Phipps, the campaign's major popular propagandist for protection, perhaps as much out of personal pique as political principle, defected first, only one month after the victory.[43]

Even more alarming to the Tories was the new strategy devised by Wright and Buchanan. Wright wrote Buchanan in early November 1878 of a scheme that had 'to be kept *sub rosa*.' The Liberal Conservative Workingman's Union of Toronto had 'within it the elements of great political power.' Wright intended

joining it and endeavouring to get the members of the different lodges to form themselves into branches of the Dominion National League so as to do away with its present exclusive character. Then I will try and induce them to adopt as their platform the progressive views and real reforms which I hold ought to be the politics of all Canadians. From what I know of the leading members of the Union I believe they are ripe for the adoption of 'our' platform and think that there will not be an insurmountable obstacle in the way of getting them to adopt the platform.[44]

Meanwhile, Wright, ever the opportunist, was also seeking financial aid for the *National* from Macdonald and permission to write a popular biography of the prime minister.[45] Even without Wright's intrigue to win the WLCU over to currency reform, the Tories were already having trouble with the obstreperous individuals controlling the WLCU. Its major Toronto leader and most visible amphitheatre campaigner, J. Ick Evans, wrote Macdonald, attacking his cabinet choices.[46] Other letters seeking patronage appointments for the WLCU faithful followed quickly.[47] WLCU leaders realized that the efficacy of the organization, and thus their own leadership positions, depended completely on their ability to deliver patronage appointments to their members. The extent to which the Tories had saddled themselves with an organizational albatross became excruciatingly clear in the East Toronto provincial by-election in December 1878.

The Tory politicos, accustomed to making their own decisions regarding candidates, apparently offered the nomination to Alexander Morris, the former Tory lieutenant governor of Manitoba, without any consultation with the WLCU lodge in the constituency. Privately outraged at the refusal of 'a few fat lambs at the U.E. [United Empire] Club' to consult with them on the choice of candidates, the WLCU were further offended when Morris, in an interview, was totally non-committal regarding their pet schemes and legislative proposals. Since he promised nothing, they refused to endorse him, leaving the decision to individual lodges. What had started as an inner-party struggle for power exploded in the party press when WLCU leader Samuel Ginner broke ranks and endorsed the candidacy of Liberal John Leys in the *Globe*.[48]

Leys had indicated to Ginner that he would 'support the claims of the workingmen' and that he favoured the WLCU's employment-expanding proposals. Not surprisingly, the WLCU, faced with this open defection, closed ranks and expelled Ginner from the organization. Morris won the election by a narrow margin of 45 votes in a constituency that had never gone Liberal.[49] The tensions between the WLCU and the party, which appeared here so clearly, were to grow.

Initially, however, the success of A.W. Wright's efforts to unite the WLCU and the Tory Populists became evident in 1879 in a series of citizen's meetings held in Toronto whose participants resembled those of former mass meetings of the now-defunct TTA. Identical in format, they pressed for legislative gains for Toronto workers. Wright was surrounded on the platform by the major celebrities of the amphitheatre campaign and the WLCU leaders. Even his old antagonist, Liberal labour leader Alf Jury, appeared and spoke at the second meeting. The first meeting concerned municipal legislation regarding a landlord's right to seize property in lieu of rent. Also discussed were an amendment to the Mechanics Lien Act to help workers collect wages from defaulting employers, along with an amendment to the Municipal Act to allow each municipality the right to make its own decision regarding tax exemptions, an action that overtly attacked the church's tax-exempt status.[50] At the second meeting in February, convict labour was condemned, as was yet another assault on workers' political rights – the Property Owners' Association's petition to the legislature seeking to impose a $5,000 ownership restriction on all City Council members.[51] The third mass meeting in May in favour of currency reform was not as well attended.[52]

The approaching 1879 provincial election led Evans to assert WLCU's intent to prevent the previous December's errors from being repeated. Thus, the WLCU forwarded two resolutions to Macdonald: the first demanded that all patronage appointments go only to tried and true Tories and the second that the WLCU should receive due consideration for all such positions.[53] In return they would operate the amphitheatre again in the provincial elections.[54] Their yeoman service, however, helped them little, and their estrangement from the party continued to grow.[55] Toronto Tory organizer Alfred Boultbee recommended that Macdonald reward WLCU members with patronage jobs. He proposed George B. Brooks for immigration agent specifically, and added that 'something must be done for half a dozen of these men who manipulated the workingmen. Then those that occupy their places can be managed through being shown what has been done for their predecessors.'[56]

This recommendation was not implemented, however, and seven months later Evans warned Macdonald again:

Understanding West Toronto is to be opened at an early date, I know from actual experience that it will take a man of no less strength than yourself to carry it if, as it is threatened Mr Blake is put up. To carry West Toronto would be a great satisfaction to the Grits and I am sorry to say sore heads and *disappointed patriots* are extremely numerous at present and what are usually termed the leaders of the Conservative Party politics in the riding are only a set of enthusiasts without any information that would guide them to a just appreciation of the danger they would encounter.[57]

The cause of Evans' concern became clear the following month when he forwarded a series of Grand Lodge motions that made the WLCU position only too clear: the WLCU had not received 'a single office of any importance, and only two or three minor ones and they not permanent.' They cited their previous party work. The amphitheatre, for example, 'did more, vastly more, to ensure the widespread and National victory of the Liberal Conservative Party then obtained, than any other organization,' and they deserved 'twelve or fifteen first class appointments and a great number of those of lower grades, and that you should give notice of vacancies.' Without such changes, members would 'become more and more discontented, the Union will to a certain extent be paralyzed and hostile, and the consequences will be altogether deplorable.'[58] A few offices resulted but not enough to satisfy WLCU members.

Strains over patronage between the WLCU and the party were intensified by Wright's increasingly critical stance towards the Tory government's economic policies. The Dominion National League had given way to a new Wright-Buchanan venture known as the Financial Reform League of Canada (FRL). Meetings were held throughout 1879 under the name National Currency League and branches were established in Hamilton, Toronto, and St Catharines.[59] The decision to create this new body was of course a serious one. Buchanan wrote Wright just before they created the FRL that 'there is no longer any use appealing to governments or Boards of Trade. The only way is to get the people enlightened so that they will demand currency reform as they did protection.'[60] The recognition of the necessity of working-class support fitted well with Wright's WLCU scheme. The 1879 FRL convention and effective lobbying began to grab the attention of the press in much the same way as had their earlier campaign for protection. The *Globe* commissioned a series of articles on 'The Currency Question' in early 1880 to counter the effective arguments advanced by League publicist Watson Griffin and others.[61]

Wright won at least the WLCU leadership to a 'Beaverback' position. At the first FRL convention in Toronto in late fall 1879, such WLCU stalwarts as

Evans, George B. Brooks, and J.I. Livingstone actively participated.[62] Perhaps inspired by the Chicago Greenback convention that launched James B. Weaver on his presidential campaign,[63] Wright returned to Toronto in 1880 committed to taking a very significant step. The WLCU, still angry at the ungrateful Macdonald, provided him with the support of an established political organization. However, a series of letters to Macdonald throughout May and June from disgruntled local Tory workers failed to win the necessary concessions. These complaints all revolved around sitting MP John Beverly Robinson's use of patronage.[64] Evans wrote the most articulate critique shortly after forwarding the official WLCU resolution; he described the discontent as 'a very bitter feeling,' complained of the MPs' 'very injudicious use of some of their privileges,' identified by name Grits who had received patronage positions, and threatened further 'open revolt' unless a group of WLCU stalwarts received their long overdue positions.[65]

Their discontent ripened throughout June and a series of letters from George B. Boyle, a WLCU candidate for a patronage position, warned Macdonald of Wright's growing plot.[66] In addition, former *Mail* editor Thomas Patteson wrote from the lofty patronage heights of the Toronto post office that Macdonald must act quickly, for 'I have heard more talk from all sorts of men the last few days than I ever did before in a like time.' After a series of specific patronage suggestions, he reiterated his warnings that West Toronto must be handled quickly. He closed with a graphic comment: 'The more it's stirred, the worse it stinks.'[67]

Macdonald failed to buy off the WLCU and instead fell back on Robinson and the old Tory elite, disparagingly termed 'the U.E. club influence' by George Boyle.[68] Robinson's attitude to the masses when they challenged his hereditary authority was made quite clear in a marginal comment he penned on a letter from a loyal Son of England congratulating him on his new appointment as lieutenant governor of Ontario: 'These are the right kind – no grievances but many votes.' This he then forwarded to Macdonald for the prime minister's edification.[69] The WLCU thus was forced to carry through with their threats, and in June they decided to nominate their own candidate and to publish a newspaper in his support.[70] Before making public this decision, both Evans and Boyle warned Macdonald again. The former maintained that feelings were running so high that any attempt to influence 'the Union or the working classes of Toronto would be utterly futile';[71] the latter again noted Macdonald's failure to reward him and closed philosophically with a rhetorical question: 'So it goes; those who have been unanswering conservatives seem to be disregarded by our leaders ... Is this always to be so?'[72]

The WCLU then met in Toronto and issued a strong statement. Now was the time for 'concerted and united' class action, they argued. Only 'the arts and wiles of cunning politicians, whose professions of sympathy and pledges of support on the eve of elections have kept us divided and widely separated.' In Parliament,

Capital alone is represented, while labour is entirely ignored. Bankers, building societies, influential and wealthy monetary institutions secure such legislation as they desire for increasing and consolidating their profits and extending their powers while laws for the improvement, elevation and comfort of the working classes receive no attention whatever.

The WLCU offered its answer:

Independence of party is our only proper course. Let us vote only for independent candidates, who will fearlessly battle with any party and every party for the furtherance of our cause; who will endeavour to sweep away class legislation from politics and who will place the interests of the country and the welfare of our people far above the designs and ambitions of individuals or party.[73]

In late July, the WLCU met to decide how to apply the above resolutions to the forthcoming by-election in West Toronto. Their new platform endorsed government Beaverbacks to support the country's public works, denounced the alienation of the people's land to other than bona fide settlers, called for the end of any assisted immigration, the abolition of prison labour, and the prohibition of Oriental immigration, demanded that mortgage holders pay a share of property taxes and that a graduated income tax be implemented, sought protection for native industry and free trade in raw materials, and recommended civil-service reform. Participants included George B. Brooks, Beaverback journalist and founder of the WLCU; William Wallace, the Tory Beaverback MP; Captain Wynne, the St Catharines Greenbacker, originally from Ohio; and A.W. Wright. Only Liberal trade-unionist Alf Jury opposed; although supporting some items of the platform, he found others contradictory and feared that such a jumble 'interfered with the work of true labour reformers.' The platform was accepted nevertheless, and the meeting proceeded to nominate Wright to contest the West Toronto seat.

In his acceptance speech, Wright acknowledged his nomination as a breach in Tory ranks but argued that now was the time to press for currency reform.[74] A new Toronto weekly, *The Commonwealth*, published only for the length of the campaign, supported the Beaverback and had among its contributors such important journalists as George Brooks, J.R. Cameron, Phillips Thompson, Louis Kribs, and Wright himself. The paper acted mainly to explain Wright's platform, although it also covered u.s. Greenback activities. In a major series of articles, George Brooks aimed 'to explain the objects of the National Currency advocates' in simple and comprehensible language.[75] After condemning usury as the major foe of the Canadian people, he accused the Canadian government of caring for and fostering 'land rings, railway rings, gold rings and rich corporations.' Now they must aid the Canadian people – the real producers of wealth. He proudly embraced the name 'repudiators':

we certainly do repudiate the idea that labour shall stand idle while usury grows sleek; we repudiate the idea of being the slave of a barbarous fashion; we repudiate the doctrine which makes Canada a mere field of speculation for foreign Shylocks; we repudiate all monopolies, all legal stealing, all rings, all extortion, and lastly all those who by word or deed endeavour to prop them up.[76]

Wright denied a charge made by the *Globe* that he was 'a conservative Puppet,' although admitting that he regretted his estrangement from the Conservative party. He even accepted their identification of him with Dennis Kearney, the California workingmen's party leader, who 'has left his mark for good on the Constitution of his State, and is beloved and respected by the down-trodden and oppressed, whose cause he has nobly championed at the risk of life and liberty.' This campaign then, ironically, was typified by a radical critique of industrial capitalist society.[77]

Isaac Buchanan himself intervened with the Conservative party to try to prevent the nomination of a candidate to oppose Wright but failed.[78] The *Mail* vigorously denounced Wright throughout the campaign.[79] He came under equally heavy fire from the *Globe*, which was convinced that his candidacy was nothing but a Tory plot to siphon off Liberal votes. Only those 'few persons afflicted with incipient insanity' would vote for Wright and his 'scheme of glorified rags.'[80] As the campaign wore on, the *Globe* became even more virulent in its attacks on Wright, ignoring his Tory opponent, Mayor Beaty. Wright was denounced somewhat incongruously as a 'Tory-Communist,' and his supporters were openly ridiculed.[81] In this heated campaign, former allies of Wright, such as John Hewitt, Edward Meek, and Alfred Boultbee, stuck closely to the official Tory candidate.[82] F.D. Barwick, an important Tory ward-heeler, also managed to bring most of the West Toronto party workers back into the fold. He accomplished this only with considerable difficulty and warned Campbell:

I promised a deputation of my workers that the Government would not appoint any person to any position in West Toronto without giving me the opportunity to consult the President of each Ward. I suppose there will be no objection to this. The Delegates intend that at the nomination of their candidate he shall agree that no appointments shall be made without a similar consideration.[83]

Tory activists, then, had forced some concessions.

The Beaverbackers ran a spirited campaign with meetings graced by a lively group of songs composed by Phillips Thompson.[84] Despite the high spirits, Wright and 'his little band of malcontents,' as the *Globe* called them, performed abysmally at the polls. The Beaverbacker ran a distant third garnering only fifty independent votes.[85] Despite their dreadful showing on election day, the Beaverbackers had at least thrown a scare into the Tory machine. Alexander Campbell, Macdonald's postmaster general, personally supervised the by-election campaign and denounced Wright 'for running on the paper money cry,' since he would 'take some of our votes among the discontented workingmen.'[86] Buchanan, the old war horse of currency reform, wrote his younger colleague immediately after the results appeared. He hoped that Wright would continue to lead the working classes and thus help convince them that paper money was crucial to all other reforms. He should not be disappointed by the results and should use the *Commonwealth*, 'To take the bull by the horns and in the first number after the election the words: "and our thought is that paper money of the aggregate people (the government) is the only basis of our independent employment of labour, on which depends the prosperity of all other classes."'[87]

Taking heart from the old agitator, the Toronto group did not quit. They organized a committee that same fall to import cheap coal through a co-operative.[88] When they discovered that all coal producers quoted them identical prices, they called a mass meeting to denounce the U.S. 'ring.' The meeting instead debated the effects of the National Policy, with Alf Jury leading the chorus for free trade to help lower the cost of living. This debate was to continue throughout the following decade. Early in the winter, the National Currency Reform League (formerly FRL) held its second convention and changed its name again.[89] Despite Buchanan's opposition, the group became the National Land, Labour, and Currency League, a name they had used in the 1880 campaign.[90] Their continued commitment to radicalism was evident in Phillips Thompson's resolution to support the new Irish Land League.[91]

These Toronto radicals continued their opposition to the Macdonald government's economic policies in January, when the WLCU recommended a government labour bureau to help the unemployed find work. They also proposed that the government establish a fund for loans to families settling upon dominion lands.[92] Both proposals had been incorporated earlier in Wright's 1880 platform. More indicative of their critical stance, however, was the series of Toronto protest meetings they organized to denounce the Canadian Pacific Railway syndicate and the entire method of financing the railway project.[93] Livingstone and J. Ick Evans of the WLCU, both prominent in this public denunciation at Toronto mass meetings, later had similar resolutions passed in the WLCU's Grand Lodge meeting in March. The first resolution noted the alarming growth of monopolies in the United States, and protested 'against the legislation approving of and ratifying the establishment of the Syndicate to construct the C.P.R.' The second resolution went even further:

The C.P.R. contract ... will be a detriment and a stumbling block to the future progress and development of the Dominion and should not be considered binding on our people or their descendants ... we shall feel at liberty hereafter to select and support candidates pledged to secure the speedy resumption by our people of the C.P.R. and all lands bartered away in large grants.[94]

Thus, in the ten years from the Trade Unions Act to the WLCU's denunciation of the syndicate, working-class politics in Toronto experienced a number of significant shifts. The early years of the Tories' glorying in the light of John A. Macdonald, the workingman's friend, lasted only a short time as the junta advanced their campaign to legalize trade-unionism. Then, as the depression deepened and trade-union activity declined precipitously, the Tories helped create a counter-institutional political centre for working-class supporters. The new WLCU delivered the vote extremely well in 1878 but, instead of providing the Tories with a long-range political counter to the trade-union movement, it quickly became a thriving centre of political and economic radicalism and ironically was extremely active in the first Toronto independent campaign identified with working-class interests. But the radical journalists such as Wright and George B. Brooks could not carry Toronto working-class voters with them, and failure drove some of the radicals back into the Tory party for a time. Their divergent post-1880 political paths, however, should not detract from their earlier efforts. Wright's 1880 campaign was an important first attempt at independent politics in Toronto. It also provided the model for the labour campaigns that the resurgent Toronto trade-union movement mounted two years later. By 1880, then, the forces of opposition to Tory political hegemony over the Toronto masses were beginning to gather. With the end of the depression and the re-emergence of a vibrant working-class movement, the seemingly feeble attempt of 1880 was to become a significant political challenge.

PART THREE
CRISIS IN TORONTO

10
Organizing all workers:
the Knights of Labor in Toronto

The economic recovery of the early 1880s which coincided with the Tory return to Ottawa led to renewed trade-union activity. The relative quiet of the late 1870s was quickly forgotten in the spring strike waves of 1881 and 1882 which swept through the Toronto crafts and in which even many unskilled workers participated.[1]

This renewed energy found its institutional manifestations in the new labour bastions – the Toronto Trades and Labour Council (TTLC) and the Trades and Labor Congress of Canada (TLC). Skilled craftsmen played the leading organizational role in the re-emergence of local and national central union bodies. The Toronto Typographical Union initiated discussions about 'a Labour League to protect the interests of unionism in our city'[2] in May 1881. Plans for reviving the TTA received an added impetus from the convention of the International Typographical Union held in June. On the last night of the convention, the TTU held a mass meeting in St Lawrence Hall. Speeches by American printers with experience in the utility of central union councils greatly impressed Toronto trade-unionists. The receptive audience also heard orations from former TTA leaders: J.S. Williams, E.F. Clarke, Alf Jury, and Alf Oakley. D.J. O'Donoghue, the former Labour MPP from Ottawa, also spoke at the meeting.[3] O'Donoghue, back at the compositor's case once again, was emerging as a leading member of the TTU, despite his recent arrival in Toronto. Over the next few years, he became the decade's most important working-class leader in Toronto.[4]

A second meeting to discuss the founding of a new city central was held in late July. An appreciable note of caution in these proceedings stemmed from the failure of the TTA; bad times were only partially to blame, it was argued, and many delegates faulted the introduction of partisan politics into the TTA. They warned that their unions were not interested in a repetition of this pattern. J.C. McMillan and John Carter, leading members of the TTA, 'defended that body very ably, and showed the good to the working classes gained for them by the Assembly, in the altering and removing of offensive laws and the passing of new ones.'[5] The meeting was adjourned to allow the delegates to consult their unions. In mid-August, they met again and founded the TTLC.[6]

The following August witnessed an equally important event in the history of the Toronto working class. In that month the city's telegraphers joined the Noble and Holy Order of the Knights of Labor as Local Assembly 2163. In four short years the order organized approximately 53 locals and, at its peak strength in 1886, it represented almost 5,000 workers. The order led the city's most dramatic strike in spring 1886, and then initiated the massive independent labour campaigns of 1886–87.[7] For a brief moment, the Toronto working class stood together united, with the Knights providing both the ideological and organizational vehicles for this new unity.

Yet the Knights of Labor present perhaps the greatest enigma in nineteenth-century working-class life. The very name – Knights of Labor – conjures up conflicting images of old and new. 'Knights' evokes almost feudal values of dignity, pride, and self-respect, whereas 'Labor' invokes a solidarity that roots the order in industrial capitalist society. Frank Foster, a printer and Knights' leader, captured this tension well in a speech in 1884: 'It [the Knights of Labor] was a nobler chivalry than that of the Knights of older times, because its object was the cause, not of a class, nor even of a nation, but of humanity.'[8] This evocative combination of chivalry and class struggle played a key role in the rhetoric of the Order. The Order's founder, Uriah Stephens, argued similarly: 'Knighthood must base its claim for labour upon higher grounds than participation in the profits and emoluments and a lessening of the hours of toil and fatigues of labour. These are only physical effects and objects of a grosser nature, and, although *imperative*, are but stepping-stones to a higher cause, a nobler nature.'[9]

The ambiguity suggested by the order's very name colours the entire experience of the Knights in Toronto. On the one hand, they were the most sophisticated local critics of the new industrial capitalist system but, on the other, they eschewed shop-floor actions and shunned strikes and other forms of confrontation. In the breadth of their vision they surpassed their more conventional trade-union brothers, but in the narrowness of their interpretation of class struggle, they surrendered much to the industrial capitalists. The order was a unique blend of tradition and innovation, an amalgam particularly suited to the transitional stage of capitalist development in Toronto.

The origins of the order in the United States have been often described, but its Canadian roots are less familiar. The order came to Canada on the telegraph lines. District Assembly (DA) 45, the National Trades Assembly (NTA) of Telegraphers, had organized over half of the first 60 or so locals in Canada by 1883. Although a significant number in itself (32 locals with about 1,200 workers), the location of these locals was even more important:[10] they followed the telegraph lines from Winnipeg to North Sydney and included such tiny Ontario villages as Hagersville and Simcoe. NTA 45 enjoyed the order's only early success in the Maritimes. Moreover, the telegraphers formed the first locals in the cities of Toronto, Montreal, Quebec, Winnipeg, Ottawa, and London. It was the international telegraphers' strike of 1883 that brought the order to prominence in Canada.[11] The strike against the monopolistic telegraph companies, symbol for much that was despised in the new industrial capitalist society, received much support from the general public and the resurgent trade-union movement. In Toronto the popularity of the strikers' cause was evidenced by significant donations to the strike fund and by a benefit performance of *The Long Strike* given by a visiting theatrical company. The 'very largely attended' play was followed a week later by a benefit concert at the Horticultural Pavilion.[12]

Besides the telegraphers, shoemakers were the next most involved in early Knights' organizing attempts. In Hamilton the shoemakers formed one of the first locals (LA 2132) and in Toronto they organized only one month after the telegraphers.[13] The prominence of former Crispins in the order in the United States, together with familiar rituals, made the order attractive to shoemakers.

The early prominence of former Crispins in the order alerts us to the important organizational innovation that the Knights represented. Craftsmen who had clearly seen the effects of machinery on their trade, such as machinists, coopers, and shoemakers, had learned in the 1870s the necessity of reaching out to all workers. In the United States, this realization gained organizational form in late 1877, when Socialist activists, who had been connected with the First International and later organized the Workingman's Party and the Socialist Labor Party, formed the International Labor Union which aimed to organize all workers, skilled and unskilled. They argued that:

The wage earning class of *every* calling must combine in trade and labor unions for the reduction of the hours of labor and increased wages. During the past 20 years the development of capitalistic production has very considerably altered the nature of every industry. As improved labor saving machinery has advanced, new divisions of labor have been created and hundreds of thousands have been driven from one trade to another or thrown in idleness on the pavement, in proof of this it is only necessary to refer to carpentry, shoemaking and other trades, thousands upon thousands of whose members have been reduced to want, and brought into competition with members of other occupations.[14]

Industrial development would continue to encroach on the old trades and render the distinction between skilled and unskilled redundant. Thus the need for a new form of labour organization: 'The barriers that have so long existed between skilled and unskilled labor must be broken down forever ... The interests of all wage workers are identical and their action must consequently be harmonious. A fraternity of interests must be established.'[15]

The International Labor Union enjoyed limited success, especially among New England and New Jersey textile workers, but more importantly its leaders and many of its members flowed directly into the Knights of Labor in the 1880s with many of these understandings intact. That craft barriers were increasingly harmful was perhaps the greatest lesson of the 1870s for some elements of the working-class leadership. When T.V. Powderly, the General Master Workman of the Knights, visited Toronto in 1884, he emphasized this point: 'In the United States fifteen years ago ... each trade had its own organization, but of concerted action among all branches of trade and labour there was no thought. Then if the question was asked of the mechanic: "Why do you not bring into your union the man who works at your side?" The answer would be, "Why he is only a common labourer."'[16] The Knights, he added, recognized no such distinction. Two years later the former Scranton machinist connected this insight with his own workplace experience:

With the introduction of labor-saving machinery the trade of machinist was all cut up, so that a man who had served an apprenticeship of five years might be brought in competition with a machine run by a boy, and the boy would do the most and the best. I saw that labor-saving machinery was bringing the machinist down to the level of a day laborer, and soon they would be on a level. My aim was to dignify the laborer.[17]

It is fitting then that the 1882 female shoe-operatives strike provided a major impetus for the Knights' introduction to Toronto. In that strike the resurgent craft-unionists came to the aid of their less-skilled sisters and presented a united labour front which had not been seen in Toronto since the nine-hour struggle of 1872. Only a few months later the male shoemakers joined the order as Local 2211.[18]

Probably the most important event in the early organizational history of the order in Toronto was the founding of Local 2305 in October 1882, which also grew out of the shoe-operatives strike. This local was formed by a number of experienced trade-unionists, who later were instrumental in the order's growth throughout Canada. The most important of these, Daniel O'Donoghue, was to play an integral part in the delicate negotiations with the Catholic Church, which featured internationally in the history not only of the Knights, but also of church attitudes to labour in North America. Joining O'Donoghue in Local 2305 were Charles March of the Painters Union, first chairman and first president of the Canadian Trades and Labor Congress, and Knights' district organizer; Alf Jury, a tailor and prominent trade-unionist, free thinker, and cooperator; John Carter, painter, first president of the CLU and president of the Central Co-operative Society; and Phillips Thompson, a famous journalist and humourist, then becoming Canada's leading labor-reform intellectual. The first three were responsible for the Canadian strategy of the Knights of Labor until summer 1886, when they were displaced first by the creation of a Toronto District Assembly, and later by the ascendancy of A.W. Wright in Canada and in T.V. Powderly's affections. All three were experienced craft-unionists to whom the events of the 1870s had suggested the need for broader strategies of labour reform.

O'Donoghue made a major contribution to the Canadian Knights in thoroughly integrating them into the already-established trade-union world by obtaining their representation in the Trades and Labor Congress of Canada and in the Toronto Trades and Labour Council. O'Donoghue saw this as an essential policy and sought Powderly's aid in 1884:

Early last Autumn the TTLC did, after the disastrous failure of the telegraphers strike, call together a Labor Congress to pass upon the situation. Now, the council is composed of (or was until two weeks ago, when it accepted delegates from 2305, of which the President of the Council, Mr. March, painters' delegate is Master Workman) delegates representing 27 local trade unions. We have among these, counting the Assembly delegates referred to above, 6 members of the Order – all of 2305. At the Congress we had K of L delegates from Oshawa, Belleville, Port Dalhousie, and St. Catharines ... The bringing together of the two bodies of trade unionists and Knights was in a great measure due to the wisdom and tact of Brothers March, Jury and Carter of 2305 ... The Congress Committee on Ways and Means, being Knights for the most part, decided that on returning home they advise affiliation with the Trades Council ... On this understanding LA 2305 elected delegates to the Council and were admitted without question. We want this step followed up by others in this city as well as throughout the Dominion in general and the Province of Ontario in particular.[19]

Powderly responded, offering the aid that O'Donoghue sought: 'I look upon the effort to bring the combined power of the labor societies of the Dominion to bear upon the government in the interest of labor agitation as a most laudable and praiseworthy one and my advice is for the LAS to bestir themselves and take an active part in it.'[20] Despite some initial hostility from TTLC trade unions, the policy succeeded, laying the basis for the Knight's effective control of both the TTLC and TLC for the next decade. This gave the Knights in Toronto and throughout Canada a significantly greater degree of influence than they held in the United States.

Even after the founding of Local 2305, however, the initial growth of the Knights was slow, a significant cause of which was the failure of the telegraphers' strike.[21] William Lane helped organize two new locals in 1883 and Charles March organized four locals the following year. The real boom began in late 1885 (10 locals) and continued into the first half of 1886 (31 locals). However, the drive which had begun in October 1885 – creating 35 locals – ended eight months later, when Powderly froze organizational efforts to give the order a chance to consolidate. After the ban was lifted, four locals were added in late 1886 and three in early 1887.

The official reports of District Assembly (DA) 125 illustrate the remarkable surge of the Knights (see Table 10.1). As of 1 July 1886, there were 41 locals with a total membership of 4,997; the next year there were 48 locals but only 2,764 members; in 1888, the last year that the General Assembly Proceedings contained membership data, there were only 968 members.[22] A second set of statistics on the order's size in Toronto, compiled by O'Donoghue for the Ontario Bureau of Industry, confirms the same general outline: 43 locals in 1886, 50 with 5,000 members in 1887, and 31 in 1889.[23]

Table 10.2 provides a complete organizational profile of the Toronto Knights and demonstrates the remarkable range of workers which the order embraced: from machinists to longshoremen, from carpenters to street-railway conductors and drivers, from plumbers to seamstresses. The names that the rank-and-file Knights chose for their local assemblies are also suggestive. They ranged from the eulogistic – Powderly, Uriah

TABLE 10.1

Membership in the Knights of Labor in Toronto, 1882–88

Date	No. of locals	No. of members	Average no. of members	Source
July 1882	3	152	52	GA, *Proceedings*, 1882
July 1883	5	515	103	GA, *Proceedings*, 1883
Dec. 1883	4	636	159	O'Donoghue to Powderly, 12 Dec. 1883, PP
July 1884	8	347	43	GA, *Proceedings*, 1884
July 1885	10	358	36	GA, *Proceedings*, 1885
Dec. 1885	14	1,800	129	*Palladium of Labor*, December 1885
July 1886	41	4,997	122	GA, *Proceedings*, 1886
July 1887	48	2,764	58	GA, *Proceedings*, 1887
July 1888	(37)*	968	26	GA, *Proceedings*, 1888

* See Table 10.3.

Stephens, George Stephenson, Victor Hugo – through the craft-oriented – Wheatsheaf, Ironworkers, St Crispin, Beethoven – to the local – Queen City, Annex, Dovercourt, Yorkville Star.

Table 10.2 also shows the order's rapid growth, but simultaneously casts doubt on explanations of its rapid demise. Despite a considerable decline in membership, the number of locals that persisted into the 1890s reveals the Knights' lasting presence in the labour world.

Tables 10.3 and 10.4 draw our attention to an extremely significant factor in the history of the Knights in Toronto; namely, their extremely volatile membership. Table 10.3 illustrates this in a static way, showing only the total ebb and flow of members at given points in time, whereas table 10.4 captures for the years of extremely slow growth the large number of workers who flowed through the organization. Since the three locals for which these data are available appear to be typical, the order must have touched and influenced directly an even larger part of the Toronto work force in this decade than the already impressive membership data had suggested.

Our profile reinforces the notion that the Knights' committment to organizing all workers regardless of craft, ethnicity, sex – and most notably skill – achieved considerable success in Toronto. The Knights also persisted in Toronto far beyond the period generally associated with the

TABLE 10.2

Toronto local assemblies of the Knights of Labor, 1882–1907

Local	Month org'd	Year org'd	Last date	Occupation	Name of local
2163	Aug.	82	83	Telegraphers	
2211	Sept.	82	93	Shoemakers	Pioneer
2305	Oct.	82	04	Mixed	Excelsior
2622	Apr.	83	96	Mixed (Massey workers)*	Maple Leaf
2782	Aug.	83	90	Harnessmakers†	Queen City
3181	May	84	93	Piano polishers	Beaver
3490	Nov.	84	90	Upholsterers	Acme
3491	Nov.	84	02	Trunk makers	Unity
3499	Nov.	84	94	Bakers	Wheatsheaf
3656	Mar.	85	87	Railroad brakemen	Dominion
3684	Mar.	85	94	Piano woodworkers	Covenant
4025	July	85	93	Watch-case makers	Eureka
4298	Oct.	85	93	Mixed	Progress
4425	Oct.	85		Railroad workers	(International Bridge)
4534	Oct.	85		Street-car employees	
4538	Oct.	85	87	Barbers	Annex
4614	Dec.	85	93	Painters	Powderly
4679	Dec.	85	87	Jewellers	Alpha
4786	Dec.	85		Silverplaters	Brittania
4999	Jan.	86	93	Mixed	Dovercourt
5087	Jan.	86	83	Labourers	Uriah Stephens
5254	Feb.	86	94	Mixed (ironworkers)*	Pride of the West
5399	Feb.	86		Cigarmakers	Ontario
5493	Feb.	86	87	Plumbers	Phoenix
5579	Feb.	86	87	Railroad workers	Headlight
5625	Feb.	86	93	Teamsters	Royal Oak
5650	Feb.	86	94	Ironworkers	Ironworkers (Parkdale)
5742	Mar.	86	96	Mixed (coopers)*	Energy
5743	Mar.	86	94	Bookbinders	Hand in Hand
5792	Mar.	86	94	Mixed (boxmakers)*	Star of the East
5845	Mar.	86	93	Tinsmiths	Star of the West
5882	Mar.	86	87	Woodworking machinists	Standard
6250	Apr.	86	93	Handsewed shoemakers	St Crispin
6290	Apr.	86		Mixed	(West Toronto)
6420	Apr.	86	93	Mixed	Onward (Parkdale)
6429	Apr.	86	93	Carpenters	Paragon
6563	Apr.	86	93	Mixed (carters)*	Primrose
6564	Apr.	86	07	Longshoremen, coal heavers	Mayflower
6724	Apr.	86	93	Boilermakers	Elite

TABLE 10.2 (concluded)

Local	Month org'd	Year org'd	Last date	Occupation	Name of local
6953	May	86		Mixed (carpenters)*	
7210	May	86		Mixed (brickmakers)*	Yorkville Star
7311	May	86	93	Carriage makers	Hub
7362	May	86		Mixed (sugar refiners)*	Freedom
7629	May	86	93	Mixed (women)	Hope
7661	May	86	93	Brassworkers	Good Intent
7814	June	86	95	Mixed (journalists)*	Victor Hugo
8235	July	86	93	Carpenters	Empire
8527	Sept.	86	93	Tailors	Golden Fleece
9005	Nov.	86	93	Machinists	Geo. Stephenson
9344	Jan.	87	93	Brewery workers	Industrial
9433	Jan.	87	94	Musicians	Beethoven
9848	Mar.	87	93	Rattan workers	True
10536		87			Happy Thought
409‡		89	93	Tailors (women)	Silver Fleece
1960		99	04	Railway teamsters	Maple Leaf
2099		99	00		Progress
2138		99	04		Victoria
2454		01	04	Coal drivers	Primrose[3]
1537		02			

* Official Knights designation 'mixed' but known to be predominantly workers in the bracketed category.
† Became mixed in 1886.
‡ Locals organized after 1888 received the numbers of lapsed locals.
§ Probably a reorganization of Local 6563.
Sources: This table is constructed from: Garlock, 'A Structural Analysis'; Forsey, 'The Knights of Labor'; Toronto City Directories; TTLC, *Minutes*; TLC, *Proceedings*; Knights of Labor, General Assembly, *Proceedings*; Powderly Papers; and my reading of the Toronto daily press and the Canadian labour press up to 1892.

order's vitality. Finally, even the high membership figures issued by the order itself obscure the extent and influence of the Knights in Toronto.

The immense gains of the Knights in 1885 and 1886 stemmed from their attempt to organize across craft lines and from their success in bringing weak local unions into the order as units. The first technique, for which the Knights are generally best known, was evident in the unionization of the shoe-factory workers (LA 2211), the Massey workers (LA 2622), workers in

TABLE 10.3

Membership in individual Toronto local assemblies, 1882–89

Local	1882	1883	1884	1885	1887	1888	1889
2163	125	200					
2211	20	191	107	31	100		
2305	12	55	25	29	45	40	40
2622		43	90	56	160	81	81
2782		26	26	25			
3181			52	48	30		20
3490			13	24	20		
3491			19	39	60		
3499			15	55	100	64	
3656				19			
3684				32	30		
4298							15
5845					30		
7814					20	21	
8527					261	200	200
Total	175	515	347	358	(856)*	(406)*	(356)*

* Data do not include all Toronto locals.

Source: Data for 1882–85 from Knights of Labor, General Assembly, *Proceedings*; and for 1887–89 from Trades and Labor Congress, *Proceedings*; *Globe*, 3 October 1887.

the Toronto musical instrument industry (LA 3181 and LA 3684), Clarke's trunk-makers (LA 3491), the Toronto Street Railway workers (LA 4535), Toronto barbers (LA 4538), Firstbrook's box-makers (LA 5792), and female garment workers (LA 7629). Secondly, the Knights replaced former independent unions of telegraphers (LA 2163), labourers (LA 5037), bookbinders (LA 5743), handsewed shoemakers (LA 6250), carters (LA 6563), longshoremen (LA 6564), and tailors (LA 8527). A third method of organizing was to create locals in crafts that already had trade unions and that continued to exist. But it was in these areas that trouble most often arose between the order and the unions. In Toronto such disputes affected the bakers (LA 3499), cigar-makers (LA 5399), and carpenters (LA 6429, 6953, and 8235). Although never as hostile as their American brothers, some Toronto trade-unionists were suspicious of the order from its inception, to the extent that the stonecutters and printers attempted to prohibit Knights'

TABLE 10.4

Volatility of membership in selected Toronto locals, 1882–85

Local	No. of members July 1882	Members added 1882–85	Members deleted 1882–85	No. of members July 1885
2211	20	272	261	31
2305	12	131	114	29*
2622	10	198	152	56
2782	26	15	16	25
3181	28	50	30	48
Total	96	666	573	189

* In 1886 Local 2305 swelled to 550 members but fell back to 45
   within the year. See O'Donoghue to Powderly, 5 April 1886, PP
Source: Knights of Labor, General Assembly, *Proceedings*, 1882–85

membership in the TTLC in 1884. Conflict also arose in 1886 in Hamilton between the cigar-makers of the International Union (55) and those of the Knights (LA 7955).[24] Still later the actions of the order in several Toronto strikes reinforced hostility on the part of craft unionists.

Nevertheless, the Knights' willingness to organize the entire working class had captured the imagination of North American workers. After their initial hostility had ended, many Toronto unionists joined Knights' mixed assemblies as individuals while retaining their union cards. In Toronto, Knights' leaders were predominantly union men: printer D.J. O'Donoghue, painter Charles March, and tailor Alf Jury, all had played active roles in their local unions, their city assemblies, and in the Canadian Labor Union. Many less-known skilled workers also joined the order's mixed assemblies. This overlapping membership added considerably to the order's strength in the TTLC and TLC, since Knights were often chosen to represent their trade unions in these bodies.[25]

Thus the order in Toronto soon embraced artisans and labourers, Orange and Green, Methodists and Freethinkers, Tories and Grits, men and women, and even black and white. For a few critical years, the cultural divisiveness of race, sex, creed, ethnicity, and partisan politics was largely overcome by the sweep of the Knights' ideology of labour reform. This new unanimity on the part of Toronto workers represented the peak of their first serious challenge to industrial capitalism. Young men recalled the experience vividly for the rest of their lives. A mayor of Hamilton, shoemaker John Peebles, reminisced in the 1940s:

I became a member of the Knights of Labor about 60 years ago when I was quite a young chap. I thought its programme would revolutionize the world, not only because of its programme which included co-operation and state ownership of all public utilities ... [but also because of its belief in] the purification of politics and of all law and state administration which also included the full belief in the honesty and sincerity of all members of the Order. In short it was a crusade for purity in life generally.[26]

Not only young men felt the Knights would revolutionize the world, for even as experienced a labour leader as Massachusetts' George McNeill felt that:

The local assemblies of the Knights of Labor, counted by the thousands, furnish the wage-workers of the continent with opportunities of association and advancement never before enjoyed. From Maine to California, from Canada to the Gulf, in all States and territories, in the lumber regions and in the mines, amidst the fluff of the textile industries, amidst the din of the iron hammer, in workshops and store, wherever men and women are congregated, – in the village and upon the plantation, – the Knights of Labor are marching on to ultimate victory.[27]

As early as 1883 the Knights' crusade, and especially their desire to organize all workers, had significant repercussions among Toronto workers. After his conversion to the principles of the Knights, Eugene Donovan, a printer by trade and the editor of the *Trade Union Advocate*, changed his paper's name in 1883 to *The Wage Worker*. His rationale was 'to give us a broader field to work in and to increase the usefulness of the paper.'[28] More to the point, 'we feel our labours ought to embrace the rights, the wrongs, and the material interests of all who earn their livelihood through the sweat of their brow.'[29] In Hamilton, the transformation of *The Labor Union* into the *Palladium of Labor* proceeded from identical assumptions. However, the Knights' goal to organize across sex and racial lines, and their refusal to stay out of the trades where unions already existed were issues that later aided in the order's demise.

Toronto Knights organized black workers for the first time. Annex Assembly 4538 (barbers), Primrose 6563 (carters), and Mayflower 6564 (longshoremen and coal heavers) all included black members. This innovation led to press jibes, especially with reference to the barbers, but the actual internal workings of these integrated locals remain unknown. A black Knight under the pseudonym 'Ethiope' defended the order against the racist fulminations of the letter of 'A Virginian' in the *World*:

... the coloured Knight is as much a representative of the toiling masses on this continent as his white brother, and the spirit which seeks to degrade him and to exclude him ... is the same arbitrary, tyrannical and aggressive spirit which seeks to rob the white as well as the colored laborer of the fruits of his toil, the enjoyment of life, and the pursuit of happiness.

Despite the rather American ring of this declaration, Ethiope went on to point out that the empire contained many loyal blacks as well as whites.[30]

In Toronto the clearest indication of the Knights' drive to organize all workers was their concerted effort to include women workers. An earlier attempt in Toronto to organize female shoemakers by the Knights of St Crispin had been wrecked on the shoals of employer intransigence. Even the relative success of the 1882 female shoe-operatives' strike proved illusory when the shoe companies later failed to fulfil their commitments to the strikers.[31] The Knights' effort began in winter 1885, resulting in Toronto's first local composed entirely of women: Hope Assembly (LA 7629), made up of tailoresses and other workers, received its charter in May 1886.[33] Unlike an earlier women's assembly of shoeworkers in Hamilton (LA 3179), which availed itself of a dispensation allowing a man to serve as master workman, Hope was completely self-governing.[34] Moreover, unlike their sisters in the Toronto shoe factories in the 1880s, Hope workers spoke for themselves and allowed their names to appear in print. Women served on the executive board of District Assembly 125 from its inception; a member of the board in 1887, Miss E. Witt became the district's Director of Women's Work in 1889. K. Lucy Shankland served with her on that year's Committee on the State of the Order.[35]

In 1887 the order held a series of meetings to try to encompass more women. In March about 70 tailoresses gathered at Richmond Hall to hear the benefits that joining the order would offer them.[36] After speeches by Alf Jury and other leading Knights, Mrs Keefer of the Women's Christian Temperance Union made an impassioned speech in support of the order. A motion was passed unanimously, and the sisters pledged to meet again the next week and to bring their friends.[37] These meetings resulted in a demand by Hope Assembly for a 20 per cent wage increase, which was backed by Local 8527.[38]

The order also brought Leonora Barry, the Knights' General Investigator of Women's Work and Wages, to Toronto in 1888 to help in the organization of women and to investigate the conditions of women workers.[39] In her week-long visit she delivered eight speeches and provided the General and District Assemblies with a detailed description of women's work and wages in the city.[40] Significantly, this was the first such attempt made in Toronto. By the time of Powderly's visit the next year, another women's assembly, Silver Fleece (LA 409), was established.[41] On the platform at Powderly's lecture were suffragette leaders Dr Emily Stowe, Mrs Parker, Mrs McDonall, and other officers of the Women's Enfranchisement Association. Although limited in effect, the Knights' efforts represented the first concerted drive to organize Toronto's women workers.

An anonymous letter to the *Journal of United Labor*, written by a female Knight, chronicled both the aims and the difficulties the drive encountered:

We are trying to get the working girls of Toronto interested and educated on the subject of labor and the industrial and economic questions which are of vital importance to them. While the conditions of our working girls in Toronto are not as bad as in some of the large cities in the U.S., yet there is much need for reform in many things. One great fault which ought to be overcome among women is their selfishness – working for selfish motives only and overlooking the interests of those who are helpless, thinking it would be unnecessary for them to join our Order unless they received immediate benefits and all the evils which have existed for years to be overcome at once.[42]

The selfishness that this writer mentions undoubtedly stemmed from the fact that for most female industrial workers in Toronto in 1889, work was generally only an interval between puberty and marriage. The Knights tried to exploit this social reality by organizing socials for men and women.

The brothers of the Order have given several 'At Homes' to the sisters and their friends to assist the girls in organization at which a good program has been prepared and addresses delivered by prominent labour agitators, to set the girls thinking and show them the necessity for, and how much good can be accomplished by thorough organization. In this way we have been able to get the working girls together.[43]

One such 'At Home' took place in May 1889 when Hand-in-Hand Local 5743 sponsored an entertainment in Shaftesbury Hall to which it invited all the women workers in the bookbinding trade. Robert Glockling chaired the meeting, and speeches by Alf Jury and Miss Witt on the values of organization were embellished by songs and recitations by men and women of the trade.[44] Another, held by Local 3491, employees in H.E. Clarke's trunk factory, attracted over 250 women.[45] Hope Local 7629 also sponsored socials. A successful 'Fruit Social' in October 1886 featured E.E. Sheppard, editor of *The News* in the chair and involved the familiar amalgam of singing and speaking.[46]

In 1886 the *Journal of United Labor* published a poem by 'a Belleville Sister' which summed up the plight of female workers on the one hand, and the hope that the order offered them on the other:

Do I belong to the Knights of Labor?
   Why yes my friend I do;
And if you'll be advised by me
   You'll join our Order too. ...

It is not any women's part
   We often hear folks say
And it will mar our womanhood
   To mingle in the fray

I fear I will never understand
   Or realize it quite
How a woman's frame can suffer
   In struggling for the right

They are only the lower classes
   Is a phrase we often meet;
And ladies sneer at working girls
   As they pass them in the street.
They stare at us in proud disdain
   And their lips in scorn will curl;
As they pass us by we hear them say
   She is only a working girl.

Only a working girl! Thank God!
   With willing hands and heart,
Able to earn my daily bread
   And in life's battle take my part.
You could offer me no title
   That I'd be more proud to own

And I stand as high in the sight of God
   As the queen upon her throne. ...

Oh workingmen and women,
   Who toil for daily bread,
Cheer up, don't be discouraged,
   There's better times ahead.
Be faithful to our Order
   Obey and keep its laws,
And never fail when you've a chance
   To advocate our cause.
And so we'll stand together
   United heart and hand
And make our cause victorious
   All over every land.[47]

The poet, Marie Joussaye, perhaps captured more than just the Knights' appeal to working women; the lines 'They are only the lower classes/Is a phrase we often meet' spoke eloquently to all Toronto workers and to their increased sense of social separation and oppression.

The extensive organizational successes of the Knights owed much to the elaborate ritual developed by the order's founder, Uriah Stephens.[48] His *Adelphon Kruptos* is often considered to have stemmed from his religious beliefs and training, but it actually resembles the secret work of other labour and fraternal societies more than any Christian ceremony.[49] Although more elaborate than many labour rituals, it shares with them, and with the complicated rites of the fraternal societies, a common masonic heritage. Thus, rather than utilizing only Christian traditions, the order drew as well on the radical heritage of secular thought. This is not to deny Stephens' religiosity, but only to suggest that there were other traditions deeply embedded in the artisan world. The order did not adopt the entire masonic ritual but rather adapted it radically to its own uses. For example, the Knights dropped the elaborate hierarchical system of degrees and proudly disclaimed the need for expensive regalia: 'The only jewels worn by the Order are those of the heart – honour and fraternity. The only regalia is that of neat, tidy dress. The only conduct, cordial, harmonious and fraternal.'[50] The order did, however, equip itself with passwords, secret signs, a coterie of officers with symbolic names, initiation rites, and a series of well-defined rules for the conduct of meetings, the founding of new locals, and the installation of officers.

The ritual reiterated the core beliefs of the order – the nobility of labour and the need for solidarity. After pledging eternal secrecy, strict obedience, and scrupulous charity towards his new brothers, the initiate was instructed:

By labor is brought forth the kindly fruits of the earth in rich abundance for our sustenance and comfort; by labor (not exhaustion) is promoted health of body and strength of mind; and labor garners the priceless stores of wisdom and knowledge. It is the 'Philosopher's Stone,' everything it touches turns to gold. 'Labour is noble and holy.' To defend it from degradation, to divest it of the evils to body, mind and estate, which ignorance and greed have imposed; to rescue the toiler from the grasp of the selfish is a work worthy of the noblest and best of our race.[51]

Later it was reiterated:

We mean to uphold the dignity of labor, to affirm the nobility of all who earn their bread by the sweat of their brow ... We shall, with all our strength, support laws made to harmonize the interests of labor and capital, for labor alone gives life and value to capital, and also those laws which tend to lighten the exhaustiveness of toil.[52]

The secret signs of the order further reinforced the centrality of class pride. The sign of recognition, for example, involved a hand motion combined with the phrase 'I am a worker.' The correct answer was 'I too earn my bread by the sweat of my brow,' accompanied by the gesture of wiping off the sweat. Secrecy, which in most fraternal societies signified little more than solidarity, was often of crucial importance in the Knights' attempts to organize. In Toronto, for example, Knights were victimized by both the Street Railway Company and the Heintzman Piano Company. Cases such as these, where jobs depended on the secrecy of the sanctuary, demonstrated the functional elements of the ritual. At the same time, the solemnity of the ritual and the values it evoked were a rich celebration of traditional working-class values.

The importance of ritual to the order was illustrated in many ways. Powderly spent much of his time as General Master Workman adjudicating disputes that arose from divergent readings of the *Adelphon Kruptos*. Some of the earliest correspondence between Powderly and Toronto Knights, for example, concerned the suspected divulgence of the order's secret work. Roger Mullen, organizer and master workman of the telegraphers' Local 2163, wrote for advice in the case of the Wynn sisters. One

Master, Orange Lodge, c. 1860

J.S. Williams, founder and editor of *The Ontario Workman (Canadian Congress Journal)*

Edward F. Clarke, Mayor of Toronto, 1888, 1889, 1890, 1891 (City of Toronto Archives)

John W. Carter, President 1873–74, Canadian Labor Union (*Canadian Congress Journal*)

Phillips Thompson   (PAC)

D.J. O'Donoghue   (PAC)

Charles March, President 1883–87,
Canadian Labor Congress   (PAC)

sister, Bella, belonged to the order, but Laura did not. Laura had aroused concern among the Toronto Knights by describing a dream: 'she dreamt she was in a strange office and shaking hands. Said she shook hands this way (giving our grip) and that one fellow had a wooden fin and could not make it properly.' Mullen decided that Bella must have revealed the order's secret work to her sister, and consequently, he sought the former's withdrawal card until Laura could be convinced to join. Since he had no proof, however, he sought Powderly's approval for his action. Powderly, who by no means answered all his copious mail, not only responded but recommended an ingenious experiment: instead of expulsion, Mullen should give a different grip to those he suspected and, if it was subsequently divulged, he would have proof of their guilt. The results of this complicated procedure unfortunately are unknown. Nevertheless, this story indicates the great importance of ritual to the Knights.[53]

Other examples of ritual abound. When A.A. Carlton visited Toronto in 1886, admission to his private lecture was by password.[54] To announce meetings, Toronto Local 2305 used a secret sign, which often appeared in the pages of the *Trade Union Advocate*.[55]

$$\begin{array}{c|l} \text{I} & 26 \\ & \underline{8} \\ & 2305 \end{array}$$

This simply announced that Local 2305 would meet at 8:00 on 26 January.

The Knights also had extensive insurance benefits for members. The importance of this aspect of the order was made clear in 1885 when D.J. O'Donoghue engaged in an extensive lobbying excursion to prevent the passage of Tory legislation which would have been detrimental to the order's benefits. The order provided more than money in death; the funeral ritual was important enough that members who failed to pay homage to their fallen comrades were fined.[57]

As with the other rituals considered in this study, the secret work of the order had tacit as well as overt functions. Because its campaign extended across craft lines and included not only Irish labourers and women workers in Canada but also poverty-stricken white and black agricultural labourers in the American South, the order needed a ritual which would create solidarity and evoke loyalties that transcended economic self-interest. No doubt the necessity of organizing workers who were still making the transition from pre-industrial to industrial work partially explains the persistence of ritual and secrecy among North American workers long after their disappearance from England. Thus, the antagonism of the clerics of Quebec, who bitterly opposed the Knights on the grounds that the order's secret work represented an infringement on the church's injunctions against secret societies, had to be overcome without sacrificing the order's important rituals.[58]

The same factors that led to the order's emphasis on ritual also accounted for the importance that Powderly and his lieutenants placed on education. One constant refrain found in their writings and speeches was the necessity of utilizing the order itself to educate the working class of the United States and Canada. One of Powderly's most highly publicized schemes was to raise enough money to recruit and send lecturers into the field on a more systematic basis than had previously been done. A financial fiasco, this scheme nevertheless brought the talents of Toronto's A.W. Wright to Powderly's attention, and he became his right-hand man on the general executive board and editor of the *Journal of United Labor* (JUL) in 1889. The other lecturer recruited for Canada was A.T. Lepine, later a Tory-Labour MP from Montreal-East.

The educational aims were also evident in the order's emphasis on newspapers. Labour papers accompanied the Knights' successes all over North America, especially in Canada. In Toronto the Knights were actively involved with Eugene Donavon's *Trade Union Advocate/Wage Worker* in 1883. Donavon, a leading member of the Toronto Typographical Union, joined the Knights as well and used his paper to promote the order. After its demise, Hamilton's *Palladium of Labor* carried on the work, and Toronto Knights intellectuals, such as Phillips Thompson, wrote copiously for this journal, which was published from 1883 to 1887. In December 1885 the *Palladium* set up a Toronto office and was published in both cities for a short time. The Toronto *Palladium* was then purchased by Wright, who transformed[59] it into the *Canadian Labor Reformer* (CLR) and published it until his departure for the United States in late 1887. Running simultaneously with the CLR was O'Donoghue's *Labor Record*, which was published from 1886 to 1887, when it merged with the CLR. After this merger and the failure of Hamilton's Palladium the CLR became the official paper of District Assemblies 61 and 125. The CLR failed in 1888 but made a short comeback in late 1889 under the editorial direction of Phillips Thompson.[60] In late 1890, the same editor started the *Labor Advocate* as a co-publication of District Assembly 125 and of the TTLC. It lasted until late 1891. The Toronto pattern of intensive labour press activity was reflected elsewhere in Canada. Vancouver, Winnipeg, St Thomas, and later Ottawa had Knights' papers; Montreal had both French and English papers. The appearance of the popular daily penny paper in this period, aimed at a working-class readership, created yet another outlet for propagandistic efforts. In Toronto, *The News*, edited by E.E. Sheppard and Phillips Thompson, ran from 1883 to 1887 as a pro-Knights paper. It was available on a joint subscription with the *Palladium*.[61] The presence of a labour press and of the new popular papers forced some of the established newspapers to rethink many of their attitudes, and even their space allocations. Thus the *Globe* invited O'Donoghue to contribute a weekly labour column.[62]

The order's leaders also made extensive public lecture tours. It was customary for the visitor to give at least one large public lecture and later to meet in private with the local Knights. Powderly visited Toronto in 1884, 1889, and again in 1891; Richard Trevellick did the same in 1883, 1885, and 1886; and other Knights' leaders, including Leonora Barry, A.A. Carlton, T.B. Barry, and Tom McGuire, also lectured there in the mid- and late-1880s.[63] Toronto, in turn, provided speakers for the Ontario hinterland. The labour papers and O'Donoghue's correspondence are filled with descriptions of speaking engagements for O'Donoghue, Alf Jury, Charles March, Phillips Thompson, and later for Sam McNab and A.W. Wright. These tours aided immensely in the spread of the order, and a subsequent visit by March often led to the establishment of new locals. O'Donoghue and the other Toronto Knights' leaders always emphasized education as their major concern. Even at the height of the 1885–86 organizational boom O'Donoghue wrote:

Organization progresses here at an extraordinary rate. The number of new charters issued to Toronto is not the full index. It is to be found rather in the quota paying up back dues. I wish to Providence I could say our *education* was increasing in a like ratio but at present I am debarred that privilege. I am very optimistic nevertheless, and do not despair as to a decided improvement in the ultimate result of our efforts. We have a small phalanx of men who never tire – out every night – spreading the light. They are 'enthusiasts', 'cranks', 'kickers', and so on according to their various critics – God bless the mark![64] [Emphasis in original]

Perhaps of more importance in the educational work than all of this, however, was the very structure of the order. All locals had to subscribe to the JUL, the organ of the Knights, which was filled with educational material about political economy and co-operation, and later about the single tax and Bellamyite nationalism.[65] Moreover, every meeting had structured into it a discussion of labour in the area, a theoretical consideration of the labour question, and the collection of statistics on the local labour situation. Knights' lecturer A.A. Carlton once described 'the local assemblies scattered over the continent [as] the schools for teaching the people to remedy the mistakes of the past.'[66] From the Canadian locals often came motions and petitions that were forwarded to the order's lobbyists in Ottawa, and the collection of data was integrated by O'Donoghue into his work at the Ontario Bureau of Industry. This job allowed O'Donoghue to appoint Knights' activists as his data collectors throughout Ontario and ensured the sympathetic collection of material.[67] Another example of statistical work by the order was the publication in St Thomas of *The Headlight*, a detailed statistical analysis of the local economy and especially of the workers' place in it.[68] All these agitational and educational efforts were an essential part of the Knights' philosophy for the transformation of North American society. Perhaps the ultimate statement of this philosophy was *The Politics of Labor*, published by Phillips Thompson in 1887.[69] This book distilled the various reform sentiments of the Knights, culminating in the necessity of education as the key behind the transformation.

Thompson, in *The Politics of Labor* and in his editorial writing in both the *Palladium* and the *Labor Advocate*, advanced the notion that workers could not gain by industrial warfare. Strikes were outmoded tools that cost the workers far more than they gained. Only through political action could the workers successfully change the society that oppressed them. These views, which were shared by many Knights' leaders, led the order into numerous ambiguous situations. Arbitration was one of the key planks of the Knights' platform, but in an age when most employers denied their workers collective bargaining rights, arbitration was often totally unworkable. Blacklisting, yellow dogs, and ironclads were constants in these early years of 'labor relations,' and the strike was a weapon that unions could ill-afford to sacrifice. The Knights did not entirely forsake the strike but regarded it as a final resort after all other avenues of action had been explored. In Toronto the Knights engaged in 18 strikes between 1883 and 1892 (mostly between 1886 and 1887), representing less than 18 per cent of the total of 91 strikes fought by Toronto workers in those ten years (see Table 10.5). Ironically, given their hope for arbitration, the Knights' major fights in Toronto were over their fundamental right to organize.

A closer study of these strikes illustrates the order's attempt to balance its conflicting goals of dignity for labour through political action with its suspicion of industrial conflict. The first strike, the telegraphers' strike in

TABLE 10.5

Strikes involving the Knights of Labor in Toronto, 1883–92

Year	Number	Industries	Local
1883	1	Telegraph Co.	2163
1886	8	Massey Agricultural Implements	2622
		Ewing & Co. Cabinets	?
		Toronto Street Railway	?
		Williams Piano Factory	3181
		Toronto Street Railway	?
		Plumbers	5499
		C. Boeckh & Sons Brushes	?
		Labourers	5087
1887	6	Clarke Trunk Factory	3491
		Heintzman Piano Factory	3181 and 3684
		Custom Shoemakers	6250
		Firstbrook Packing House Factory	5792
		Toronto Upholstery Co.	3490
		Carpenters	6429 and 8235
1889	1	Custom Shoemakers	6250
Total	16*		

* Professor Forsey reports a strike by Local 3499 at Dale's Bakery in 1885 on the basis of evidence in the TTLC, *Minutes* for 16 October, and 4, 14, 18, 29 December 1885. All these references are extremely ambiguous, referring to 'trouble' but never explicitly to a strike. There are also no references to such a strike in the daily press. Thus I have not included it since the weight of evidence appears to be against it.

1883, has been described well by Eugene Forsey.[70] Let us turn instead to 1886, a critical year for the North American working class in general and of crucial importance to Toronto's workers in particular.

The Massey agricultural implements manufacturing works was relocated in Toronto in 1879 after a fire destroyed its factory in Newcastle. It immediately prospered in Toronto and doubled its size by buying out its major competitor in 1881. Employing somewhere in the neighbourhood of 700 workers, it quickly became Toronto's largest factory.[71] In over thirty years of production in Newcastle and for the first five years in Toronto, the Masseys knew nothing of organized industrial unrest. Their methodist conscience led them to supply their workers with a memorial hall, a library and reading room, a band, a Workmen's Library Association, a mutual benefit society, and even an in-house workingman's paper called *The Triphammer*.[72] In contrast, their major American competitor, Cyrus McCormick, was waging an all-out war against his workers in Chicago, an anti-union campaign that was to culminate in 1886 in the events at Haymarket Square.[73]

Despite this tradition of peaceful relations with their workers, storm clouds appeared at the Massey works as early as 1883. In that year the company reduced the wages of skilled workers from $2 to $1.75 a day and of labourers from $1.25 to $1.10. Approximately one year later, blacksmith Sam McNab of Local 2622 wrote to Powderly complaining of the Masseys' latest cut. The plant had been switched to eight hours from the customary ten and wages reduced accordingly. 'Now the skilled workmen and they are few get $1.50, the labourers and they are many get 88c.' McNab, who had just received his organizer's commission from Powderly, proposed that when the Masseys decided to return to ten hours, the workers should refuse. Instead they should demand eight hours and a wage increase of 10 or $12\frac{1}{2}$ per cent to cover the previous reduction. McNab did not expect to win both demands but thought that combining them would ensure the wage increase at least. He advised Powderly that 'to win this shop is to win the town and to lose it would make it bad for the Order in this city.' The shop was 'pretty well organized,' and with a demand like this 'we could depend on a majority in all the departments.' Powderly disagreed, however, and hurriedly responded that they should not ask ten hours' pay for eight hours' work but rather that they should demand shorter hours first and only after that success, ask for a raise. But he cautioned McNab against any action before consulting the more experienced Toronto Knights' leaders – O'Donoghue, March, and Jury.[74]

The advice of Powderly had its effect, and the Masseys escaped their first strike for another eighteen months – until February 1886.[75] On 18 January a committee of dissatisfied employees waited on the superintendent of the works and asked that a price list be posted and that they be paid on a fortnightly basis. Superintendent Johnson agreed. Five days later, the men sent up another committee to ask why this promise had not been carried out. The committee was one man short this time, for Josiah Ablett had been fired. This time Johnson refused to post the price list, claiming that wages were a private matter between each employee and the Masseys, and that they did not want visitors to the plant to be able to estimate the company's costs. The men then sought aid from Knights' leaders. A delegation consisting of O'Donoghue, March, Jury, and George Beales set out to interview Massey. Massey refused to meet with them and added that he would fire any employee who joined a union. He carried out this threat the following Saturday when five prominent Local 2622 members were dismissed without cause. On Sunday the Knights called an emergency meeting and decided to demand that Johnson rehire the five men. When he refused the next morning, they struck. Only then did the Masseys learn how extensive was the organization in their factory. Their own estimate was that approximately 400 men struck.[76]

Daily strike meetings were held at Crocker's Hall near the plant, and Knights and trade-unionists rallied to the support of the Massey workers. Order and control typified the workers' actions throughout; the event's tenor was best exemplified in the parade to city hall on the second day of the strike. The procession protested the massive display of force by Toronto police at the plant. The workers met with W.H. Howland, the recently elected mayor, and complained bitterly that the police presence was a gratuitous attack on the order, unfairly favoured management by implying potential violence, and was a misallocation of their taxes. Not only would the workers guarantee the safety of the Massey's property, they would personally guard it. As one old striker emphasized, 'The act was a direct personal insult to every man who had come out on strike.' Howland, whom the Knights had helped to elect, promised to investigate their charges and to talk to the Masseys. The next day, at the mayor's request, the Police Commission ordered the chief of police to remove his guards from the Massey plant.

The strikers' cause was also aided immensely on the second day of the strike, when the 40 to 45 members of the International Iron Moulders Union struck in support of the Knights. The precise relationship between the Knights and the IMIU remains unclear, but it appears that, as in the McCormack works in Chicago, the moulders cooperated closely with all other workers in the plant.[77] Even more important than the moulders' action was the decision by the highly skilled tool-room workers to strike on the third day. This was the critical turning-point, since tool-room workers were crucial to the production process, and ended any possibility for the Masseys to hire scab labour. It also gave further evidence of the solidarity of all the Massey workers – Knights, unionists, and the unorganized.[78]

Faced with such unity, the Masseys surrendered on the fifth day of the strike. The intervention of Mayor Howland, the choice of both organized labour and Massey himself in the mayoralty race of the previous month, certainly helped the workers, but it was their unanimity that won the day. The terms of the settlement, according to O'Donoghue, were a complete victory: the five men were reinstated, and Massey agreed to recognize the

Knights of Labor in his factory. After the strike, *The Triphammer* spoke of the Masseys' old faith that industrial conflict would never touch them. The strike had arisen 'out of a misunderstanding and if the explanations which were made after the strike had been made before there would have been no strike at all.' After invoking the workingman's right, and even duty, to organize, the editorial continued:

So long as the union keeps itself honestly and faithfully within its own right and does not try to infringe the rights of others, so long it is entitled to the respect and good will of the community. But the moment the divine command 'Thou shalt love they neighbor as thyself' is forgotten or overridden in the pursuit of any object, no matter how worthy, that moment the all powerful lever of right is deprived of its virtue and its strength and has to be cast aside. And with it must assuredly fall away the sympathy and support of all good men.

Labour, then, had the right to combine and to withdraw its labour but never to try to force others to do the same. Not surprisingly, the Masseys discontinued their employees' journal with this issue, whose editorial board had, with only one exception, consisted entirely of supervisory personnel.[79] The Masseys learned from their first taste of industrial conflict. On 10 March they announced that they would begin to pay their men fortnightly and would now withhold only five days' pay instead of the previous ten.[80] Later that year they promoted Sam McNab, the District Master Workman of District Assembly 125, to foreman of their blacksmith's shop.[81] They were to have no further labour trouble in the 1880s with the Knights, but the moulders, as we have seen, had a very different history at Masseys'. The Knights also learned from the Massey conflict. In a letter to Powderly, O'Donoghue explained their actions:

Much as I dread fighting ... I saw that it was better in this case to risk a contest and all it implied than to desert the men who faced Massey on the strength of their faith in their brothers and the Order in general. Not to have taken the action would have ruined our character. Better far honorable defeat than that it should be said that we had not the pluck to fight for our existence and the rights even of the few.[82]

Faced with a similar situation in spring 1886, the Knights again proved their willingness to fight. The victory at Masseys', based on class solidarity throughout the plant, extensive public sympathy, and political support from the mayor, undoubtedly prepared them for the battle with the Toronto Street Railway Company. The owner, Senator Frank Smith, opposed all attempts by his workers to organize. The intransigence of this Roman Catholic Tory cabinet minister led to a lockout in March and a strike in May 1886, probably the most bitter labour dispute fought in nineteenth-century Toronto.

The story began in winter 1885, when Smith, undoubtedly worried by the labour upsurge, demanded that his men sign an ironclad. As a direct result, the previously unorganized, but now insulted, employees sought out the Knights.[83] O'Donoghue addressed them in secret at the Knights of Labor Hall in early November. A press leak resulted in a report that the 'old hands' had done most of the speaking and urged organization 'as the only means by which they could fight the spies and obtain justice from the company.'[84] Thirty-one drivers and conductors created Local 4534 that night. Only one week later, O'Donoghue reported that a Catholic priest and intimate of Smith was trying to interfere with the new assembly. O'Donoghue promised to 'floor' him, and wrote that 'we now have a footing on the street railway system and we are determined not to surrender it.' O'Donoghue, however, was too optimistic. The next week it was discovered that 'among these 31 there was an informer – a Judas – who told the Superintendent the names of the officers elected as well as the names of all who took the obligation. During the past two weeks these men have been, one by one, discharged.' A blanket command followed from management for the remaining Knights to sever their relationship with the order or be fired. Faced with this ultimatum, O'Donoghue and Jury convinced the men to allow Local 4534 to lapse after only two weeks' existence. The decision was based on a realistic assessment of the available resources:

As old fighters and keeping in view the interests of the men as well as the Order we thought this course best. Cowardice was not the cause for we intend to fight. Without means financially to keep these men idle all winter it would have been cruel and impolitic to have forced them into idleness. Now the Company is keeping them for us ... Besides without lapsing they could not rid themselves of the Judas amongst them.

O'Donoghue, however, issued an ominous warning: 'Now we are taking steps to fight the Company and Jury and the rest have lost their cunning if this Company has not a hot time of it before we are through with them.'[85]

The plans for this coming battle were immediately put into effect. Members from the lapsed assembly of street-railway employees were taken into O'Donoghue's own mixed Assembly 2305. The platform provided by the Toronto Trades and Labour Council, together with the coming mayoralty race, was utilized to attack the street railway for its labour relations and for a score of other issues. The street railway franchise was a relatively easy target for O'Donoghue's 'whip of scorpions.' A chartered monopoly, it dealt with public complaints in an arrogant fashion, infringed its charter with depressing regularity, and was thought by all to have the city council in its pocket. It also oppressed its workers in many blatant ways, paying extremely low wages, demanding excessively long hours, and providing abysmally poor working conditions.[86]

The trouble finally came in early March 1886, a far more propitious season for the workers than the previous winter.[87] The Knights began to meet with the street-railway employees again and held a large meeting on Sunday, 7 March, at which the workers decided to form a new local. The men called an emergency meeting at midnight the following Tuesday after it became evident that Smith and his superintendent, J.J. Franklin, had again discovered the workers' plans. When the men arrived at work on Wednesday morning, they found the assignment board blank. The company claimed later that it had intended to fire only the men whom it had identified as violating the ironclad by joining the Knights (about 32). The Knights, however, claimed that the company had, in effect, locked out its entire work force. The company's intentions mattered little, for whatever their reasons, all street-car workers walked out en masse with their fellow conductors, drivers, and stable hands. The company attempted to run cars for the duration of the strike, using a few loyalists who remained at work (approximately 12) and a force of strikebreakers hired that week.[88]

On the first morning the men gathered at the Knights of Labor Hall on Yonge Street, and O'Donoghue and Jury became spokesmen for the strikers. That morning set the pattern for the other days. Almost immediately crowds began to gather. The pro-Knights' *News* provided graphic coverage of these events:

The scene on the streets at various points this morning was a lively one. A large crowd of working men took up a position on the corner of King and George Streets [near the stables] and hooted the drivers and conductors as the cars passed ... That the men have the sympathy of the great mass of workingmen was shown by the conduct of the drivers of wagons, coal carts, etc., who got in the street tracks and refused to turn out until the cars had been greatly delayed ...[89]

By early afternoon the few cars that had managed to leave the stables found themselves surrounded by hostile crowds and blockaded by coal carters, wagons, and drays. The good-natured crowd unhitched the horses but allowed them to be return to the barns. They then derailed two cars. The company wisely decided not to run any more cars that day.

On Thursday the company again tried to run cars, but the crowds, estimated in the thousands, used the same tactics to prevent normal service. After they dehitched and derailed two cars, the company suspended service for the second time. Mass working-class support for the strikers was evident again in the crowd's actions and also in the city's enthusiastic support of the carters, the heroes of the first two days: 'Everywhere the coal carters drove yesterday they were loudly cheered. Had it not been for their hearty co-operation the cars could not have been so easily stopped.'[90] The scabs received more than just the jeers and insults of the crowd; they were forced to dodge mud, stones, and bricks and were threatened with ostracism. One scab driver reported that 'a woman with a child in her arms had rushed out of a tavern on King Street West and yelled at him, "Don't you ever dare come into my place for a drink."'[91]

While the crowd controlled the streets, the street-car workers sent a deputation, led by Alfred Jury and A.W. Wright, to meet Mayor Howland. As in the Massey strike, the Knights regarded the use of police as an insult. Moreover, they pointed out that the company was violating its charter by not maintaining service and emphasized that the striking workers had nothing to do with the crowd and could not be held responsible for its actions. Howland responded in a public letter to Smith. He denounced the Tory senator's actions unhesitatingly: 'You are not in the position of an ordinary employer of labour. You have a trust from the city in occupying its streets and have undertaken to provide a certain convenience for the citizens in return; which convenience you have by your act withdrawn.'[92] This assertion echoed the strikers' position, but Howland went even further:

You have by your act produced this trouble, having in its face the knowledge of the result (as your application for police protection in advance of your act proves) deliberately locked out a large body of your men, not on account of any claim for higher wages or shorter hours, but simply for exercising a legal liberty, in joining a lawful body or society.[93]

This unequivocal declaration from the city's chief magistrate contributed considerable legitimacy to the workers' position and, unintentionally, to the crowd's actions.

On the third day the crowd ceased to be good natured as the police were given carte blanche for the first time. An initial show of force was insufficient to intimidate the crowd, estimated at 7,000, far larger than on the previous day: 'The coal carts, express wagons, railway lorries, and vehicles of every conceivable description continued to arrive, and as each obstacle caused the driver to "down brakes", a wild cheer broke from the crowd, which continually received accessions to its numbers from all the side streets and factories.'[94] The crowd forced this first car to return to the stable, but the police, a phalanx of 100 men, won the following encounters. After many arrests and a number of serious injuries, the police were successful in breaking a car free of the crowds. The street fighting continued all morning, however, and at lunch time on Yonge Street the mounted police rode briskly through the crowd, fighting individual battles. All papers reported that the police had engaged in indiscriminate clubbing in the afternoon, but that the police chief, buoyed by his men's success in breaking free a few cars, suggested that the militia was not necessary 'as yet.'[95]

That same afternoon, faced with accelerating violence, a group of aldermen arranged a compromise between Smith and the Knights which ended the conflict for a time. Smith agreed to take all his workers back, which news the Knights greeted with enthusiasm, voting overwhelmingly to return to work. The Toronto street cars ran normally on Saturday, 13 March.

The three-day conflict had sparked crowd action on a scale unprecedented in a Toronto labour dispute. The police had made 18 arrests during the strike, most of them in Friday's vicious battles. Those arrested included Toronto workers from all strata, from labourers to skilled craftsmen. Popular support for victimized workers was not unusual in the annals of Toronto labour disputes, but the virulence of the crowd action was. What transformed the street-car lockout into open street warfare between the crowd and the police?

The strike's most perceptive analyst has argued persuasively that the crowd's actions stemmed from a pervasive working-class culture which unanimously condemned the tyrannical behaviour of the Toronto Street Railway Company. Noting the crowd's control, David Frank argues:

The crowd's attitude was one of obstruction not destruction. The 'moral economy' of the Toronto crowd included several elements. Sympathy with the working conditions of the street railway men and support of their right to form a union were supplemented by the scorn of 'scabs' and the notion that the corporation, in locking out its men, was breaking a public trust ... The crowd's moral consensus was further legitimized by Howland's letter and the sympathetic attitude of the press, both of which offered a certain license to the crowd.[96]

This analysis can be extended even further, for the street railway was regarded by Toronto workers as a central part of their everyday life. Totally dependent on it, they had come to incorporate its service in their definition of their rights. Attempts by the monopolists to abridge and to exploit these rights had to be dealt with severely.[97] This then accounted for Toronto workers' willingness to rush out of their shops and factories to stop the operation of the monopolist's street railway in support of their fellow workers. It was no accident that the Knights of Labor were at the centre of the conflict, for in many ways their organization embodied the same emerging working-class consensus. Moreover, the carters and other drivers who had supported their fellow transport workers so militantly joined the Knights the next month as Primrose Assembly 6563. Their fellow workers on the docks, the longshoremen and coal heavers, organized simultaneously as Mayflower Assembly 6564.

Unfortunately, the consensus that was evident in the streets in March against the Toronto Street Railway began to break down after the street-railway workers returned to their jobs. The Knights claimed victory too early in the struggle. A jubilant O'Donoghue wrote Powderly on the day after the settlement: 'Only a few of the street car employees were or are members of the Order but we would not tell the public. *We have won their battle.* LA 2305 last night had 240 propositions of these men. Jury steered them yesterday to success.'[98]

The Knights' successes that eventful spring gave the already frenzied organizational drive even more impetus, but further trouble was imminent. The settlement that Jury had obtained in March was ambiguous from the start. The workers and their representatives claimed that they had won total victory and that Smith had not only agreed to take the men back but had also accepted their right to organize. Smith, however, argued that he had taken the men back only on his original terms – no labour organization. The debate ultimately could be resolved only in one way, and in May the conductors and drivers were back on the streets.

It is somewhat surprising that the settlement lasted even two months for, as early as mid-April, the employees reported that Smith was flagrantly violating the agreement.[99] One conductor complained:

Mr. Franklin tyrannizes over us the same as ever and many have got the sack for no cause whatever; it is one continuous round of petty fault finding for no other reason than to gradually weed all us union men out. But if Senator Smith and Mr. Franklin think they can buck against the Knights of Labor they make a great mistake. The new hands join the union as soon as they come on, and we've got the whole order at our backs.[100]

Only considerable pressure from the Knights' leader kept the men at work.[101] The local's secretary, Conductor Donagher, was sent to Smith with a list of grievances. Smith refused even to hear the demands for the reinstatement of fired Knights, for a wage increase from $8 and $9 to $10 for all, and for a reduction of hours from twelve to ten. The Knights then sought the intervention of the aldermen who had helped settle the March lockout, but Smith also refused to see them. In a final attempt at compromise, a TTLC committee visited Smith's partner, George Kiely. He too refused to listen to the demands of the men. Exasperated by further dismissals and having exploited every available means in accordance with Knights' principles, the workers struck on Saturday, 8 May.[102]

This time, both sides in the struggle were well prepared. The company did nothing but hire scabs to keep as many cars running as possible. This time the mayor and aldermen, agitated by the March riots, placed their major emphasis on retaining law and order. Crowd rule could not be allowed to recur. The mayor's initial statement on this occasion was not an attack on the company, as it had been in March, but a warning to all to remain peaceable as well as a proclamation 'forbidding gatherings on the street during the strike.'[103] Dire warnings of severe punishment were quickly forthcoming. York County's Judge McDougall, a member of the city police commission, warned gratuitously that intimidation would not be permitted. The police, who had been caught in the middle during the previous dispute, were given a free hand in May, even though charges of brutality against them in March had been partially sustained. Finally, Police Magistrate Denison declared that any defendant found guilty of any strike-related violations would face fines and imprisonment on an ascending scale of severity as incidents multiplied.

The public also responded differently during this second altercation; the mass actions of March were noticeably absent. No doubt the civic authorities' dire threats of repression were partially responsible. One also suspects that Smith's fervent denials that he had promised in March to withdraw the ironclad confused some people. In addition, there had been a significant shift to the right in public opinion following the Haymarket bombing; the sympathetic *News* suggested that this reaction was at the root of Toronto's less fiery support of the strikers.[104] But the major factor was the strategy of the Knights' leaders. Seemingly embarrassed by the crowd violence of March, they carefully dissociated the order from those actions. Instead they called on the public to boycott the street railway. The predominantly Irish street-railway employees were only too familiar with this tactic imported from their homeland and recently used with great success by the Toronto printers.[105] Thus, at their Sunday meeting at the Irish Catholic Benevolent Union Hall, they 'confidently' issued an 'appeal to the general public, and to the working classes in particular, to withhold all patronage, even though at some present inconvenience, from this company in its effort to tyrannically deprive their unfortunate employees of their undoubted right to join or belong to any legal organization they may deem advisable.'[106] The boycott's effectiveness, however, depended on the availability of an alternative mode of transport and so, initially out of necessity, was born the Free Bus Company. On 11 May, the third day of the strike, four buses decorated with union jacks appeared on the Toronto streets. The *News'* perspicacious city hall observer enthused: 'This is the right way to do business; it not only gives the men work but hits the company in the fountain of monopolistic life – the pocket. Never bother appealing to a capitalist's brain when you can reach his pocket. That is the vital spot.'[107] The buses carried an enthusiastic clientele at the start, and contributions were generous. Nevertheless, as each day passed, more street cars ran until by 14 May the *World* reported that the day-time schedule was almost back to normal, and by the following Friday the cars even dared to run at night.[108]

Toronto workers did not totally accept the Knights' strategy. There were a number of crowd or individual incidents of violence against the scab cars. For example, on 12 May,

While a King street car was passing Clarke's trunk factory on King St. West, a bottle said to have contained carbolic acid, was thrown at the driver ... At noon a large number of workingmen from the west end factories hooted and jeered the cars that passed along King St. In front of Clarke's factory a line was formed across the street but the men were dispersed by the police.[109]

Moreover, many individuals acted in various ways to obstruct the street cars. Among the many who were arrested were Edmund Livisky, a planing-mill employee; Joseph Donelan, a factory shoemaker; Bernard McGuffin, a Shedden drayman; and Chris Conway, a black ice-wagon driver. All were dealt with harshly by Police Magistrate Denison and none received the popular acclaim that had been the reward for such actions in March.[110] The one concerted street action occurred on 25 May, when a large crowd gathered to greet the arrival of nine new buses from Oshawa. Led by the Irish Catholic Benevolent Union band, the parade of buses and strike supporters proceeded through the Toronto streets. The trouble began when they encountered their first street car, which they cursed, jostled, and stoned. The crowd, estimated by the *News* at an exaggerated 40,000, then commenced to attack all the street cars in their path. Knights' District Master Workman Sam McNab intervened to end the parade, counselled non-violence, and ordered the band to lead the crowd away from the street-car routes. The next day, the Knights again disclaimed any connection with the violence, which they condemned unequivocally.

The general lack of violence in this strike was contrasted sardonically with the demonstrative show of civic force:

The police authorities' superhuman efforts to preserve order, when no attempt is being made to break the law is quite touching ... I will leave it to the public whether it is not slightly silly to see mounted police capering up and down the streets as though the city were in a state of seige ... Perhaps the police authorities are taking excessive precautions through fear that someone will steal them.[111]

The strikers' high spirits were evident throughout the first few weeks of the strike. In speeches, proclamations, poems, and songs, they asserted their demand for the right to organize.

Drive on my lads! no slaves are we,
But sons of Canada the free,
Who prize as life our liberty
   Drive on, my lads! Drive on!

From early morn till night is old,
Unceasingly the reins we hold,
For our employers gathering gold.
   Drive on, my lads! Drive on!

'Tis not enough, we needs must sell
Our manhood – liberty as well:
Renounce our birthright, sooth to
    tell!
   Drive on, my lads! Drive on!

Never! The day of wealth is past;
The day has dawned for *MAN* at last;
The stake is won – the die is cast.
  Drive on, my lads! Drive on!

Drive on! Drive over tyranny!
Drive on for love of Liberty;
Drive on, my lads, to victory!
  Drive on, my lads! Drive on![112]

Another popular theme – the contrast between monopoly's riches and the poverty of the workers – can be seen in the following verse by striker James Downs:

I am a simple labouring man,
  I work upon the car,
To keep those hungry wolves away,
  From the poor street car man's door ...

The rich man rides in his carriage,
  His horses are swift and strong;
But should a poor street car man ask fair play,
  He will tell him that he's wrong.

Give us fair play for every day,
It's all we ask of thee.
Our cause is right
We're out on strike,
For a poor man's family.[113]

Yet, despite the overt sympathies of Toronto's working class and despite the initial militance and spirit of the strikers, the strike failed. It failed largely because the free-bus strategy worked only too well. In effect, the combination of buses and street cars provided Toronto with a vastly better transportation system than it had previously possessed, and thus the crisis activated by the strike was dissipated. With the crisis ended, the conflict settled into a contest between the rich and well-organized street-railway monopoly and the new co-operative bus company organized by the strikers and Local 2305 under the leadership of Alfred Jury and John O'Brien, the chairman of the strike committee. What had started simply as a fight against an ironclad agreement was transformed into a contest between capital and co-operation. Most Toronto workers recognized that the ironclad was 'a menace against their personal liberty,' as one trade-union leader told the *World*;[114] few Toronto workers, however, were ready for the co-operative millennium envisioned so often by Knights' leaders.

The problem was further complicated by a growing split between the strikers and the Knights' leadership over the direction of the co-op. Basically, the terms of the dispute were predictable. The strikers were primarily interested in winning the strike and found themselves somewhat unwilling partners in a scheme that left settlement of the strike a non-issue. Moreover, as managers of the new co-op, the Knights were sinking much of the money that was raised in aid of the strike into the co-op instead of using it for strike pay. In the first month of the strike, the men complained bitterly that they had received only a little over $20 each. The debate, which commenced in the third week of the strike, grew ever more bitter. The response of the Knights in the press to these complaints appears indicative of the core of the problem. The leaders constantly reminded the workers that they had counselled caution; the strikers continually complained that the leaders were arrogant and made decisions without consultation – ironically protests similar to those they had made against Smith. The leaders' answers to public discontent certainly did little to assuage the men's growing anger. Unidentified members of the executive committee called the protesters 'weak kneed,' 'snakes in the grass,' and dismissed them as 'kickers.' O'Donoghue added fuel to the already smoldering fire:

Those who struck to assert a principle are still fighting and have no doubts, only those who expected to have a holiday at the expense of those who were making sacrifices, and were disappointed, were dissatisfied that they did not get a 'haul' before deserting the men whom, in so far as their votes and voices could influence, they encouraged to strike.[115]

This particular conflict disappeared for a while after the founding of District Assembly 125 brought renewed support to the strikers, but flared up again in mid-June when the *World* astutely noted that

[The] real trouble is between the superior power of the Knights of Labor, as represented by the management committee of the Co-operative Company, and the street car men's assembly; that the latter are naturally and strenuously opposed to allowing money, which they rightly consider their own, and of which they can get none, going in chunks to sleek outsiders, who are not street-car men, nor even Knights of Labor.[116]

The *World* had also hinted at a less overt conflict, but no doubt one that the strikers would have found most disconcerting:

As usually happens the Knights and strikers are having their 'legs pulled' by the politicians. The head men in the strike are Mr. O'Donoghue (in the employ of the Ontario Government) and Mr. Jury, a prospective labour candidate in the Reform interest for West Toronto. The big thing they are working for is to arouse the workingmen against Sir John, who keeps Frank Smith in his cabinet. It is not to be all that way, however. Aleck Wright has arrived in town, started a labour reform paper and spoke at Wednesday's mass meeting. He has been a faithful organizer and candidate for the Conservatives and men with half an eye are imagining that Aleck is here to checkmate Jury and O'Donoghue. He will have his hands full – the others have got a big start.[117]

The *World*'s cynicism was answered by Wright's assertion the following day that 'men may have differences on such outside issues as party politics and yet come together in the cause of labour reform.'[118] Nevertheless, additional seeds of doubt had been sown in the strikers' minds.

By the third week in June it was evident to all that the Knights had lost. On 24 June the District Assembly stepped in directly to take over the co-operative. They agreed to investigate charges of financial mismanagement against Jury and O'Donoghue, to assume the co-op's debts, and to wind up the operation. All this was done under an initial façade of continuing the struggle, but most observers understood the action as a face-saving effort. Nevertheless, when 57 strikers petitioned the District Assembly to call off the strike so that they could attempt to regain their jobs, Sam McNab refused. The refusal led to yet another round of public recriminations that culminated in striker Charles Gibbons' letter to the *World* appealing for rank-and-file Toronto Knights to consider the position of 'men who have worked hard and faithfully since the strike commenced till the last ray of hope had gone.'[119]

Thus ended, rather dismally and sordidly, the Knights' fight with Frank Smith. After two strikes, considerable effort, many arrests, a great outpouring of public support, and untold suffering by the strikers themselves, the Knights were totally defeated. Smith ran his franchise without organized workers until his charter expired in 1891.[120] In November 1890 a notice was sent from Toronto to the JUL, addressed 'To our Parisian Brothers.' The letter warned that Superintendent Franklin of the Toronto Street Railway was on his way to Paris to manage a similar enterprise. After expressing their gratitude that he was leaving Toronto, the workers advised the Paris brothers to treat him as they would 'any other bullly or Blackguard.'[121] The bitterness of 1886 did not die quickly. One should also note that just before the city ended Smith's lease in 1891, the men again attempted to form a local, and threatened a strike to shorten their work day, which still lasted twelve hours.[122]

For the Toronto Knights of Labor, the failure of the street-railway strike left both a legacy of bitterness and serious debts from which the order never fully recovered. Strife in the order had begun to surface even before the strike, and opponents were rising to contest the, until then, unchallenged leadership of 'the boys from 2305.' The founding of District Assembly 125, which O'Donoghue had bitterly opposed, and the election of Sam McNab as district master workman were early signs of conflict. Perhaps of most significance, however, was the action the assembly took in ending what must have been O'Donoghue's and Jury's most ambitious scheme in careers that had already spanned twenty years of labour-reform agitation.

How did such seasoned leaders get themselves involved in a scheme such as the Co-op Bus Company? One can only speculate that the remarkable successes of late 1885 and early 1886 led them to believe that the times were propitious for such an adventuresome undertaking. Thus their customary caution gave way to the enthusiasm for labour reform that inspired their long years of work for the cause. That year the membership of the order had increased to 5,000 workers in Toronto alone, and to 1,000,000 on the North American continent. It was also the year of their first great electoral success, when they replaced Tory mayor Alexander Manning with Howland, an avowed friend of the Knights.[123] That year had also seen their great triumphs over the Tory *Mail*, the huge Massey enterprise, and the initial, illusory victory over Frank Smith. But perhaps above all, it was the year in which finally they had a united working class behind them, as evidenced not only in the massive increases in organization but also in the March street actions and in the initial public response to the second strike.

Although there were no mass demonstrations, the second strike also had the support of the public. Scabs were unable to find boarding houses to reside in; teamsters and carters again did all they could to obstruct the street cars; another ten workers were arrested for various infractions against the franchise; the public overwhelmingly boycotted the cars and donated large sums to the strike when they used the free buses; a city-wide public meeting, chaired by Howland, pledged community support to the strikers by passing unanimous motions that were proposed by Knights' leaders; and the unions and locals of all Ontario donated funds and materials in an unprecedented show of solidarity.

Certainly, there were good reasons for the leadership's passionate enthusiasm. Although it is easy to criticize the innocence of their challenge to the immensely rich street-railway company, one is forced to admire their audacity. This is what the Knights of Labor stood for – an eclectic collection of beliefs that included the boycott, co-operation, and ultimately faith in social change through the concerted efforts of the working class and whatever allies it could recruit among the middle classes.[124] Thus O'Donoghue's cautious concern about the educational level of the Toronto Knights in November 1885 and his strong support of Powderly's order to cease organizing gave way to his enthusiasm and hope of early summer 1886. After all, had not Powderly himself proposed in 1880 that the way to 'banish the curse of modern civilization – wage-slavery [was to use] co-operation, as the lever of labour's emancipation'?[125]

Only a year later, in spring 1887, the order was forced again to fight for its right to exist. The piano manufacturing firm of Heintzman and Son dismissed three wood polishers with no explanation. Beaver Assembly, Local 3181, sent a deputation to demand from Heintzman the reason for the firing. The deputation was told it was due to incompetent work. All three men, however, were long-time employees and active unionists; the local refused to accept this explanation and instead requested the intervention of District Assembly 125, upon which a committee requested permission to inspect the allegedly faulty work. After investigation, the committee ruled that the work was up to standard except for one piece, which they suspected had been placed there to deceive them. On the strength of this report, the assembly asked the company to rehire the men. When the company refused, the assembly suggested arbitration and even proposed that the arbitrators be chosen from the Toronto Board of Trade. The company twice refused this offer, and the assembly appeared ready to back down when the company suddenly fired the local's master workman, again not offering any reason. When the company once again refused arbitration, Heintzman workers struck, with the District Assembly's consent. The other local in the plant (LA 3684), of piano woodworkers, also took a strike vote and decided by a vote of 41 to 1 to support their brother Knights. Seven weeks later, the General Executive Board sent D.R. Gibson to Toronto to try to settle the strike. After discussions with both sides, he proposed that the firm rehire all their men and submit the original conflict to an arbitration board in which the Knights would be represented by Sam McNab. The company accepted this arrangement, and the men returned to work.[126]

The pattern, typified in this strike, of avoiding conflict at almost any cost became more evident as 1887 progressed. This was partially due to the District Assembly's embarrassed financial situation. It sent its recording secretary, Robert Glockling, to Philadelphia to plead before the General Executive Board for monetary aid to settle the debts it incurred before it was founded.[127] The failure of this mission, combined with the ideological reluctance to resort to strikes, led to a series of unfortunate incidents which substantially undermined the order's position in Toronto.

The first of these occurred during the strike of Local 5792 in May 1887 against the Firstbrook Packing House Factory. Knights workers claimed to have struck after the dismissal of two members, but Firstbrook argued that this claim was only an attempt to force a closed shop on him. The District Assembly intervened, supported Firstbrook against the men, and ordered the Knights back to work.[128] A second incident occurred during Local 3490's strike against the Toronto Upholstery Company for a wage increase. The assembly again intervened and ordered its members back to work; in this case the employers even reported that the assembly would aid them in finding replacements if the workers refused. The assembly issued an angry rebuttal of the latter charge but did not comment on its action in ordering the men back.[129]

A different but related problem became evident in the building trades early in 1887 when plasterers and plasterers' labourers went out on strike because of the presence of non-union lathers. The lathers on the job were, however, members of the Knights of Labor. The trade-unionists objected against these lathers because of their willingness to work at piece rate, a method of pay strongly resisted by skilled building-trades workers for fear of the usually concomitant speed-up. One Knight's response, 'We're Knights of Labor, and that's as good as being in the union, ain't it?' was to meet shortly with a resounding 'No' from Toronto carpenters also.[130]

This final and most damaging incident occurred in August towards the end of the carpenters' strike that lasted almost ten weeks before ending in defeat for the Brotherhood and the Amalgamated: the Knights, after joining the strike in a half-hearted manner, unilaterally ordered their men back to work early.[131] This again brought to the fore craft-union antagonism toward the order.

The District Assembly's sentiments on the strike question were also made clear in 1888 when DA 125 co-operated with Powderly in having T.B.

Barry expelled from the order. The major evidence against him was the testimony of DA 125's executive board; one of their main charges was that Barry had deprecated education and co-operation, and instead counselled strikes and boycotts when he spoke in Toronto.[132] These pacifist policies damaged the order seriously in Toronto. It lost most of its carpenter members after the premature end of the 1887 strike; other groups who left later, such as the factory shoemakers, complained bitterly of the order's failure to support shop-floor struggles.[133] When the new Boot and Shoe Workers International Union led its first strike in Toronto in 1890, one commentator noted that the strike was 'being run by a new society chiefly under the management of young men, who have discarded the old Knights of Labor platform of 'no strike till all other means have failed.'''[134]

Moreover, there can be little doubt that the failure of the independent labour campaigns of 1886–87, together with the resulting cesspool of charges and countercharges, damaged the order in Toronto. Ironically, it was again the order's ambition that endangered its longevity – as we shall see in the following chapters.

Nevertheless, District Assembly 125, headed by bookbinder Robert Glockling, continued to play an active role well into the 1890s, and the leadership cadre developed by the order retained the most important positions in the TTLC and even in the national TLC. There was a slight resurgence of interest in the order in summer 1891, which prompted the General Executive Board to meet in Toronto that October.[135] There can be no doubt that this tenacity was inflated and manipulated by Knights' leaders for a variety of purposes. After the revolt at the General Assembly in 1893, which elected Powderly as General Master Workman, the new General Executive Board sent T.B. McGuire to Toronto to investigate charges that a Powderly-Wright axis had allowed District Assembly 125 to retain its charter only to provide General Assembly credentials to Powderly supporters. McGuire's report confirmed these charges and stripped the assembly of its district status. McGuire seized its books but allowed Glockling to retain the seal, since the Toronto bookbinder claimed that there was some hope of reorganizing dormant locals.[136] The order did not disappear completely from Toronto and a number of locals carried on the Knights name. O'Donoghue, for example, continued to represent Local 2305 at TLC meetings until the 1902 Berlin decision.[137] The other lasting contribution of the order was the foundation it laid for the further emergence of international unions in Toronto in the late 1880s and early 1890s. In a number of cases, former Knights locals joined these unions as a unit just as independent unions had joined the Knights in the 1880s. The importance of this local continuity of personnel and of trade organization transcends the discontinuities of national or international units.

The order's extreme and increasing reluctance to support strike action damaged the Knights irreparably in the struggle with craft unionism. The unions of the skilled were strongest precisely where the order was weakest – at the point of production. Toronto printers, moulders, and other craft-unionists in the 1880s and 1890s engaged in militant struggles to maintain old – or to establish new – traditions of control over production. A striking paradox resulted: whereas the Knights viewed industrial militancy far too sceptically, the craft-unionists failed to translate their shop-floor strength into political gains for their class. The Knights conceived social transformation grandly but shunned conflict; the craft-unionists fought fiercely but for narrowly defined goals.

Eugene Donavon had argued in 1883 that 'The Order of the Knights of Labor is not a benevolent society exclusively; nor is it a trade union alone; nor is it a political party – it combines the best elements of all of these.'[138] This statement pointed to the order's greatest strength. The Knights spearheaded a social movement, both in the United States and in Canada, that confronted the new industrial capitalist society in all realms – at the workplace, in the cultural and intellectual spheres, in local politics, and in the end, even in the national political arena. Although ultimately an organizational failure, the Knights' influence on future developments should never be underestimated. An entire leadership cadre of both the trade-union movement and of the emerging socialist movement came to prominence through the Knights. An entire generation of workers was deeply touched by the Knights' experience and took part, for at least a short period, in a class movement that for the first time organized all workers regardless of race, sex, or skill.[139] The deep political commitment of the Knights was maintained by the Canadian working class, whose independent political tradition was cemented in this decade.

Discontinuities of organization are vastly overrated in labour history; most Knights' locals reorganized under other banners in the 1890s and the total experience lived on in working-class memory. For, as the Boston *Labor Leader* reflected, one of the Knights' most important contributions lay 'in the fact that the whole life of the community is drawn into it, that people of all kinds are together ..., and that all get directly the sense of each others' needs.'[140] This was indeed a discovery of invaluable worth and it came to Toronto's working class only through the Knights of Labor.

11

Partyism in decline

We cannot safely leave politics to politicians, or political economy to college professors. The people themselves must think, because the people alone can act.
Henry George

The relationship between the economy and trade-union activity largely determined the political behaviour of the working class in the 1870s. The economic militancy and organizational gains of the early years of that decade shaped the political contours of the subsequent period. Class struggle in 1871 and 1872 created the climate which forced the Canadian government to take the initial steps towards legitimizing trade-unionism as an integral component of industrial capitalist society. By the latter years of the decade, however, the failure of trade unions to resist the employer encroachments accompanying the ever-deepening depression once again shifted the balance of class forces significantly. The few working-class leaders who remained visible found themselves increasingly implicated in the economic debates of Canadian capitalists, desperately seeking a successful development strategy. With the economic upturn of the early 1880s, the working-class seat on the seesaw of power relations lifted skywards – never again to be grounded totally.

Although the focus in the following chapters will be the political dimensions of class struggle in the 1880s, the reader should constantly keep in mind that these political struggles were dialectically intertwined with the economic activities and workplace struggles of the trade-union movement.[1] Indeed, these struggles deeply influenced the political environment in Toronto in the 1880s. The printers' struggle with the *Mail* and the Knights' struggle with Smith and his Toronto Street Railway set the scene for the emergence of the workers' first attempts at independent labour politics. Partyism, however, had developed deep roots in the working-class world in the 1870s. It would not be easily eliminated.

The roots of partyism were not solely ideological. By the 1880s a number of working-class leaders had reaped the rewards of political prominence. Junta members, especially, had profited from their co-operation with the Tories. Printer J.S. Williams, for example, had become a full-time party organizer in Toronto. Cooper John Hewitt had left his trade to work as a clerk at the Toronto Water Works and as an assistant editor of the *Orange Sentinel*. At the *Sentinel*, his boss was E.F. Clarke, who had been arrested during the printers' strike of 1872. Clarke would build on his Orange and trade-union connections further to become a four-term mayor of Toronto and a Tory MPP and later MP. Meanwhile, on the other side of the political divide, D.J. O'Donoghue received a clerical position in the Mowat government's Bureau of Industry, and his close friend, tailor Alfred Jury, was named to a provincial Royal Commission on Ontario prisons. This is only to elaborate on a few of the socio-economic ramifications of partyism for Toronto working-class leaders. The fierce struggle between partyism and independent labour politics raged throughout the 1880s.

The new labour bastions of the early 1880s were the Toronto Trades and Labour Council and the Knights of Labor. In its first few months of activity, the TTLC devised methods of effective political work. Initial lobbying activities were related to the Factory Investigation Committee, appointed by the Macdonald government to survey working conditions and recommend legislation. The TTLC's new Legislative Committee supplied a list of provisions that they demanded be part of any factory act.[2] Commissioner Lukes visited the council and used its information extensively in his report.[3] The council also named a committee to study the perennial question of trade-unionists' attitudes to prison labour.[4] One additional early activity demonstrated well the council's continuity with TTA activities and tactics. The Legislative Committee devised a proposal for an improved Mechanics' Lien Act (MLA) and brought it before the council in a special meeting.[5] After much discussion, the proposal was approved and a mass meeting to direct public pressure at the Mowat government was planned. After speeches by Alf Oakley, Thomas Moor, Alf Jury, O'Donoghue, and others, this meeting demanded MLA amendments to protect workers from bankrupt employers. The meeting called for the organization of all workers and for the working classes to seek direct class representation in Parliament.[6]

All of this activity closely resembled that of the junta years and both

O'Donoghue and Jury acknowledged this fact in their speeches, but there had been a significant change in the balance of class forces in which the labour movement operated. The resurgence of Toronto and Ontario labour made the Mowat government particularly responsive to trade-union pressure. Premier Mowat, after two visits by the TTLC Legislative Committee in February had provided him with considerable documentation of the losses incurred by building-trades workers under the MLA, responded quickly by introducing corrective legislation.[7] The TTLC enthusiastically 'Resolved that ... the MLA ... will give the workingmen a great measure of justice, and will not be detrimental to the interests of any section of the people.'[8] The council then visited the legislature en masse to demonstrate their support.

This event taken singly, or out of context, would have had little significance, but it set the pattern for the rest of the 1880s. The 1870s were the years of federal focus and of Tory dominance, whereas the 1880s were to witness a shift to the provinces and to the Liberals.[9] Although most apparent in Ontario, the same pattern also held in Nova Scotia. The TTLC, the Knights of Labor DA 125, and their allies throughout the province enjoyed an intimacy with the Mowat government unknown before the 1880s and seldom seen after in Canadian working-class history. If the MLA set the tone in provincial politics for the period, then the election of 1882 did the same for federal politics.

Working-class issues dominated the 1882 campaign in Toronto. The *Globe* launched a major attack on Macdonald's national policy as detrimental to Canadian workers. The Tory's massive claims in the 1878 amphitheatre campaign were unearthed. In addition, the *Globe* called on Liberal workingmen to describe the effects of Tory tariff changes on their trades.[10] Prominent TTLC leader and stonecutter Alf Oakley and Toronto Journeyman Shoemakers Association leader John Giblin responded with searing attacks on the national policy. Oakley argued that the tariff on Ohio free stone had almost ended the use of stone in Toronto building, since the only available local substitute was twice as expensive to work. The tariff's overall effect on the stonecutters' trade had been to reduce the number of working cutters in Toronto from well over 100 to between 10 and 30. Giblin, prominent in the 1882 female shoe-operatives' strike, argued that whereas prices had increased, wages had not. The women, he claimed, had actually seen their wages decline. He concluded succinctly that 'they never expected anything from the NP [national policy], but depended upon good times and their own organization as the sources of prosperity.'[11] These letters set off a predictable debate in the Toronto press. The *Mail*, backed by Tory stonecutters and contractors, claimed that Oakley had exaggerated and that the problem was caused by changing building styles, not by the tariff.[12]

In the 1882 campaign the Tories managed to reconstruct their fractured alliances for one last outing. The WLCU was brought back into the fold by the awarding of lucrative land grants to colonization societies, which involved leading lights in the Grand Lodge.[13] A.W. Wright also returned to the Tory camp, after a short absence in the United States. He had been rewarded with the secretary-ship of the Ontario Manufacturers Association, the leading pro-national-policy lobbying body. He used his position as a propagandist for protection to keep his hand in the working-class world as well and maintained his contacts with the 1,200-strong WLCU which, he was sure, would 'work alright' this time. Perhaps the Tory organizer closest to the Toronto working-class vote, Wright was quite concerned, however, about the security of the Toronto seats. He warned Macdonald that there was considerable discussion in Liberal circles of running labour leader O'Donoghue in East Toronto and that, if he ran, 'he would probably poll a strong vote.'[14]

Perhaps Tory insecurity about this election accounted for their particularly vituperative campaign for the working-class vote. The TTLC was almost wrecked only a year after its rebirth by the internecine strife carefully seeded by the *Mail*. The *Globe*'s 1870s role of discovering partisan political motivation underlying every action of the TTA was mimicked with a vengeance by the *Mail* in 1882. The *Mail* opened the campaign with a strong denunciation of the TTLC's Legislative Committee for its critique of the Tory government's withdrawal of its Factory Act. Arguing that its reintroduction in the Senate indicated the government's continued interest, the *Mail* launched a full-scale attack on the committee for being 'partisan.'[15] Committee member Alfred Oakley responded in a letter to the *Globe*: the committee was certainly interested in politics but it was political economy not party politics that motivated them. The *Mail* had had no complaints when the TTLC lobbied Mowat for the new Mechanics' Lien Act, but when they raised questions about Ottawa, it viewed them as 'mad dogs.' Oakley countered the *Mail*'s claim that the Tories had an excellent record on social legislation by arguing forcefully that 'every measure tending to elevate the masses has been forced by the people from their rulers.'[16] This was but the opening salvo in the dispute. The following TTLC meeting launched a major campaign against clauses in the Seaman's Act that denied trial-by-jury for a series of offences which carried sentences of up to five years in prison. The committee was instructed to interview prospective candidates and learn their positions on the Seamen's Act,

Chinese immigration, and the Factory Act. The candidates' responses would then be published as a guide for trade-unionists to use in the coming election.[17]

The *Mail* responded with an anonymous attack by 'A Trade Unionist,' which identified the committee members as 'pronounced Reformers' and one 'ultra-grit.' The anonymous unionist claimed that the committee had discovered the Seaman's Act issue to be a 'good political move'; then he went on to attack Oakley and carpenter Thomas Moor specifically. The only evidence offered was the presence of a *Globe* shorthand reporter when the key committee report was read, which led the trade unionist to conclude that the TTLC was being prostituted 'by a few tricky men.'[18]

Oakley again responded that the committee was appointed by the president, who at present was a Tory;[19] the committee had two non-Tory members of five; and it even included a *Mail* employee.[20] The charge that the committee had discovered the Seaman's Act for partisan purposes conveniently ignored the real inequities of the Act. Denying the slur that he was in the pay of the Ontario government as a political operative, Oakley noted with pride his twelve years as a journeyman stone-cutter in Toronto. After this carefully phrased defence, he could not resist going on the offensive and he asked why the Tories did not

devote a little more attention to the so-called Workingman's National Union of Canada – whose officers, executive and members consist of a few unsuccessful manufacturers, briefless barristers, third rate journalists, full-fledged Yankee Greenback orators, paid spouters of the NP interests with their high-sounding titles of colonel and general when on the war path in Uncle Sam's Dominions?

He also speculated on the cause of this new Tory assault: '[The Tories] begin to see that the workingmen have an intention to use the franchise to suit themselves. They fear their hold on the cities, and especially on Toronto, is being loosened. Hence this splutter.'[21]

On 16 June, the committee reported that it had sent questions to the various candidates for office in the city. Only the Liberals had responded, and all three of them gave the council full support on all issues. This set off a storm of debate with Tory workingmen, such as printer John Armstrong, 'putting some close questions as to who was served with these questions and how they were presented and if the Premier had been asked these questions. And why these questions were not put verbally as requested by the Council.' The report was accepted, but no action was taken on the candidates' responses, indicating that all decided to act with caution lest they destroy the fragile TTLC. Oakley and Moor rose later in the meeting on points of personal privilege to defend themselves against the *Mail's* charges.[22] The *Mail's* only response was yet another rather weak letter from the anonymous 'Trade Unionist' who accused the committee of 'grit juggling' and claimed that, if Moor and Oakley had spent less time campaigning for McMurrich, the Liberal candidate in West Toronto, they might have found more time to carry out the work of the committee. He also refused to withdraw his earlier accusations that they were 'political tricksters.'[23]

The *Mail*, in the closing week of the campaign, discovered a more effective issue to take to the working-class voter. The *Globe*, as part of its campaign against the national policy, had commissioned its most-skilled journalist, Phillips Thompson, to conduct an investigation of the Canadian textile industry.[24] A radical moving increasingly towards the working-class movement, Thompson included in his reports an assessment of the conditions of workers in the industry. The *Mail* seized on one paragraph with great effect. In describing the long hours and unhealthy conditions of the female workers, Thompson questioned their moral state as well:

If the mill life and home life of the operatives is deplorable, their moral condition is more so. There is something in the social atmosphere that – according to the testimony of the most intelligent and best informed gentlemen I have met there, and according to my own observations – produces a feeling of utter apathy in the hearts of most of the operatives. They move through the world, enervated mentally and physically, with stolid indifference, and little object in life, even the excitements of the hour which stir the most commonplace minds scarcely rousing them from their stupor.

He then gave the views of one of his informants who felt that:

Their morals are bad, very bad. The conduct of the girls is immodest in the extreme, and a deep degradation reveals itself in both sexes when anything awakens them for a time from a mode of mental life which can scarcely be said to be more than mere existence … I do not think there are ten virtuous girls in a hundred. A good-looking girl is almost certain to fall before she has long lived in the surroundings of cotton mill life.[25]

Thompson qualified these statements, but not sufficiently to spare himself the *Mail's* wrath. The *Mail's* lead editorial, under a banner headline, A MOST DISGRACEFUL TISSUE OF MISREPRESENTATION: MEN AND GIRLS

ALIKE INSULTED, launched a polemic, vehement even by nineteenth-century newspaper standards. The *Globe*'s article was 'disgraceful to the man who wrote it. it is disgraceful to the journal which published it. It is a libel on the operatives, male and female, of all the factories of the Dominion.' The *Mail* rose to new heights of eloquence in defending the insulted workers: 'The pathos of poverty is theirs at times; its struggles and its troubles are theirs; but theirs too are its heroism, its self-sacrifice, its charity, its virtues. We protest against the degradation which the *Globe* would cast on their way of life.'[26] Thompson's critique of wages, hours, employment of children, housing conditions, and so on was lost in the *Mail* counter-offensive which focused only on morality.

In addition to its editorial critique, the *Mail* sent its Montreal correspondent to investigate the Hudon Mill at Hochelaga, and to interview some of the town's leading figures concerning the *Globe* articles. Needless to say, the manager of the mill, the local Catholic priest, the protestant minister, and the town physician all denied the charges.[27] The *Mail* also featured prominently the letters that poured in from textile manufacturers across the province vehemently denouncing the *Globe*.[28] But perhaps most important were the reports of the spontaneous demonstrations among the operatives at mills in Paris, Ontario, and in Cornwall, where 1,500 operatives paraded an effigy of the *Globe* correspondent through the town and then burned it.[29] The *Mail* appealed very cleverly in this case to working-class respectability. In late-Victorian Canada, this had an immense impact, and although we cannot be certain what was in the minds of Toronto workers as they voted on 21 June, it seems likely that the *Globe* had once again alienated Toronto workers – ironically on this occasion – by being overly solicitous. Phillips Thompson, especially, must have felt the irony as his investigative reporting was turned to partisan advantage by the Tories. Thus the Tories, despite their early worries about the working-class vote, again swept the three Toronto seats.[30]

The longer-range effects of the 1882 campaign, the last campaign of the decade without labour candidates, deserve consideration. The emerging independent labour position was probably best depicted in the pages of Toronto printer Eugene Donavon's *Trade Union Advocate*. It defended the TTLC against the *Mail's* charges of partisanship and called for 'a platform upon a purely labour basis.' This, combined with effective organization, would allow Toronto workers 'to have representatives from their own class not only in Dominion and Local parliaments but also in Municipal institutions.' This was one way to avoid the destructive infighting created by partyism.[31]

Earlier, the *Advocate* had refused to take a position on the upcoming election:

We have been repeatedly asked what course we shall pursue in the coming election? Our position is easily defined. As we hold decided views on the labour question, we deem it our duty to the workingmen to stand aloof from party politics pending the formation of a labour platform, to be shortly promulgated by the TLC of this city.[32]

These noble *Advocate* sentiments did not save the TTLC from significant partisan strife. The mid-year TTLC election almost turned into a crippling fiasco because of partyism. On 16 June, Alf Oakley, Thomas Moor, and W. Hawthorne were nominated for president. Four other nominees, including printer John Armstrong, declined to run.[33] At the following meeting, Moor withdrew, leaving only Oakley and Hawthorne, but Griffiths introduced a motion to reopen nominations. Oakley had no personal objections to the motion but suggested that it was quite irregular. The president, however, permitted the procedure, and Griffiths then renominated John Armstrong, who accepted this time. Hawthorne then retired in favour of Armstrong. Objections were immediately raised that the nominations had been reopened for ulterior political motives, but the election took place and Armstrong defeated Oakley, 17 to 13.[34] Lengthy and heated procedural debates about the constitutionality of the election dominated the next two meetings. A tortured compromise was finally arranged which voided the election, but then returned the previous winners by acclamation. The Armstrong victory definitely had Tory political roots. TTLC Liberal delegates, however, seem to have been satisfied to expose this and did not choose to jeopardize the council's very existence by forcing a final confrontation.[35]

Meanwhile, plans for the development of a labour platform proceeded. These were not free from strife either. The motion to form a committee who would draft a labour platform was introduced by carpenter Sam Heakes. His aims were questioned, especially by Oakley, who feared that a platform was premature and that, at the very least, it should be referred to the Legislative Committee rather than to a special committee.[36] The special committee was appointed nevertheless, but its proceedings were slow and difficult. The *Advocate* complained in late September that either apathy or partyism was obstructing the creation of the platform.[37] Heakes finally introduced the platform on 6 October. The preamble read:

The complete revolution in the manufacturing industry consequent upon the rapid production of labour-saving inventions has given an impetus to business that has never been equalled; and as labor is the creative power of all wealth, so had the capital of the country increased in proportion; but while capitalists have amassed riches, the conditions of the toilers has remained but little changed. While the one class lives in luxury, and the other exists in comparative poverty, there can be no harmony between capital and labor under existing conditions; for capital, in its modern character, too often consists of unpaid labor in the shape of profits, legally, though unjustly taken from the producer, who is compelled to sell his labor and skill at such price as the grasping employer may choose to offer. The only hope of changing this state of affairs is with the working classes themselves ... By sinking party differences and uniting on a common platform to improve our condition, success will not be long in crowning our effort.[38]

The platform asserted the need for workers and unionists to represent the working classes in Parliament and then enumerated demands ranging from extension of the franchise to restricted immigration, and from shorter hours to a factory act. The relatively uncontroversial platform 'could be concurred in by all sections of the working classes.' The TTLC passed it with little debate and the *Advocate* endorsed it.[39]

The political scene quickly heated up again, when master carpenter J.J. Withrow announced his candidacy for mayor. The *Advocate* led the campaign against Withrow:

As a large employer Mr. Withrow does not appear to great advantage ... When he enters into a combination not only to prevent the men getting fair wages, but also to prevent all who went on strike getting work in the city, he oversteps the mark of everything that savours of honour or manliness ... Withrow and his accomplices would make men slaves. He would rob them of their liberty ... and place on them the yokes of serfdom.[40]

The issue was introduced to the TTLC by Tory harnessmaker W. Hawthorne, who moved that the council instruct workers to oppose Withrow. Liberal Alf Oakley opposed the move, claiming it was a blatant attempt to introduce politics into the council. Oakley's constitutional objections were overruled by President John Armstrong, and the council voted Withrow out by a sound 34 to 4 majority. Oakley recovered gracefully and asked for the floor after the vote to record three words: 'Alas! poor Withrow.'[41]

The debate, however, was not over. Oakley wrote to the *Advocate*, denying charges of personal partyism and suggesting instead that the council and the paper were opposing Withrow only because of his Liberal party identifications. If all anti-unionists were to be opposed, why had they not fought against Robert Hay, the Tory MP for Centre Toronto, who, as an employer of labour, had hardly proved himself a friend of trade-unionism? The *Advocate*'s response to Oakley's 'insinuations bordering on accusations' was to reassert that opposition to Withrow was based solely on his record and that in the future Oakley should remember his own advice on the question of partyism.[42]

When Withrow publicly denied all the charges of the TTLC and the *Advocate*, the council met to consider their response. After some debate, Oakley convinced his colleagues to hold a mass meeting at which Withrow would be allowed to answer his accusers. A ten-point indictment was drawn up, focusing mainly on his actions in 1872 and in the carpenters' strike in the spring of 1882. At the meeting Armstrong, Moor, and Heakes read the charges. Withrow's defence rested mainly on denials that convinced no one.[43] The subsequent election was extremely close and the TTLC's opposition was credited as a major factor in Withrow's defeat.[44]

The victory provided a major impetus to further political activity. The *Advocate* viewed the result in class terms:

The struggle developed into a direct contest between capital and labor, employers irrespective of politics, rallying around Mr. Withrow, determined to assist him in gaining a crowning triumph over labor. With all the efforts of capital, church influence, temperance associations, and personal popularity to combat, labor has come out victorious.[45]

Several lessons could be learned from the campaign. First and 'chief among them was the now well recognized fact that capital is determined to crush labor.' Second was the desirability of further political activity.[46] The TTLC had already discussed, in a preliminary fashion, the possibility of nominating labour candidates in the upcoming Ontario election, and the mayoralty results encouraged further activity.[47] In early January the Legislative Committee reported that candidates chosen from a group consisting of Moor, Heakes, Oakley, Armstrong, and John Carter would run well.[48] The *Advocate*, however, began to express deep concern with the explicit partyism that it perceived in the council. It called for 'a radical change in the personnel of the Council [for there was] no mistaking the fact that Grit and Tory is "sticking out" too plainly for the Council's welfare.'[49] After much debate, the TTLC arrived at a method of choosing their candidates and a list of potential nominees.[50] The infighting was so fierce that the *Advocate*'s concern continued to grow. Editor Eugene Donavon thought it 'unpolitic' to nominate candidates, since there was not enough time to prepare an effective campaign and because of the 'fatal diversity of opinion' that existed in labour's ranks.[51] The TTLC did not follow his advice and, after another heated controversy about the method of balloting, proceeded to choose candidates. Although not acknowledged formally, the TTLC attempted to avoid virulent partisan strife by recognizing one nomination as a Tory seat and the other as Grit. Thus, in Toronto East, Tory carpenter Sam Heakes was chosen by a vote of 35 to 8 over old junta member and bricklayer Andrew McCormack. The battle for the Toronto West nomination took a total of five ballots before Grit painter J.W. Carter defeated the prominent Liberal carpenter Thomas Moor by one vote. In both cases strife prevented making the choice unanimous; in Heake's case only Blain of the Harnessmakers refused, but in Carter's, approximately half the delegates refused to make the choice unanimous, and Oakley hinted blackly at 'outside influence.'[52]

At a special meeting the following night, Carter indicated that he would not accept the nomination unless it were made unanimous, since the only chance of success was if all 'threw party feelings to the wind.' Armstrong moved to make it unanimous despite his earlier support for Moor. After a heated debate, which again centred on Oakley's vague charges, the resolution passed. Council plans for the campaign included a mass meeting to ratify the nominees.[53] This apparent resolution of all difficulties lasted only briefly, however, for TTLC President Thomas Moor forced another special meeting, when he charged that the results of the original nomination meeting were illegal on the basis that one of Carter's major supporters had been ineligible to vote because his union had previously withdrawn from the council. Heakes was acclaimed for the Toronto East nomination, but yet another election was held for the nomination in Toronto West. Carter again defeated Moor, and on this occasion Moor moved, seconded by Oakley, that the nomination be made unanimous.[54]

The first independent labour campaign in Toronto then did not get off to an auspicious start. Nevertheless, it caused considerable concern among Toronto Tories. The incumbent Tory MPP in Toronto East, Alexander Morris, warned Macdonald: 'The Trade Labour Union [sic] threaten working men candidates here and in Hamilton and it would hurt us and help the Grits. I would like an easier seat as I may break down in fighting East Toronto.'[55] In Morris' riding, Heakes found himself opposed by both parties. Carter, however, was opposed in West Toronto only by Tory trunk manufacturer H.E. Clarke.[56] The Liberals' willingness to allow Carter to run unopposed against Clarke was no doubt motivated by his Grit party ties. Pledging himself to independence, however, Carter did receive the support of Hawthorne, Heakes, Armstrong, Wilson, McCormack, and other self-acknowledged Tory workingmen. Similarly, Liberal Alf Jury pledged his support to Tory Sam Heakes in West Toronto: 'No matter what he was outside of Toronto he would be for workingmen first and Grit afterward in the city.'[57] The *Mail* again campaigned vigorously for the working-class vote. It tried to place the national policy at the centre of the campaign, and even returned to the Thompson scandal of the previous year.[58] Nevertheless, Carter ran extremely well in West Toronto, losing to Clarke by only 200 votes, and winning 48 per cent of the total vote; but Heakes, opposed by both parties, was overwhelmed and gained only 300 votes (7 per cent).

Although disappointed, the TTLC and the *Advocate* were not disconsolate about the results. In a balanced assessment Donavon argued:

The attempt to lead the masses of manual and mechanical labor out of the usual rut of party politics in the city of Toronto was a brave one, and although not thoroughly successful yet a great stride was made in that direction. The defeat is but a momentary check to the efforts of those who fought, and will continue to fight for that recognition on the floor of Parliament to which the working classes are in justice entitled.[59]

This innovative political departure demonstrated a growing maturity on the part of the Toronto labour movement. Although the articulated rationale for independent labour politics had been present as early as the 1870s, the new-found ability to unite and contest an election cannot be underestimated. The 1883 electoral experience constituted stage one of a labour upsurge that was building towards the most tangible and significant political challenge in the late-nineteenth century.

The following year was spent consolidating previous gains. The TTLC became an increasingly effective lobby. In early March, the council appointed a committee to investigate factory conditions in Toronto as a method of publicizing the continued need for a factory act.[60] In early April, when the Tories finally introduced a factory act, the council sent a delegation to Ottawa to lobby for it, after Jury informed them that the manufacturing interests were trying to 'burke' the bill.[61] This special committee, composed of Heakes, Moor, and Sheppard, interviewed Macdonald and others in Ottawa but with inconclusive results.[62]

In May the new TTU delegate, O'Donoghue, was appointed to the Legislative Committee.[63] This action shaped the politics of the council for the remainder of the decade, brought the TTLC into international prominence, and increasingly put them in direct conflict with the Macdonald government.

Before O'Donoghue's appointment, the committee's interest in the question of immigration had been limited to opposing the recruitment of Chinese workers. After his appointment, the immigration question in all its aspects became the major preoccupation of the TTLC and, in the process, became the major labour critique of the national policy.[64] O'Donoghue initiated a policy of carefully scrutinizing the actions of both Ontario and Canadian immigration agents in the British Isles, and under his guidance the Legislative Committee circulated petitions and literature to unions all across Canada.[65] Both innovations, plus his voluminous correspondence with British newspapers and trade-unionists, projected the TTLC beyond local significance. In addition, O'Donoghue played an active role in the TTLC's initiative in convening the December 1883 Labor Congress.[66]

This first congress was important. It not only marked the birth of one component of the present Canadian Labour Congress, but also its resolutions set the lobbying goals for the next decade of political labour activity. Finally, the congress also heralded the arrival of the Knights of Labor as an important force in the Canadian labour scene.

The lobbying campaigns that the new congress selected were predictable, given earlier TTLC activities. Resolutions were passed demanding the end of assisted immigration and the abolition of pauper and Chinese immigration; a factory act and a nine-hour working day; manhood suffrage and the abolition of property requirements for municipal office; a Bureau of Labor Statistics; and the endorsement of temperance.[67] Resolutions demonstrating newer and more radical influences included a call to unionize women, equal pay for equal work, a strong Georgite plank opposing the monopolization of land,[68] and a call for labour representation on the basis of grouped constituencies and voting reform. This last measure would have created larger ridings with many members where voters would plump for individual candidates.[69]

The Knights of Labor had leaped into Canadian prominence the previous summer during the international Telegraphers' strike.[70] The new (October 1882) mixed assembly (LA 2305) of self-conscious labour-reform trade-unionists began to plot a strategy for control of the TTLC. The TLC provided their first major opportunity, with O'Donoghue and painter and Knights' organizer Charles March being in excellent positions to promote Knights' aims. O'Donoghue's Legislative Committee was responsible for planning the congress, and it invited all trade-unionists and Knights.[71] Charles

March, president of the host TTLC, was elected chairman of the congress. In his opening speech, he commented on the presence of the Knights, which 'was right in principle ... as between the two bodies [trade unions and Knights] antagonism should not exist.'[72] Of the 45 delegates, at least one-third were Knights, and they dominated the key Ways and Means Committee.[73] From TLC meetings sprouted the plans for the Knights' entry into local trades councils, for, as O'Donoghue explained to Powderly, 'the TTLC is a power recognized, I am proud to say, by legislators and the governments take note of its proceedings and opinions.'[74] O'Donoghue's strategy led Local 2305 to join the TTLC in January, and it was followed by Locals 2211 and 2782 in early May and Locals 3181 and 2622 in mid-May.[75] Entrance into the TTLC proved more difficult than into the TLC. The Toronto Typographical Union, ironically represented by O'Donoghue, protested against the admission of the Knights.[76] The debate took place in early April, when O'Donoghue resolved, seconded by John Armstrong, that 'it is detrimental to our interest that Knights of Labor should be represented by delegates in the Council and that the Trades Council be memorialized to prevent the admittance of delegates of that body to the Trades' and Labor Council.'[77] Although O'Donoghue introduced this TTU motion, he later opposed it, arguing that the order was not detrimental to the interests of trade-unionists. After much discussion, the resolution was referred back to the TTU for more information. O'Donoghue, not surprisingly, attended the next meeting as a representative of Local 2305, not of the TTU.[78]

The carpenters, the stonecutters, and the iron moulders also recorded their initial opposition to the Knights' presence over the next few meetings.[79] The issue came to a head again when Willard (of the moulders) moved, seconded by Merredith (of the printers), that the present relations between the TTLC and the Knights cease and the Knights' money be refunded. This motion was soundly defeated, and the issue did not surface again in the 1880s.[80] O'Donoghue and the Knights had scored a major tactical victory, by managing to avoid a vote until they already had 15 delegates on the council. This voting block guaranteed their victory. A reflective O'Donoghue wrote Powderly a month later, blaming Orangemen for the Knights' difficulties:

I have told you before that the 'isms' of other lands have a strong hold here. Notwithstanding all this however we are gradually gaining some headway, and by the exercise of prudence, firmness and tact will ultimately gain a firm hold on the mind of the laboring classes. Persons less sanguine than a few of us here would in view of the vilification, contumely and deliberate misrepresentation of our motives, 'throw up the sponge' and pursue the 'even tenor of their way' disgusted at the criminal foolishness as well as perverseness of those in their own ranks. But while this is but too true we recognize the still plainer fact that some body or bodies must 'face the music' for the sake of humanity and as a consequence our motto is '*Nil Desperandum*.'[81]

Despair was hardly called for, since O'Donoghue and 'the boys from 2305' effectively controlled the Toronto labour scene during the next few years. For the first time the Toronto labour leadership passed from the Orange-Tory craftsmen. 'The boys from 2305,' although of Liberal persuasion, transformed themselves into a new junta with extensive influence over the entire Canadian labour movement. Their control of the TTLC, especially its Legislative Committee, and of the Knights of Labor gave them an extremely powerful base from which to work. O'Donoghue had earlier explained the conflict to Powderly:

You will bear in mind, too, that we have an element to contend against here that you are not cursed with in the United States – I refer to the Orange body which is sworn to uphold a certain form of creed, and upholds the crown (*which can do no wrong*!!) This element is frowning down, in so far as it can, the K. of L. Order, as they dread, and justly, the broad platform of 'live and let live' upon which the members of the latter stand together. We find the malicious influence of the Orange Order ever operating against the Knights and particularly such of them [who] are known to be Catholic.[82]

By mid-1884, then, the Grit takeover of the TTLC was complete. On the political spectrum the new leadership was clearly Liberal. Jury had been the most highly visible Toronto Liberal workingman since the amphitheatre debates of 1878. O'Donoghue, although initially elected to the Ontario legislature in 1874 with the endorsement of one faction of the Ottawa Tory party, soon became a Mowat Liberal in everything but name.[83] Certainly by the 1880s his party ties were clear; he was rewarded with employment in Mowat's new Bureau of Industry as a collector of labour statistics, and later became the labour columnist for John Cameron's *Globe*.[84] Charles March, the third member of the new triumvirate, kept his politics in the background, but his closeness to Jury and O'Donoghue and his Roman Catholicism suggest his close ties to the Liberals. As we have seen, partyism was virulent in the TTLC in the early 1880s. The Liberal faction's ascendance, however, ironically reduced the tension. Residual charges of partyism surfaced periodically in the TTLC,[85] but by 1885 there was a new unanimity in Toronto labour circles, forged by the Knights, by O'Donoghue's clever use of the immigration issue, and by the *Mail's* attack on the TTU.[86]

The unprecedented success of the Liberal party in attracting working-class support in Toronto increasingly worried the Tories. Tory MP John Small wrote Macdonald a letter of introduction for the 1883 TTLC delegation, which identified them as 'Grits of the worst kind [who] worked hard against us in the election.'[87] In 1884 A.W. Wright proposed a complicated scheme to Macdonald, by which 'the working classes could be more firmly attached to the Conservative Party, than they are, and whereby we could frustrate the conspiracy to draw them into the Grit ranks, of the existence of which conspiracy the doings of the Toronto Trades and Labor Council are ample evidence.' The scheme was similar to one he had proposed earlier when the Hamilton *Labor Union* had appeared to be failing in 1883. This time, the *Palladium of Labor* had ceased publication and Wright sought $4,000 from Macdonald for its takeover by the Tories:

My plan is to have a paper started which will be made the organ of the Knights of Labor and perhaps of the Trades and Labor Council. Put it in the form of a joint stock company allotting a *minority* of the stock to the more active and prominent members of the labor organizations, thus identifying them with the paper without running the risk of letting them actually get control of it. My idea is that in order to fully obtain and retain the confidence of the working classes the paper should be conducted editorially on a purely labor platform, even antagonizing the Conservative Party where it could be done harmlessly but whenever opportunity offered putting in a word where it would do good.[88]

The plan did not work on this occasion, as the *Palladium* was refinanced as a co-operative paper of District Assembly 61; nevertheless, the Tories' concern about losing their working-class base was again very evident.

The fight between the Toronto Typographical Union and the *Mail* (which was briefly discussed in chapter 6) further decimated the Tories' ties with organized labour. As early as 1884 leading Tory printers warned Macdonald of the possible repercussions of the *Mail's* antagonistic stance. J.S. Williams, for example, had written in August: 'Not only will the matter complained of [*Mail* lock-out] alienate a very large proportion of the working men who have hitherto nobly supported the party, but it places a barrier in the way of any prominent or representative workingman actively working or speaking in the future.' Moreover, he predicted that the *Mail's* reactionary policies could cost the Tories two to three seats in Toronto and perhaps seats in other urban centres as well. E.F. Clarke, a prominent Tory politician and a member of Local 91, wrote to the same effect: 'A reduction of wages at a week's notice and a refusal of the Mail to leave the settlement of the question to arbitration will alienate the sympathies of a large number of workingmen who have hitherto supported the Conservative cause, and will weaken the influence of the journal with the masses.' A non-working-class Tory politico wrote that the labour friends of the party were now in an impossible position since they 'cannot support the party that treats them so shabbily,' and expressed the fear that the loss of the whole Toronto Trades and Labor Council might result in electoral defeat in the city.[89] Nevertheless, these warnings were ignored.

The dire predictions nearly became fact in the December 1884 mayoralty race in Toronto. As early as September, Alfred Boultbee expressed concern about the necessity to find a strong Tory candidate to oppose Liberal J.J. Withrow who had come close to victory in 1883.[90] They finally settled on Alexander Manning but entered the race with grave trepidations:

Something must be done to secure the *workingman's vote*. The T.L.C. are opposed to our candidates in consequence of the actions of the *Mail* with members of the Typographical Union. They explained their case to Manning yesterday and told him distinctly that they had made up their minds to oppose anyone advocated for any position by Mr. Bunting.[91]

As it turned out, the TTLC actually remained neutral in the campaign, seeing little reason to support either candidate. Their stance was understandable given Withrow's labour record, which had been so thoroughly exposed in the 1883 campaign. Their refusal to support Manning, however, showed how far the antagonism against the Tories had progressed. Consequently, Tory fears ran so high in the 1885 campaign that Macdonald was asked to intervene to force certain Tory aldermen to support Manning more strongly.[92] Boultbee took charge of the campaign personally, since it was 'enormously important that we don't have a Grit mayor now' and because things 'looked very nasty.'[93] After their narrow 145 vote victory, he complained that 'the whole conservative system here is rotten to the core, [demanding that] it be thoroughly reorganized or some fine day we shall be cleaned out root and branch.'[94]

If Tory concern was rampant in Toronto, what did the Knights' Liberal triumvirate do to increase their new leadership power? In lobbying style there was actually little to choose between their policies and those of their

Tory predecessors. In policy matters, however, there were crucial differences. O'Donoghue and March, through their control othe TTLC Legislative Committee, led a massive campaign against Canadian immigration policy. Although initially they were charged with partyism because of their focus on federal programs without a corresponding critique of Ontario provincial schemes, they later won near-universal approval. By 1885, for example, the acknowledged leader of the Tory faction in the TTLC, printer John Armstrong, proposed that the council send a representative to England to combat the Macdonald government's misleading propaganda aimed at recruiting British workers to Canada.[95]

The campaign to end Chinese, assisted, pauper, and orphan immigration was the TTLC's major fight in the 1880s. O'Donoghue dedicated his committee's work almost single-mindedly to exposing the lies, deceptions, and distortions of the Canadian immigration agents, the English philanthropists, and the agents of Canadian railroads and steamship lines. Legislative committee reports were filled with exposés of the actions of these individuals, whose motives ranged from nefarious to altruistic. O'Donoghue consistently condemned them all. Although the Chinese question led the labour spokesmen into racist excesses on occasion, in most other cases the critique was not nativist. Instead, it revolved around the considerable and growing problems of unemployment and poverty in Canada's industrial cities.

O'Donoghue's techniques in this regard were those of the skilled propagandist and lobbyist. He described some of them for Powderly:

We have done a great deal in checking wholesale immigration to Canada, and our influence has been acknowledged in other directions. I send papers to every Trades Council in Great Britain (33), to many separate Trade Unions, to Gladstone, Northcote, Roseberry, Justin McCarthy, and to 46 newspapers and a large number of correspondents.[96]

A few months later he sent Powderly a copy of a pamphlet prepared by the Legislative Committee for the British Trades' Union Congress. It described 'the condition of the labour market, the rate of wages, etc., in Canada during the year,'[97] and was intended to counter the government's glowing descriptions.

These lobbying techniques were also used domestically.[98] O'Donoghue, as committee secretary, circulated prepared petitions before every parliamentary session (both provincial and federal) to all union and Knights' locals. All the locals had to do was sign and return them either to

O'Donoghue or to their parliamentary representatives. O'Donoghue also instructed the locals, as a final act to ensure the effectiveness of the petitions, to telegram their representative inquiring if he had received their petition and requesting acknowledgment. The avowed rationale of this style of petitioning was 'that the Parliaments appealed to for justice *must* by reason of our persistence devote more than a passing careless thought to our Petitions.'[99]

Another O'Donoghue innovation was the recommendation for a TTLC municipal committee in 1885.[100] Formerly part of the Legislative Committee's work, local government activities which impinged on wage earners could be analysed in far more detail by the new committee. The committee was also established to allow the council to evaluate seriously the work of aldermen. The new municipal focus stemmed from increased interest in taxation, which was being brought to the fore by the ideas of Henry George,[101] who visited Hamilton in August 1884. In late 1885 this combined with the Toronto Typographical Union's continuing campaign against the *Mail*[102] and the Knights' campaign against the Street Railway Company[103] to ensure a heated mayoralty race, with labour playing a prominent role in the campaign.

In early December the TTLC resolved to ask the mayoralty candidates to express their views on the proposed changes in the method of electing the mayor, on the need to take strong action to compel the Street Railway Company to live up to the terms of its charter, and on the use of prison labour in municipal public works.[104] At the same meeting, they also appointed ward committees to interview the alderman candidates on labour questions so that the council could endorse a slate of pro-labour candidates. A special meeting evaluated the ward committees' reports and drew up lists of approved and unsatisfactory candidates. The challenger in the mayoralty race, W.H. Howland, answered all the questions satisfactorily, but the committee was instructed to interview Mayor Manning again about his rather ambiguous answer on the question of prison labour.[105] TTU delegates reported that the printers wanted trade-unionists to oppose all candidates who had received the *Mail*'s support. After some debate, the TTLC endorsed the request with the proviso that if the candidates 're-pudiated over their own signatures the stand of the *Mail* towards organized labour,' they would be removed from this labour version of the *Mail*'s blacklist.[106] Union after union endorsed the TTU position, and thus Manning attempted desperately to dissociate himself from the *Mail*.[107] Reports near the end of the campaign, that the TTU had lifted their opposition to him, were denied vehemently by the TTLC[108] and the TTU.[109] A fight erupted at the last TTLC meeting before the election, when Tory bricklayer Andrew McCormack claimed that Manning had repudiated the *Mail*, and O'Donoghue argued that he had not.[110] The decision was left to the TTU,[111] and they decided that Manning's letter did not suffice.[112] A large TTU advertisement in the *Globe* called on Toronto workers to oppose Manning.[113] The Knights of Labor also endorsed Howland, who scored a smashing victory over Manning. The working-class vote had been crucial. O'Donoghue wrote happily to Powderly: 'We had a great victory here on Monday last. Labour combined and defeated the *Mail*'s candidate for Mayor by a majority of 1786 ... The victory of organized labour in Toronto has created dismay in the ranks of party heelers.'[114] The burgeoning growth of the Knights of Labor was breaking the established patterns of Toronto working-class politics. The Hamilton *Palladium of Labor* had noted in December: 'It [the order] ought to destroy the pig-headed and unreasoning partyism which has so long prevailed among the working people of that city – under which time and time again the interests of labour have been subordinated to those of tricky politicians and ringsters who court the workingman's vote only to betray him.'[115]

Other political observers noted the same events but drew different conclusions. After January's humiliating defeat, the Tories immediately began to mend their disintegrating political fences. Their first step was to end the *Mail*'s embarrassing battle with the TTU.[116] Tory ward-heeler Harry Piper wrote Macdonald only a month after Howland's victory that the difference between the *Mail* and the TTU had now 'assumed a very serious aspect [since] our oldest and best committee men worked for the enemy' in the mayoralty election. Through the good offices of former junta member J.S. Williams and Toronto TTU leader John Armstrong (who had lost his own job at the *Mail* during the 1884 strike), Piper arranged for the *Mail*'s total capitulation to the TTU. This had become absolutely necessary since the 'union was *killing our party* and the Grits were reaping the benefits of the trouble and using our friends.'[117] On the next day, the gleeful Piper noted that 'The *Iron Clad document* will be burnt tonight in the *Mail* office before all the printers and that important fact will come up before the unions Saturday night next.'[118] The *Mail* boycott had ended in a glorious labour victory.

O'Donoghue also noted this victory over the *Mail*[119] but saved his real enthusiasm for the Grit response to this new Tory stratagem:

As I told you the *Mail* 'caved' and is now a 'square' union office. The *Globe* was never a thoroughly union office – simply an open office. Well through the efforts of

Jury and March, and whatever little I could help, it has been 'worked' and it agreed to arbitrate with the union and named as its arbitrators A.F. Jury, Charles March, George Beales – all of LA 2305.[120]

If the timing alone was not sufficient to indicate the political rationale of the *Globe*'s new stance on labour questions, then their bargaining position should have:

Oh, I forgot, I am included as one of the arbitrators, although known to the *Globe* as a radical trade unionist and a member of the Typographical Union. The Manager said: 'These men know all about the circumstances and I have full confidence in their impartiality and leave the whole matter to their judgement and will stand by their decision.' Just fancy – 4 *trade unionists*, and one of them interested, chosen by an employer to arbitrate between himself and a trade union. What are we coming to?[121]

The *World* and some Toronto printers, however, took a more critical view of these proceedings. In protesting the arbitration decision which allowed six or seven old non-union printers to remain at the *Globe*, they pointed out that a single arbitrator was normally chosen by each party and those two then chose a third. In this case the *Globe* had appointed all the arbitrators, and even though they were all trade-unionists, only O'Donoghue was a printer and he no longer practised his trade. Moreover, they pointed out the striking coincidence that all four arbitrators were Knights and, more importantly, Reformers.[122] Nevertheless, the TTU wisely accepted the settlement.

Thus in the spring of 1886, almost anything seemed possible in Toronto. The TTU, largely because of its wise political strategy, had just won major concessions not only from its recent major enemy, the *Mail*, but also from its ancient antagonist, George Brown's *Globe*. One suspects that the reality of class politics in Toronto, which accompanied the rise of the Knights of Labor, must have caused considerable discomfort for the spirit of the assassinated Grit leader.

12

1886–1887: a year of challenge

The Local Assemblies of the Knights of Labor, counted by the thousands, furnish the wage-workers of the continent with opportunities of association and advancement never before enjoyed. From Maine to California, from Canada to the Gulf, in all the states and territories, in the lumber regions and in the mines, amidst the fluff of the textile industries, amidst the din of the iron hammer, in workshop and store, wherever men and women are congregated – in the village and upon the plantation – the Knights of Labor are marching on to ultimate victory.
George McNeill

The Howland victory, labour's first major political success, set the tone for the turbulence of 1886. Not since the unrest of 1872 had the Toronto working class been so visible. The organizational surge of the Knights, their victory over the Masseys, and the upheaval of the street-railway strikes, all led to the enthusiastic labour campaigns in the following winter's Ontario and federal elections. *News'* cartoonist S. Hunter captured the spirit of 1886 in his warning to Blake and Macdonald, 'A Political Cold Snap.' *News'* columnists were no less enthusiastic:

The [mayoralty] contest ... has left organized labour in a position far in advance of what it has ever occupied before. Men who, a few weeks ago, were called demagogues, cranks and agitators, are today spoken of as leaders in the cause of labour, and in the future no election calculations will be complete which do not take into consideration the votes of the union workingmen of Toronto ... And this is but the first step ... Let there be no cessation of the good work of organization. Let it not be confined to Toronto alone, but let it spread, as it is doing, over the Province and the Dominion, and the day is not far distant when labor will secure its rights, and when its voice will be felt in national as well as in municipal affairs.[1]

The *News* had correctly identified the approaching political battles.

The *Mail*'s February concession to the Toronto Typographical Union did little to reassure Tory strategies. Tory bagman Alfred Boultbee expressed continued concern to Macdonald that spring:

Since you spoke to me about Toronto I have been investigating matters here very carefully and think I now understand the situation. When I last talked to you on the subject I think I expressed the opinion that the whole situation was bad but that East Toronto was possibly allright and capable of being carried by Small, now I feel satisfied that he cannot get the nomination except subject to such a split as will render a loss of the constituency.[2]

Boultbee suggested one possible solution: convince Mayor Howland to run as a Tory candidate. If they could do so, they would 'have his influence in the other divisions with the labour vote.' If they failed and he ran for the Grits, however, 'we might possibly lose all three seats.'[3] Such was one Tory politico's appraisal of the impact of the 1886 surge. (Howland later refused both parties.[4])

Frank Smith's unpopularity with Toronto workers caused even further distress. In the wake of the street-railway struggle, A.W. Wright, another Tory who kept a close eye on the labour front, arrived on the scene. After a short sojourn as secretary of the Canadian Manufacturers' Association, Wright quickly identified himself with elements in the Knights of Labor who were pushing for a district assembly in Toronto. O'Donoghue 'personally opposed it' for, as he wrote to Powderly:

I dread interference with the usefulness of the Trades Council. Men may reach the DA whose presence on the TTLC would not be acceptable and not without good reason. We have men who *appear* to be good Knights but we never knew them to be good trade *unionists*, so that these people do not win the utmost confidence of Jury, March, myself and others as yet.[5]

O'Donoghue and his friends in Local 2305 pushed for a provincial assembly instead. O'Donoghue argued:

To checkmate the 'District' movement March, Jury and myself have set about forming a Provincial Assembly. This will, or at least may, enable us to do more than is now being accomplished in the way of the enactment of laws by our legislatures. Up to date, and for years, Toronto stood the whole cost – does still, of such work. It is time those of other localities 'put up' a little in the cause. The District 'racket' was being worked with the object of killing our trades council, which has too many old and tried trades unionists. You tumble.[6]

Only a few weeks later, O'Donoghue asked Powderly to send a circular letter to the Knights in Ontario calling for a referendum on a provincial assembly. This would 'obviate a District in Toronto,' would compel all parts of the order to pay their share of lobbying costs, and, most importantly, would 'prevent the local big frogs from having a little puddle of their own to wallow in.'[7] Powderly refused to play O'Donoghue's game and 'the boys from 2305' lost this battle when an application for district assembly status arrived in Philadelphia in March. O'Donoghue sought Powderly's intervention one last time:

In the interest of the Order, and at the urgent request of Jury and March, *do not allow* this Charter to be granted. Some of the locals loudest for the charter are only in existence some one or two months. Several politicians – municipal and parliamentary – have crept into one or two of the mixed assemblies and the object is to disintegrate the Trades and Labor Council which is obnoxious to one of the political parties – the Tory. Of course a District would soon clash as to jurisdiction and then would come trouble with the several international unions represented in the council.[8]

Powderly did nothing, and on 17 May 1886, at the height of the street-railway struggle, Toronto became District Assembly 125. O'Donoghue's fears proved well founded; the unanimity that had existed between the Knights and the TTLC was to break down in 1887 and those who, to O'Donoghue, only appeared to be 'good Knights' were to gain a foothold in the organization through the assembly. These men, of whom Wright was the most prominent, used the assembly as a base from which to challenge O'Donoghue and 'the boys from 2305' for dominance.

The Knights' surge in spring 1886 invited even more partisan attention. The old parties seemed frightened of the emergence of an independent political working-class movement. A.W. Wright, for example, during the second street-railway strike, warned Macdonald that unless Smith settled it,

The effect on the Conservative Party not only in Toronto but wherever the Knights of Labor and trades unions are organized will be this. If the fight is kept up the Grit wirepullers will be able to get them pledged to oppose all candidates who support the government of which Mr. Smith is a member ... If for any reason the men are beaten the feeling will only be intensified. The Conservatives who are in the Order are powerless to prevent this as the weapon placed in the hands of the Grits is too strong.[9]

Wright also reminded Macdonald that in September, the TTLC had called another congress. Belabouring the obvious, Wright added that, 'D.J. O'Donoghue will be a leading spirit and I need hardly say that the opportunity to make Grit campaign ammunition will not be neglected.'[10]

One hundred and ten delegates, the largest number at any national congress in this period, attended the second TLC meeting in Toronto in September. The predicted Grit manipulation, however, was not so evident. The motions passed in 1886 did not differ substantially from those of the 1883 congress. The Tory government certainly could take no solace in the congress resolutions, but this had been true in 1883 as well. The overt political motions, all in support of independent working-class political activity, were almost identical in wording to those of 1883:

... the working classes of this Dominion will never be properly represented in Parliament or receive justice in the legislation of this country until they are represented by men of their own class and opinion, and the members of this congress pledge themselves to use their utmost endeavours to bring out candidates at the ensuing local and Dominion elections in the constituencies in which they reside.[11]

A committee report on practical political action led to a considerable debate. Wright offered an amendment stipulating that wherever there were no labour candidate's in the race, organized workers should vote as a block for candidates pledged to carry out the policies of the congress. This debate saw O'Donoghue come to the amendment's defence, when W.H. Bews, the former editor of the Toronto *Palladium of Labor*, attacked the record of H.B. Witton, Hamilton's Tory-Labour MP in the early 1870s. O'Donoghue joined with Wright and the vast majority of the delegates in endorsing the policy of supporting workingmen's friends in ridings where no independent candidates were running.[12]

The only significant, potentially divisive issue that surfaced at this congress arose on the last day when an embarrassingly frank motion was tabled without recorded debate. This motion deplored 'the dissension which seems to exist between Knights of Labor and trade unions, [blaming it on] the arbitrary action of a few leaders.' With an overwhelming majority of Knights at this congress (85 of 110 delegates), it certainly could have been passed.[13] O'Donoghue and the Knights' leaders, however, sought solidarity in 1886, not potentially divisive resolutions.[14]

Although Tory strategy for the coming elections did not include concessions to the Knights of Labor in the street-railway strike as recommended
by Wright, Macdonald had a different scheme up his sleeve. In summer
1886, he decided that a royal commission on labour would serve a number
of useful functions: first, it would buy his government time by placing a
lengthy investigation in the way of labour's immediate legislative demands;
second, it would stand as evidence of the Tory government's continued
interest in the problems of Canadian workers; and third, it would provide
the party's formerly faithful trade-unionists with patronage appointments
that might ensure their support in the forthcoming campaigns. Thus was
born the Royal Commission on the Relations of Labor and Capital.[15]

Discussions concerning the two Toronto appointments to the commission made clear the immediate electoral aims of Macdonald's scheme.
Toronto MPP H.E. Clarke played a key role in choosing the local commissioners. In a letter to Macdonald promoting Sam Heakes and John
Armstrong, who were subsequently named to the commission, Clarke
pointed out that the commission 'would help very considerably at the next
election.' He then articulated the Tory quandary:

We want the workingmen who are gradually drifting away from us, and to get them,
and keep them, it will be necessary to give much prominence to the planks they
favour ... I take it the report would favour the National Policy. It would also most
likely recommend some mode of arbitration for trade disputes which would be
immensely popular with workingmen everywhere.

He went on in a similar vein to recommend the abolition of tax exemptions
('very popular with nearly all classes') and an end to 'the large expenditure
on immigration.'[16] Clearly the Tories were listening to labour's message.

In this same letter, Clarke warned Macdonald that he did not 'think too
much care can be exercised in the formation of this commission, [since it
would] be subject to severe criticism by Tories, Grits, and workingmen.'
Unfortunately for the prime minister, Clarke's nominations were less than
astute, despite his caution. He first chose Armstrong, a highly respected
and popular Toronto union leader who, although a Tory, had proved his
labour credentials by campaigning for John Carter against Clarke in the
1883 provincial election. He had also served the party well by arranging the
TTU's acceptance of the *Mail*'s surrender in early 1886. Clarke erred badly,
however, in bypassing Sam McNab, recommended by the Toronto Knights
of Labor. Rejected for working against Tory MP Clarke Wallace in York
West, McNab would have been far more acceptable to Toronto workers
than Clarke's choice, Sam Heakes.[17]

Presentation of the Workingmen's Testimonial to Lady Macdonald (*Canadian Illustrated News*)

The Workingmen's Reception of Mackenzie (*Canadian Illustrated News*)

Sir John A. Macdonald Addressing the People (*Canadian Illustrated News*)

Sunday Preaching in Queen's Park (*Canadian Illustrated News*)

OLD TO-MORROW ABROAD.

'Old To-morrow Abroad': 'SIR JOHN (*to workingmen's and Chinese representatives*), – Grievances on both sides, hey? Well, put 'em into these famous pigeon
holes, and I'll give 'em my consideration.' (*Grip* 1886)

Howland, supported by the Knights of Labor, trounces Blain in the 1887 mayoralty
election (*Grip* 1887)

LABOR
DAY
SOUVENIR

ISSUED BY THE UNION LABEL LEAGUE OF TORONTO 1896

'Division of Labor' (*Grip* 1886)

Sir John A. Macdonald threatens to drop Frank Smith during the street railway
strike (*Grip* 1886)

The labour press immediately attacked Heake's appointment. Even Wright and O'Donoghue agreed on this issue, and both the *Canadian Labor Reformer* and the *Labor Record* roundly denounced Heakes.[18] Initially, opposition focused on Heakes' use of shady credentials at the recent TLC meeting, but later his appearance in support of Tory candidates in the winter provincial election became the major issue. The political advantage gained by appointing the commission were certainly offset by the choice of Sam 'Sneakes,' his nomenclature in the labour press. Macdonald's refusal to withdraw the appointment infuriated Toronto labour leaders, and subsequently both the TTLC and District Assembly 125 refused to testify before the commission when it visited Toronto in fall 1887.[19]

Tory concerns about the working-class vote became even more evident in winter 1886 when Mowat finally called the expected provincial election. In the usual discussion of suitable candidates, F.D. Barwick, Toronto Tory party chairman, recommended Clarke and foundry owner Edward Gurney to Macdonald, 'because they are both trade and labour supporters.' How these two manufacturers, especially the latter with his history of bitter struggles with the moulders, could be considered labour supporters is not clear. Barwick simultaneously reminded Macdonald of Mowat's clever electoral ploy: 'You will remember that Mr. Mowat gerrymandered Toronto so that an elector can only vote for two candidates and the whole city has become one constituency. So that in any event the Reformers will get one member.'[20] The incumbent Tory MPP for Toronto East, Alexander Morris, wrote in the same vein:

The position is one of difficulty – Toronto is now one constituency embracing in addition to the old East, Centre and West, Parkdale, Yorkville, Brockton and St. Matthews Ward – electing three members but each elector only casting two votes. How it will work nobody can tell – there will be regular party candidates, perhaps two on each side, and possibly Labour and Temperance candidates.

He also thought the Tories would win two seats at best but refused to seek re-election himself.[21] The nomination for his seat was not made until late November, when the Tories followed Barwick's general advice, but chose E.F. Clarke, ITU member and Orange leader, to run with H.E. Clarke.[22] The *World* immediately dubbed them 'Sentinel' Clarke and 'Saratoga' Clarke, respectively – the former after his Orange newspaper, the latter for his trunk factory.[23] Both Clarkes wrote Macdonald in early December requesting that he finalize his appointments to the Royal Commission since it would 'help us very much in the local contest.'[24] Both

Clarkes also sought his permission to use Heakes and Armstrong on the stump during the campaign. 'They are willing,' the Clarkes noted, but demanded permission from Macdonald.[25]

The Tory nomination of their first Toronto workingman, and the party's willingness to risk the impartial façade of their Labour Commissioners were both further evidence of its extreme concern about the workers' political initiative. John Armstrong, faithful to his labour roots, did not campaign in Toronto for the Tories but instead supported the labour candidates.[26]

Toronto labour had been preparing for the next elections since the Howland mayoralty victory of the previous winter. The *Palladium of Labor* greeted that 'splendid victory' by announcing that 'the Labor Reform faction in politics has come to stay.' 'No temporary splurge,' the major task was to build toward the coming provincial and federal elections.[27] The *Labor Record* and the *Canadian Labor Reformer* promoted the forthcoming labour candidates throughout the summer of 1886. When Mowat issued the election call in late October, the TTLC passed O'Donoghue's motion to form a committee which would meet with District Assembly 125 to discuss a call for a labour nominating convention.[28]

The preliminary closed meeting on 12 November was chaired by labour reformer Phillips Thompson, with Robert Glockling as secretary. After the meeting ended, the joint committee reported that a nominating convention would be held on 30 November, that all union and local assembly delegates would need official credentials, and that representation would be one delegate for 100 members or less, and a delegate for each additional 100 members.[29] The only note of discord was the joint committee's failure to agree on a satisfactory committee to work on a detailed platform based on the recent TLC convention resolutions.[30]

Approximately 80 voting delegates attended the nominating convention at Richmond Hall, which was chaired by printer J.H. Lumsden.[31] After deciding to nominate candidates for both the federal and provincial elections, the delegates proceeded to accept the TLC resolutions as the platform for both campaigns. The only significant debate of the evening revolved around the number of candidates to nominate in the peculiar provincial electoral arrangement in Toronto. A number of delegates favoured only one candidate, but O'Donoghue and Jury spoke strongly in favour of two candidates, arguing that with almost 10,000 workers represented at the meeting, surely they could elect two labour members. They won the argument and the convention then proceeded to nominate two Knights, John Roney and Charles March. The other contestants ran weakly: J.S.

Williams won a high of 18 on all four ballots and John Carter won a high of 10 in the first four ballots.[32] The federal nominations followed. E.E. Sheppard, editor of the *News*, narrowly defeated Alf Jury (41 to 38) for the West Toronto nomination. Jury was then acclaimed as the East Toronto candidate, after John S. Dance refused to stand. It was also decided not to nominate a labour candidate in Centre Toronto.[33] In effect, the 1883 pattern, by which Toronto workers nominated one Tory (Heakes) and one Grit (Carter) as their standard-bearers, had been broken. There is no clear indication in the press as to whether this was intentional or rather a reflection of the balance in the convention. In either case, Roney and Sheppard had, at best, loose populist Tory ties, whereas March and Jury were self-acknowledged Grits. Tory workingmen might well have trouble with this arrangement.

One week later, the labour troops again gathered in Temperance Hall. This mass meeting enthusiastically endorsed the nominees and heard speeches from the candidates. As in 1883, the meeting also saw numerous well-known partisan labourites appear on the platform to demonstrate their open support for the labour ticket. Wright, O'Donoghue, and others spoke in support of the labour candidates and gave notice that they were suspending their party allegiances, at least for the term of the election. The meeting also organized a network of ward committees to work for labour and to help get out the vote on election day.[34] The spirited and enthusiastic crowd chanted constantly throughout the evening under the leadership of 'a little man with a big voice' who cried persistently, 'Whoop'er up, boys.' 'Whoop'er up' became the labour campaign's slogan.[35]

The next night the TTLC voted in $250 to defray campaign expenses.[36] The labour campaign certainly benefited from the experiences of 1883; the organization was far more extensive, focused on ward work, and held many small meetings throughout the city. There was only one monster Saturday-night rally toward the end of the campaign, which included a torchlight parade with numerous bands and banners from each ward association, with slogans such as 'No Sectarianism,' 'We Work and Win,' 'Down with Monopoly,' 'Just Laws,' 'Equal Representation.' The men marched in factory and union groups, and there were especially strong contingents from the Massey Works and from the Knights' Boxmakers Assembly, which carried a tombstone inscribed 'In memory of the late Liberal Conservative and Reform Parties. Died December 28, 1886,' and a box labelled 'All party prejudices securely closed and nailed down in this box.'[37]

The procession culminated in a mass meeting in Shaftesbury Hall, which had been filled long before the arrival of the marchers. The overflow crowd heard speeches from Jury, March, Roney, Sheppard, and from guests Garson and J.T. Carey of St Catharines. Garson, the Knights of Labor candidate in Lincoln, emphasized that he and Carey represented Orange and Green, respectively. Success in Toronto, he continued, depended on the workers' ability to work together and avoid the pitfalls of sectarianism. The meeting ended with the unanimous passage of a resolution condemning 'the efforts of certain sections of the press in Ontario to set creed against creed by appealing to the prejudices of religious bigotry.'[38]

Charges of bigotry echoed through the campaign. The Tory forces played sectarianism for full value in Toronto. The *Mail* focused not on the great success of the national policy as previously, but instead directed its major attack against Mowat's supposed educational concessions to Roman Catholics.[39] How effective this was in Toronto is difficult to evaluate, but the labour candidates spent much of their time denouncing sectarianism and emphasizing class issues. Jury, for example, explained early in the campaign:

Every means would be taken by the two political parties to divide the workingmen. In their trade societies the workingmen stood together, irrespective of creed or nationality, and to succeed now they would require to do the same thing in respect to politics. National and sectarian cries were introduced by politicians for the mere purpose of keeping workingmen from being united. If they stood true to each other there was nothing to prevent them from attaining success, and thereby placing the working classes in a position they never occupied before.[40]

The campaign speeches of 'Saratoga' and 'Sentinel' Clarke and of their major labour supporter Sam Heakes, however, did not replicate the *Mail*'s sectarian strategy. Indeed, Heakes' major role was constantly to represent E.F. Clarke as a legitimate workingman's candidate. Clarke's ITU connection and his arrest during the printers' strike of 1872 appeared in absolutely every campaign speech. Heakes described Ned Clarke as a 'man who worked for the masses ... the very embodiment of the labour movement.' Heakes also spoke of his own independent labour candidacy in 1883, accusing Grits in the labour council of abandoning him in that race. More specifically, he accused Thomas Moor, then TTLC president, of offering him the Liberal nomination if he would guarantee to support the Mowat government. Heakes refused and thus lost the support of the Grit labourites.[41] He offered no substantiation of these charges; Moor emphatically denied them, wondering why these charges had not been made in 1883.

Moor also suggested that it had been clever politics on his and some friends' part to convince the Reform party not to oppose Carter. Why, he asked, had not Heakes done the same with the Tories?[42] Although this begged the question of labour men's partisan attachments, it satisfied most labour supporters.

Meanwhile Heakes, himself, became a significant issue in the campaign, and the TTLC debated his actions. After a heated discussion the council, by a vote of 27 to 10, expressed:

its total want of confidence in the usefulness and impartiality of the Labour Commission recently appointed by the Dominion Government, and recommend that all members of labour organizations throughout Canada decline giving any evidence before the same, while the name and person of Samuel R. Heakes is continued thereon, and that a certified copy of this resolution be forwarded to Sir John Macdonald.[43]

District Assembly 125 passed a similar motion of denunciation:

We as workingmen cannot view with anything but contempt the action of Mr. Samuel Heakes in taking the public platform in favor of party nominees, in company with an unfair scab printer [W. Joyce?], and therefore repudiate him as a fair representative, and unfit to represent the best interests of the working classes of this city on the Labor Commission, and so call upon the Dominion Government to recall him from the same.[44]

The *Canadian Labor Reformer* had earlier commented that the Tories were 'welcome to such a recreant; ... the Labor Party wanted no such traitors in its camp.'[45] Wherever Heakes spoke throughout the campaign, he met with unmerciful heckling.[46] This reached a peak at a Tory meeting in Parkdale which was disrupted by labour supporters who, after hearing speeches by Jury and others outside the Tory hall, marched through the town singing 'We'll hang Sam Sneakes on a Sour Apple Tree.'[47] Not all the attacks on Heakes were so good-natured. 'Don' (E.E. Sheppard) dismissed him in the *News* as a 'Judas Iscariot.' Sheppard also argued that although 'designated a "commissioner" [he was] utilized as a spy.' Finally Sheppard accused the Tories of 'travelling Sneakes as a purchase' to prove that a former labour candidate could be bought. Thus 'the workingmen, seeing how low a point this man has sunk, will believe that every man may sink to the same low level.'[48]

Meanwhile the Grits, quietly pursuing their own strategy, had nominated only one candidate in Toronto, John Leys. This had necessitated a vigorous debate at the Reform convention, where 'boss' J.D. Edgar had had to fight hard to convince the delegates not to oppose March. Grit workingmen, such as Thomas Moor, had endorsed Edgar's strategy. Although opposed by some, Edgar's strategy prevailed and the Grits fought the campaign with only one candidate.[49]

On election night, 'Sentinel' and 'Saratoga' Clarke topped the poll, in that order, and John Leys, the single Reform candidate, finished third. March ran a strong fourth for labour, and Roney finished fifth. The results demonstrated two interesting new political facts. First, Mowat had indeed gerrymandered Toronto in such an effective way that even though the Liberal vote dropped from 1883, they still won a seat. John Leys took only 36 per cent of the total vote in 1886 – but won a seat nevertheless – whereas in 1883 he had lost with 45 per cent. Second, the labour vote had definitely increased in the three years. Although March did not come as close to victory as Carter had in 1883, the labour vote was considerably improved. In a five-way race, March took 27 per cent of the total vote and Roney took 23 per cent. March's vote can be partially dismissed, since he undoubtedly picked up Reform votes, but it is quite clear that the independent labour vote, which in 1883 had delivered only 7 per cent of the vote to Heakes in a three-way race, now gave Roney a vastly improved 23 per cent. If taken as a base figure for labour votes, this would account for most of March's count as well.[50]

The candidates also assessed the election results. In a speech to his supporters on election night, E.F. 'Sentinel' Clarke noted that

He was indebted to the working classes for standing so nobly by him. The result of the election was the best possible evidence to him that the great majority of them had not been led away from their allegiance to the party whose policy, in his humble judgement was most conducive to their interests. He hoped the election was only the precursor of the greater victory to be achieved for the defence of the National Policy when the Dominion elections came on.[51]

Clarke, who had basically campaigned as a Tory-Labour candidate, finished well ahead of his mate, H.E. 'Saratoga' Clarke, who had had the advantage of incumbency.

Labour response was predictably more mixed. O'Donoghue commented bitterly on election night that March and Roney had not been defeated by the two old parties but 'by the apathy of the workingmen.' Irish Land Leaguer and Knight Brian Lynch described his extreme disappointment but attributed the defeat to 'lack of knowledge of organization and political tactics.' However, Jury and Sheppard, the nominees for the upcoming federal election, both found the results encouraging. Jury compared the results favourably to those of 1883, and Sheppard noted that 4,000 labour votes could not be dismissed. Jury also suggested that 'the lesson they had learned from the day's work was the necessity of a standard organization ... They should establish the Workingman's Political Party.'[52] Meanwhile Sheppard, in a *News* editorial, pointed to the 'tremendous odds they were fighting against, [namely] party and sectarian prejudices, old time associations, and the power of the machines.' Moreover, their candidacies had forced excellent nominations on the old parties, especially E.F. Clarke. Finally, labour must learn from the defeat, for 'it is precisely by such experiences that new political parties, like undisciplined soldiers, learn by degree the art of veterans.'[53]

March and Roney, the defeated candidates, both pledged themselves to work hard in the coming federal campaign. The general consensus then, even in their immediate disappointment, was to look to the next election. Wright took a similar position, but also noted the continuing strength of partyism:

We have learned that the Labour movement cannot expect support from either Tories or Grits, as such. In order to win them we must convert them to our principles and take them out of the rank of parties ... The elections have taught us that the principles of Labour Reform have only to be fairly and with reasonable ability placed before the people ... to secure the support of a large number.

He too called for a more thorough and systematic political organization.[54]

O'Donoghue, after further reflection on the election, came to a similar analysis. In his report to the TTLC, he noted not only the London, Hamilton, and Toronto defeats, but also Garson's Lincoln victory. The lesson was simple – the labour party must work harder in the future. Full manhood suffrage had become an absolute necessity and should be made the highest lobbying priority. At the next TTLC meeting, the Legislative Council called on all council members to work actively in the Jury and Sheppard campaigns.[55]

Only one week after the provincial election, Toronto voters went to the polls to elect a new city council. Labour, which had been busily involved in the provincial campaign, played a less prominent role than it had in the previous municipal contest. Nevertheless, it helped re-elect Mayor Howland, who had defended labour faithfully against both the Masseys and

Frank Smith's Toronto Street Railway Company. He returned to office with a smashing victory over former York West Liberal MP David Blain, whom the *World* promoted strongly as pro-labour because of his role in supporting the Brotherhood of Locomotive Engineers in the 1877 Commons debate which followed the Grand Trunk Strike.[56] Although the TTLC had decided against over-extending itself and therefore refused to recommend local candidates, the Knights of Labor and the *News* had supported Howland. The TTLC position undoubtedly reflected the prevailing peace between the TTU and the Tory party. Blain was clearly the approved candidate and received support from Tory working-class figures such as Williams.[57] The Knights, however, put out for Howland; not only did District Assembly 125 endorse his candidature but District Master Workman Sam McNab published he following letter in the *News* on the day before the election:

Fellow workingmen: Who are you going to vote for? For W.H. Howland, the man who has stayed by us through thick and thin all the year round; the man who helped us to fight and win; the man whom none of us ever went to look for without finding him ... or Mr. Blain, the President of a bank that would not open an account with the Knights of Labor ... ; Mr. Blain, the intimate and particular friend of Frank Smith, our avowed enemy ... P.S. – I have questioned Mayor Howland, and he assures me that he voted for March and Roney in the late elections.[58]

Given that endorsement, Howland not only won a smashing victory with an increased majority, but did so with what the opposing *World* called 'nearly the whole of the labour vote.'[59] Moreover, there was a noticeable decline in 'old-guard' fortunes in the 1887 alderman races, and labour favourites such as aldermen Hunter and McMillan were returned while four Howland enemies went down to defeat. Labour had a friend in the mayor's chair for another year,[60] and McNab appeared at the Howland victory celebration 'to whoop-er up.'[61]

Labour's attention quickly switched to the long-expected federal election, which Macdonald finally called in mid-January. Tory politicos were somewhat apprehensive about their chances; Toronto brewer Eugene O'Keefe wrote Macdonald: 'The labour vote is the one I most dread, as it goes in chunks, and can't be depended on.'[62] The campaign proceeded much along the lines of the provincial contest. The labour party held frequent meetings in both ridings, and its platforms were sprinkled with Toronto labour leaders of both parties. March and Roney repaid the speaking efforts of Jury and Sheppard, appearing often throughout the contest. O'Donoghue, Wright, Armstrong, Moor, Thompson, and various other TTLC and Knights figures also loaned their oratorical talents to the labour candidates.

The Tories again emphasized the national policy in this campaign. Their new Toronto paper, *The Daily Standard*,[63] printed an open letter to workingmen:

Every workingman knows that in almost every town and village in Canada new establishments, and in some instances new industries, have sprung up since the adoption of the National Policy, and because of its adoption ... To say that this doesn't mean an increase for labour is to insult the intelligence of the people. To say that the tendency of such an increased demand is not to raise the price of labour – wages – is to fly in the face of a well understood law.[64]

Lest this seem to deny any role to labour, the writer quickly pointed out that 'workingmen must depend largely on themselves, and on their own combined efforts to obtain increases of wages.' Workers had to struggle to ensure that they benefited from the national policy. But if manufacturers' business was bad, as it would be without protection, then 'no efforts on the part of his employees to obtain an increase would be successful.' In the eyes of *The Daily Standard*, the main question in the 1887 campaign for workers was, 'Shall the National Policy be continued or abandoned?'[65]

In Toronto, the Reform party ran no candidates against labour in 1887. This decision followed Blake's general campaign strategy, which focused heavily on attempting to win the working-class vote. He had appeared on a Toronto stage with Powderly during the Knights leader's 1886 Toronto visit, and the Liberal platform leaned heavily to labour-reform proposals. O'Donoghue, although hardly an objective observer, enthusiastically claimed that 'Blake virtually accepts and adopts the Platform of the Order.'[66] Blake's 1887 campaign speeches supported the thrust of O'Donoghue's assertion. In election meetings through Ontario's industrial belt, Blake appealed openly for the Knights of Labor vote. In Toronto he claimed credit for his 1870s labour legislation, explained his modified views on the tariff question ('Manufacturers have nothing to fear'), attacked Macdonald's immigration policy, called for the abolition of assisted passages, attacked combinations and price fixing, supported higher taxes on the rich, denounced the CPR monopoly, and promised an arbitration scheme.[67] Later, in a speech to the Knights of Labor in Welland, he also called for protective dominion factory legislation. Additional speeches in Deseronto, Belleville, and Hamilton reiterated these themes, promised an end to Chinese immigration, and denied Macdonald's version of the 1872 events which the Tories were again unearthing in their perennial quest for the working-class vote.[68]

In East Toronto a few of the local Liberals refused to abide by the party's decision not to oppose the labour ticket. At a stormy nomination meeting, the party leaders were able to get majority agreement not to run a candidate against Jury but were unable to pass a motion supporting him.[69] A Liberal splinter group later nominated Alderman E.A. Macdonald to oppose Jury without party endorsement. Among Macdonald's supporters, J.J. Withrow, apparently still smarting from his 1883 defeat by labour, was especially prominent.

The campaign saw none of the enthusiastic mass meetings of the December election. The Labour party held by far the most meetings, whereas the Tories avoided all public discussion:

The contest in the city is beginning to wax warm, but none except the Labor Party seem to have much liking for public discussion ... Col. Denison is conducting his campaign as if he were on a sort of secret diplomatic mission up the Nile ... Mr. Small also doesn't appear to cotton to public meetings, either his own or his opponents. He seems to fancy that if the electors don't find out that he is running he may get in.[70]

The two labour candidates made strong bids for the seats. Sheppard took 47 per cent of the vote in his two-way race with Denison, although Jury won only 35 per cent in the battle in East Toronto.[71] Yet this time the results were extemely disappointing to labour supporters:

There was a good deal of surprise and even indignation expressed by the supporters of the labour candidates at the comparatively poor showing made by them. It was evidently felt that a real combination of the Labour and Reform vote should have totalled up more strikingly ... The opinion which received most acceptance was that the Conservative workingmen had gone back on candidates who showed such decidedly Liberal leanings as the Labour candidates in East and West Toronto.[72]

Tory workingmen were certainly much in evidence in the rhetoric of the victory celebrations. Denison credited his victory 'to the Conservative workingmen of West Toronto, [promising that] he would not forget it.' E.F. Clarke and Louis Kribs both added their thanks for the Tory workingmen's votes that they had both worked so hard to deliver. In East Toronto, where J.S. Williams had been the returning officer, Sam Heakes made a similar speech.[73] Apparently, Clarke and Heakes had helped deliver the Tory working-class vote, preventing its full flight from the national policy.

The *Mail* provided an interesting post mortem on the election from its new position above the party fray:

it is not difficult to understand why the labour candidates in Toronto failed. There was really a combination of circumstances against them. As labour men they had not a policy sufficiently definite to warrant workingmen who differed from them on general political issues to come to their support. In addition their alliance with the Liberals, though it was better for them than an independent candidature, drove Conservatives from them, while it failed to attract the full Liberal strength. The lesson of the contest is that workingmen after all will not sever old party ties for the sake of electing men whose only claim upon their support is that they, too, are workmen.[74]

O'Donoghue, not surprisingly, saw events differently. He had written Powderly before the vote: 'Those who defeated March for being a Catholic will work to defeat Jury as being an agnostic. One believed *too much* and the other *does not believe enough* for the Liberal minded and highly educated Orangemen and bigots of Toronto.[75] After the campaign, he believed his earlier remarks to be prophetic: 'But Jury is a *Secularist* and because of this our Protestant *Christians* would not nor did not vote for him when we "ran him" for the House of Commons. But I am proud to say that *every Catholic* voted for him even to the priests. Brother Jury, though an Englishman is an honest Home Ruler and the "Micks" don't forget the fact.'[76] As usual O'Donoghue saw only the blindness and bigotry of the Tory voters. No matter how sincere a labour reformer he was, O'Donoghue failed to understand that his, Jury's, and March's close ties with the Liberal party were extremely suspect to Tory workers and thus equally damaging to independent labour-reform politics. O'Donoghue saw only Tory plots; Wright, in contrast, saw only Grit conspiracies. This battle, which they had partially laid aside during the 1886 and 1887 campaigns, re-emerged triumphant in the bitter aftermath of the electoral defeats.

Thus ended the 1886–87 independent labour campaigns. Labour supporter Howland retained the mayor's chair but clearly with the support of a reform coalition of which labour was, at best, one component. The provincial and federal campaigns had not gone well and beneath the façade of labour independence, party feelings still burned. Nevertheless, despite the electoral failures, labour had emerged in 1886–87 as one of the most potent political forces in Toronto. All politicians, all businessmen recognized that no longer could the workers be taken for granted. The struggle towards a class identity which transcended party, sect, and ethnicity had not totally triumphed in Toronto but positive steps had been taken. Moreover, it had also become clear that a militant labour base could prevent trade-union leaders from the easy partyism of the earlier period. Sam 'Sneakes,' for example, never again held a trade-union position in Toronto. Nevertheless, were the militant base to weaken, partyism still had much to offer.

13

Partyism ascendant

I will speak of them as the three prejudices. The first I would refer to is that of Party ... as soon as we help the old parties to power they laugh at our simplicity and we richly deserve our reward. The second is that of religious differences and this I consider the most despicable and unworthy of all ... The third and last element of dissension is race prejudice ... These three then – race, religious and political prejudices – are the prime elements of discord in our ranks.
'Niger,' Toronto letter, *Iron Molders Journal*, 31 January 1887

The year 1887 had not started well for Toronto labour. The electoral defeats led to a round of acrimonious wrangling in which all the participants lost. The immediate issue was the interpretation of the election. A.W. Wright's *Canadian Labor Reformer* argued that the Toronto and Hamilton results made clear that Grit voters had abandoned labour. This point was debatable, but the editorial then attacked D.J. O'Donoghue, Thomas Moor, and John Armstrong for taking the stump for the old-line parties during the campaign, especially since some of them (read O'Donoghue and Moor) had earlier attacked Sam Heakes for precisely the same offense.[1]

In the following issue of the *Reformer*, both Armstrong and O'Donoghue responded to the charges. Armstrong wrote a carefully phrased account of his actions, defending himself on the grounds that he spoke only in two constituencies where there were no labour candidates, and that he attempted to vindicate his character after a fellow Knight attacked him in the press. The *Reformer's* editor reprimanded him mildly, suggesting that he should have made use of the Knights' court to defend his character.[2] O'Donoghue, in contrast, was outraged. He termed the editorial 'intentionally impertinent and grossly insulting,' demanding to know 'by what authority does A.W. Wright call upon me for explanations?'[3] The *Reformer* then denied Wright's authorship and again demanded an explanation from O'Donoghue in the name of the labour condidates whose chances he had impaired. What they received was another vituperative attack on Wright. After citing his long experience in the labour movement, O'Donoghue commented:

During all these years I have met, more than once, with the sometimes open and other times covert hostility of a class of transparent frauds – cunning, conniving and unscrupulous fellows – who had floated into the ranks of organized labour for every purpose other than that of doing an honest part in practically improving the general condition of the working classes.

He admitted speaking in Lincoln for the Liberals but denied that there was any reason why he should have refrained from doing so, since Garson was a Liberal labour candidate. Finally, he reviewed Wright's own career and suggested that he was simply a Tory sojourner in the working-class movement. As evidence he cited Wright's candidacy in the December Ontario election in Lambton where, although nominated by the Knights, he appeared on a platform with John A. Macdonald and was named the Conservative candidate by the *Mail*. O'Donoghue also accused Wright of trying to manipulate trade-unionists to gain the Tory nomination in Centre Toronto in the recent federal election.[4]

Wright responded in kind, and the fight went on for a few additional rounds. Little new evidence emerged, but the hostility mounted.[5] What was accomplished by this public mud-slinging? The accusations of political intrigue probably did not surprise Toronto workers, since these and similar charges had been appearing in the party papers for years. Rumours and allegations in the party press were not the same, however, as a vicious dispute in the labour press in which two of Toronto's most prominent working-class leaders provided concrete evidence to the workers that their previous scepticism about the possibilities of independent labour politics had been only too well founded. Thus the unanimity and new opportunities that had opened up to labour following the remarkable upsurge in 1886 and that had culminated in the enthusiasm and excitement of the 'whoop'er up' campaigns were now being dissipated in a round of senseless partisan accusations.

Nevertheless, the impact of the labour campaigns affected the Ontario Legislature's spring session. Even Wright and O'Donoghue agreed that December's campaigns had resulted in a vastly more responsive House. In addition, the new labour members provided the trade-union movement with an access to power that they had never previously had. O'Donoghue's assessment was enthusiastic:

The session of the legislature closes next week. The Knight members have done well so far – particularly, Brother Garson. He was elected a straight Labour candidate. Ingram, *it is alleged*, used the K. of L. until he got a political *party nomination* and then ignored the labor party and Brother Picard was endorsed by a political party. Be these things as they may, and although *we* of Toronto, Hamilton and London were defeated with *our* candidates, the Labor Party has made its impress in Ontario, as is evidenced by the fact that we have had more weight before the House this session than we ever had before – and more legislation respecting wage earners. [Emphasis in original.]

Never modest, O'Donoghue claimed with some justification that 'even though we are not by any means as well organized as we should be, or will be in time, yet we in Ontario exercise much more influence in the Legislative councils of our Province than do a great majority of our Brothers in the United States.'[6] Any final evaluation of the 1886 and 1887 labour campaigns then is extremely difficult. The failures and subsequent internecine warfare must be weighed against the less obvious legislative gains and the even less tangible evolution of working-class political awareness.

The bitter interpersonal conflict between O'Donoghue and Wright continued throughout 1887. Wright turned his considerable energies to the promotion of an independent Canadian Knights of Labor. The motivation for this nationalist campaign remains unclear, but the intrigues that it engendered certainly further damaged the order's reputation in Canada. O'Donoghue first warned Powderly of his intention in April 1887. As usual he had no trouble in locating the source of the trouble: 'The enemies of the Catholics, the enemies of our Order are again at work trying to get up a severence of our connection with the Order in the u.s. ... You will see by my editorial in the *Record* that we have taken strong ground against such a step.'[7] A few weeks later, he asked Powderly to support Glockling's request for financial assistance from the Knights' General Executive Board for the impoverished District Assembly 125: 'I am more than anxious to be in a position to show that Canada, where deserving, is treated just as would any state of the Union under like circumstances. You know I have no doubts on the matter myself, but I desire to checkmate this 'Independent Order in Canada' movement which is being worked vigorously by some although very quietly.'[8] The District Assembly did not receive financial assistance, however, and the campaign for a separate Canadian general assembly continued. The issue surfaced in a *Journal of United Labor* letter from a Tilsonburg Knight:

The all-absorbing topic of discussion here is, of course, 'Home Rule', or the formation of a Provincial Assembly, partaking of the nature of a State Assembly, with a Canadian Executive Board, and for the retention of a certain portion of the funds for legislative purposes, but acting in conjunction and harmony with the General Executive Board. The project is meeting with much favour, and the matter will in all probability come before the GA at Minneapolis in October.[9]

In early September, Master Workman Edward Cannon of Toronto Local 9648 wrote Powderly to complain of the 'painful decrease in membership in D.A. 125.'[10] 'The Order was growing weak in Canada,' he argued one week later, [because of] religious ignorance and feelings, and political speculators.'[11] He was also very worried about 'the program now working in Canada to have a GA for Canada almost independent of the GA of America ... The principal advocate in DA 125 is the editor of the *Canadian Labor Reformer*.' Of Wright, he worried anxiously, 'I hope he is free from selfishness.'[12]

Wright's plans came to fruition in late September, when representatives of Assemblies 61 and 125 met in Toronto to consider the question of Canadian independence. This convention called for the General Assembly or the General Executive Board to appoint a committee to meet with a Canadian committee to arrange for the creation of a dominion assembly, which would be chartered by the General Assembly but would have 'exclusive control over all members within its jurisdiction [and would] collect all moneys, levy all assessments, and distribute all supplies in Canada.' A second set of resolutions sought a Canadian legislative committee equivalent to the Knights Washington committee, a Canadian member in the General Executive Board, and the abolition of compulsory payment of dues to the General Co-operative Board.[13]

When O'Donoghue was informed, he immediately provided Powderly with a version of the events. After denouncing all the participants as 'disguised *traitors* to their obligations,' he singled out Sam McNab, who 'had played a double game throughout. He is desirous of getting on the Executive Board and it suits his purpose to be in a position to point out that dissatisfaction exists in Canada, and that if we had a representative on the Executive Board it would be all right.' The constitutionality of the whole affair was questionable since 'the action was never submitted to all the

Local Assemblies in DA 125. All the Assemblies in Toronto who had the subject *before them in its true light* declared against his attempt at drawing the *national* line.' (Emphasis in original.) The whole affair left O'Donoghue spluttering about 'the crookedness' of the scheme and about the 'emissaries of our political parties who desire to prevent unity in our ranks at political elections.'[14] In addition, O'Donoghue's Local 2305 passed motions condemning the move, as did St Catharines Local 7025.[15]

Forewarned by Cannon and O'Donoghue, Powderly dealt with the Canadian question carefully at the Minneapolis General Assembly. In his annual report he noted the rumours that Canadian members might either seek a separate jurisdiction or even secede from the order. The executive board had not ignored Canada, and indeed, Canadians had managed their affairs so well that the board had fewer calls from them than from 'the smallest state in the Union.' He proposed that two provincial assemblies (equivalent to state assemblies) should be set up instead of a separate general assembly and that a legislative committee for Canada should be named and sent to Ottawa. He concluded assertively: 'In any event there can be but one GA of the Knights of Labor in North America. Every artery and nerve of this organization must work in harmony. There must be no divisions ... the needs of the hour require at our hands an observance of the maxim: We must tolerate each other or else tolerate the common enemy.'[16] Powderly's concessions apparently satisfied the discontended Canadians, and only the provision of a legislative committee was debated, but it passed easily.[17] The rest of the September resolutions made in Toronto were introduced but were allowed to be referred to the executive board without debate, an act which guaranteed their demise.[18]

O'Donoghue was delighted with the results. He commended Powderly highly: 'We desire to thank you from our hearts for the tact displayed by yourself in so nicely and withal justly offsetting the treachery and recreance of those in our midst who contemplated the formation of a Canadian GA.' Moreover, he took heart from this success and re-entered the fray on Wright's home ground by finally accepting his election by local 2305 as a delegate to the District Assembly. Wright, whom he now identified as *'no friend of Powderly* and the actual "head and front" of the secession movement,' would be unhappy with this decision. In addition, O'Donoghue immediately recognized the political importance of a Canadian Knights' legislative committee and pressed Powderly to implement the General Assembly's resolution:

We know by our experience that such a committee is *very necessary*, and if composed of the *right* material, it can accomplish a great deal more in our interest than can be accomplished at Washington, for many of our leading members are *personally* acquainted with our Cabinet Ministers. If the appointment of this Committee has been neglected or not provided for through you or the Executive Board, as per your recommendation, then indeed have we a grievance, and one that will be magnified to the fullest by those who thoughtlessly or otherwise advocated separation.[19] [Emphasis in original.]

O'Donoghue's delight at the new initiative grew at least partially from his experience in Ottawa during the 1887 session. In early June the TTLC Legislative Committee had noted with alarm a bill, introduced by Quebec Tory MP Guillaume Amyot, which would have withdrawn the protection of the Trade Unions Act. Although specifically aimed at the Quebec Ship Laborers' Benevolent Society, O'Donoghue saw the bill as 'a blow at the liberties of the workingmen all over the Dominion, and, if allowed to pass, it would be an act of great injustice.' The council had decided unanimously to send a delegate to Ottawa 'to oppose the Bill by every possible means.'[20]

O'Donoghue rushed to Ottawa to discover that the government had killed Amyot's bill but had introduced a worse proposal in its place. The TTLC denounced the new measure 'as a direct blow to the rights and privileges of organized labour throughout the Dominion.'[21] O'Donoghue had some success in forcing amendments to the modified bill which 'rendered it relatively unobjectionable.' The lesson was clear, however; labour needed permanent representatives in Ottawa.[22]

The General Assembly's proposal then came at a particularly convenient time. O'Donoghue was even more pleased when Powderly turned to him for advice on the choice of members for a Canadian legislative committee. In the best traditions of cabinet selection, a series of letters passed between Scranton and Toronto weighing the possible combinations for the committee. Powderly initially suggested Wright on the ingenious grounds that 'being an enemy I furnish him with work not on the principle that the devil finds work for idle hands but that I find work for the devil to do.' More seriously, Powderly suggested:

If I could even the thing up by putting on a Catholic, an Orangeman, and a person who is not troubled with religious views of any kind it would be to my mind the very best thing that could happen provided of course that they would not annihilate one and other on these grounds. My choice would be Jury as a Liberal man, the others I am not decided on yet.

From O'Donoghue he sought 'a key to all these problems so that I may have a little more knowledge of the situation.'[23]

O'Donoghue, alarmed by Powderly's suggestion of Wright for the delicate Legislative Committee, proposed different work for 'the devil.' Given that District Assembly 125 had already nominated Wright for the job of general lecturer, O'Donoghue suggested that as a far safer appointment to Powderly. He reminded Powderly of Wright's role as 'one of the strongest connivers at securing a *split* in the Order by promoting the scheme for an Independent Order in Canada,' and accused him of being '*Anarchistic* to some degree in his editorials in his paper.' O'Donoghue implored the General Master Workman not to put Wright on the Legislative Committee. He also rejected Sam McNab totally, giving no reason for this judgment, 'as I desire to be charitable.' J.T. Carey of St Catharines was too valuable as the order's organizer of Great Lakes sailors. The Hamilton scene was extremely complicated because of the current war between the two obvious candidates, George Collis and D.R. Gibson. If a choice had to be made, Collis, although a Son of England ('as bad in its own way as Orangeism'), 'would be by far the strongest and best man of the two.' Thus O'Donoghue recommended, if the committee were composed of three men, Jury, Collis, and Redmond (of Montreal); if four, Little of Quebec, Jury, Collis, and March; if the judgment were to be made on quality alone, Jury, March, and Collis. Since the last alternative was unlikely, he also suggested March for Ontario Examining Organizer.[24]

Powderly accepted O'Donoghue's first combination and named Collis, Jury, and Redmond to the committee. He joked, perhaps a little nervously, that 'if they kill themselves on religious grounds they will have to go to different planting grounds.'[25] O'Donoghue, pleased by this vote of confidence in his judgment, assured Powderly that they were 'too sensible to quarrel over religious matters.' However, he also cautioned:

You must not lose sight of the fact, in 'summing up' after the Parliamentary session, that what they have succeeded in doing may not be of a character to enumerate as specific work done, but that the good result of *their presence* and their *influence* must of necessity take time to develop itself. I know from experience that their presence, as duly accredited representatives at Ottawa of our Order will be a *surprising* innovation to those who *know* that there are Assemblies of the Knights of Labor in their constituencies.[26] [Emphasis in original.]

If O'Donoghue and Powderly thought that the naming of this committee would solve all the order's immediate problems in Canada, they were sadly mistaken. Shortly after their selection, the committee members met in Toronto to plan its work. They elected Redmond as secretary and Jury, who was also to attend the parliamentary session in Ottawa, as chairman.

They chose to give priority to a familiar litany of labour demands: the reduction of immigration expenditures, the establishment of a bureau of labour statistics, and dominion factory legislation, workshop regulations, and employers' liability legislation.[27]

Before the month was over, however, protests began to flood in against the method of appointing the committee.[28] St Thomas District Assembly 138 denounced General Master Workman Powderly's failure to consult the Canadian Knights before naming the committee. District Assembly 125 passed a resolution demanding that all Canadian appointments be made only after consultation with the Canadian order.[29] Powderly defended himself, explaining that with no provincial assemblies, he had no formal body to consult.[30] George Collis warned Powderly a week later that the storm was growing.[31] Powderly considered sending a circular letter to the Canadian assemblies defending his choice but decided instead to let the opposition burn itself out.[32] Collis believed that the controversy had familiar roots:

The action of these men show that they have not laid aside their political party leanings when they joined the Knights of Labor. They charge us with being Grits but they are evidently supporters of the present administration ... I am firmly convinced that the whole trouble is caused by supporters of the present administration who have never shown any inclination to introduce any measures of benefit for the toiler.[33]

The decision not to respond succeeded, and Assembly 138, which had led the attack, explained in early March that 'we have no objection to the Brothers whom you appointed and have no sympathy with the politicians' objections that have been raised.'[34] Nevertheless, Powderly had been starkly reminded that the Canadian section of the order could not be treated cavalierly. Perhaps even more important, this episode demonstrated that O'Donoghue's control of the Canadian order was waning. Although no surprise to anyone familiar with Ontario events, Powderly had depended almost totally on O'Donoghue's views of Canadian developments and therefore could not have obtained the total picture. In the future, he would seek advice elsewhere.

Meanwhile, Jury proceeded to Ottawa where he remained for the entire parliamentary session.[35] His activities there suggested the importance of this new lobbying presence. O'Donoghue felt

that the presence there [Ottawa] of Bro. Jury will be of inestimable value to the Labor cause in Canada. He is laying a good foundation for good legislation in the future and credit for which may fall to those who may succeed him ... He is the most indefatigable worker I have ever known. From early morning until the House adjourns, let it be at midnight or in the 'sma wee hours' of the morning, Jury is to be found either in the Press Gallery or in the Library hunting up materials for his purpose.[36]

Although hardly an objective view, one is still struck by the stark contrast with March's comments of only one year before regarding the TLC's episodic lobbying activities: 'Through no fault of your executive of the past year but rather through the want of power to act, they were unable to reflect credit on themselves, or be of any weight in furthering the aims of the body whose officers they were.'[37] March therefore recommended a standing committee on legislation with funds for future lobbying efforts. Accepting his argument, the TLC elected its first permanent legislative committee, which met in December to decide on its immediate legislative priorities; March and Wright were delegated to lobby in Toronto for the TLC. No action was taken regarding Ottawa until the Knights committee was chosen, after which the TLC also decided to appoint Jury to represent them in Ottawa.[38] In April the TTLC also endorsed Jury as their representative in Ottawa.[39]

Jury's presence in Ottawa represented a major break with past practice. On arrival he interviewed Macdonald and other members of the government in an attempt to have factory, workshop regulations, and employers' liability legislation enacted. In all three areas the government now claimed that such acts were *ultra vires* of federal jurisdiction. After this refusal, Jury turned his attention to the protection of sailors and railroad workers with the result that the government finally introduced a bill 'in reference to the safety of ships.' However, the bill was not satisfactory since it did not include a load line and had very weak enforcement clauses. The ministry, when faced with these criticisms, decided to withdraw the bill until the next session.[40] Similarly, Jury attempted to have clauses introduced into a railway bill to provide additional safety measures such as wider running boards and the packing of 'frogs.' Later he tried to have an amendment made to this bill to offset a number of severe clauses regarding the punishment of railroad employees for negligence in the line of duty. Although he failed, he did force a division of the House on the amendment and some Tory MPs (including G.R.R. Cockburn of Toronto) broke party ranks to support the labour-backed amendment.[41] Basically Jury prosecuted his tasks diligently, vigorously, and effectively. He made labour's presence felt in Ottawa and was a thorn in the side of the complacent Tory government.

The Tories made an important recovery in January 1888 when E.F. Clarke won the mayoralty race. Howland's second term had not produced results for the labour movement in Toronto. Moreover, Howland's hand-picked successor, Elias Rogers, a rich coal merchant, won the emnity of the TTLC Municipal Committee when, as an alderman, he opposed shorter hours for civic employees. He also came under a cloud of suspicion when Clarke Wallace (Conservative, York West) made revelations in the House of Commons about monopolists in general and the Toronto coal ring in particular. Ned Clarke's nomination represented an ingenious strategy to rebuild the old Tory-Labour alliance which had been so badly damaged in the years from 1884 to 1887. The plan worked exceptionally well and labour reformers as diverse as Thompson and Wright supported Clarke's candidacy. The only Toronto daily paper which endorsed him was the *News* which, although under new editorial control, still purported to be a people's paper. The TTLC did not formally endorse Clarke, narrowly overruling a motion that they do so.[42] The Knights of Labor also stayed out of the race, and this represented a major victory since the Knights had formerly been an important complement of the Howland reform alliance.[43] The TTLC did, however, blacklist five aldermen[44] and, although four of them were returned in the election, their leader, G.F. Frankland, sought peace shortly after his re-election. He met with the TTLC Municipal Committee, was 'full of sympathy for everybody and everything, and if he had been wrong in the past, he sincerely regretted it and promised to never do so any more.'[45]

Clarke, 'The People's Candidate,' easily defeated Rogers, 'The Citizens' Candidate,' even with a slight split of the Tory vote due to Tory Alderman Defoe's refusal to withdraw from the race.[46] Clarke, TTU member, hero of the printers' strike of 1872, and publisher of the *Orange Sentinel*, had thus matched his earlier achievement in the 1886 Ontario election of rebuilding the Tory-Labour alliance in Toronto. The celebration of the Clarke victory by the TTU symbolized the return of the city's older political alliances. The union presented Clarke with a beautifully printed resolution of congratulations and chose old junta members J.C. McMillan and J.S. Williams to deliver it. Clarke's accomplishment, not only in recreating the old alliance but also in transforming that alliance into a seat in the Ontario legislature and the Toronto mayoralty for himself, demonstrated the ever-increasing importance of Toronto workers in politics.[47]

The Tory labourites scored another important victory when Powderly reluctantly acted on District Assembly 125's recommendation to appoint Wright Lecturer and Examining Organizer for Ontario.[48] O'Donoghue expressed his dismay immediately: 'Wright is a fluent speaker and a shrewd man and should make his mark as a lecturer – that is, if he is ''in the cause'' because of its mission and its principles, and not for A.W. Wright. Time will unravel which, and we shall see.' Wright's appointment as Examining Organizer infuriated O'Donoghue, who termed it 'a slap in the teeth to the old and tried as well as tireless men.' The insult appeared even greater because Wright had also just defeated Jury by three votes to become District Assembly 125's delegate to the 1888 General Assembly. O'Donoghue threatened war on Wright and promised Powderly some startling revelations: 'If all I learn here is true, and the facts are pressed to an issue, as I anticipate they will be, he may lose all the honours and be forced to figure in a new *role*. We shall see in time. It is an old adage that the mills of the gods grind slowly but nevertheless surely.' In closing, O'Donoghue mentioned that the subject of this tirade was on his way to Philadelphia, and that Powderly would soon be able to form his own opinions. In a revealing juxtaposition he 'strongly urged [that Powderly] continue Bro. Jury in the capacity of one of Canada's Parliamentary Committee, *no matter who advises otherwise.*'[49] Powderly's characteristic response appears to have been to remind O'Donoghue that Wright's appointment had been O'Donoghue's own suggestion the previous winter. O'Donoghue answered that his suggestion had only been intended to keep Wright off the Legislative Committee. He again warned that Wright was 'shrewd and slippery':

If only Wright is sincere in our cause (I will not say positively that he is not, but I do say that I am justified in many ways in asserting that I have very grave doubts on the matter) he can do much good because he is a very good and pleasing speaker. If time and experience proves me wrong in judgement respecting him no one will be more ready to acknowledge the error than will be Dan O'Donoghue.[50]

Wright's new status raised additional howls of protest from Toronto. His appearance at a banquet for Tory Secretary of State Sir J.-A. Chapleau, led Master Workman Michael O'Halloran (Toronto Local 2622) to complain: 'I cannot see how any officer of this Order can do his duty while toadying to any party and particularly as they are the same party who always raise the race and religion cry at election time and every other time they wish to try and keep the workingmen alienated or divided.'[51] The same banquet led O'Donoghue to comment that 'it is hard to change the spots on a leopard.' More seriously, he accused Wright of 'carefully keeping an eye to the chances of getting to Parliament on our backs whether we want him or not.'[52]

Wright scored his major triumph in the General Assembly, where he initially won Powderly's attention and later his trust. As a result, Powderly nominated him as one of the candidates for the four positions on the General Executive Board. Wright led the balloting and became the first Canadian to win a high office in the order.[53] From this period on, Powderly had no closer a confidant in either country than Wright. O'Donoghue noted these developments with considerable bitterness: 'Accept my congratulations and for numerous reasons. Owing to the fact that you *now* have an immediate adviser from Canada and having no desire to interfere in the remotest way with that advice I will very rarely trouble you in the future.' He made two initial exceptions to this pledge, however. First, he reiterated that it was absolutely crucial that Jury be named to the order's Legislative Committee, adding that perhaps his long-time ally Brother Carey of St Catharines should also be sent to Ottawa. Second, he asked Powderly to discuss with Wright the Toronto District Organizers' jobs because District Assembly 125 had just named Brothers Beales and Gibbons, passing over long-time Toronto organizer March. O'Donoghue thought that the injustice was so clear that even Wright would agree.[54]

The Legislative Committee became O'Donoghue's major passion. He recommended Jury again in mid-December:

He is not in the Order for office or emolument. On the same night and at the same meeting of LA 2305 in the spring of 1883 Jury and I were initiated into the Order: we joined it because its principles commended themselves to us. The Order was not very popular then and no one can say that a man's ambition had much chance of being furthered much at that time; neither was there any money in it. In fact neither of us entered as an apprentice in the Labor cause at that late date – we began that eighteen years earlier as members of separate Trade Unions.[55]

Those recommended by the Canadian General Assembly representatives were 'all good honest men, [but] they are not the men for that work.' O'Donoghue carefully disguised his comments, but his fears of another Wright manipulation were clear:

When I see the way the chips are floating I have no difficulty in determining how the current of a stream is running. The drift in this matter, whoever manipulated the intended course of the stream, is not for our good as an Order. I feel this in my bones. The whole affair, as to the nominations of these men, whether they themselves saw it or not, has been conceived in mature deliberation by someone, and with a motive foreign to our interests as an Order. There are those who desire that

the old committee *shall not* come back here again in a representative capacity –
those who so desire are not of our Order, but they are very prominent politicians of a
partisan party. I am not quite clear that they are not being assisted in this by some of
our membership whose 'spots' are not very well hidden as yet.[56]

These and other protests were of no avail, and the new committee of W.R.
James of St Catharines, O.D. Benoit of Montreal, and R.R. Elliot of
Uxbridge took office in January 1889.[57]

When the TLC met in fall 1888, it thanked prolifically the Knights Legislative Committee under Jury for its aid the previous year.[58] It also en-
shrined the lobbying role of its own executive committee in a new constitution: '[It] ... shall watch the provincial legislatures and Dominion Parliament, and shall as far as possible, endeavour to further the legislation
decided on by the Congress at each session, or such other legislation as
shall by them be deemed advisable'[59] Following O'Donoghue, the TLC
refused to endorse the Knights' lobbyist, R.R. Elliot, and instead sent
their president, J.T. Carey, to Ottawa. In Carey's report to the 1889
congress, we find no grateful acknowledgement of fellow lobbyist Elliot;
indeed a studied silence followed his commendation of O'Donoghue's TTLC
Legislative Committee.[60] The TTLC also refused to recognize Elliot as a
representative, defeating a motion by Armstrong that they do so.[61]

Elliot proceeded on a very different set of assumptions in Ottawa than
Jury. In January he met with Macdonald in Toronto, who informed him that
there could be no new labour legislation until the Labour Commission
report came out. Apparently accepting this decision without complaint,
Elliot then went to Ottawa. There, he explained,

your committee thought it their duty to devote their energies to the Government or
the Liberal-Conservative Party. But in doing so we studiously avoided doing
anything that could give offence to the other political organization; ... Knowing that
this jealousy [between parties] exists the members of your committee scrupulously
avoided attending any Liberal-Conservative caucuses in order that the grits might
not take umbrage.[62]

Previous lobbying efforts by labour had been orchestrated on the basis of
petitions and public campaigns for legislation, not on the basis of access to
party caucus. Moreover, the notion that only access to government policy
was useful to labour interests broke significantly with the critical role that
O'Donoghue and Jury had developed in Ottawa and even in Ontario.

The most important piece of legislation introduced in the 1889 session,

Clarke Wallace's Combines Bill,[63] provided an interesting case study of the two lobbying theories in action. Wallace had led an exposé of a number of rings and trusts in the 1888 session. In 1889 he followed his investigation with a bill to limit combinations in Canada. The bill first went to the House Banking and Commerce Committee, where it was expected to die, especially when the Wholesale Grocers' Guild hired B.B. Osler, one of Canada's most prominent lawyers, to oppose it. The bill was reported out of committee, however, and when Wallace voluntarily amended it, Macdonald accepted it as a piece of government legislation. The amendment attempted to prevent combines from disguising themselves as trade unions and thus from avoiding the impact of his legislation: 'The foregoing provisions of this act shall not apply to the exercise of any handicraft, or to the performance of any labour, but, subject to such exception, they shall be construed as if Section 22 of the Trade Unions Act had not been enacted.'[64] The bill then proceeded to the Senate, where the appointed moguls in all their wisdom cleverly deleted the section of the above clause which exempted trade unions from prosecution. The new version read, 'The foregoing provisions of this Act shall be construed as if Section 22 of the Trade Unions Act had not been enacted.'[65] After Wallace and the Tory government accepted the Senate-amended bill, it became law.

Predictably, the trade-union movement responded with outrage. Not so predictably, the Knights' major lobbyist, R.R. Elliot, contented himself with gaining reassurances from Sir John Thompson, the minister of justice, to the effect that 'the Act was not intended to apply and did not apply to labor organizations.'[66] This may have been sufficient guarantee for Elliot, but it was not for the rest of the labour movement. The TTLC Legislative Committee, which had approved Wallace's bill in its original form and which then had petitioned the Senate to delete Wallace's entire qualifying clause, now condemned the government and the Act.[67] Alf Jury bitterly wondered: 'What Mr. Elliot ... was doing when this little bill went through. The papers have been talking of his bright eyes: they should have been wide open when a measure was passed that will assuredly render the Trades Union Act inoperative in all its clauses.'[68]

The TTLC organized mass protest meetings to condemn the measure. At the first of these, held before the Senate delted all protection, a motion condemning Wallace's amended bill had passed with only two dissenting votes (those of John Armstrong and R.L. Simpson of the *Canadian Labor Reformer*).[69] The two dissidents defended Wallace vocally but were unable to sway the meeting. At a later mass meeting sponsored by the TTLC and District Assembly 125, Wallace appeared to explain the Act. The only defender Wallace had was Wright, who offered a more moderate motion, calling on Wallace to amend his Act if in its operations it proved harmful to trade-unionists. Wright's attempt failed, and motions were passed condemning the Act and calling on Wallace to introduce legislation at the next session of parliament to protect trade-unionists.[70]

The TLC meeting in September also opposed the Act.[71] Their earlier refusal to allow Elliot to represent them in Ottawa now seemed extremely wise, and the howl of protest that greeted his report, when it was finally published in late November, more than confirmed their previous suspicions. The *Globe* did not have to stretch the evidence very far in summarizing it as 'an advanced issue of Conservative campaign literature.' The generally positive tone of Elliot's comments on the session contrast sharply with the discontent produced by the Combines Bill and also with J.T. Carey's TLC summary that efforts for labour legislation in 1889 had been 'altogether abortive.'[72] The TTLC Legislative Committee also condemned Elliot's report for its misleading claim that the Macdonald government had met all of labour's demands regarding immigration practices.[73]

Elliot's partisan political performance in Ottawa necessitated another round of political intrigue regarding future legislative committees. Powderly had defended the Elliot committee against Toronto Knights' criticisms, claiming that he took the advice of the Canadian General Assembly representatives only.[74] This defence had been suggested by Wright, who had warned Powderly of the agitation in Toronto: 'The O'Donoghue-Jury crowd here are very wrathy regarding the appointment of the Legislative Committee with Jury left off. A resolution has been passed at the D.A. and will be forwarded to you protesting against the appointment without consulting the Order here.'[75] In August, after almost an eight-month break in communication, O'Donoghue wrote Powderly. As usual the subject was the Knights Legislative Committee. O'Donoghue sought as a 'personal favour' a copy of the Elliot Committee's report. In addition, he suggested that

the G.M.W. should offer to Congress [T.L.C.] to defray one half the cost of its Parliamentary Committee, conditioned upon having one half (3) of its members Knights of Labor, but all to be elected by the Congress which will be composed of both Knights of Labor and trade unionists. This step while doing away with two such Committees, as at present, would at the same time *relieve* you of a source of more or less annoyance.[76]

Not surprisingly, Powderly refused this offer, which would have removed his control over the Knights' Legislative Committee.[77] O'Donoghue, in his response, abandoned indirection. The Elliot Committee

was *worse than apathetic*: it was positively an injury because, while giving no assistance to President J.T. Carey of the Dominion Trades and Labor Congress who was at Ottawa during the session, its very presence even though doing nothing indicated a division of authority in our councils which did not tend to imporve our chances of securing required legislation. [Emphasis in original.]

The committee had lost the confidence of Canadian Knights: 'as it is presently constituted [it] should cease to exist.'[78] By this point, Powderly had lost all patience with O'Donoghue and answered sharply:

If men who growl would work as hard and energetically as they growl the effect would be very beneficial ... The Order in Canada sends men of her own selection to the G.A. to make laws and to be chosen as officers. And if the Order is not gifted with that vitality that it ought to have or if other counsellors than those of your own selection, and which now predominate, are not given some consideration the fault is not mine.

He demanded that O'Donoghue lay formal charges and cease making allegations against Wright, Lepine, and others:

If you don't like Wright for some reason or other why don't you fight it out over there and let me and the Order make the best use possible out of him. Either that or take him home. In appointing the last Canadian Committee I did as I did before, act on the recommendations of the Canadian representatives and yourself. I was asked by the whole Canadian delegation to appoint the present Committee and I did so. Would you have me slap the representatives of Canada in the face by refusing to honor their choice and then select my own favorites? If they didn't do right by Canada or the Order there, they are to blame and not me.[79]

O'Donoghue's response was both long and distressed. To Powderly's demand 'to write plainly, what you want me to do – what the Order in Canada wants me to do,' O'Donoghue answered:

1st *I don't want you to do anything*. 2nd As I don't represent the Order in Canada ... I can't say what the Order in the Dominion wants you to do ... In my last letter I

RECOMMENDED, and I *now repeat that recommendation*, that as the Dominion Trades and Labor Congress at its session in Montreal last September elected a Parliamentary Committee of seven ... with the President of the Congress, Bro. J.T. Carey of St. Catharines as the Chairman of that Committee, as the seven elected are all Knights of Labor and prominent in the Order in their respective localities, it would be a wise and judicious act on your part to choose three out of that seven – one from Ontario and from the province of Quebec and the chairman to be the present chairman of the Congress. [Emphasis in original.]

He suggested Charles March, P.J. Jobin of Quebec, and J.T. Carey. 'My reason for offering this suggestion is this,' O'Donoghue continued, 'by so doing the existence at Ottawa of *two* Committees representing Labor would be done away with and the power for good of the then Committee (or Joint Committee as it would be) would be greatly enhanced and the Government would not be in a position, as it was last session, to say that they did not know which Committee deserved their first attention.' (Emphasis in original.) He also pointed out that the new Congress Committee with a new provincial component was an improvement over the former Knights' structure which had focused entirely on Ottawa.[80]

Powderly hedged, claiming that he might not 'appoint another Legislative Committee for Ottawa.' The major problem in Canada as seen from Scranton, Pennsylvania, was partyism:

If it were possible to find someone in Canada who was not a Tory or a Liberal or whatever they are over there, I would like to see him. No matter who I select he will not give satisfaction to the other party and instead of assisting to gain results each party would rather have a committee that would make capaign thunder for his own little principles. It is impossible for me to know the men of Canada personally and it seems to be equally impossible to find independent men there.[81]

The battle continued in Toronto; Local 2305 passed a series of resolutions accusing Wright of a serious misappropriation of funds while he was a lecturer for the order. Powderly helped Wright orchestrate his response and offered him full support. Powderly reminded Local 2305 that Wright had been the nominee of their District Assembly, and had subsequently been twice elected representative to the General Assembly. Surely that indicated that the order in Toronto had some considerable faith in him? He then asked:

Now what am I to do? You send men to represent you and then find fault with me for associating with them or treating them with even less consideration than you have shown them. If Bro. Wright is not what he is supposed to be point out the why and wherefore and I will act carefully upon your report. I shall ask of DA 125 to read this letter in connection with the one you send in so that they may hear both sides.

Powderly then upbraided them, suggesting that their complaints were inspired by other than Knightly principles:

If Bro. Wright is not the man to represent you then he should be called home and a better man sent in his stead, but in electing him pick out a man who never made enemies in his own home, who has never opposed anyone, who agrees with his neighbours without dispute. When you send such a man to me I will label him fool and send him back to be placed in some anatomical museum as a freak. I know of no man who has the esteem of all his townsmen and thank God I do not base my opinions of men on what their enemies say, for if I did I would've carried some queer impressions away from Toronto the last time I left there, but I do that every place I go to, so Toronto has no monopoly on the back-biting business, it flourishes all around.

After reducing the charges to back-biting, Powderly concluded:

Until you have placed facts before the court of his local and followed it until DA 125 or its court has settled it I should not be treated to any insinuations in the shape of resolutions which only resolve. The G.A. is to act on all accounts, if they are not right that body must say so and act accordingly. If there is anything else the matter it must be remedied at home for I believe in home government of officials for offences committed at home.[82]

After sending this letter to Gilmour and another to Glockling of District Assembly 125, Powderly wrote Wright to assure him that 'the growlers, with jaws of resolution will not like what they have received.'[83] Indeed, O'Donoghue wrote an irate response attacking Wright as 'a dastardly rascal' and rebutting his charge that O'Donoghue and Jury would 'stab anyone whom they believed to be inimical to their schemes.' O'Donoghue self-righteously asserted that 'our only scheme is to defend the Order against those who by acts of omission or commission justify us in believing are of its membership for selfish purposes only.'[84] This time Powderly answered carefully: 'There is something astir in Toronto concerning Wright and those who are in opposition to him that I do not understand and it does seem to me that in the interest of the labour movement. Your own people should settle it, whatever it is without making it harder for me to accomplish anything by useless complaints.'

Powderly in the early spring ignored District Assembly 125's advice and reappointed the old legislative committee. Any possibility of cooperation with the TLC disappeared with this move, and Elliot's rather ineffectual 1889 lobbying was replicated in 1890, especially since the Knights, for economic reasons, reduced his stay in Ottawa to the first three weeks of the session.[85] Powderly, in refusing a request by Elliot to remain in Ottawa longer, noted that at the next General Assembly, he intended 'to recommend that the committees at Ottawa and Washington be done away with, for their work is neutralized by fault finding.'[86] Elliot's 1890 report gave further evidence of partisan Toryism. He commended the government for the passing of a bill to set up a Canadian Bureau of Labour Statistics – a bill so ineffectual that it was never implemented and one that both the TTLC and TLC requested be held over for further consideration.[87]

In spite of his recent failures, O'Donoghue tried once again in 1891 to influence Powderly:

When the House of Commons meets, Bro. Carey will be at Ottawa representing the Dominion Trades and Labor Congress and I once again urge that *you* officially appoint him, at least, as the representative of the Order to watch and work in the interests of the labor cause in respect of legislation introduced or sought for, as well as to prevent, if possible, the passage into law of acts which are, or may be, inimical to labor interests.[88]

Powderly had had enough and in 1891 decided not to name a Canadian legislative committee.[89] This decision effectively ended the Knights' national influence in Canada, although they continued to play important local roles.

Elliot had been the centre of a different controversy in the fall of 1890 which also demonstrated the demise of the Knights and their new utility for politicos in the labour movement. The TLC met in Ottawa that year with 26 Knights delegates present, 'many of them representing nobody but themselves,' as R.J. Kerrigan noted unkindly. Elliot represented Port Perry Local 5330 and in a minor Tory victory was elected secretary-treasurer in a close race against the incumbent, Toronto printer George Dower. His credentials were challenged the next day, however, when a letter arrived from William Hogan, the master workman of District Assembly 236, who claimed that Local 5330 had lapsed and that Elliot was a member of a different local anyway. After a heated floor debate, the matter was left to the executive with the proviso that Dower hold his old office until the matter was resolved. The final resolution unfortunately went unrecorded, but Dower remained in office for the whole year. Moreover, in October it was discovered that a number of the Windsor delegates had also presented forged credentials.[90]

Partyism then had re-emerged strongly in the late 1880s. Yet partyism generated its own critique as well. The most perspicacious of the Toronto labour reformers, Phillips Thompson, analysed well in his powerful *The Politics of Labor* the dialectical tension that existed between the emergence of the working class and its residual commitment to the old political parties. On the one hand, 'nothing could be more sickening [than] the deference which each party feels called upon to pay labor in the caucus and the convention'; but, on the other hand, the partisan quest to capture the labour vote, no matter how hypocritical, was a hopeful sign, for it evidenced the new political importance of the working class.[91] 'Hitherto the politicians have used labor. The time has come when labor must use the politicans. The politicians have been able to use labor because workingmen have put party first. When they put labor first and let party interests look out for themselves they can make the politicians their obsequious servants.'[93] The tension, however, was not just between the actual and the potential, for although 'the hold which party associations and traditions have obtained over the masses ... is the greatest obstacle to any present advance,'[93] that hold, even in the present, was increasingly contingent on 'repeated concessions and pledges to labor.'

Slight and insincere as these may be, nevertheless they are an indication too plain to be misinterpreted of the influence of the new factor in public affairs. They are the thin edge of the wedge. When the people learn in the process of political education now going forward that the concessions are futile so long as the wage system remains intact, ... a new departure on a broader scale may be looked for.[94]

Thompson understood well what later critics had not seen. He cautioned all not to 'underrate what has already been achieved by labor reformers in politics.'[95] The time had certainly come for the labour movement to transcend these gains, or 'palliatives' as Thompson termed them, but labour could not be ignored.[96] Thompson was to lead one attempt to transcend palliatives in 1891 which captured well the tensions and ambiguities of labour in politics at the end of the period of transition to industrial capitalist society.

14

Radicalism and the fight
for the street railway

Are we whose interests are alike to make common cause against the common enemy or are we to remain forever divided and forever the victims of injustice and oppression? Do you not see that the struggle the world over is becoming less one of race or religious ascendancy, less one of political ascendancy, but is becoming more and more one of class against class – the one fighting for domination, the other for emancipation? Can we who at the very name of freedom feel a thrill of pride course through our veins longer refrain from working out our own deliverance.
'Niger,' Toronto letter *Iron Molders Journal*, 31 January 1887

Partyism then remained a strong force in the Toronto working-class world, but there were other political traditions and new modes of thought available to Toronto workers with more radical implications. These ideas were never seized upon by all Toronto workers but, nevertheless, they occupied a prominent place in the cultural landscape that surrounded and influenced workers' choices. We can deal only fleetingly with a few here – Irish Nationalism, Anti-Poverty and Single-Tax Societies, and Bellamyite Nationalism.[1]

Irish Nationalism had travelled a precarious course in Orange Toronto especially after the Fenian raids' fiasco in the late 1860s.[2] Nevertheless, it emerged from its subterranean existence in the early 1880s with the founding of a Toronto Irish Land League branch.[3] The organization started on a wave of enthusiasm and unanimity that disappeared almost immediately, when the more radical members of the group condemned Gladstone's Irish policies.[4] The organization was composed of Irish from many walks of life, including Toronto's few Irish Catholic politicians such as Alderman Ryan and ex-Liberal MP John O'Donohue. The Land League also attracted prominent labour leaders such as Dan O'Donoghue, and more surprisingly, the English-born Jury and Thompson. Wright, another prominent Toronto radical, gave the league's first St Patrick's Day address. His address condemned the Irish land system as 'murderous,' a form of 'slavery.'[5]

Political differences plagued the organization, and in early May 1881 Thompson denounced

the attempts which have been made to prejudice the movement by raising sectarian and national issues, and contending that the question was broader than any mere party one, and that it was one in which men of all creeds and countries were interested. Landlords and monopolists were not foolish enough to quarrel over differences of race and sects, and the masses should learn wisdom in this respect.[6]

Thomspon also suggested that one way of bridging this gap would be by agitating for the abolition of property seizures for defaulting on rents. The attempt to broaden the movement was also evident in their invitation to Henry George to lecture in Toronto.[7] George, whose *Poverty and Progress* was just becoming famous, addressed a large, enthusiastic audience which included many labour leaders. He assailed landlords and private ownership of land, and described the growth of socialism in the United States.[8] In July, the league sent Thompson to Montreal, when Fanny Parnell visited there on a North American promotional tour for the Land League.[9]

The whole Irish question demanded so much press attention, especially after Parnell's arrest in October, that the *Globe* sent Thompson to Ireland as a special commissioner to investigate the land question. His articles describing conditions in Ireland appeared every few days for almost a month.[10] The series closed with an attempted interview with the jailed Parnell and interviews with Anna Parnell and with Henry George.[11] The logic of the Irish situation and the exposure, through it, to other radical thinkers had a profound effect on Thompson and on other Land Leaguers in Toronto and elsewhere. Georgism, for example, certainly strengthened itself as one important critique of industrial capitalism by embedding itself in the North American working-class movement through platforms of the Land League.[12]

John McCormick provides an even clearer example of the connection between the Irish question and North American radical traditions. Starting off as a correspondent of Pat Boyle's Fenian *Irish Canadian* in the early 1870s, McCormick found little of a positive nature in Canadian politics. He dismissed the Grits as the 'John Calvin Ring [who were] of the same kidney as their confreres, the Cromwellians of the New England States.' Although they had 'Reform on their tongues, [they had] an awful amount of bigotry, intolerance, and narrow selfishness in their hearts.' Yet the Tory 'Orange Ring' was even worse. The Canadian Catholic Irish had to create a third force under 'their own flag.' McCormick turned to the labour movement for potential support in his campaign but found the Toronto junta with its Orange ties unattractive.[13] By 1880, he had turned to currency reform and the land question. An avid reader of the *Irish World* (New York), he also endorsed the platform of the Socialist Labor Party. This curious synthesis, so typical of labour reformers in the 1880s, appeared in his remarkable pamphlet on the labour question, *The Conditions of Labour and Modern Civilization*.[14] McCormick then, like many of his countrymen in North America, followed the logic of the Irish question to the conclusion that independent working-class politics were necessary.

The process of broadening out from Ireland is also clear in Thompson's later invitation to George to lecture in Toronto:

The lecture that would take best here I think would be one dealing with the question from a general rather than from an Irish standpoint – though of course illustrations and allusions drawn from the Irish situation would be telling. Those principally interested in land nationalization as a principle are mostly of other than Irish nationality though of course we might expect a considerable Irish attendance.[15]

The Land League throughout North America splintered when Parnell and Davitt again parted ways over the tactics to be pursued in the Irish struggle.[16] Nevertheless, the broader ideas that had been propagandized by the land struggle did not disappear, and Henry George made another Canadian tour in early 1883 under the auspices of the Knights of Labor.

With the later shift in the Irish struggle in 1885, Toronto was the centre for another round of Irish nationalist activity. In late September 1885, the Irish National League in Canada was organized to raise funds to sustain Parnell's parliamentary fund.[17] This organization attracted many of the same figures as before, including O'Donoghue, Jury, and Thompson, and was extremely active in the independent labour campaigns of 1886–87, again showing the tendency of the Irish struggle to merge with labour reform. Bryan Lynch, one of the major Irish nationalist leaders, was particularly prominent in the labour campaigns. No labour demonstrations throughout the 1880s, ranging from strike support for the street-railway workers through the campaign parades for the labour candidates, were complete without bands from the city's Hibernian societies – societies that most often functioned as front-groups for physical-force Fenianism.[18]

None of this should surprise us, for the rise of the Knights in Toronto, especially its organization of unskilled workers, meant that for the first time the Irish Catholic working-class was finding its own voice – a voice free of the church and of the middle class.

The Toronto labour campaigns of 1886 and 1887 were part of a massive political upsurge of working classes across North America, of which the most dramatic and visible campaign was the Henry George candidacy for mayor of New York.[19] Eric Foner recently demonstrated how closely tied that electoral contest was to the Irish Land League and the rise of the Knights of Labor:

The social dominance of this triple alliance [Catholic Church, Democratic Party, Irish-American middle class] was challenged in the 1880s by the organized social radicalism articulated and institutionalized in the Land League's radical branches and the Knights of Labor. Here was the only organized alternative to the Tammany-oriented saloon and local clubhouse, as a focus for working class social life in the Irish-American community. The discussions of political issues, the emphasis on temperance, the reading of the radical labor press, and the very process of union-building across divisions of ethnicity, skill, and craft, all embodied a social ethic that challenged the individualism of the middle class and the cautious social reformism of the Democratic Party and Catholic Church.[20]

The Irish Catholic working class in Toronto benefited from the same social process.

From the links with labour that Henry George forged in the New York mayoralty race, he began to build a social movement. Commencing with a weekly newspaper, *The Standard*, a new organization called the Anti-Poverty Society was founded.[21] George visited Toronto again in May 1887, only a few months after his electoral defeat. For over two hours George lectured his overflow audience. 'a large proportion of them evidently mechanics,' on the intricacies of the single tax. At the end, he urged them to spread the light by forming clubs, circulating literature, talking to others, and so on.[22] Two weeks later, a number of his followers organized an Anti-Poverty Society (APS) in Toronto.[23] The society almost instantly became a city institution. It received considerable press coverage because of its extensive propagandistic efforts, which ranged from the distribution of literature to weekly addresses in Queen's Park, Toronto's version of Hyde Park Speakers' Corner.[24] The society also held educational meetings at which Toronto social reformers presented their favourite schemes and thoughts for their comrades' consideration. For example, consecutive

Single Taxers turned out to hear Thompson lecture on his European experiences. He 'related in graphic style his investigations into the social question in France, England, and the Scottish highlands during his year abroad.'[38] Later that year, Thompson was greeted less enthusiastically by his audience when, in a lecture on capitalism, he tried to explain systematically some of the ideas he had been exposed to in Europe. The more orthodox Georgites responded with hostility to his attempt 'to show the need for not only land nationalization but also for reforms in the commercial system, under which, at present, capital is made the means whereby one class lives in idleness, condemning the other to double toil.'[39] The Georgites maintained their links with the labour movement through a constant interchange of lobbying support on various measures. At the 1889 TLC meeting in Montreal, Single Taxers asked to be seated as delegates. After considerable debate, the Credentials Committee turned them down. An appeal to the floor against this decision resulted in a tied vote which was broken by the chair in support of the Credentials Committee's decision to refuse them seats. Nevertheless, the support they won indicated their strength in the labour movement.[40]

In July 1890 another organization with even broader interests in social reform was founded in Toronto.[41] Modelled on the nationalist clubs which originated in Boston after the publication of Edward Bellamy's *Looking Backward*, it was called the Toronto Nationalist Association. Prominent among the Toronto organizers was Phillips Thompson. Although differing with Single Taxers about the proposed remedy for the injustices of industrial capitalist society, the two associations maintained friendly relations and overlapping memberships in Toronto. Thompson, for example, retained his membership in the Single Tax Association, as the APS became known in 1890.[43]

The nationalists also played an active role in lobbying and educational work in Toronto; they maintained close links with the labour movement and enjoyed a considerable overlapping of membership with the TTLC. Thompson, their most prominent leader, gained a position of great influence in 1890 when, as a result of extended negotiations between District Assembly 125 and the TTLC, the *Labor Advocate* appeared under his editorial direction.[44] This new paper was fully endorsed by the two labour bodies. The *Labor Advocate* published for only ten months, but in that period it led the Toronto radicals in quite new directions.[45] Its successes and failures were indicative of the strength and weaknesses of both the working-class movement and of its radical middle-class supporters.

Of the six labour papers published in Toronto in the years covered by this study, Thompson's *Labor Advocate* was by far the most impressive. Attractively printed, its columns were filled with the major debates of the emerging socialist movement and of labour reform. The interesting eclecticism of *The Ontario Workman*, the committed unionism of the *Trade Union Advocate*, and even the elegance of Wright's *Canadian Labor Reformer*, all fade before the *Labor Advocate's* excellence. Yet, although of a high intellectual and literary tone, it never lost contact with the workers' struggles. Thompson, at his most devastating, commented on the role of intellectuals, journalists, and others, who regarded themselves as educated beyond daily concerns:

The shallowness of what passes as modern intellectual culture is shown by its lamentable failure to meet the problems of the time, or even to make an attempt in that direction ... Never since the dark ages was there a greater lack of creative power or originality, of the boldness and mental grasp necessary in dealing with a new situation ... In place of a literature touching the strongest and most deep seated emotions, dealing with great problems of life, and appealing to the hearts of the mass of mankind, we have the 'society' novel and the 'society' poem, written for a class and embodying the caste idea.[46]

His newspaper, while noting and criticizing the major intellectual and literary currents of the time, also engaged in direct political interventions. Its major campaign was the attempt to municipalize the Toronto street railway.

Frank Smith's street railway company was easily the most despised symbol of corporate capitalism in the city. The lease for monopoly control of the city's streets was up for renegotiation in 1891.[47] The TTLC, remembering only too well the struggles of 1886, set up a special committee in September 1889 to consider the question of the next street-railway charter.[48] This committee met immediately with representatives from District Assembly 125 to form a joint committee on the street-railway question. Thus in December, when the TTLC's municipal committee met to discuss the issues it considered important to pose in the January 1890 municipal election, city takeover and operation of the street railway figured prominently on the list.[49] In late December a public meeting at St Lawrence Hall passed resolutions calling for the city council 'to take the necessary steps for the acquirement of the franchise and to arrange for such disposition of it as shall prove most profitable for the citizens.' In support of this motion, Thompson specified that he thought public ownership would be best. Alf Jury introduced a second resolution calling for voters to support only those aldermen who would support municipalization of the franchise. Other labour spokesmen echoed these sentiments.[50]

When the new city council met in January, Alderman E.A. Macdonald moved that they form a street-railway committee to prepare a policy for the 1891 negotiations. Meanwhile, the Toronto Street Railway Co. (TSR) was trying to avoid its fate by appealing to the Ontario Legislature to award it new rights to electrify the system with an understood implication that its franchise would then be safe from municipal interference. City opposition successfully killed this scheme. The city council then called a referendum on a money by-law which would provide the necessary funds to take over the assets of the TSR. Despite a lobbying campaign by the company which focused on the horrors of potential municipal ownership, Toronto voters overwhelmingly supported the by-law (5385 to 427).[51] Unfortunately, it was not clear what alternative they favoured; civic politicians, frightened by the street-railway campaign against municipal ownership, indicated that all they wanted was the power to lease new tenders – not permission to run the road themselves.

The Street Railway Committee (of the city council) commenced arbitration procedures with the TSR to arrive at a purchase price for the franchise. The TSR continued to behave arrogantly and even refused the city access to its books. Simultaneously, the committee began to commence private meetings to consider questions of contract requirements for the next lessee. The TTLC and Knight's joint committee was strangely silent on the whole matter given the TTLC Municipal Committee's earlier endorsement of public ownership, which was reiterated in May 1890.[52] The joint committee condemned the secret meetings of the Street Railway Committee in July, but only on the grounds that all discussion of the disposition of the franchise should be public.[53] Then in late November they warned, rather indirectly, against the rumoured possibility that the city committee might relet the contract to the TSR. At this point the TTLC named two additional members to its joint committee, John Armstrong and George Harris, which suggested that the council was becoming impatient with their committee's relative inactivity.[54]

In fall 1890 both the Single Tax Association (STA) and the Nationalist Association took up the street-railway question as an important local issue. STA leader S.T. Wood raised the question in an October letter to the *Globe*, and then the Nationalist Association made it a tangible public issue by lobbying for public ownership at the TTLC meeting in November.[55] The nationalist's effort encouraged the TTLC to resume interest in the question.[56] Speaking for the nationalists, Thompson addressed the city council

Nationalist Association to sponsor a late-January mass meeting on public ownership. The 300 persons in attendance heard speeches from prominent trade-unionists and labour reformers in favour of civic control. Motions were passed which almost unanimously favoured the TTLC's proposal for civic operation under a commission.[64] After this meeting, things remained relatively quiet until early March when the Toronto Board of Trade entered the fray with a predictable denunciation of municipal ownership.[65]

Shortly after the Toronto Board of Trade's pronouncement, the city council opened tenders for the franchise but extended the old company's charter until mid-May to provide more time for consideration. The *Labor Advocate* greeted this decision with enthusiasm, since it provided two more months of agitation for municipal ownership. Thompson called for intensified work, for

the monopolies and other interested opponents of civic ownership are active, vigilant, and aggressive. They have a great prize to work for, and will use every exertion to carry their point and bring influence to bear upon the aldermen. Their machinations can only be defeated by steady, resolute work, and all true labour reformers will do their share in the most important battle for popular rights against monopoly privileges which has yet been fought in the municipal arena.[66]

At the end of April, the Street Railway Committee rejected both tenders that it had received and issued a call for another set of offers. At the same time, it modified its proposals to make the franchise more attractive to capital. This led to vigorous denunciations by the *Labor Advocate* and by the TTLC. At the same TTLC meeting, the Street Railway Committee indicted the person who had informed Alderman McDougall that the council cared little about the issue. On a motion by Davey and Cribben of the committee, the council reaffirmed its commitment to public ownership and then added T.W. Banton, the vice-president of the TTLC, to the committee.[67] On the basis of the close work that the joint committee had been doing with the other social reform groups in the city, Davey and Cribben also moved that the TTLC join with District Assembly 125, the Single Tax Association, the Nationalist Association, and the Canadian Women's Enfranchisement Association to co-operate 'for the purposes of uniting the strength of the said organizations or associations upon questions of social reform.'[68] Thus, out of the campaign for the street railway emerged the first organizational link between the labour movement and other progressive groups.

On 16 May the city took over the street railway from Frank Smith, although not without another round of mock heroics on his part. He refused to turn the property over to the city on the appointed date, and only threats of vigorous legal action forced him to do so.[69] The city kept Smith's manager and had him implement changes in hours and pay that it had demanded as part of the tenders for the new franchise.

Thompson and his allies enthusiastically greeted this first experiment in public ownership. The new joint committee of progressive organizations echoed Thompson's advice to the aldermen to go slow and to give public ownership a realistic trial.[70] The TTLC and District Assembly 125 issued a joint circular directed to their 'fellow workers' which called upon them to resist the arguments of the monopolists' press and to realize that the time was ripe for significant change: 'Wake up! Do not by your apathy give to the great money autocrats a still firmer grip over the masses. Be masters of your own property and streets.'[71] The joint committee followed with a submission to the Street Railway Committee in which Banton of the TTLC, Dower of the Knights, Thompson of the nationalists, and S.A. Jones of the Single Tax Association called for civic operation for a year at the minimum, 'in order to obtain sufficient practical information as to the real value of the franchise, and the possibility of successful municipal management, as a basis for final action.'[72]

In late June municipal ownership received another boost when the financial statement for the first three weeks' operation of the street railway became available. The profit for that period was over $13,000, which was down from that under private ownership only by the amount now paid in higher wages and that paid out for additional horses. Effective use was made of the evidence that the profits of the old franchise had actually outstripped the total of its employees' wages.[73] In mid-July a meeting of progressive groups again contacted the Street Railway Committee. Emphasizing their representative character and the fact that they had no personal interest in the matter, unlike many who made representations to the council, they reiterated that there was no adequate reason for council to award the franchise to any syndicate and reminded the vote-conscious aldermen that those who gave away the franchise would have to face an enraged electorate in January.[74]

This particular threat had less impact than usual as many of the aldermen knew this was their last term because of a drastic municipal reform scheme which would reduce the number of wards from thirteen to six and the number of aldermen from 39 to 24 in the coming election. Thus the Street Railway Committee, by a narrow vote of eight to seven, rejected municipal ownership and then, rejecting Mayor Clarke's call for yet another set of tenders, awarded the franchise to the Kiely-Everett syndicate by a vote of nine to seven. This decision was greeted with howls of outrage. The *Labor Advocate* immediately reported in an editorial entitled 'Our Boodle Alder- men' that there was 'every reason to believe that their decision is due to bribery of the most flagrant kind,' a charge echoed by one of the competing syndicates. Such 'a shameless clique of ringsters ... should be in the penitentiary,' insisted the angry Thompson.[75]

The decision still required ratification by the city council and so plans to oppose it immediately focused on a mass protest rally to be held at City Hall on the evening of the key vote. The call for a demonstration went out from the TTLC and the Knights, and was supported by the other groups which had campaigned vigorously for municipal ownership. At a stormy TTLC meeting at which plans were made for the demonstration, the TTLC mem- bers of the Street Railway Committee implored the members to defeat the defecting aldermen in January. T.W. Banton also gave notice of a motion 'that it was both desirable and necessary that labour run direct candidates in the next municipal election,' in conjunction with the joint Social Reform Committee. The most prominent members of the Street Railway Commit- tee, Bradley and Cribben, were then elected president and secretary of the TTLC respectively. The fight for municipal ownership was having profound effects on the Toronto labour movement.[76]

The mass meeting attracted more than 2,000 angry citizens who, after numerous speeches attacking the deal, voted overwhelmingly to condemn the city council. Only the Knights' Alfred Jury spoke against the motion, arguing that the tender that had been accepted was a good one. A.W. Wright followed this speech with a blistering attack in which he denounced any labour reformer who took the course that Jury had followed. Wright announced that he would sooner 'see the road mismanaged by the city than well run by a monopoly.' Phillips Thompson then denied that the council had the right to take any decision because of the already mounting evidence of corruption. Needless to say, the council, unswayed by the oratory, proceeded to ratify the agreement by a vote of 24 to 14.[77]

Even that convincing vote did not end the debate, however, for in the next weeks increasing evidence came to the fore that the bargain had indeed been a corrupt one. Ex-Alderman Macdonald initiated court pro- ceedings to get an injunction to stop Mayor Clarke from signing the agreement.[78] In his opening testimony, he suggested that Alderman Hall, who had figured prominently as a Kiely-Everett supporter, had originally offered his services and vote to a rival syndicate for $50,000. Macdonald then mysteriously discontinued his case and, when the demands became of malfeasance in office' and citing that $4,500 was paid to prevent an inquiry, that $10,000 was paid to a Cleveland commission merchant and experienced 'lobbyist' Baruch Mahler (affectionately known at home as 'the clean skater'), that extraordinary enthusiasm was shown by certain aldermen for the Kiely-Everett franchise, and that these same aldermen opposed all investigations. The Street Railway Committee refused to take action on this petition.[82] At the next TTLC meeting, O'Donoghue moved that the council make clear 'that it has taken no steps in the direction of, nor has it sought, an injunction ... and further that no person or persons whatsoever had authority from or sanction of this council in any such proceedings.'[83] The president ruled this motion out of order on the grounds that it ran counter to the previous motion that had conceded that there was sufficient evidence to justify an investigation. Printer Gilmour's appeal against the ruling of the chair failed – after a lengthy debate. He then introduced a substitute motion, backed by O'Donoghue, which endorsed the Street Railway Committee's demand for an investigation, but dissociated the council from Thompson's injunction.[84]

Thompson responded bitterly to this attack on his injunction. He denounced 'O'Donoghue and his small following of rabid Grit factionists [and credited his behaviour to] the petty jealousy and partisan malignity which so frequently governs his actions, and have done so much to offset any really useful work he may have accomplished in the past.' Nevertheless, the struggle went on, and in appealing for financial support, Thompson noted that it was 'costly and the means available for the purpose limited.'[85]

The hearings on the application for an injunction lasted just over two weeks and, although they did not lead to any new and devastating revelations about the corruption of aldermen, they amply confirmed everyone's suspicions. Kiely confessed to frequent discussions with Aldermen Hall, Hewitt, Saunders, Score, Bell, and Piper but denied any knowledge of bribes or of the $4,500 paid to Macdonald. Mahler, 'the clean skater,' claimed weakly that his connection with the whole affair was simply a business venture, denying any claim to his fame as a 'fixer' of city councils. Henry A. Everett did not even deny that the syndicate might be behind Marshall's payment to Macdonald; instead, he just insisted that he had had no prior knowledge of such a payment. Marshall then testified that he was not financially interested in the syndicate and had not told them of his payment to Macdonald. He did so only in the interests of his friend and partner, William Mackenzie, who knew nothing of this favour. Perhaps even more telling was the testimony of J.F. Coleman, another syndicate lobbyist, who, after admitting that he received additional money from

Marshall, was unable to remember what he did with it. He did admit, however, that he had visited many of the aldermen on the Street-Railway Committee. E.A. Macdonald gave considerable evidence of corrupt deals, but none of it was sufficiently conclusive to support legal action. He described, for example, how 'in the early part of last year Kiely, unsolicited by him invested some money in land over the Don and when the matter of bringing out the former Street Railway Company came up he was given to understand by a mutual friend that he was expected to be more friendly to Kiely on account of this transaction.' Macdonald also supplied hearsay evidence that Mahler had been brought to Toronto to buy the requisite number of aldermen's votes to ensure the syndicate's success. He claimed that he had been told of a conversation in which Mahler and Everett had discussed the price of various Toronto aldermen. Thompson's funds ran out at this point and he was forced to allow the application for an injunction to expire.[86]

The *Labor Advocate* announced on 4 September that the fight was over.[87] Thompson, in a post mortem editorial, blamed the 'slavish indifference of the citizens (especially those of the wealthy and self-styled intellectual and respectable classes) [and the] influence of boodle.' The working class did not escape criticism, however, for 'they have foolishly thrown away the best opportunity offered them in many years for dealing a crushing blow to a monopoly.' He ended on a more affirmative note, claiming that those involved in the struggle for municipal ownership had 'nothing to be ashamed of, nothing to apologize for, and nothing to regret. [Moreover,] sooner or later the whole shameful story will come out,' and they would be vindicated.[88]

Labor Advocate columnist 'Ben' (George A. Howell) was more bitter than Thompson:

The mention of the street railway makes me mad. If there's anything I hate its getting whipped in a fight, especially where it's so near a win as the street railway fight was … Jealousy and politics as usual were at the bottom of it, and, for fear that some one of the opposite party would get a position on the Commission, or that the younger workers in the Labor Reform cause would put the older men in the shade, there was a division among the fighters. Traitors weren't wanting to belittle the efforts of those who still fought on and, as a result of this, we have lost the fight, and capital again triumphs.[89]

Ben's critique was confirmed by the final report of the Street Railway Committee. It blamed the previous committee under O'Donoghue and

March for the defeat. Echoing their earlier theme, they suggested that the previous committee 'had gone slow' to prevent the council from making the street railway a major issue in the 1891 municipal election. Having lost that opportunity, the current committee had been unable to work effectively. They felt, however, that the whole campaign had allowed quite beneficial educational work among Toronto workers, many of whom were now more favourably disposed to public ownership.[90]

The same council meeting saw yet another debate on political action by labour. The split in the council, which had become obvious in the street-railway campaign, was again evident as the new labour reformers, such as Tom Banton and other members of his committee, pushed a strong independent labour party line while the old Grit leadership of O'Donoghue and March promoted a policy of supporting candidates pledged to labour planks no matter which party they represented. O'Donoghue managed to have the resolution referred back to the constituent unions for discussion.[91]

Thompson had called for the punishment of the aldermen who had given away the franchise. The TTLC blacklisted fourteen aldermen in 1892, only six of whom were re-elected to council.[92] However, on the greatly reduced council only six of the fourteen aldermen who had voted against the syndicate won re-election.[93] Some of the corrupt were defeated, but it was hardly a complete vindication. Thompson's remark that the whole truth would emerge proved far more prescient. In 1895 after a series of scandals involving the Kiely-Everett franchise, a serious investigation was finally conducted. Judge J.E. McDougall's reports confirmed all the 1891 rumours. Various aldermen had received money from the syndicate, and the $4,500 supplied Macdonald by Marshall had indeed come out of William Mackenzie's pocket.[94] It is not clear how much consolation this provided Thompson and his 1891 allies, but it certainly added impetus to the emerging campaign for public ownership of utilities in Ontario. The radical 1891 campaign under Thompson's control thus ironically laid some of the groundwork for the progressive business campaigns for public ownership in the first decade of the twentieth century.[95]

The campaign of 1891 prefigured other emerging progressive alliances also. The joint Social Reform Committee continued. Its attempts to embarrass the Toronto clergy into a concern for social problems, combined with the increased prominence of the Social Gospel in the United States, created the Toronto Social Problems Conference.[96] A clear line can be drawn from that organization to the full blossoming of the Social Gospel in Canada and the emergence of professional organizations which concerned themselves with social problems.[97]

Such a movement lies beyond the period of this study, but the crisis of 1891 starkly demonstrated the maturity of industrial capitalist society in Canada. Its existence was no longer debated; its effects were. The old reform alliances, based strongly in the ambiguity of the period of transition and strongly influenced by memories of other forms of social organization, were on the wane. In Ontario they surfaced for one last dramatic moment in the provincial election campaign of 1894, when the Patrons of Industry challenged the assumptions of industrial capitalist society. In this campaign, their forces were greatly augmented by the political alliance with labour and by the intellectual contributions of labour-reform intellectuals such as A.W. Wright, Phillips Thompson, and George Wrigley, the editor of their major organ, *The Canada Farmers Sun*.[98]

Wrigley and Thompson moved beyond the populist alliance into the Canadian Socialist League and then later merged it with the Socialist Party of British Columbia to create the Socialist Party of Canada. Wright remained loyal to his Tory roots and became the principal party organizer for Ontario and later head of the Ontario Workmen's Compensation Board. He became prominent in the campaigns for public ownership of hydro-electric power in Ontario. The 1891 public ownership campaign led in various directions.

Denounced as Grit factionists in 1891, O'Donoghue and Jury later received rewards for their party loyalty. Jury became a commissioner on the 1891 Ontario Royal Commission on Prisons and later, when Laurier came to power in Ottawa, was appointed an immigration agent in his native England. O'Donoghue followed a young admirer of his, Mackenzie King, to Ottawa as the dominion's first Fair-Wage Officer.

Different parts of Toronto's labour movement travelled in these various directions. The mainstream continued to involve itself in the currents of reform that became the Canadian Progressive movement, working through the two old political parties. Simultaneously, some Toronto workers embraced the radically different path of socialism. The debates of 1870–90 about labour's role in politics continued to bedevil the TTLC for the next 30 years, with three identifiable positions challenging for control: those who supported the two old-line parties; those who supported the Socialist Party of Canada, or later the Social Democratic Party of Canada; and finally those who worked for an Independent Labour Party along the lines of the British model. The latter two groups usually controlled the TTLC, but their ability to co-operate was always strained and often broke down.

15

Summary

The cultural, organizational, and political activities of Toronto workers in the late-nineteenth century were deeply rooted in the transition to industrial capitalism and in the rapid economic growth that ensued. Toronto was a vastly different city in 1891 than it had been only 25 years before. It had almost tripled in population, its industrial production had quadrupled in value, and the capital invested in its industries had increased by 725 per cent. In 1891 Toronto stood poised to enter yet another phase of capitalist development. A huge influx of American capital and a massive merger movement in the years before the Great War would again reshape Toronto's economic contours. Having struggled with industrial capital for the previous 30 years, Toronto workers were about to face a revamped enemy with entirely new strategies of control.[1] Those struggles against monopoly capital lie beyond this study but they were deeply influenced by the formative years of working-class development treated here.

Industrial capitalism, born in the 1850s and 1860s in Toronto, grew to maturity in the 1870s and 1880s. The working class emerged in these decades and struggled to keep pace with the vast changes wrought by the new economic system. In its attempt to comprehend and to cope with the wrenching transformation of capitalist industrialization, the working class tenaciously maintained the political and cultural traditions of its ancestors. These traditions ranged from the peculiar Orange trinity of crown, empire, and Protestantism (reminiscent of eighteenth-century 'church-and-king' crowds in England) to the customary methods of work associated with pre-industrial craft production. But Toronto workers adapted these traditions to the new context of industrial capitalist society. Those that failed to be adapted, such as the Orange ritual riot, slowly disappeared in these transitional decades. The Orange Order itself, however, continued to play an important institutional role in the world of Toronto workers. Orangeism lost most of its rough edges in the 1880s; in the process it became increasingly divisive when stripped of its earlier functions as a mass political vehicle for the disenfranchised and as an important ethnic aid society.

The artisan traditions deeply entrenched in the pre-industrial world provided Toronto workers with innovative strategies to combat their employers who tried to enforce industrial capitalism's new work styles. From medieval craft lore, the shoemakers brought forth St Crispin as a symbol of their historic roots and of their importance to the community. Building on traditions of craft pride and solidarity, Toronto shoemakers even resorted to breaking machines in their desperate attempt to maintain decent wages and conditions in the shoe industry. Most striking was their ability to adapt the older means of artisan resistance to their new situation. Thus they extended craft traditions to encompass all workers in the industry, including women, quickly realizing that a narrow view of production was destined to fail. This aim, which would have organized the entire work force, in the industry, brought a combined employers' assault on the union.

Similarly, Toronto coopers built on their craft experience to form the initially successful Coopers International Union to protect the trade from the capitalist innovations that were destroying older styles of work and ways of life. Other crafts joined with the shoemakers and the coopers to create the Toronto Trades Assembly, the nine-hours movement, and the Canadian Labor Union in the early 1870s. These new institutional forms proved too fragile to survive the depression of the 1870s but re-emerged in the 1880s when the economy recovered.

Other craft workers, such as the printers and moulders, established solid institutional forms that lasted throughout this period. The uneven nature of industrial capitalist development meant that printers and moulders were free for most of this period from the onslaught of mechanization. They were not free from attacks by employers, of course, but retention of their skills provided them with considerable collective strength. Class conflict in these industries was intense, but the printers especially were able to adapt their traditions successfully to the new contingencies of industrial capitalist society. By the time the linotype machine arrived, the ITU was strong enough to protect the compositors. Moulders enjoyed similar success until the early 1900s, when the metal trades became the focus of class conflict when capital strove to gain control of the shop floor.

Trade unions emerged out of older craft associations and traditions when it became necessary to institutionalize work rules and standard wages. This process commenced in Toronto in the 1840s when George Brown challenged the notion of customary wages. In the 1850s the railroad boom led to an increase in these wage struggles and unions became more prevalent. When capitalists tried unilaterally to impose new conditions of work and new notions of payment (based on market value as opposed to custom), workers organized. There was no collective bargaining in the 1860s and 1870s on these issues; conflicts between workers and employers were resolved by strength alone. This strategy succeeded for the skilled 'who had progressed but part way down the path from journeyman artisan to factory wage labour.'[2] It was far less satisfactory for the unskilled who, instead, 'relied on massive solidarity supplemented by intimidation of dissenters through social ostracism, threats, or riots.'[3] The arrival of factory production demanded new union strategies. The Knights of St Crispin pioneered these strategies in Toronto in the early 1870s – by aiming to control the labour supply not only through union rules and craft solidarity but also through the notion of organizing the entire potential work force regardless of skill. In addition, unions in this period turned to arbitration, centralization, and bureaucratization as other possible resolutions of their new problems.

The experiences of the 1870s made a deep impact on many workers whose skills were increasingly undermined by the development of industrial capitalism. They began to recognize that their strength no longer lay in their skill but rather in their ability to organize all workers. This strategy became the keynote of the Knights of Labor, who preferred arbitration to strike action to as a way of resolving industrial conflict. The Knights arrived in Toronto in the early 1880s and proceeded to organize large segments of the Toronto work force previously untouched by craft unionism. As had been true in 1872, when labour united in the nine-hours movement, however, capital responded vigorously to this new challenge and defeated the Knights dramatically in the second street-railway strike in 1886 and in a series of lesser struggles in 1887. These defeats, together with an economic downturn, decreased the Knights' influence. The re-emergence of partisan politics among the order's leaders, and of heated conflict between trade-unionists and the order, quickened its demise.

Class conflict was not restricted to the workplace in late-nineteenth-century Toronto; the working class played an important role in politics as well. In the 1870s, workers tended to support the Tory party because of its ties with the Orange order, Macdonald's responsiveness to the legalization of trade unions in 1872, and its high-tariff policy to encourage the development of Canadian industry. It was the populist left wing of the party that the workers joined in support of currency and land reform. Winning the working-class vote, however, became increasingly problematic when workers organized the Workingmen's Liberal Conservative Union. From this base stemmed a devastating critique of the railroad and land-settlement policies of the Tory party.

The organized labour movement of the 1870s developed effective lobbying techniques through its new central bodies. It gained important legislative reforms which further clarified the legal status of unions, strikes, and employment contracts. In the 1880s labour perfected its lobbying style and enjoyed considerable success with Mowat's Ontario government. Success with Mowat and an increasing disenchantment with Macdonald's national policy, especially its encouragement of unrestricted immigration, slowly eroded the Tory hold on the working-class vote. This shift, combined with the *Mail*'s serious error in blacklisting the TTU, led to the election of a labour-reform mayor and strong independent labour candidacies in the 1886 provincial and 1887 federal elections. The middle years of the decade, then, saw a vigorous struggle for political control of Toronto workers, the competing platforms being a new labour reform ideology versus the older Tory philosophy. Electoral defeats, partisan political intrigues, and economic recession ended that struggle, the Tories regaining their overt electoral control but not their total ideological hegemony.

The 1880s also saw the revitalization of various independent political strains, which joined with labour in 1891 to force into public debate the issue of municipal versus private ownership of the street railway. Antimonopoly sentiments were sufficiently strong to end the TSR's reign, but not powerful enough to gain public ownership of the franchise. Partyism emerged in this struggle, with Grit labour leaders undermining public support of civic ownership.

By 1891, trade-unionism in Toronto was strong and stable. The TTLC and TLC had established themselves as powerful central bodies with permanent committee structures and highly developed lobbying techniques. The District Assembly of the Knights, however, was in rapid decline and lost its charter two years later. The Toronto Knights had, at best, a tenuous existence until their final expulsion from the TLC in 1902 for dual unionism.

However, the new institutional strength of 1891 also had weaknesses. The major loss was the Knights' concerted effort to organize all workers regardless of skill, sex, ethnicity, and race. Other potential dangers lay in the increased centralization and bureaucratization of the international unions, of the TTLC, of the TLC, and of the American Federation of Labor.

In the political sphere the situation was similar. The stronger institutions provided a far more effective lobbying force, but at the same time represented a narrowing of vision – the gain in focus was lost in perspective and overview. Simultaneously, socialism appeared in Toronto, with its more sophisticated and consistent critique of the totality of industrial capitalist society. It provided a minority of workers with both focus and perspective but was unable to build a mass movement to match the labour upsurge of 1886 and 1887, which Edward Aveling and Eleanor Marx so aptly described as 'unconscious socialism.'[4]

Curiously, when S.T. Wood, a single-taxer and prominent Toronto journalist, tried to invoke satirically the world of the late-nineteenth-century labour-reform intellectuals, he caught their essence. Wood commented that they congregated 'in friendly unity, joined by the bond of an unfaltering belief that if things were only not as they were they might have been otherwise.'[5] If we ignore his satirical thrust, surely this captures the Canadian labour reformers' inspiration in the late-nineteenth century. Their utopia was not fully developed, for they stood on the edge of what Edward Thompson has called 'the river of fire.' Many, like Phillips Thompson, were about to cross that river, but many others would not. After Thompson crossed it, he was invited to debate the merits of socialism at the University of Toronto with a former comrade, Grit labour leader Alfred Jury. Jury had spoken at the university many times previously as a representative of labour. However, this debate never occurred for the university administration intervened and refused to allow Thompson to speak on campus. Such divisions came only after the river had been forded.

The transitional nature of the 1870s and 1880s bred a labour reform ideology and a labour movement which simultaneously looked backward and forward. Much of the movement's strength lay in the workers' knowledge of a past that was totally different from their present. They knew that industrial capitalism was a social system with a history; it was neither natural nor pre-ordained. This realization injected their struggles with a precocious vigour, based on their comprehension that the economy had been, and thus could be, organized in radically different ways. This commonly shared understanding disappeared in the twentieth century, and only socialist workers maintained an alternative social vision. The precision of the socialist critique was a major gain for the Toronto working class, but the declining numbers of those whose vision transcended the established system was a major loss. Class conflict, of course, continued.

APPENDICES

I

Toronto's industrial revolution tables

TABLE I.1

Clothing* industry in Toronto, 1871

Size of work force	No. of estabs.	Total no. of employees	% of emps. in industry	Value added in $000s	% of value added
100+	5	671	31	115.9	25.4
50–99	6	421	19	99	21.7
30–49	10	358	17	90.3	19.8
0–29	73	711	33	151.8	33.2
Total	94	2,161	100	457	100.1

Largest employers

Name of firm	Product	No. of employees					Value of production in $000s	Value added in $000s	Motive force (hp†)
		Adult		Child					
		M	F	M	F	Total			
Henderson	Straw	12	175	14		201	88	44.9	15†
Barker	Straw	15	80	5	30	130	62	12	8
Livingstone	Clothing	20	100	2	2	124	110	24	H‡
Walker	Clothing	50	60	4	2	116	100	20	H
[No name]	Clothing	25	75			100	90	15	H
Sillup	Tailor	18	70			88	83	8	H
Hughes	Tailor	24	60			84	60	24	H
Simpson	Wool knitting	11	60	3	3	77	50	10	20

TABLE I.1 (concluded)
Largest employers

Name of firm	Product	No. of employees					Value of production in $000s	Value added in $000s	Motive force (hp†)
		Adult		Child					
		M	F	M	F	Total			
Finch	Clothing	5	50		5	60	45	5	H
Kay	Millinery		50		6	56	40	15	H
Thompson	Clothing	16	30	10		56	70	37	H

* Clothing includes tailors, dressmakers, millinery, hats and furs, straw, and knitting.
† Horse power, steam
‡ Hand power
Source: Canada, Census of 1871, Industrial Mss., Toronto. This is true of all tables in Appendix I unless otherwise specified.

TABLE I.2
Female and child labour, Toronto, 1871

Industry	No. of women employed	No. of children employed	Total no. employed	% women and children
Clothing	1,411	201	2,161	74.6
Shoe	359	169	1,565	33.7
Printing	269	114	869	44.1
Tobacco	60	124	364	50.6
Furniture	50	4	479	11.3
Total	2,149	612	5,438	50.8
All industries total	2,238	1180	9,999	34.2

TABLE I.3

Boot and shoe industry in Toronto, 1871

Size of work force	No. of estabs.	Total no. of employees	% of emps. in industry	Value added in $000s	% of value added
100+	4	1,047	66	106.8	48.7
50–99	4	290	19	63.2	28.8
30–49	2	79	5	18.5	8.4
0–29	39	149	11	30.6	14.0
Total	49	1,565	101	219.1	

Largest employers, 1871

	No. of employees					Value of production in $000s	Value added in $000s	Motive force (hp)
	Adult		Child					
Name of firm	M	F	M	F	Total			
Sessions, Turner	330	90	50	40	510	300	20	15
Childs & Hamilton	134	42	13	3	192	160	10	H
Damer, King	105	60	1	25	191	250	48	15
Paterson, Murphy, & Braid	100	50	4		154	160	28.8	H
Holmes	50	24	2	7	83	100	14	H
Barclay, Evans	66	8	2	4	80	75	10	H
Sanderson & Williams	50	15	3	2	70	45	6.8	H
Dack, Forsythe, & Leslie	37	20			57	60	32.4	H
Cobley	13	30	3	3	49	35	7.2	H
McEntee	25	4	1		30	18	11.3	H

TABLE I.4

Metallurgy in Toronto, 1871

Size of work force	No. of estabs.	Total no. of employees	% of employees	Value added in $000s	% of value added
100+	4	730	57	788.6	71.3
50–99	3	196	15	73.2	66.0
30–49	3	135	11	88.0	8.0
0–29	17	221	17	156.0	14.1
Total	27	1,282	100	1,105.8*	100

Largest employers

Name of firm	Product	No. of employees Adult M	F	Child M	F	Total	Value of production in $000s	Value added in $000s	Motive force (hp)
Dickey Foundry	Mach.	230				230	275	82.7	50
Hamilton Foundry	Mach.	200				200	620	485.0	60
Gzowski Rolling Mill	Rails	180	20			200	500	41.0	250
Beard Bros.	Stoves	60	40			100	250	179.9	15
Gurney	Stoves	90	3			93	75	23.0	25
Currie	Boilers	50	3			53	45	8.2	12
Armstrong	Stoves	45	5			50	80	42.0	20
Levey	Mach.	40	6			46	90	60.0	30
Harte Foundry	Stoves	47	2			49	55	20.0	15
Taylor & Co.	Safes	40				40	35	8.0	15

* This figure is approximately triple the published census version for this group of industries. The value-added figures for Hamilton and Beard seem suspiciously high. The anomaly, however, remains unresolved. In cases of doubt I have trusted the manuscript version.

TABLE I.5

Publishing in Toronto, 1871

Size of work force	No. of estabs.	Total no. of employees	% of employees	Value added in $000s	% of value added
100+	2	299	34	77	22.1
50–99	5	383	44	214	61.3
30–49	2	91	11	40	11.5
0–29	10	96	11	18	5.2
Total	19	869	100	349	100.1

Largest employers

		No. of employees					Value of production in $000s	Value added in $000s	Motive force (hp)
		Adult		Child					
Name of firm	Product	M	F	M	F	Total			
Hunter Rose	Books	70	100	3		173	160	62	25
Campbell	Bindery	35	90	1		126	100	15	15
Daily Telegraph	Paper and books	75		20		95	200	30	10
Leader	Paper and jobshop	70		10		80	250	90	20
Globe	Paper and jobshop	70		10		80	220	40	H
A. Dredge	Binder	10	30	4	20	64	126	35	H
Copp Clark	Books	50	10	2	2	64	60	19	10
Brown Bros.	Binder	30	18			48	50	10	H
Belford		23	7	11	2	43	126	30	H

TABLE I.6

Furniture industry in Toronto, 1871

Size of work force	No. of estabs.	Total no. of employees	% of employees	Value added in $000s	% of value added
100+	1	430	89.8	30	71.7
0–29	7	49	10.2	11.8	29.2
Total	8	479	100	41.8	99.9

Largest employer

	No. of employees							
	Adult		Child			Value of production	Value added	Motive force
Name of firm	M	F	M	F	Total	in $000s	in $000s	(hp)
R. Hay & Co.	380	50			430	500	30	40

TABLE I.7

Tobacco, Toronto, 1871

Size of work force	No. of estabs.	Total no. of employees	% of employees	Value added in $000s	% of value added
50–90	3	224	62	5.35	11.5
30–49	2	85	23	21.27	45.7
0–29	4	55	16	19.93	42.8
Total	9	364	101	46.55	100

Largest employers

		No. of employees							
		Adult		Child			Value of production	Value added	Motive force
Name of firm	Product	M	F	M	F	Total	in $000s	in $000s	(hp)
C.P. Reid	Cigars	56	6	16	2	80	73.2	9.15	H
Scales	Tobacco	20	25	15	20	80	105.0	6.50	16
Wallace	Tobacco	33	10	15	6	64	25.0	−10.30	Water
Peniston	Tobacco	12	9	15	12	48	42.0	.70	8
Benner	Tobacco	25	10	2		37	48.0	20.57	12

TABLE I.8

Brewing and distilling, Toronto, 1871

Size of work force	No. of estabs.	Total no. of employees	% of employees	Value added in $000s	% of value added
100+	1	150	63.6	960	82.6
0–29	10	86	36.4	202	17.4
Total	11	236	100	1,162	100

Largest employer

		No. of employees							
		Adult		Child			Value of production	Value added	Motive force
Name of firm	Product	M	F	M	F	Total	in $000s	in $000s	(hp)
Gooderham & Worts	Liquor	150				150	1,470*	960	116

* This figure appears to be that before the subtraction of government excise taxes.

TABLE I.9

Bakeries and confectioneries, Toronto, 1871

Size of work force	No. of estabs.	Total no. of employees	% of employees
50–59	1	50	25
10–29	3	35	17
0–9	32	116	58
Total	35	201	100

Largest employer

	No. of employees							
	Adult		Child			Value of production	Value added	Motive force
Name of firm	M	F	M	F	Total	in $000s	in $000s	(hp)
Hessin Confectionery	27	5	18		50	130	28	25

TABLE I.10

Brass, tin, and sheet iron, Toronto, 1871

Size of work force	No. of estabs.	Total no. of employees	% of employees
10–29	3	56	40
0–9	20	83	60
Total	23	139	100

TABLE I.11

Carriage-making, Toronto, 1871

Size of work force	No. of estabs.	Total no. of employees	% of employees
30–49	1	33	24
10–29	4	88	63
0–9	5	18	13
Total	10	139	100

Largest employer

| | No. of employees | | | | | Value of production in $000s | Value added in $000s | Motive force (hp) |
| | Adult | | Child | | | | | |
Name of firm	M	F	M	F	Total			
Wilby	25	2	6		33	15	10	12

TABLE I.12

Harness-making, Toronto, 1871

Size of work force	No. of estabs.	Total no. of employees	% of employees
10–29	3	47	62
0–9	8	29	38
Total	11	76	100

TABLE I.13
Employment in major Toronto industries, 1871–91

Industry	1871*			1881			1891		
	No. of employees	Rank	% of employees	No. of employees	Rank	% of employees	No. of employees	Rank	% of employees
Clothing	2,156	1	23	2,775	1	22	6,287	1	26
Boot and shoe	1,565	2	17	1,232	3	10	742	4	3
Foundries and machinery	1,279	3	14	728	4	6	2,390	3	10
Publishing	869	4	9	1,618	2	13	2,872	2	12
Furniture	479	5	5	354	6	3	500	7	2
Tobacco	364	6	4	389	5	3	154	10	1
Distilling and	236	7	3	333	7	3	550	6	2
Agricultural implements				322	8	3	575	5	2
Musical instruments	141	8	2	270	9	2	320	8	1
Meat packing	117	9	1	136	10	1	303	9	1
Total top 10	7,206		77	8,157		64	14,733		60
Total in city	9,400			12,708			24,470		

* 1871 data are based on published returns to be consistent with 1881 and 1891 returns. This accounts for any inconsistencies with previous 1871 data which were drawn from the manuscripts.
Source: Canada, Census, 1871, 1881, 1891

TABLE I.14
Annual product in major Toronto industries, 1871–1891

Industry	1871*			1881			1891		
	Value in $000s	Rank	% of product	Value in $000s	Rank	% of product	Value in $000s	Rank	% of product
Clothing	1,817	1	13	2,782	1	15	7,345	1	17
Distilling and brewing	1,814	2	13	1,692	3	9	2,195	4	5
Foundries and machinery	1,585	3	12	1,002	6	5	3,838	2	9
Boot and shoe	1,334	4	10	1,290	5	7	1,157	7	3
Publishing	1,193	5	9	2,227	2	12	3,683	3	9
Meat packing	983	6	7	1,371	4	7	1,638	5	4
Furniture	517	7	4	382	9	2	800	8	2
Tobacco	351	8	3	402	8	2	212	10	1
Musical instruments	184	9	1	311	10	2	565	9	1
Agricultural implements				580	7	3	1,250	6	3
Total top 10	9,778		71	12,039		63	22,683		53
Toronto total	13,686			19,100			42,489		

* See note, Table I.13.
Source: Canada, Census, 1871, 1881, 1891.

TABLE I.15
Value added in major Toronto industries, 1871–91

Industry	1871* Value added in $000s	Rank	% value added	1881 Value added in $000s	Rank	% value added	1891 Value added in $000s	Rank	% value added
Distilling	1,003	1	26.2	209	7	3.7	275	6	2.3
Clothing	457	2	11.9	723	1	12.9	2,207	1	18.1
Engineering	330	3	8.6	313	5	5.6	1,024	2	8.4
Publishing	298	4	7.8	519	3	9.2	877	3	7.2
Shoe and boot	219	5	5.7	239	6	4.3	265	7	2.2
Meat packing	193	6	5.0	334	4	5.9	156	10	1.3
Brewing	160	7	4.2	540	2	9.6	418	5	3.4
Musical instruments	70	8	1.8	70	11	1.2	187	9	1.5
Tobacco	53	9	1.4	165	8	2.9	51	11	.4
Furniture	38	10	1.0	128	10	2.3	264	8	2.2
Agricultural implements				142	9	2.5	651	4	5.3
Total top 11	2,821		73.7	3,382		60.2	6,375		52.3
Toronto total	3,826			5,617			12,219		

* See note, Table I.13
Source: Canada, Census, 1871, 1881, 1891

TABLE I.16

Garment industry in Toronto, 1871–91*

		No. of estabs.	No. of employees					Value of annual product in $000s	Value added in $000s
			Adult		Child				
			M	F	M	F	Total		
1871	Dressmaking	25		164	3	26	193	121	28
	Furriers	10	42	114	9	17	182	163	47
	Hosiery	1	11	60	3	3	77	50	12
	Straw	2	27	255	19	30	331	142	53
	Tailors	51	466	764	22	47	1,299	1,341	317
	Total	89	546	1,357	56	123	2,082	1,817	457
1881	Dressmaking	72	7	393	7	76	483	284	81
	Furriers	15	85	197	5	3	290	325	113
	Hosiery	2	26	49	9	3	87	112	31
	Straw	2	19	69	3	3	94	46	15
	Tailors	61	537	927	16	23	1,503	1,596	397
	Corsets	2	19	232	4	8	263	180	34
	Shirts	8	6	68			74	128	26
	Woolcloth	5	28	43	4		75	114	26
	Total	167	727	1,978	48	116	2,869	2,782	723
1891	Dressmaking	402	30	1,547	15	85	1,677	1,487	486
	Furriers	30	230	412	4	1	647	1,316	493
	Hosiery	4	21	64	13	29	127	123	43
	Tailors	216	1,034	1,575	28	17	2,654	3,172	793
	Corsets	6	50	314	2	11	377	397	111
	Shirts	19	53	535	2		590	480	154
	Woollens	2	41	57	14	7	119	210	51
	Knitting	1	38	82	4	12	136	160	76
	Total	680	1,497	4,586	82	162	6,327	7,346	2,207

* The data for 1871 in Tables I.16 to I.27 are drawn from the published returns to be consistent with 1881 and 1891 returns. This accounts for any discrepancies with data in Tables I.1 to I.8.

Source: Canada, Census, Industrial Tables, 1871–91

TABLE I.17

Machinery and foundry products (including agricultural implements) in Toronto, 1871–91

		No. of estabs.	No. of employees				Total	Value of annual product in $000s	Value added in $000s
			Adult		Child				
			M	F	M	F			
1871	Foundries and machinery	15	801		59		860	817	192
	Boilers	2	53		3		56	48	9
	Engines	2	49		6		55	95	56
	Safes	2	45		1		46	41	9
	Foundries (iron & brass fittings)	14	86		16		102	85	23
	Rolling mill	1	180		20		200	500	41
	Total	36	1,214		105		1,319	1,586	330
1881	Foundries (machinery)	25	350		22		372	448	115
	Boilers	2	40		6		46	96	19
	Engines	2	86		4		90	81	24
	Safes	1	65		10		75	82	12
	Foundries (fittings)	25	248		15		263	386	126
	Pumps	2	13				13	40	17
	Agricultural implements	3	317		5		322	580	142
	Total	60	1,119		62		1,181	1,713	455
1891	Foundries	36	1,250	1	21		1,272	1,975	545
	Boilers	1	15		3		18	200	62
	Engines	2	300				300	375	73
	Safes	1	130				130	115	25
	Iron & brass fittings	15	349	8	27		384	454	102
	Pumps	3	65	1	1		67	120	43
	Agricultural implements	1	575				575	1,250	651
	Furnaces	9	123	2	8		133	332	174
	Total	68	2,807	12	60		2,789	4,821	1,675

Source: Canada, Census, Industrial Tables, 1871–91

TABLE I.18

Publishing industry in Toronto, 1871–91

			No. of employees					Value of production in $000s	Value added in $000s
		No. of estabs.	Adult		Child		Total		
			M	F	M	F			
1871	Printing	11	331	100	72		503	913	237
	Book	5	80	140	5	25	250	280	61
	Total	16	411	240	77	25	753	1,193	298
1881	Printing	32	862	116	233	24	1,235	1,223	291
	Book	6	135	190	16	22	363	1,003	228
	Total	38	997	306	249	46	1,598	2,227	519
1891	Printing	74	1,790	441	147	6	2,384	3,094	741
	Bookbinding*	9	225	254	8	1	428	589	136
	Total	83	2,015	695	155	7	2,872	3,683	877

* It would appear that the 1891 bookbinding category is more specific than the 1871 and 1881 book categories. The rest of book production has probably been added to printing in 1891.

Source: Canada, Census, Industrial Tables, 1871–91

TABLE I.19

Brewing and distilling industries in Toronto, 1871–91

		No. of employees					Value of production in $000s	Value added in $000s
	No. of estabs.	Adult		Child		Total		
		M	F	M	F			
BREWING								
1871	5	73		6		79	281	160
1881	10	217		3		220	1,078	540
1891	9	396	1	3		400	1,395	418
DISTILLING								
1871	2	157				157	1,533	1,003
1881	2	111		2		113	625	209
1891	1	150				150	800	275

Source: Canada, Census, Industrial Tables, 1871–91

TABLE I.20
Boot and shoe industry in Toronto, 1871–91

	No. of estabs.	No. of employees					Value of production in $000s	Value added in $000s
		Adult		Child				
		M	F	M	F	Total		
1871	47	1,032	361	87	84	1,174	1,334	219
1881	76	838	269	91	34	1,232	1,290	239
1891	149	576	152	13	1	742	1,157	265

Source: Canada, Census, Industrial Tables, 1871–91

TABLE I.21
Furniture industry in Toronto, 1871–91

	No. of estabs.	No. of employees					Value of production in $000s	Value added in $000s
		Adult		Child				
		M	F	M	F	Total		
1871	7	398	50	4		452	517	38
1881	16	316	14	24		354	382	128
1891	68	415	51	33	1	500	800	264

Source: Canada, Census, Industrial Tables, 1871–91

TABLE I.22
Musical instrument industry in Toronto, 1871–91

	No. of estabs.	No. of employees					Value of production in $000s	Value added in $000s
		Adult		Child				
		M	F	M	F	Total		
1871	5	137		4		141	184	70
1881	9	254		16		270	311	70
1891	13	306	2	12		320	565	187

Source: Canada, Census, Industrial Tables, 1871–91

TABLE I.23

Tobacco industry in Toronto, 1871–91

			No. of employees					Value of production in $000s	Value added in $000s
			Adult		Child				
	Product	No. of estabs.	M	F	M	F	Total		
1871		9	180	60	84	40	364	331	53
1881		13	237	80	63	9	389	402	165
1891	Cigar	6	54	2	1		58	65	18
	Tobacco	4	107	22	8		137	147	33
	Total	10	161	24	9		195	212	51

Source: Canada, Census, Industrial Tables, 1871–91

TABLE I.24

Bakeries and confectioneries in Toronto, 1871–91

			No. of employees					Value of production in $000s	Value added in $000s
			Adult		Child				
		No. of estabs.	M	F	M	F	Total		
1871		33	132	19	36		187	585	154
1881		45	263	61	27	27	378	980	160
1891	Bakery	58	500	208	35	7	750	1,550	367
	Confectionery	24	151	123	13	18	305	570	190
	Total	122	651	331	48	25	1,055	2,120	557

Source: Canada, Census, Industrial Tables, 1871–91

TABLE I.25

Tin and sheet iron in Toronto, 1871–91

| | | No. of employees | | | | | Value of production in $000s | Value added in $000s |
| | No. of estabs. | Adult | | Child | | | | |
		M	F	M	F	Total		
1871	20	99		24		123	101	23
1881	40	202	11	101	16	330	259	70
1891	53	404	30	34	7	475	731	196

Source: Canada, Census, Industrial Tables, 1871–91

TABLE I.26

Carriage-making in Toronto, 1871–91

| | | No. of employees | | | | | Value of production in $000s | Value added in $000s |
| | No. of estabs. | Adult | | Child | | | | |
		M	F	M	F	Total		
1871	12	128	2	22		152	99	39
1881	23	173	1	20		194	146	37
1891	30	307		4		311	336	107

Source: Canada, Census, Industrial Tables, 1871–91

TABLE I.27

Largest Toronto employers, 1885–91

Industry and firm	1885	1886	1888	1891
CLOTHING				
Livingstone (1867)†			250	
Laley (1844)	450*		200*	
Petley & Petley	150			
Thompson & Son	200			
Martin		50		
Gray (1862)			80	
Walker			200	
Murray				
Bilton Bros. (tailors)		50		
Jameson (tailors)	150			
Score & Son (tailors)	60			
Spain (tailors)		60		
Pittman Millinery		80		
McCall Millinery		125		
McArthur (furs)		50	75	
Allan (hats and furs) (1877)	60		65	
Christie (hats and furs)	40			
Lugsdin (hats and furs)	60		60	
Gillespie (furs) (1862)	75	80	100	
McPhail (furs)		40	75	
Crompton Corsets (1874)	350		250*	
Simpson Knitting (1865)	120	150*	120	136
Universal Knitting		100		
Latham (overalls)	100			
Gale Shirt Co.	135		170	
A.H. Sims (shirts)	300			
BOOT AND SHOE				
Charlesworth (1874)	150			
Cooper Smith (1852)		500		
King (1869)			300	
Hamilton		300		
FURNITURE				
Hay	575			
CIGARS				
Taylor		65		
Eichhorn		80		

TABLE I.27 (continued)

Industry and firm	1885	1886	1888	1891
METALS AND MACHINERY				
Massey (agricultural implements) (1847)	400			700
Abell (agricultural implements)	300	200		
Dominion Bridge (1879)		100		
Inglis & Hunter (machinery) (1857)		100	100	130
Taylor Safes (1855)	140*	125	150	175
St. Lawrence Foundry (1851)	150	150	150	
Polson Iron Works (1882)	30		200	
Gurney (stoves) (1868)	150*		300	
Dominion Saw	50	50		
Northey (pumps) (1881)	50			
Doty (engines)	100			
Ontario Bolt				500
Morrison (brass)	100		115*	150
Toronto Radiator				100
Toronto Rolling Mill	300			
MUSICAL INSTRUMENTS				
Heintzman (1871)	150	150	150	150
Williams (1854)	150			
BREWING AND DISTILLING				
Toronto Brewery		75	50	
Copland		50	50	
Dominion			100	
O'Keefe			63	
Davies			60	
Gooderham & Worts				150
MISCELLANEOUS				
Gage (publishers)		125		
Toronto Lithographing		75		
Copp Clark (publishers)			120	
Boeckh (brushes) (1856)	95		100	
Nelson (brooms)			125	
Ellis (jewellery)	100		125	
Hemming (jewellery)			50	
Clarke (trunks) (1854)	45			
Toronto Bag Works		50*		
Kilgour Paper Bags		110*		
Taylor Paper	100			

TABLE I.27 (concluded)

Industry and firm	1885	1886	1888	1891
Cobban (mouldings) (1874)	125			
Ewing Mirrors (1862)		100		
McCausland Stained Glass	50			40
Christie Brown (1856)		120	175	
Robertson (confectionery) (1863)	100	150	125	
Hessin (confectionery) (1854)		150	100	
R.T. Watson (confectionery)		100*		
Gutta Percha Rubber	100			
Acme Silver		50		
Toronto Silver Plate (1881)		110		
Lyman (drugs)		55		
Morse (soap)		40	50	
Davies Meat Packing		125		
Firstbrook (boxes)			90*	
Dixon Carriages	50			

* 1885, *Globe*; 1886, *Mail*, 19 November; 1888, *Royal Commission on the Relations of Capital and Labour* (Toronto Evidence) (Ottawa 1889).
Bracketed dates after company names are date of founding, as given in Canada, Parliament, *Sessional Papers*, 1885, no. 37.
Sources: *History of Toronto and the County of York* (Toronto 1885); *Industries of Canada: Historical and Commercial Sketches of Toronto* (Toronto 1886); *Globe*, 'Board of Trade Edition,' July 1888; G. Mercer Adams, *Toronto: Old and New* (Toronto 1891) and 1891 Census.

II

Toronto strikes 1867–1892

TABLE II.1
Strikes in Toronto, 1867–92

Year	Number
1867–69	8
1870–74	27
1875–79	9
1880–84	44
1885–89	55
1890–92	13
Total	156

Sources: Toronto Press;
Ontario, Bureau of Industry
Reports; trade union data

TABLE II.2
Strikes in Toronto, 1867–92

Year	Number
1867	5
1868	1
1869	2
1870	2
1871	5
1872	11
1873	5
1874	4

TABLE II.2 (concluded)
Strikes in Toronto, 1867–92

Year	Number
1875	2
1876	1
1877	3
1878	2
1879	1
1880	2
1881	11
1882	12
1883	11
1884	8
1885	2
1886	19
1887	14
1888	13
1889	7
1890	9
1891	2
1892	2

TABLE II.3
Toronto strikes by month of origin, 1867–92

Month	Number
January	7
February	10
March	25
April	18
May	24
June	18
July	11
August	8
September	11
October	11
November	3
December	6
Unknown	4
Total	156

Sources: Toronto Press; Ontario, Bureau of
Industry, *Reports*; trade union data

TABLE II.4

Strikes by craft, industry, and year

Trade and year	Number
BUILDING TRADES	
Bricklayers 1872, '77, '86, '90	4
Bricklayers' labourers 1879, '81, '88	3
Building labourers 1881, '85, '88	3
Carpenters 1867, '72, '81, '81, '82, '82, '83, '87, '88	9
Painters 1867, '82, '83, '88, '91	5
Plumbers and steamfitters 1886, '88, '88	3
Plasterers and lathers 1874, '81, '82, '83, '86, '86, '86, '87, '88, '88	10
Plasterers' labourers 1882, '83, '84, '84, '89	5
Stone cutters 1874, '89, '90	3
Stone masons 1887, '90	2
Total	47
TRANSPORTATION	
Carters and teamsters 1883, '86, '86, '88	4
Cabmen 1868, '69, '73	3
Street-railway workers 1886, '86	2
Sailors 1891	1
Various railroad-running trades 1875, '77, '80, '80, '84	5
Communications 1873, '74, '83, '88	4
Total	19
METAL TRADES	
Blacksmiths 1872	1
Boilermakers 1883	1
Brass finishers 1872	1
Massey works 1886	1
Moulders 1867, '70, '71, '72, '74, '75, '81, '87, '90, '90, '92	11
Total	15
PRINTING TRADES	
Printers 1872, '77, '78, '83, '84, '88, '89, '92	8
Bookbinders 1872, '72, '86	3
Pressmen 1887	1
Total	12
BOOT AND SHOE	
Shoemakers 1869, '70, '71, '81, '81, '85, '87, '89, '90	9
Female shoe operatives 1882, '82	2
Total	11

TABLE II.4 (concluded)

Strikes by craft, industry, and year

Trade and year	Number
CLOTHING TRADES	
Tailors 1871, '73, '83, '86, '87, '87	6
Corsetmakers 1888, '90	2
Sewing machine operators 1883, '84	2
Total	10
FURNITURE AND MUSICAL INSTRUMENTS	
Furniture 1872, '72, '86, '87, '87, '87	6
Musical instruments 1886, '87	2
Total	8
FOOD AND TOBACCO	
Bakers 1881, '89	2
Cigarmakers 1867, '71, '72, '73, '78, '88	6
Total	8
MIXED CRAFTS 1867, '76, '81, '82, '84, '86, '89, '89, '89, '89, '90	11
LABOURERS	
Longshoremen 1871, '82, '84	3
Railroad navvies 1883, '84	2
Gardeners 1882	1
Freight porters 1881, '82	2
Labourers (unspecified) 1873, '82, '86, '86, '86, '87, '87	7
Total	15
GRAND TOTAL	156

Sources: Toronto Press; Ontario Bureau of Industry, *Reports*; trade union data

III

Selected biographies of Toronto labour leaders 1867–1892

This list should not be regarded as definitive or complete. It has been compiled largely on the basis of accessible material. Many important figures are not included.

ARMSTRONG, JOHN, printer, labour leader, and Conservative spokesman. Active in the TTU and frequent officer from the 1870s on, he also served three terms on the ITU executive, holding the office of president in 1878. The major Tory figure in the TTLC, he was president in 1882 and was always active in the TLC. Fired from the *Mail* after the 1884 strike, he led the working-class defection from the Tory party, which so alarmed Macdonald. After the party succumbed in 1886, he arranged the truce and was subsequently appointed to the Royal Commission on the Relations of Labour and Capital in which he served the labour movement faithfully. He was later appointed secretary of the Ontario Labour Bureau. He died 22 November 1910.

CAREY, DAVID A., machinist and union leader, born in Dublin 1859, emigrated to Canada in 1861. Joined KOL Local 2622 in 1882, of which he later became DMW. He was later president of the TLC. He died 26 March 1927.

CARTER, J.W., painter and union leader, born in England, where he was active in the trade-union movement before arrival in Toronto in 1871. Appears to have carried Lib-Lab politics to Canada. Also active co-operator and frequent president of the Central Co-op Society. Active in TTA and first president of the CLU. He ran as a provincial labour candidate in Toronto West in 1883. He served as a TTLC trustee throughout the 1880s. He was also a prominent member of the Oddfellows and Sons of England.

CLARKE, E.F., printer, Tory MPP, born in Ireland in 1850, came to Canada in 1864. As a *Globe* printer and TTU leader, was arrested in 1872. A prominent Orangeman, he became editor of the *Orange Sentinel* in 1877. Sat as a Toronto MPP from 1886 to 1894 and was mayor of Toronto, 1887–91. Later MP for Toronto West. He was also a member of the 1892 Royal Commission on the Liquor Traffic. 'The People's Ned' was a major force in Toronto working-class politics.

DANCE, JOHN, moulder and union leader, born in London, England, 1843, died in Toronto, 1893. Brought to Toronto in 1845, apprenticed as moulder at St Lawrence Foundry in 1858. Joined IMIU No. 28 in 1862. Elected vice-president of IMIU in 1870. Moved to St Catharines in 1872 to take charge of St Catharines' Stove Works. Returned to Toronto in 1881 to take charge of Morrison's Foundry. Elected vice-president of IMIU again in 1882. Also a prominent figure in TTLC.

DAVEY, JOHN W., machinist, born in Bruce County, Ontario 1859. Started to study law in Toronto in 1875 but went to sea instead. Returned to Toronto as machinist and joined LA 9005 in 1887. He served as recording secretary and master workman each for two terms. Became member of DA 125; executive board in 1889 and DMW in 1890. He also served on the TTLC as a local chairman. He was active in both the Single Tax and Nationalist associations.

DONAVON, EUGENE, printer and labour editor. Prominent in the TTU, he left the case in 1882 to edit the *Trade Unions Advocate*, through which he promoted KOL principles. After the paper's failure in 1883 he ceased to be prominent in Toronto labour circles.

DOWER, GEORGE, printer and labour leader, born in Toronto, 1852. Joined TTU in 1872 and worked in various Canadian and U.S. cities. Prominent in TTU, K of L, TTLC, and TLC in 1880s and 1890s, he became ITU district organizer in 1893. Associated closely with D.J. O'Donoghue.

GLOCKLING, ROBERT, bookbinder and Knights leader; born in London, England, 1854. Began apprenticeship in London before arriving in Canada in 1869. Travelled and worked throughout the United States after leading Toronto bookbinders' strike during nine-hours movement of 1872. After return to Canada in 1873, became active in Bookbinders' Benevolent Society which he led into the KOL in 1886. DA financial secretary in 1887, recording secretary in 1888, and treasurer from 1889 into the 1890s, he also was president of the TTLC in 1889–90 and 1895–96. Later he was president of the Bookbinders International Union after being secretary of Ontario Labour Bureau from 1900 to 1906. Close to O'Donoghue and other Toronto Lib-Labs.

GLOCKLING, WILLIAM, bookbinder and union leader, born in London, England, 1861. Arrived in Canada in 1869 and apprenticed in jewellery trade. Later switched to bookbinding. Prominent in Bookbinders' Benevolent Association, KOL, and frequent representative at TTLC and TLC. Robert's brother.

HARRIS, GEORGE, painter and union leader. A major force among Toronto painters, frequent president of their union, and two-term president of the TTLC. Also first vice-president of Brotherhood of Painters and Decorators of America, founded in 1887.

HEAKES, SAMUEL R., carpenter and trade-unionist. Came to Toronto in 1849, becoming active in union politics as Tory. Worked in Montreal in 1860s and organized union there. Chairman of the TTLC platform committee in 1882. He ran for provincial office in 1883 in Toronto East as a labour candidate. Became a figure of great controversy in 1886 when, after being named to the Royal Commission on the Relations of Labour and Capital, he campaigned for Tory candidates against labour. After that, not active in trade-union movement.

HEWITT, JOHN, cooper and labour leader. After working in New York he returned to Toronto, where he was secretary of the Toronto Coopers. He played an active role in the Coopers' International Union of which he was a vice-president. He was also instrumental in the founding of the TTA and the CLU. A prominent protectionist he moved towards the Tories and was rewarded with a job at the Toronto Water Works with the co-editorship of the *Orange Sentinel*. A radical thinker, he promoted land and currency reform despite his party ties.

HOLMES, A.W., machinist and labour leader, born in Ayr, Ontario, 1858. Apprenticed at 14 and came to Toronto in 1880. Joined LA 2622 in 1882 and was twice MW. Went on to organize LA 9005 (machinists). After three terms as its MW he became DMW for two terms. Active in TTLC and the TLC, he later became a member of the General Executive Board of the International Association of Machinists.

JURY, A.F., tailor and Knights leader, born in Kent, England, 1848. Active in the Amalgamated Tailors at home, he came to Canada in 1873. After joining Toronto Tailors Union, became a prominent member of TTA and CLU. In 1880s joined KOL and with O'Donoghue and March used LA 2305 as base. He was eight-term president of Toronto Co-op Society. An active Lib-Lab, he ran federally as a labour-reform candidate in Toronto East in 1887. Served on Ontario Prison Commission in 1891 and was named Dominion Immigration Agent in England by federal Liberal government in 1897. Jury was also a prominent free thinker and single-taxer. He died in October 1916.

LOWES, E., shoemaker and Knight, born in 1836. A charter member of LA 2211, he twice served as MW and was a Toronto delegate to the Richmond Knights convention.

MCCORMACK, ANDREW, bricklayer and union leader. A leader of the Toronto bricklayers union and important personage in the TTA and CLU. Unlike other junta leaders, he remained active in the TTLC in the 1880s. Later he became vice-president of International Bricklayers Union. An active Tory and frequent critic of O'Donoghue.

MCMILLAN, J.C., printer and trade-union leader; born in Scotland, 1836, died in Toronto, 1889. Arrived in Toronto in 1867 and joined the TTU. He became vice-president in 1870 and president in 1871. As president he was arrested in 1872 when Brown attacked the union. With David Sleeth and J.S. Williams, he purchased *The Ontario Workman* in fall 1872. A delegate to the TTA from 1872 to 1878, he served in various offices including president. In 1880 he played a key role in the founding of the TTLC. An important member of the junta, he played a key role in the CLU as well. He passed his craft on to all three of his sons who became printers in the 1880s.

MCNAB, SAMUEL, blacksmith and Knights leader; born in the United States in 1853. Finished his apprenticeship at the St Lawrence Foundry when it was struck as part of the nine-hours movement in 1872. He then tramped in Buffalo and throughout the United States. Returned to Toronto when Massey Co. moved there. A member of the blacksmiths union until 1882, when helped form LA 2622. Twice MW, he led the successful 1886 strike against the Masseys. Later DMW and promoted to foreman at Masseys. Although considered for the Royal Commission of 1886, he was rejected as politically too independent. Nevertheless, he seems to have co-operated closely with A.W. Wright in opposing the Grit 'boys from 2305.' Certainly O'Donoghue regarded him as an enemy.

MARCH, CHARLES, painter, trade-union leader, and Knight; born in Toronto, 1850. A member of the painters union, he was president of the TTA in 1874. He joined LA 2305 in 1882 and played a key role with O'Donoghue and Jury in developing Grit Knight strategy. He also served as Ontario Knights organizer in mid-1880s and then as DA 125 organizer. A two-term president of the TTLC, he was also the first president of the TLC. He ran as an independent provincial labour candidate in 1886, winning over 4,000 votes. One of the few Roman Catholics prominent in the labour movement, he died in May 1908.

MOOR, THOMAS, carpenter and union leader. One of the founders of the Toronto branch of the Brotherhood of Carpenters, he led the important 1882 strike. As a result he was blacklisted by Toronto employers and thus hired as the first full-time TTLC organizer. Also served as TTLC president. Closely associated with the Grits, he received an Ontario government patronage job in the mid-1880s.

OAKLEY, ALFRED, stonecutter and trade-union leader; born in England, 1846; died in Toronto, 1883. He arrived in Toronto about 1872 and became prominent as a representative of the stonecutters union at the TTA in an 1875 prosecution of five stonecutters for breach of the CLAA. An active Lib-Lab, he was the centre of some controversy in the early 1880s at the TTLC. He died of consumption, an occupational disease, at the young age of 37.

O'DONOGHUE, DANIEL J., printer, labour MPP, Knights' leader, and Liberal public servant; born in County Kerry, Ireland, 1844; died in Toronto, 1907. Came to Canada in 1852 and five years later apprenticed as a printer in Ottawa. An active Irishman in the St Patrick Society, he left for the United States at time of Fenian raids. In Buffalo joined the ITU, returned briefly to Ottawa to commence organizing there, and then tramped throughout the U.S. Returned to Ottawa, where he organized the Trades Council and lobbied for Trade Unions Act. Active in the CLU, he was elected MPP in 1874, returned in 1875, but soundly defeated in 1879. Moved to Guelph and then to Toronto. Joined TTU, was active in TTLC but switched to Knights. Major force in Toronto labour world throughout decade especially as secretary of TTLC Legislative Committee and as Powderly's Canadian advisor. Appointed clerk in Ontario Bureau of Industries in 1885 and later Federal Fair Wages Officer. His son John became Canada's first prominent labour lawyer.

PARR, W.H., printer and union leader; born in Toronto, 1853. Apprenticed at *Telegraph*, 1868–72, then worked as journeyman for various Toronto papers. Active in TTU, ITU, TTLC, and TLC. Also member of LA 2305. Active Methodist.

RONEY, J., painter and union leader; born in Brockville, 1845. Apprenticed in Ottawa, then worked widely throughout United States, including in Illinois railroad shops. Returned to Canada in 1878. Became foreman of Northern Railroad paint shops in Toronto in 1880 and later moved to Credit Valley Railroad. In 1885 became foreman of Toronto Upholstery Co. A charter member of LA 2305, he left to form LA

2622. He became its first MW and Toronto delegate to the Richmond General Assembly. Also at TLC in 1883 and 1886. An active Baptist and temperance advocate, he ran as an independent provincial labour candidate in 1886.

ROSE, JAMES, carpenter and labour leader, born in England. Came to Canada in 1873 and settled in Almonte. Later moved to Toronto, where he was very active in Brotherhood of Carpenters and TTLC.

SHEPPARD, E.E., journalist and editor; born Elgin County, Ontario, 1855; died California, 1924. Educated in United States, returned to Canada in 1878 as a journalist. Edited St. Thomas Journal 1881–83 and then took over Toronto News until 1887. Ran it as a KOL popular daily. As a result became federal labour candidate in Toronto in 1887. After defeat, founded Saturday Night.

THOMPSON, PHILLIPS, journalist and socialist intellectual; born in Newcastle-on-Tyne, England, 1843; died in Oakville, 1933. Came to Canada in 1857 and became solicitor in 1865 but never practised. Instead commenced working as journalist in St Catharines and joined Toronto Telegraph in 1867. Worked on various Toronto papers and established reputation as humourist under pseudonym, Jimuel Briggs. Founded National in 1874. Moved to Boston for a few years and returned to Toronto in late 1879. Worked as investigative reporter for Globe, editor of News with Sheppard, and major columnist for Palladium of Labor under pseudonym Enjolras. Active in radical politics as a currency reformer, labour reformer, single-taxer, Ballamyite nationalist, and later socialist. Wrote The Politics of Labor in 1887, edited Labor Advocate in 1891, and published Labor Reform Songster in 1892. One of Knights' major thinkers. Continued to move left in the 1890s and was a founding member of Socialist Party of Canada.

TODD, WILLIAM V., cigarmaker and union leader; born in Quebec, 1852. Active in Toronto Cigarmakers Union from inception and became vice-president of international in 1880. Frequent TLC and TTLC delegate.

WILLIAMS, J.S., printer and union leader. Active in the TTU and the ITU in the early 1870s, he became the central junta figure as editor of The Ontario Workman, and key TTA and CLU delegate. Helped found TTLC in 1881, but most of his energy focused on Tory party in 1880s, which had appointed him major Toronto organizer. For a short time was also member of Knights. Died 27 September 1929.

WRIGHT, A.W., journalist and labour leader; born Markham, Ontario, 1845. Worked briefly in woollen industry before becoming journalist in 1870s. Active editor in

1870s and proponent of protection, currency, and land reform. Ran as Beaverback candidate in Toronto West in 1880. Active in WLCU, Currency Reform League, etc. Later secretary of Ontario Manufacturers' Association. Returned to labour politics through Knights. Editor of *Canadian Labor Reformer* and major force behind creation of DA 125 and proposed independent Canadian General Assembly. Used this scheme to become lecturer for Knights and a Powderly confidante; then elected to General Executive Board. Also editor of *Journal of United Labor*. Frequently wrote under pseudonym 'Spokeshave.' Later, Ontario Tory organizer and first head of Workmen's Compensation Board.

IV

Toronto franchise and election results 1867–1891

Toronto provincial franchise, 1871–91

Year	Eligible voters (male only)	All males 21+	Percentage eligible
1871	9,892	13,825	71.6
1881 (1883)*	20,362	21,506	94.7
1891 (1890)*	43,351	40,237	+100.0

* Ontario, Legislative Assembly, *Sessional Papers* for franchise in election closest to census year
Sources: Canada, *Census*, 1871, 8181, 8191 for population

Toronto federal franchise, 1871–91

Year	Eligible voters (male only)	All males 21+	Percentage eligible
1871 (1872)*	10,990	13,825	79.5
1881 (1882)*	20,456	21,506	95.1
1891	38,391	40,237	95.4

* Canada, Parliament, *Sessional Papers* for franchise in election closest to census year
Sources: Canada, *Census*, 1871, 1881, 1891 for population

TABLE IV.3 Toronto federal election results, 1867–91

Year	Conservative No.	%	Liberal No.	%	Labour No.	%	Independent No.	%	Total no. of votes	Total no. eligible	Percentage turnout
TORONTO EAST											
1867	1,113	53.2	980	46.8			1	0	2,094	4,294	48.8
1872	872	52.9	775	47.1					1,647	2,949	55.9
1874	1,152	47.2	1,289	52.8					2,441	4,116	59.3
1875*	1,396	58.7	982	41.3					2,378		
1878	1,743	62.4	1,055	37.6					2,792	5,339	52.3
1882	1,992	57.1	1,496	42.9					3,488	6,141	56.8
1887	2,858	61.8			1,603	34.7	164	3.5	4,625	9,925	46.6
1891	3,520	63.1	2,056	36.9					5,576	14,237	39.2
TORONTO WEST											
1867	1,477	58.5	1,048	41.5					2,525	4,746	53.2
1872	1,043	64.5	574	35.5					1,617	3,897	41.5
1873*	1,006	39.1	1,564	60.8					2,570		
1874	1,440	46.6	1,651	53.4					3,091	5,024	61.5
1875*	1,935	54.9	1,584	45.1					3,519		
1878	2,165	58.6	1,528	41.4					3,693	7,461	49.5
1880	2,097	52.3	1,836	45.8	49	1.2	23	0.6	4,005		
1882	2,714	54.3	2,283	45.7					4,997	9,121	54.8
1887	3,895	53.2			3,428	46.8			7,323	13,781	53.1
1891	5,048	60.5	3,291	39.5					8,339	17,084	48.8
TORONTO CENTRE											
1872	1,188	49.4	1,216	50.6					2,404	4,144	58.0
1874	1,225	44.8	1,509	55.2					2,734	4,366	62.6
1875*	Acclamation										
1878	1,631	58.8	1,141	41.2					2,772	4,973	55.7
1882	1,620	53.2	1,422	46.8					3,042	5,194	58.6
1887	2,282	55.5	1,828	44.5					4,110	6,553	62.7
1891	2,414	55.8	1,912	44.2					4,326	7,070	61.2

* By-elections

Source: Canada, Parliament, *Sessional Paper*

TABLE IV.4

Toronto provincial election results, 1867–90

Year	Conservative No.	%	Liberal No.	%	Labour No.	%	Independent No.	%	Total no. of votes	Total no. eligible	Percentage turnout
TORONTO EAST											
1867	1,178	56.3	914	43.7					2,092	4,485	52.3
1871	1,232	52.6	1,112	47.4					2,344	6,312	54.4
1875	1,849	53.8	1,579	46.0			7	0.2	3,435		
1878*	1,891	50.6	1,846	49.4					3,737		
1879	2,132	50.7	2,075	49.3					4,207	8,230	51.1
1883	2,135	47.9	2,011	45.2	308	6.9			4,454	8,909	50.0
TORONTO WEST											
1867	1,439	57.3	1,074	42.7					2,513	5,407	51.8
1871	1,316	46.9	1,487	53.1					2,803	7,648	55.3
1875	2,145	50.7	2,085	49.3					4,230		
1879	2,324	50.7	2,256	49.3					4,580	10,123	45.2
1883	2,634	52.0			2,427	48.0			5,061	11,453	44.2
TORONTO COMBINED (3 elected at large)											
1886$_1$	7,032	47.1	5,380	36.0	4,055	27.2			14,916	33,296	44.8
1886$_2$	6,883	46.1			3,408	22.9					
1890$_1$†	5,862		5,359				703		31,166/2‡	43,351	(36)
1890$_2$	5,542		5,197								
1890$_3$	4,001		4,502								

* By-election

† Official returns did not indicate actual number of voters but simply added the votes.

‡ Due to Mowat's gerrymander, Toronto received 3 members but each voter had only 2 votes.

Source: Ontario, Legislative Assembly, *Sessional Papers*

TABLE IV.5
Federal election results, Toronto East, 1867–91

Year	Name (party)	No. of votes	% of vote
1867	Beatty (c)	1,113	53.2
	Aikins (L)	980	46.8
	Allen (I)	1	0
1872	Beatty (c)	872	52.9
	O'Donohue (L)	775	47.1
1874	O'Donohue (L)	1,289	52.8
	Coatsworth (c)	1,152	47.2
1875*	Platt (c)	1,396	58.7
	O'Donohue (L)	982	41.3
1978	Platt (c)	1,743	62.4
	Galley (L)	1,055	37.6
1882	Small (c)	1,992	57.1
	Thompson (L)	1,496	42.9
1887	Small (c)	2,858	61.8
	Jury (Lab)	1,603	34.7
	Macdonald (I)	164	3.5
1891	Coatsworth (c)	3,520	63.1
	Wheeler (L)	2,056	36.9

* By-election
Source: Canada, Parliament, *Sessional Papers*

TABLE IV.6
Federal election results, Toronto West, 1867–91

Year	Name (party)	No. of votes	% of votes
1867	Harrison (c)	1,477	58.5
	Macdonald (L)	1,048	41.5
1872	Crawford (c)	1,043	64.5
	McLellan (L)	574	35.5
	Capreol (I)	0	0
1873*	Moss (L)	1,564	60.8
	Bickford (c)	1,006	39.1
1874	Moss (L)	1,651	53.4
	Robinson (c)	1,440	46.6

TABLE IV.6 (concluded)
Federal election results, Toronto West, 1867–91

Year	Name (party)	No. of votes	% of votes
1875*	Robinson (C)	1,935	55.0
	Turner (L)	1,584	45.0
1878	Robinson (C)	2,165	58.6
	Hodgins (L)	1,528	41.4
1880*	Beaty (C)	2,097	52.3
	Ryan (L)	1,836	45.8
	Wright (I)	49	1.2
	Capreol (I)	23	0.6
1882	Beatty (C)	2,714	54.3
	McMurrich (L)	2,283	45.7
1887	Denison (C)	3,895	53.2
	Sheppard (Lab)	3,428	46.8
1891	Denison (C)	5,048	60.5
	Mowat (L)	3,291	39.5

* By-election
Source: Canada, Parliament, *Sessional Papers*

TABLE IV.7
Federal election results, Toronto Centre, 1872–91

Year	Name (party)	No. of votes	% of votes
1872	Wilkes (L)	1,216	50.6
	Shanly (C)	1,188	49.4
1874	Wilkes (L)	1,509	55.2
	Morrison (C)	1,225	44.8
1875*	Macdonald (L)	Acclamation	
1878	Hay (C)	1,631	58.8
	Macdonald (L)	1.141	41.2
1882	Hay (C)	1,620	53.2
	Edgar (L)	1,422	46.8
1887	Cockburn (C)	2,282	55.5
	Harvie (L)	1,828	44.5
1891	Cockburn (C)	2,414	55.8
	Kerr (L)	1,912	44.2

* By-election
Source: Canada, Parliament, *Sessional Papers*

TABLE IV.8

Provincial election results, Toronto East, 1867–83

Year	Name (party)	No. of votes	% of votes
1867	Cameron (c)	1,178	56.3
	Stock (L)	914	43.7
1871	Cameron (c)	1,232	52.6
	Metcalf (L)	1,112	47.4
1875	Cameron (c)	1,849	53.8
	Crooks (L)	1,579	46.0
	Allen (I)	7	0.2
1878*	Morris (c)	1,891	50.6
	Leys (L)	1,846	49.4
1879	Morris (c)	2,132	50.7
	Mowat (L)	2,075	49.3
1883	Morris (c)	2,135	47.9
	Leys (L)	2,011	45.2
	Heakes (Lab)	308	6.9

* By-election

Souce: Ontario, Parliament, *Sessional Papers*

TABLE IV.9

Provincial election results, Toronto West, 1867–83

Year	Name (party)	No. of votes	% of votes
1867	Wallis (c)	1,439	57.3
	Crooks (L)	1,074	42.7
1871	Crooks (L)	1,487	53.1
	Wallis (c)	1,316	46.9
1875	Bell (c)	2,145	50.7
	Thomson (L)	2,085	49.3
1879	Bell (c)	2,324	50.7
	Ogden (L)	2,256	49.3
1883	H.E. Clarke (c)	2,634	52.0
	Carter (Lab)	2,427	48.0

Source: Ontario, Parliament, *Sessional Papers*

TABLE IV.10

Provincial election results, combined Toronto riding, 1886–90*

Year	Name (party)	No. of votes	% of votes
1886	E.F. Clarke (C)	7,032	47.1
	H.E. Clarke (C)	6,883	46.1
	Leys (L)	5,380	36.0
	March (Lab)	4,055	27.2
	Roney (Lab)	3,408	22.9
1890	E.F. Clarke (C)	5,862	
	H.E. Clarke (C)	5,542	
	Tait (L)	5,359	
	McDougall (L)	5,197	
	Armour (L)	4,502	
	Bell (C)	4,001	
	Moses (I)	703	

* Mowat gerrymandered the Toronto seats by giving the city three members to be elected at large but granting each voter only two votes. This almost of necessity meant that the Liberals, as the minority party, would elect one member.

Source: Ontario, Parliament, *Sessional Papers*

Notes

CHAPTER I

1 For an early description of this school see J.M.S. Careless, 'Frontierism, Metropolitanism, and Canadian History,' *Canadian Historical Review*, 35 (1954), 1–21. See also W.T. Easterbrook and M.H. Watkins, *Approaches to Canadian Economic History* (Toronto 1967), ix–xviii.

2 The following discussion owes much to the brilliant pioneering economic histories of H.C. Pentland and Stanley Ryerson. Pentland's 'The Role of Capital in Canadian Economic Development before 1875,' *Canadian Journal of Economics and Political Science* (1950), 457–74, and his 'Development of a Capitalistic Labour Market in Canada,' *Canadian Journal of Economics and Political Science* (1959), 450–61, are examples of fine, innovative, scholarly work. This is even more true of his 'Labour and the Development of Industrial Capitalism in Canada' (unpublished PH D thesis, University of Toronto 1960). Stanley Ryerson, Canada's leading Marxist historian, attempted a brave synthesis (*Unequal Union* [Toronto 1968]) which, despite its dismissal by bourgeois historians and the recent attacks on it by left-wing nationalists, remains the best overview of Canadian economic development in the nineteenth century. My debts to both these scholars are evident throughout this work.

3 The new econometrics literature in Canada, while problematic in many respects, has made recent strides in debunking some of the older notions of Canadian economic development. Three areas of work have importance for the arguments made here. First is the recent discussion of the impact of the Reciprocity Treaty of 1854 which de-emphasizes it as a factor in colonial economic growth. See L.H. Officer and L.B. Smith, 'The Canadian-American Reciprocity Treaty of 1855 to 1866,' *Journal of Economic History*, 28 (1968),

598–623; and Robert Ankli, 'The Reciprocity Treaty of 1854,' *Canadian Journal of Economics*, 4 (1971), 1–20. Second is the important literature which re-evaluated the period 1878 to 1896 and reasserted that economic growth took place especially in manufacturing. See O.J. Firestone, 'Development of Canada's Economy, 1850–1900,' in *Trends in the American Economy in the Nineteenth Century* (Princeton 1960), 217–52; Gordon Bertram, 'Economic Growth in Canadian Industry, 1870–1915,' *Canadian Journal of Economics and Political Science*, 19 (1967), 159–84; and Duncan M. McDougall, 'Canadian Manufactured Commodity Output,' *Canadian Journal of Economics*, 4 (1971), 21–36. Third is the work which indicates that the 'wheat boom' of the years after 1896 has been given a disproportionate place in Canadian economic history and that continued manufacturing growth was of great import in the prosperity of the Laurier years. See Edward J. Chambers and Donald F. Gordon, 'Primary Products and Economic Growth,' *Journal of Political Economy*, 74 (1966), 315–32. For a useful survey of all this literature, written for a literate audience, see Peter J. George and Ernest H. Obsanen, 'Recent Developments in the Quantification of Canadian Economic History,' *Histoire Sociale*, 4 (1969), 76–95. See also Trevor J.O. Dick, 'Frontiers in Canadian Economic History,' *Journal of Economic History*, 36 (1976), 34–9.

4 This new group of left-wing nationalist scholars is avowedly attempting 'to stand Creighton on his feet.' One can only assume Harold Innis has always stood on solid ground in this view. The major member of this school is Tom Naylor, whose 'The Rise and Fall of the Third Commercial Empire of the St. Lawrence,' in Gary Teeple (ed.), *Capitalism and the National Question in Canada* (Toronto 1972), 1–41, was the first major work. More important is his recent *The History of Canadian Business*, 2 vols. (Toronto 1976). Another scholar working along these lines is Daniel Drache, who has recently argued the critical strength of the staples approach in his 'Rediscovering Canadian Political Economy,' *Journal of Canadian Studies*, 11 (1976), 3–18. Glenn Williams in 'Canadian Industrialization: We Ain't Growin' Nowhere,' *This Magazine*, 9, 1 (1975), 7–9, and 'Canada – the Case of the Wealthiest Colony,' *This Magazine*, 10, 1 (1976), 28–32, has corrected some of Naylor's excesses and has reinserted labour into this discussion of political economy quite beneficially. Most important is his recent 'The National Policy and Import Substitution Industrialization,' unpublished Canadian Political Science Association paper, 1978, which includes a devastating critique of Naylor. Other substantive critiques of Naylor are L.R. MacDonald, 'Merchants against Industry: An Idea and Its Origins,' *Canadian Historical Review*, 56 (1975), 263–81, and Stanley Ryerson, 'Who's Looking After Business: A Review,' *This Magazine*, 10, 5 and 6 (1976), pp. 41–6. Robert Storey, 'Industrialization in Canada: The

Emergence of the Hamilton Working Class, 1850–1870s,' unpublished MA thesis (Dalhousie University 1975), and Bryan Palmer, 'Most Uncommon Common Man: Craft, Culture and Conflict in a Canadian Community, 1860–1914' (unpublished PH D thesis, State University of New York at Binghamton, 1977), provide excellent accounts of Hamilton's industrial revolution. Other implicit critiques are Stephen Langdon, 'The Political Economy of Capitalist Transformation, Central Canada from the 1840s to the 1870s' (unpublished MA thesis, Carleton University 1972). See also Leo Johnson, *History of the County of Ontario, 1815–1875* (Whitby 1973).

5 Joan MacKinnon, *A Checklist of Toronto Cabinet and Chair Makers, 1800–1865* (Ottawa 1975), 3, 165.

6 Pentland, 'Labour and the Development of Industrial Capitalism,' 341–3.

7 Robert Baldwin Sullivan, *Lecture Before the Mechanics' Institute, on the 17th November, 1847*, Hamilton, 1848 [?]. Quotations are from pp 6–7, 7–8, 9–10, 40, 41.

8 See also his 'Memo, re: Corps of Military Labourers' in *Elgin-Grey Papers*, IV, 1436 ff.

9 Sullivan, *Lecture*, 20–36. One of the only discussions of commodity production in the 1840s is Ryerson, *Unequal Union*, ch. 9.

10 British-American League, *Minutes of the Proceedings of a Convention of Delegates*, Kingston, 1849, p. 8. For the only detailed discussion of the League see Gerald A. Hallowell, 'The Reaction of the Upper Canadian Tories to the Adversity of 1849: Annexation and the British-American League,' *Ontario History*, 62 (1970), 41–56.

11 British-American League, *Proceedings*, Kingston, p. 20.

12 Ibid., 21.

13 For a detailed biography see Barrie Dyster, 'John William Gamble,' *Dictionary of Canadian Biography*, X (Toronto 1972), 299–300.

14 Text of speech is from Samuel Thompson, *Reminiscences of a Canadian Pioneer for the Last Fifty Years* (Toronto 1884), 251–60.

15 British-American League, *Minutes of the Proceedings of ...*, Toronto, 1849, pp. 5, ii, xiv–xvi, and passim. In addition to the British-American League, there was also a Montreal association for home manufactures which advocated protection. For a description of their 1849 meeting see William Weir, *Sixty Years in Canada* (Montreal 1903), 98–104. This organization also presented a 4000-name petition to the Legislative Assembly in 1849 in favour of protection. See Elizabeth Gibbs (ed.), *Debates*, 1849, 699.

16 For a discussion of Gamble in the legislature see Edward Porritt, *Sixty Years of Protection in Canada, 1846–1912* (Winnipeg 1918), 174–80.

17 On capital imports see Leland H. Jenks, *The Migration of British Capital to*

1875 (New York 1927), 198–206. The best discussion of the railroad era is probably still G.P. de T. Glazebrook, *A History of Transportation in Canada* (Toronto 1938). For details on the connection of business and government see Gustavus Myers, *History of Canadian Wealth* (Toronto), and H.V. Nelles (ed.), *The Philosophy of Railroads* (Toronto 1972). The most insightful discussions of the broad impact of railroads on the Canadian economy are predictably Ryerson, *Unequal Union*, ch. 12 and 13, and Pentland, 'The Role of Capital,' 463–70.

18 Pentland, 'Role of Capital,' 463.

19 Leo Panitch, 'The Role and Nature of the Canadian State,' in *The Canadian State* (Toronto 1877), 3–27. See also Peter Baskerville, 'Professional vs. Proprietor: Power Distribution in the Railway World of Upper Canada/Ontario, 1850–1881,' paper delivered at the Canadian Historical Association, 1978.

20 *Report of the Toronto Board of Trade* (Toronto 1856), 9–10; John E. MacNab, 'Toronto's Industrial Growth in 1891,' *Ontario History*, 47 (1955), 61. For a useful discussion of the importance of railroads to industrial development see Albert Faucher, *Quebec en Amérique au XIXᵉ siècle: Essai sur les caractères économiques de la Laurentie* (Montreal 1973), ch. 3, 7.

21 On Weir see his *Sixty Years in Canada*.

22 *Canadian Merchants' Magazine*, I (1857), 1. Weir later (in *Sixty Years*, p. 248) described it as 'a monthly magazine advocating the development of Canadian Industry.'

23 Ibid., I (1857), 29–30, 163–5; 215–1; II (1858), 205–9; III (1858), 97–106, 407–40.

24 Ibid., I (1857), 193–6; II (1858), 198–205.

25 Ibid., II (1858), 198 ff.

26 Ibid.

27 Ibid., III (1858), 35, 26.

28 Weir, *Sixty Years*, 105–18. Buchanan's importance has not yet been sufficiently understood, but his influence over an entire generation of Canadian economic thinkers was profound. The major work on him to date, Douglas McCalla's, 'The Buchanan Businesses, 1834–1872: A Study in the Organization and Development of Canadian Trade' (unpublished PH D thesis, Oxford University 1972), unfortunately ignores Buchanan's role as an economic thinker. Craufurd D.W. Goodwin's, *Canadian Economic Thought* (Durham, NC 1961), 49–51, treats Buchanan in passing but is not very useful. A more useful brief treatment is Peter Warrian, ''Sons of Toil'': The Impact of Industrialization on Craft Workers in Late 19th Century Ontario,' in David F. Walker and James H. Bater (eds.), *Industrial Development in Southern On-*

tario (Waterloo 1974), 69–99, which discusses two of Buchanan's publishing ventures: *The Workingman's Journal* (1864) and *The Peoples' Journal* (1869–72). See also Robert Storey, 'Industrialization in Canada: The Emergence of the Hamilton Working Class, 1850–1870s' (unpublished MA thesis, Dalhousie University 1975).

29 *Report of the Public Meeting of Delegates ... and Proceedings of the Association for the Promotion of Canadian Industry.* Toronto, 1858, p. 5.

30 Ibid., 6.

31 Ibid., 4, 7, 14. There was an overt attempt to keep the profile of manufacturers low for fear that they would appear too self-interested. See Weir, *Sixty Years*, 130, and Isaac Buchanan to W.H. Howland, 2 October 1878, Buchanan Papers, PAC.

32 See among others his: *Letters Illustrative of the Present Position of Politics in Canada* (Hamilton 1859); *A Permanent Patriotic Policy* (n.p. 1860); *Britain the Country versus Britain the Empire. Our Financial Distresses – Their Legislative Cause and Cure* (Hamilton 1860); *Relations of the Industry of Canada with the Mother Country and the United States* (Montreal 1864); and *The British American Federation, A Necessity. Its Industrial Policy also a Necessity* (Hamilton 1865).

33 Isaac Buchanan, *Britain the Country ...,* I, xxxiv.

34 Douglas McCalla, 'The Commercial Politics of the Toronto Board of Trade, 1850–1860,' *Canadian Historical Review*, 50 (1969), 51–67; and Toronto Board of Trade, *Reports*, in the 1860s.

35 *Canadian Merchants' Magazine*, III (1958), 407–40. This essay won the Board of Arts and Manufacturers of Upper Canada's essay contest in 1858. For more about the board see below.

36 D.F. Barnett, 'The Galt Tariff: Incidental or Effective Protection?' *Canadian Journal of Economics*, 9 (1976), 389–407. Compare this convincing view, based on a detailed analysis, which concludes that 'evidence strongly supports the protective character of Galt's tariff changes' with Tom Naylor's argument that 'the objectives of the tariff were in fact clearly revenue-oriented.' This is a good example of the empirical weakness of Naylor's polemical *The History of Canadian Business, 1867–1914*, 2 vols. (Toronto, 1975). The quotation is from I, 28.

37 Hon. A.T. Galt, *Canada 1849 to 1859* (Quebec 1860), 33–4.

38 Weir, *Sixty Years*, 115.

39 Dominion Board of Trade, *Proceedings*, 1871, 26; 1877, 116–17; and passim.

40 John MacLean, *The Complete Tariff Hand-Book* (Toronto 1880), 3.

41 *Canadian Merchants' Magazine*, IV (1859), 321–2.

42 *Canadian Illustrated News* (Hamilton), 20 December 1862.

43 *Journal of the Board of Arts and Manufacturers of Upper Canada*, III (1863), 12–15.

44 Isaac Buchanan, *British American Federation*, 4.

45 Association for the Promotion of Canadian Industry, *Its Formation, By-Laws*, (Toronto 1866). Quotations are from pp. 7, 6.

46 For a very sketchy account see S.D. Clark, *The Canadian Manufacturers' Association* (Toronto 1939), 1–7.

47 Dominion Board of Trade, *Proceedings*, 1871, 24–8.

48 Ibid., 1874. Quotations are from pp. 65–6, 73–84, 113–15.

49 The convention rejected a free-trade resolution by a vote of 34 to 20.

50 Ibid., 1876. Quotations are from pp. 109–11, 135–8, 175.

51 Ibid., 1877, 116–18, 126, 133.

52 Ibid., 1878, 72–9, 88, 200.

53 Manufacturers' Association of Ontario, *Proceedings of Special Meeting ...* , *1875* (Toronto 1876), pp. 2–4.

54 Ibid., passim.

55 Dominion National League, *Country Before Party* (Hamilton 1878). See also the earlier *Home Industries. Canada's National Policy. Protection to Native Products. Development of Field and Factory. Speeches by Leading Members of Parliament* (Ottawa 1876). Although this pamphlet fails to identify its source, considerable advertising by Ontario manufacturers suggests that the MAO was involved.

56 Clark, *Canadian Manufacturers' Association*, 7.

57 For perhaps the most comprehensive western indictment see Porritt, *Sixty Years of Protection in Canada*, especially ch. XI.

58 Ibid., 260.

59 For a totally unapologetic defence of the staple theory see Mel Watkins, 'The Staple Theory Revisited,' *Journal of Canadian Studies*, 12, 5 (Winter 1977), 83–95.

CHAPTER 2

1 For general works on the economic history of Toronto see: Edith Firth (ed.), *The Town of York*, 2 vols. (Toronto 1962 and 1966); F.H. Armstrong, 'Toronto in Transition: The Emergence of a City, 1828–1838' unpublished PH D thesis, University of Toronto 1965); Armstrong, 'Metropolitanism and Toronto Reconsidered, 1825–1850,' *Canadian Historical Association Annual Report* (1966), 29–40; Barry Dyster, 'Toronto 1840–1860: Making It in a British Protestant Town' (unpublished PH D thesis, University of Toronto 1970); E.C. Guillett, *Toronto from Trading Post to Great City* (Toronto 1934); D.C. Mas-

ters, *The Rise of Toronto, 1850–1890* (Toronto 1947); Masters, 'Toronto vs. Montreal,' *Canadian Historical Review*, 22 (1941), 133–46; and G.P. de T. Glazebrook, *The Story of Toronto* (Toronto 1971).

2 W.H. Smith, *Canadian Gazateer* (Toronto 1846), 193–7.

3 Canada, *Census*, 1848, 1851.

4 MacKinnon, *Toronto Cabinet Makers*, 69–77, 184–91.

5 *Journal of the Board of Arts and Manufacturers of Upper Canada*, IV (1864), 193–96. See also testimony of R. Hay to the Select Committee on the Extent and Condition of the Manufacturing Interests of the Dominion, *Journal of the House of Commons*, 1874, Appendix III, 46–8.

6 Bruce Sinclair, et al., *Let Us Be Honest and Modest: Technology and Society in Canadian History* (Toronto 1974), 158–9.

7 Ibid., 138; G.P. de T. Glazebrook, *The Story of Toronto* (Toronto 1971), 113.

8 *Journal of the Board of Arts and Manufacturers of Upper Canada*, IV (1864), 1–3.

9 For a discussion of Armstrong's painting see Gregory S. Kealey, 'Toronto Rolling Mills,' *Canadian Labour History*, 7 (1975), 1–2.

10 Toronto Board of Trade, *Report*, 1865.

11 Barrie Dyster, 'Francis Henry Medcalf,' in *Dictionary of Canadian Biography*, X (Toronto 1972), 503–4.

12 George Mainer, 'William Hamilton,' ibid., 330–1.

13 Toronto Board of Trade, *Report*, 1863.

14 Mainer, 'Hamilton,' 361. For a general description of developments in iron and secondary metal which is generally in agreement with my line of argument see William Kilbourn, *The Elements Combined* (Toronto 1960), ch. 1–3.

15 *Canadian Illustrated News* (Hamilton), 3 January 1863.

16 Smith, *Canadian Gazateer*, p. 196.

17 Canada, *Census*, 1851.

18 For developments in the Montreal shoe industry see Jean Hamelin and Yves Roby, *Histoire economiques du Québec* (Montreal 1971), and Joanne Burgess, 'L'industrie de la chaussure à Montréal: 1840–1879,' *Revue de l'histoire de l'amérique française*, 31 (1977), 187–210.

19 Toronto Board of Trade, *Annual Report*, 1856.

20 *Canadian Merchants' Magazine*, III (1858), 418–19.

21 Ibid.

22 For a brilliant discussion of the shoe industry see Ross Thomson, 'The Origin of Modern Industry in the United States: The Mechanization of Shoe and Sewing Machine Production' (unpublished PH D thesis, Yale University 1976). For an equally useful local study, see Alan Dawley, *Class and Community: The Industrial Revolution in Lynn* (Cambridge, Mass. 1976).

23 Hamelin and Roby, *Histoire économique de Québec*, passim.

24 Canada, Parliament, *Sessional Papers*, 1885, no. 37, 28.

25 Canada, Parliament, House of Commons, *Journals*, 1874, Appendix 3, 63 ff. and 1876, Appendix 3, 90–115.

26 Toronto Board of Trade, *Report*, 1860, 41.

27 Ibid., 28, and *Report for 1861*, 1862.

28 Toronto Board of Trade, *Report for 1863*, 1864, 24.

29 Toronto Board of Tarde, *Annual Report for 1865*, 1866, 39–40.

30 *Globe*, 18 November 1870.

31 Toronto Board of Trade, *Annual Report for 1862*, 1863.

32 Ibid.

33 *Journal of the Board of Arts and Manufacturers of Upper Canada*, III (1863), 84–5, 321–5.

34 Raphael Samuels, 'Workshop of the World: Steam Power and Hand Technology in Mid-Victorian Britain,' *History Workshop*, 3 (1977), 57.

35 *Canadian Illustrated News* (Hamilton), 25 April 1863.

36 J. Clarence Ingram, 'The Financial Depression of 1873 and Its Effects on Canadian Industry' (unpublished MA thesis, Queen's University, Kingston 1929), and Edward J. Chambers, 'Late Nineteenth Century Business Cycles in Canada,' *Canadian Journal of Economics and Political Science*, 30 (1964), 391–412.

37 William Wycliffe Johnson, *Sketches of the Late Depression* (Montreal 1882), and Sarah Common, 'A History of Business Conditions in Canada, 1870–1891' (unpublished MA thesis, Queen's University, Kingston 1930).

38 *Globe*, 13 January 1883; *Canadian Labor Reformer*, 13 November, 25 December 1886. See also Hector Charlesworth, *Candid Chronicles* (Toronto 1925), 68–70, for a description of his father's failure.

39 Canada, House of Commons, *Journals*, 1874, Appendix 3 and 1876, Appendix 3.

40 *Globe*, 9, 23 February 1876.

41 Ibid., 24 May 1879; 17 April 1880. On the agricultural implement industry in Canada see Merrill Denison, *Harvest Triumphant: The Story of Massey-Harris* (Toronto 1949), and W.G. Phillips, *The Agricultural Implement Industry in Canada* (Toronto 1956).

42 *Globe*, 17 May, 26 June, 17 July 1880.

43 Clipping Files, Volume One, Massey Archives. From *Mail*, 9 March 1888; *News*, 10 March 1888; *Empire*, 27 December 1888; *World*, 25 October 1888.

44 Toronto Trades and Labor Council, *Minutes*, 1888–9, passim.

45 Canada, Parliament, *Sessional Papers*, 1885, no. 37, 5.

46 Ibid., 20–2.

47 For a discussion of the early Toronto meat-packing industry see Michael Bliss, *A Canadian Millionaire: The Life and Business Times of Sir Joseph Flavelle* (Toronto 1978), esp. 27–52.

48 James M. Gilmour, *Spatial Evolution of Manufacturing: Southern Ontario, 1851–1891* (Toronto 1972), 153–68.

49 *Globe*, 5 September 1891.

50 Gilmour, *Spatial Evolution of Manufacturing*, especially ch. 7; David F. Walker and James H. Bater (eds.), *Industrial Development in Southern Ontario* (Waterloo 1974); Peter Goheen, *Victorian Toronto, 1850 to 1900* (Chicago 1970); Warren R. Bland, 'The Location of Manufacturing in Southern Ontario in 1881,' *Ontario Geography*, 8 (1974), 8–30; Warren R. Bland, 'The Changing Location of Metal Fabricating and Clothing Industries in Southern Ontario, 1881–1932,' *Ontario Geography*, 9 (1975), 35–57; J. David Wood (ed.), *Perspectives on Landscape and Settlement in Nineteenth Century Ontario* (Toronto 1975), ch. 9–10. See also J. Spelt, *Urban Development in South-Central Ontario* (Toronto 1972).

51 Denison, *Harvest Triumphant*, ch. 5 and 6.

52 This legislation is elaborated on later in the discussion of working-class politics.

CHAPTER 3

1 E.J. Hobsbawm, *Age of Revolution* (New York 1962), 259.

2 E.J. Hobsbawm and George Rude, *Captain Swing* (London 1969), 18, 63–4.

3 Albert Soboul, *The Sans-Culottes* (New York 1972).

4 E.P. Thompson, *The Making of the English Working Class* (London 1963), 549.

5 Paul Faler, 'Workingmen, Mechanics and Social Change: Lynn, Mass. 1800–60' (unpublished PH D thesis, University of Wisconsin 1971), ch. 3 and Conclusion; Alan Dawley, *Class and Community, the Industrial Revolution in Lynn* (Cambridge 1976).

6 Charles Lindsey, *The Life and Times of Wm. Lyon Mackenzie* (Toronto 1862), Appendix 1.

7 David N. Johnson, *Sketches of Old Lynn* (Lynn 1880), 4–8.

8 Fred Gannon, *The Ways of a Worker a Century Ago* (Salem 1918), 2; Fred Gannon, *A Short History of American Shoemaking* (Salem 1912), 18–19. See also Herbert Gutman, 'Work, Culture and Society in Industrializing America,' *American Historical Review*, 78 (June 1973), 531–88.

9 George McNeill (ed.), *The Labor Movement* (Boston 1887), 192.

10 Thomas Wright, *The Romance of the Shoe* (London 1922), 51–6.

11 Charles Lipton, *The Trade Union Movement of Canada* (Montreal 1968), 6, 21;
James Richard Rice, 'A History of Organized Labour in St. John, New Brunswick' (unpublished MA thesis, University of New Brunswick 1968), ch. 1.

12 Thomson, 'The Origins of Modern Industry in the United States,' describes
the process brilliantly. Dawley, *Class and Community*, ch. 1–3, presents an
excellent description of the transformation of shoe production in Lynn, Mass.
These two descriptions of the coming of industrial capitalism in the shoe
industry are the best we have for any North American industry and are a model
for further economic and community studies. For a good, but older, general
description of changes in the methods of shoe production, see Edith Abbott,
Women in Industry (New York 1919), ch. 8, and for Canada, see Canadian
Reconstruction Association, *The Boot and Shoe Industry in Canada* (Toronto
1920).

13 *Globe*, 18 November 1885.

14 Bray, *Canada under the National Policy* (Montreal 1883), 123–5. See also
Joanne Burgess, 'L'industrie de la chaussure à Montréal: 1840–1870 – le
passage d'artisanat à la fabrique,' *Revue de l'histoire de l'amérique française*,
31, 2 (1977), 187–210.

15 Wright, *Romance of the Shoe*, 224–6; Alan Fox, *A History of the National
Union of Boot and Shoe Operatives, 1874–1957* (Oxford 1958), 13–14. See also
Samuel, 'Workshops of the World,' 34–6.

16 Faler, 'Workingmen, Mechanics and Social Change,' ch. 11; Dawley, *Class
and Community*, ch. 3.

17 *Annuaire du Commerce et de l'Industrie de Québec pour 1873* (Quebec 1873),
8–9.

18 Paul C. Appleton, 'The Sunshine and the Shade: Labour Activism in Central
Canada, 1850–1860' (unpublished MA thesis, University of Calgary 1974), 44.

19 Ibid., 119–24.

20 *Globe*, 13 January 1858.

21 The events of 1858 are drawn from: *Globe*, 9, 12, 15, 26 January 1858; and
Appleton, 'The Sunshine and the Shade,' 98–100.

22 David Montgomery, *Beyond Equality* (New York 1967), 143–5.

23 *Globe*, 20 September 1869; *Leader*, 20 September 1869; *Daily Telegraph*, 20
September 1869.

24 Data from Don Lescohier, 'The Knights of St. Crispin, 1867–1874' in *Bulletin
of the University of Wisconsin, Economic and Political Science Series*, VII
(1910), 1–102; from a perusal of the Toronto press from 1867–1886; and from
the *Proceedings of the International Grand Lodge of the Order of the Knights
of St. Crispin*, 1869, 1870, and 1872. The only previous Canadian study of the
order is A.E. Kovacs' brief 'The Knights of St. Crispin in Canada,' *Canadian
Labour* (1966), 35–6.

25 The secondary literature on the KOSC was until recently woefully repetitive.
John Commons used the experience of American shoemakers to develop his
thesis about the importance of market relations in the history of labour. His
seminal article, 'American Shoemakers, 1648–1895' in *The Quarterly Journal
of Economics* (1909), was expanded in Lescohier's Wisconsin thesis in 1910.
These two works became the standard interpretation. A subsequent volume by
Blanche Hazard, *The Organization of the Boot and Shoe Industry in Mass.*
(Cambridge 1921), added little. Augusta Galster's, *The Labor Movement in the
Shoe Industry* (New York 1924), was a slightly more perceptive work, showing
many of the flaws of the Commons' approach: an over-emphasis on national
developments, a dependence on official publications, a narrow institutional
framework, and a theoretical emphasis on the centrality of market relations
which de-emphasized the conflict of capital and labour. The KOSC, in this view,
became an organization almost totally preoccupied with controlling the operation of machinery and closing off the factory to non-shoemakers. Conflicts thus
became shoemaker versus green hand and ultimately shoemaker versus market. Struggles between workers and employers almost disappeared.

Only in the last twenty years has this interpretation come under attack. The
first historian to question these views was John Hall who, in his unpublished
PH D thesis 'The Gentle Craft: A Narrative of Yankee Shoemakers' (Columbia
University 1953), discovered that in Massachusetts the order had been far
more interested in wages and hours than in green hands. Hall's 'The Knights of
St. Crispin in Massachusetts, 1869–1878,' *Journal of Economic History*, 18
(1957), 161–75, is an excellent summary of the major points of his dissertation
and adds a useful invocation for labour historians to turn away from a national
and leadership focus and concentrate instead on the local and the rank-and-file.
Two recent theses, Pual Faler's 'Workingmen, Mechanics, and Social Change'
and Allan Dawley's 'The Artisan Response to the Factory System: Lynn
Mass.' (unpublished PH D thesis, Harvard 1971), acted upon this invocation
and the results are excellent. Faler's sensitive community study of Lynn
shoemakers up to 1860 showed the development of a working class with a
distinct culture, which by 1860 had moved into direct conflict with their
employers. Dawley traced the Lynn story into the 1870s and put to rest notions
of the Crispins as a labour elite of custom shoemakers fighting off other
workers. Lynn Crispins represented a complete cross-section of the factory
labour force and found themselves in direct conflict with their employers on a
wide range of issues. Alan Fox's *History of the National Union*, a study of
English shoemakers, suggests the relative uniqueness of the Crispin success in
creating a union which combined the old artisans with the new factory workers.
Alan Dawley's Harvard thesis has been extensively revised and recently
published as *Class and Community*. Finally Ross Thomson's 'The Origins of

Modern Industry' provides us with a thorough Marxist analysis of the development of the modern shoe and sewing-machine industries.

26 Dawley, *Class and Community*, 130–1.

27 *Globe*, 28 November 1868, 27 November 1869, 9 August 1870, 23 December 1870, 11 February 1871, 3 September 1871, 1 September 1873; *Irish Canadian*, 2 December 1868, 1 December 1869; *Ontario Workman*, 9 May 1872, 24 April 1873, 28 August 1873.

28 For the importance of funerals see Brian Harrison, *Drink and the Victorians* (London 1971), 43.

29 KOSC, London Lodge (No. 242), *Constitution, By-laws, and Rules of Order* (London 1872), p. 23.

30 *Ritual of the Order of the Knights of St. Crispin* (Milwaukee 1870), 16–17.

31 For a description of Crispin funerals in Toronto see *Globe*, 15 December 1873, 5 July 1881.

32 Dawley, *Class and Community*, 80 ff.

33 *Spectator* (Hamilton), 2 July 1867, as cited in R. Storey, 'Industrialization in Canada: The Hamilton Working Class, 1850–1870's.'

34 *Workingman's Advocate* (Chicago), 25 May 1872.

35 *Ritual*, 9.

36 Lescohier, KOSC, 93–4. On Masonic rites in general see Eric Hobsbawm, *Primitive Rebels* (London 1959), ch. 9; Noel P. Gist, 'Secret Societies,' *University of Missouri Studies*, XV (October 1940).

37 *Ritual*, 8.

38 Ibid., 10.

39 Hobsbawm, *Primitive Rebels*, ch. 9; see also Thompson, *Making*, especially ch. 14–15.

40 *Globe*, 13 April 1870; *Daily Telegraph*, 13 April 1870.

41 KOSC, London Lodge, *Constitution*, p. 12.

42 *Leader*, 10 April 1871. For evidence of a fourth lodge in Toronto (366) see *Globe*, 26 January 1872, and *Ontario Workman*, 20 February 1873.

43 *Leader*, 10 April 1871.

44 David Montgomery, *Beyond Equality* (New York 1967), 395–9, 457–61.

45 After compiling lists of Knights of St Crispin, I checked their personal biographies by following them through the Toronto city directories of the 1870s and 1880s.

46 KOSC, London Lodge, *Constitution*, p. 12.

47 For details of events see *Leader*, 10 April 1871; *Globe*, 25 January 1871, 26 January 1871, 10 April 1871; *Daily Telegraph*, 24 January 1871. The following narrative is reconstructed from a reading of the Toronto press.

48 Dawley, *Class and Community*, 185–6.

49 KOSC, London Lodge, *Constitution*, 3.

50 *Globe*, 26 January 1871.

51 See Frederick Rudolph, for the New England case 'Chinamen in Yankeedom: Anti-unionism in Massachusetts in 1870,' *American Historical Review*, 53 (1957); Hall, 'The K.O.S.C. in Massachusetts,' 165–8.

52 *Leader*, 10 April 1871.

53 Ibid., 4 April 1871.

54 *Daily Telegraph*, 8 April 1871.

55 *Monetary Times*, 4 (1871), 686.

56 *Globe*, 10 April 1871.

57 Eric Hobsbawm, 'The Machine Breakers,' in *Labouring Men* (London 1964), 7. On this subject see also Thompson, *Making*, ch. 14; Malcolm Thomis, *The Luddites* (New York 1972); and Lionel Munby (ed.), *The Luddites and Other Essays* (London 1971), 35–56.

58 Hall, 'The Gentle Craft,' ch. 9–10.

59 Toronto Trades Assembly, *Minutes*, 2 June 1871, 20 October 1871, 3 November 1871, 22 November 1871.

60 *Monetary Times*, 5 (1871), 491.

61 *Ontario Workman*, 20 February 1873, 27 March 1873, 12 June 1873, 28 August 1873, 27 November 1873, 11 December 1873, 19 February 1874, 5 March 1874; *Mail*, 26 July 1873, 21 July 1875, 22 July 1875; *Leader*, 1 September 1873, 12 February 1874, 22 July 1875; *Globe*, 14 February 1874, 22 July 1875, 24 July 1875.

62 Toronto Trades Assembly, *Minutes*, December 1872.

63 Ibid., 1875.

64 *Globe*, 22 July 1876.

65 William Wycliffe Johnson, *Sketches of the Late Depression* (Montreal 1882), 160–2. See also the testimony of shoe manufacturers before House of Commons' committees in 1874 and 1876, *Journals*, 1874, Appendix 3 and 1876, Appendix 3.

66 *Globe*, 7 April 1886.

67 Jean Hamelin, et al., *Répertoire des Grèves dans la province de Québec au XIXᵉ siècle* (Montreal 1970), 73.

68 Rice, 'Organized Labour in St. John,' ch. 4.

69 *Globe*, 15 February 1877, 21 October 1879.

70 Ibid., 11 March 1885; *Telegram*, 11 March 1885.

71 *Globe*, 22 October, 23 October 1879, 29 October 1879, 28 April 1881, 30 April 1881, 18 May 1881, 24 May 1881, 18 May 1882, 30 June 1882, 17 May 1883, 17 November 1883; *Mail*, 14 October 1879, 21 October 1879, 22 October 1879; *Telegram*, 29 April 1881, 23 May 1881.

72 See *Globe*, *Mail*, *Telegram*, and *News* for April and early May 1882 for details. Also see *Trades Union Advocate*, May 1882.

73 *Trades Union Advocate*, 4 May 1882.

74 Gerald Grob, *Workers and Utopia* (Chicago 1961), 122–4. For a local version see James Morris, 'The Cincinnati Shoemakers' Lockout of 1888: A Case Study in the Demise of the Knights of Labor,' *Labor History*, 13 (Fall 1972), 505–19. For events in Toronto see below, 'The Knights of Labor,' ch. 12. For NTA 216 see *Report of the First Annual Session of the Boot and Shoe Workers of the U.S. and Canada* (Boston 1887).

75 Norman Ware, *The Labor Movement in the U.S., 1860–1925* (New York 1929), 200–9, and Montgomery, *Beyond Equality*, 199, 426–70.

76 Knights of Labor, Pioneer Assembly, No. 2211, Toronto, *By-laws*, Toronto, 1887. Quotations from pp. 3, 6–7.

77 *Globe*, 13 January 1883; *Labor Reformer*, 13 November 1886, 25 December 1886. See also Hector Charlesworth, *Candid Chronicles* (Toronto 1925), 68–70, on his father's failure.

78 *Globe*, 15, 19, 21 February 1890. For the Boot and Shoe Workers International Union, especially its socialist politics, see: Henry F. Bedford, *Socialism and the Workers in Massachusetts, 1886–1912* (Amherst 1966); and John Laslett, *Labor and the Left* (New York 1970), especially ch. 3.

79 R. McDougall to T.V. Powderly, Hamilton, 6 January 1883, Powderly Papers, Catholic University of America.

80 *Shoe and Leather Reporter Annual*, 1888.

81 *Monetary Times*, 27 (1893–94), 736.

82 Ibid., 21 (1897–98), 304.

83 Ibid., pp. 1389, 1579–80, 1649. (My thanks to Craig Heron for these references.)

84 McNeill, *Labor Movement*, 213.

85 Hall, 'The Gentle Craft,' 356.

CHAPTER 4

1 Bob Gilding, *The Journeymen Coopers of East London: Workers' Control in an old London Trade* (Oxford 1971), 49.

2 Franklin E. Coyne, *The Development of the Cooperage Industry in the United States, 1620–1940* (Chicago 1940), 24. On a similar note Gilding relates: 'I remember back in 1912–1913 some old coopers in the shop one Monday morning having a glass of "bull" in the chimney corner and saying very seriously "Who is our Patron Saint?" – "Don't know" was the reply, "All I

know is that it was on a Monday.'' ''Well,'' said all the coopers together, ''It might be today so we'd better honour her''' (p. 38).

3 *Coopers' Journal* (henceforth CJ), May 1871, 210–11.

4 *Workingman's Advocate*, 19 March 1870.

5 H.G. Gutman, 'The Labor Policies of the Large Corporation in the Gilded Age: The Case of the Standard Oil Company,' unpublished paper, 10.

6 Coopers International Union (henceforth CIU), *Cooper's Ritual* (Cleveland 1870), 6.

7 Ibid. The value and importance of the new union was well expressed in the following excerpt from a poem written by a Baltimore cooper for the CJ (December 1870):

THE COOPER
The Cooper is not such a dolt;
He is no dunce or useless drone,
But worth a king upon his throne.
Society cannot ignore
His services on sea or shore.
And commerce whitening every sea
With ships of every country,
Whose piled up decks and crowded holds,
The truth of prosp'rous trade unfolds,
But for his aid, would soon be shorn
Of much importance now her own; ...

Now then 'tis clear beyond a doubt
The Cooper can't be done without;
And all the world must plainly see
A skill'd and useful man is he,
And if his wages fall below
The average as the facts will show,
It is because he has been blind
To his best interests–which defined
Means that he has, until of late
Neglected to inaurgate,
The one thing needful to be made,
A UNION TO PROTECT HIS TRADE.

8 CIU, *Proceedings*, 1871.

9 CJ (August 1871), 263.

10 CIU, *Proceedings*, 1873.

11 Organizational data is drawn from CJ, 1870–75; CIU, *Proceedings*, 1871 and 1873; and CIU, Executive Department, *Names and Addresses of the Cor[responding] Secretaries of all the Unions* (Cleveland 1873).

12 *Workingman's Advocate*, 20 January 1872.

13 Benson Soffer, 'A Theory of Trade Union Development: The Role of the Autonomous Workman,' *Labor History*, I (1960), 141.

14 CJ (August 1871), 319.

15 Ibid. (April 1872), 254; CIU of North America, Executive Board, *Price List* (Cleveland 1872), 32–3.

16 CIU, *Ritual*, 9.

17 CJ (October 1872), 633; (March 1873), 133–4; (June 1873), 278. Subsequent quotations are from ibid. (Sept. 1872), 566 (June 1871), 248 and (June 1872), 373.

18 CIU, *Ritual*, 8–9.

19 CJ (May 1871), 211.

20 Ibid. (December 1870), 50.

21 Gilding, *Journeymen Coopers*, 84–6.

22 David Montgomery, 'Workers' Control of Machine Production in the Nineteenth Century,' *Labor History*, 17 (1976), 491–2.

23 Martin Foran, *The Other Side: A Social Study Based on Fact* (Washington 1886). The novel originally appeared in serial form in CJ commencing in December 1871 and was reprinted in Toronto's *Ontario Workman* in 1872. See also David Montgomery, *Beyond Equality*, 220–1, for a discussion of this novel.

24 CJ (July 1872), 426–9.

25 Ibid. (March 1871), 153.

26 Ibid. and *Proceedings*.

27 Gutman, 'Standard Oil.'

28 H.B. Small, *The Products and Manufactures of the New Dominion* (Ottawa 1868), 139–41. For a good description of hand production see T.A. Meister, *The Apple Barrel Industry in Nova Scotia* (Nova Scotia Museum, Halifax, n.d.).

29 *Journal of the Board of Arts and Manufactures of Upper Canada*, 3 (1863), 248.

30 CJ (January 1872), 47–8.

31 For Gooderham see CJ, passim; Toronto *Mail*, 23 April 1872; *Canadian Illustrated News*, 25 April 1863.

32 CJ (April 1871), 188.

33 CIU, *Proceedings*, 1871.

34 The information and quotations in the following paragraphs are from the CJ: (October–November 1870), 25; (July 1871), 268; (March 1872), 182; (April 1872), 235; (August 1872), 500; (September 1872), 566; (December 1872), 741; (December 1874); (June 1875).

35 Greg Kealey (ed.), *Canada Investigates Industrialism* (Toronto 1973), 113–16.
36 B. Soffer, 'The "Autonomous Workman,"' 148.
37 CJ (June 1875).
38 CIU, *Proceedings*, 1871.
39 CJ (July 1871), 263 ff. Quotations are from CJ: (July 1872), 426–9; (December 1872), 754–5; (March 1872), 144–5.
40 See also Martin Foran's earlier attack on machinery in CJ (May 1871), 200–2. Foran pointed out that 'capitalists used machines for the same pupose as labor – to make money.' He argued that machines had never benefited the trade – their purpose was 'simply to make money and enslave coopers.'
41 *Globe*, 15, 24 April 1882.
42 *Iron Molders' Journal*, August 1883.
43 G.S. Kealey, 'The Knights of Labor in Toronto,' ch. 12.
44 *Globe*, 28 August 1889.

CHAPTER 5

1 See Herbert Gutman, 'Class, Status and the Gilded Age Radical: A Reconsideration' in Gutman and Kealey (eds.), *Many Pasts: Readings in American Social History*, vol. 2 (Englewood Cliffs 1973), 125–51; and his 'Work, Culture, and Society in Industrializing America, 1815–1919,' *American Historical Review*, 78 (1973), 531–88; see also E.J. Hobsbawm, 'Custom, Wages, and Work-load,' in *Labouring Men: Studies in the History of Labour* (London 1964), 344–70.
2 David Montgomery, 'Workers' Control of Machine Production in the Nineteenth Century,' *Labor History*, 17 (1976), 485–509; see also Montgomery's 'Trade Union Practice and the Origins of Syndicalist Theory in the United States' (unpublished paper) and his 'The 'New Unionism' and the Transformation of Workers' Consciousness in America, 1909–1922,' *Journal of Social History*, 7 (1974), 509–29. All these are part of Montgomery's ongoing study, tentatively titled 'The Fall of the House of Labor, 1800–1920.'
3 Raymond Williams, 'Base and Super-structure in Marxist Cultural Theory,' *New Left Review*, 82 (November-December 1973), 3–16. For an application of these categories to U.S. working-class history see Leon Fink, 'Class Conflict and Class Consciousness in the Gilded Age: The Figure and the Phantom,' *Radical History Review*, 3 (Winter 1975), 56–72.
4 Benson Soffer, 'A Theory of Trade Union Development,' 141–63.
5 Montgomery, 'Workers' Control,' 487–95.
6 On scientific management in the U.S. see Milton Nadworny, *Scientific Man-*

agement and the Unions (Cambridge, Mass. 1955); Katherine Stone, 'The Origin of Job Structures in the Steel Industry,' *Radical America*, 7 (1973), 19–66; and Bryan Palmer, 'Class, Conception and Class Conflict: The Thrust for Efficiency, Managerial View of Labor and the Working Class Rebellion, 1903–1922,' *The Review of Radical Political Economics*, 7 (1975), 31–49. For Canada see Bradley Rubin, 'Mackenzie King and the Writing of Canada's (Anti) Labour Laws,' *Canadian Dimension*, 8 (January 1972); Michael Piva, 'The Decline of the Trade Union Movement in Toronto, 1900–1915' (unpublished paper); and Craig Heron and Bryan Palmer, 'Through the Prism of the Strike: The Contours and Context of Industrial Unrest in Southern Ontario, 1901–1914,' *Canadian Historical Review*, 58 (1977), 425–58. For a brilliant overview of these developments see Harry Braverman, *Labor and Monopoly Capital* (New York 1974). The most incisive critique of this work to date has been the review by Russell Jacoby in *Telos*, 29 (1976), 199–207.

7 Robert Storey, 'Industrialization in Canada,' 187–90.

8 *Times* (Hamilton), 23 March 1865 as cited in ibid., 130.

9 C.B. Williams, 'Canadian-American Trade Union Relations: A Study of the Development of Bi-national Unionism' (unpublished PH D thesis. Cornell University 1964), 93.

10 Palmer, 'Most Uncommon Common Men,' 251–2.

11 *Royal Commission on the Relations of Capital and Labor*, Ontario Evidence, 294–300.

12 Paul C. Appleton, 'The Sunshine and the Shades: Labour Activism in Central Canada, 1850–1860' (unpublished MA thesis, University of Calgary 1974), 97.

13 The best work on the IMIU in Canada is C.B. Williams, 'Canadian-American,' ch. 3–4. Although limited in scope, the discussion of the union is insightful.

14 IMIU, *Constitution*, 1859, as cited in Williams, 'Canadian–American,' 105.

15 The discussion of wages in the industry is drawn from John P. Frey and John R. Commons, 'Conciliation in the Stove Industry,' *Bulletin of the Bureau of Labor*, 62 (1906), 124–96, especially 125–30; Frank T. Stockton, *The International Iron Molders Union of North America* (Baltimore 1921); and David A.M. McCabe, *The Standard Rate in American Trade Unions* (Baltimore 1912), 47.

16 Carroll D. Wright, 'Regulation and Restriction of Output,' *Eleventh Special Report of the Commissioner of Labor* (Washington 1904), 149–85; and McCabe, *The Standard Rate*, 110.

17 Peterborough Iron Moulders International Union, No. 191, *Minutes*, 4 September 1882, in Gainey Collection, Trent University Archives (henceforth *Minutes* no. 191).

18 Wright, 'Regulation and Restriction of Output,' 151.

19 *Minutes* no. 191, 19 June 1891.

20 Jonathan Grossman, *William Sylvis, Pioneer of American Labor* (New York 1945), 153.
21 *Globe*, 21 January 1871.
22 Palmer, 'Most Uncommon Common Men,' 254. Miller had been Toronto's delegate at the international convention in 1861.
23 *Minutes* no. 191, 8 February 1889, 15 May 1891.
24 *Royal Commission on the Relations of Capital and Labour*, Ontario Evidence, 147, 153, 294–300.
25 *Iron Molders Journal* (henceforth IMJ), October 1873.
26 John H. Ashworth, *The Helper and American Trade Unions* (Baltimore 1915), 36.
27 Ibid., 68.
28 Ibid., 70.
29 Frey and Commons, 'Conciliation,' 126–27, 176; Stockton, *International Molders Union*, 170–85.
30 Williams, 'Canadian–American,' 120.
31 Ibid., 122. In the end the notice was withdrawn and 'apprentice and helper rules were controlled by the union, and shop committees continued to enforce shop rules and customs.'
32 IMJ (August-December 1874, February 1876). See also the testimony of foundry owners Gurney and Smart before House of Commons' Committees in *Journals*, 1874, Appendix C, and 1876, Appendix C. The quotation is from Smart's 1876 testimony, p. 177.
33 IMIU, *Proceedings*, 1863.
34 Ibid.
35 IMJ (March 1864).
36 *Globe*, 22 March, 3 April 1867; IMJ (May 1867).
37 *Globe*, 21, 23, 27 December 1870; 20 January 1871; IMIU, *Proceedings*, 1872.
38 *Globe*, 24 May, 2 June, 26 September 1890; 10 January 1891. Massey Clipping Files, Vol. 1, 1886–91, Massey Archives, Toronto. IMIU, *Proceedings*, 1890.
39 IMIU, *Proceedings*, 1895.
40 See especially J.H. Barnett to John Robertson, Toronto, 20 August 1903 and 30 May 1904 in IMIU no. 191. *Correspondence*, Gainey Collection (henceforth *Correspondence* no. 191).
41 *Globe*, 22 March 1867.
42 Ibid., 6 April 1867.
43 Ibid., 20 January 1871. See also 21, 23, 27 December 1870; 21 April 1871.
44 IMJ (January 1871).
45 *Globe*, 15, 18 July, 18 November 1871. For the moulders' response to these legal initiatives see IMJ (31 January 1871).

46 *Globe*, 28 February 1871. Subsequent quotations are from *Globe*, 30 September, 31 December, 31 October 1871; 10 February, 1875. For similar cases see IMJ (30 September 1871, 31 December 1870).

47 *Globe*, 8 January 1887, 6 January 1888; *Canadian Labor Reformer*, 8 January 1887.

48 Frey and Commons, 'Conciliation,' 104–47.

49 *Royal Commission on the Relations of Capital and Labor*, Ontario Evidence, 294–300.

50 Williams, 'Canadian–American,' passim.

51 Grossman, *Sylvis*, 110.

52 Ontario Bureau of Industry, *Annual Report*, 1892; IMIU *Proceedings*, 1892–95.

53 *Globe*, 27 February 1890, 22 August 1890, 26 September 1890, 3 October 1890, 10 January 1891; *News*, 25 August 1890; *Monetary Times*, 31 October 1890.

54 *Globe*, 10 January 1891.

55 Ibid., 22 August 1890.

56 David Black to R.W. Parkes, Peterborough, 29 June 1890, *Correspondence* no. 191.

57 *Globe*, 24 May, 2 June 1890.

58 'To the Canadian Public,' Toronto, 1 September 1890, *Correspondence* no. 191.

59 *Labor Advocate*, 16 January 1891.

60 *Globe*, 10 January 1891. Encouraged by his temporary victory in Toronto, Gurney attacked his Hamilton moulders the next year. For this bitter struggle see IMIU, *Proceedings*, 1895; Fred Walters to F.W. Parkes, Peterborough, 20 March 1892; Executive Board IMIU, 'Circular letter,' 3 March 1892; Hamilton IMIU Local No. 26, 'Labor Struggle against Capital,' 28 March 1892. The last three items are in *Correspondence* no. 191.

61 For general material on the employee offensive see works cited in note 6 supra and especially Wayne Roberts, 'Toronto Metal Workers and the Second Industrial Revolution, 1896–1914' (unpublished paper).

62 J.H. Barnett to John Robertson, Jr., Peterborough, 20 August 1903, *Correspondence* no. 191.

63 Barnett to Robertson, 30 May 1904, ibid.

64 Robert Ozanne, *A Century of Labor-Management Relations at McCormick and International Harvester* (Madison 1967), ch. 1.

65 Massey Account Books, Massey Archives, Toronto. For the best discussion of technological innovation in the moulding industry see James Cooke Mills, *Searchlights on Some American Industries* (Chicago 1911), ch. 7.

66 For the Massey strike see 'Knights of Labor,' ch. 10; for the Peterborough–Lindsay connection see *Minutes* no. 191, 1886–87. Ozanne's *A*

Century provides similar evidence of co-operation between Chicago moulders and the Knights.

67 *Royal Commission on the Relations of Capital and Labor*, Ontario Evidence. Quotations are from pp. 143–50, 169–73, 294–300.

68 IMJ, 31 December 1892. For a historical reminiscence which depicts the early moulder's life, see Joseph A. Barford, 'Reminiscences of the Early Days of Stove Plate Molding and the Union,' *International Molders' and Foundry Workers' Journal*, 94 (July 1958), 8–11.

69 Eugene Forsey Papers, PAC.

70 *Royal Commission on the Relations of Capital and Labor*, Ontario Evidence, 62–70.

71 *Machinists and Blacksmiths Journal* (June 1871), 234. Subsequent quotations are from (June 1871) 324, (June 1872) 654–5, 668.

72 Wright, 'Restriction of Output,' 102. See also *By-laws of Machinists and Blacksmiths Union No. 1* (Milwaukee 1876).

73 For details on an attempt to revive the IMBU see *Constitution and Rules of Order of the Central Council of Mechanical Engineers* (Milwaukee 1878).

74 David Montgomery, 'Trade Union Practice,' 16–25.

75 *Fincher's Trades Review*, 15 August 1863.

76 IMJ, February 1868.

77 James C. Sylvis, *The Life, Speeches, Labors and Essays of William H. Sylvis* (Philadelphia 1872), 390.

78 For similar events in Vancouver see Bartley, *Outline History*, 11. There, during a strike in 1892, the printers founded *The New World*.

79 Russel Hann, 'Brainworkers and the Knights of Labor: E.E. Sheppard, Phillips Thompson and the Toronto *News*,' in Kealey and Warrian (eds.), *Essays*.

80 Harkness, *Atkinson*, 25–47.

81 *Machinists and Blacksmiths' Journal* (December 1871), 451, (January 1872), p. 486.

82 *Globe*, 30 October; 5, 18, 27 November; 14 December 1878.

83 *Cigar Makers Journal*, March 1879, April 1880.

84 *Palladium of Labor*, 29 May; 3, 10 July 1886.

85 *Globe*, 30, 31 January; 5, 8, 22, 25, 28 February; 17 March; 28 April; 9, 15 May 1884. See also *Journal of United Labour*, 25 October 1885.

86 *Fincher's Trades Review*, 23 April 1864.

87 *Globe*, 5 April 1882.

88 Ibid., 14 July 1887.

89 For example see David Frank, 'Class Conflict in the Coal Industry: Cape Breton 1922,' in Kealey and Warrian (eds.), *Essays*. The socialism of the IAM, for example, was no accident.

90 F.W. Taylor, *The Principles of Scientific Management* (New York 1967), 32. For a brilliant discussion of modern management strategies see Braverman, *Labor and Monopoly Capital*.
91 Taylor, *Principles*, 49.
92 Ibid., 53.
93 Palmer, 'Class, Conception and Conflict,' 31–3.
94 Wright, 'Restriction of Output,' 174.
95 Montgomery, 'Workers' Control,' 487.

CHAPTER 6

1 On the union's early history see: James McArthur Conner, 'The Early Printers Unions of Canada' in International Typographical Union, *69th Annual Convention Souvenir*, Toronto, 1924; Sally Zerker, 'A History of the Toronto Typographical Union,' (unpublished PH D thesis, University of Toronto 1972), ch. 1; Edith Firth, *The Town of York, 1815–1834*, pp. xxxii–iv, 85–6; and F.H. Armstrong, 'Reformer as Capitalist: William Lyon Mackenzie and the Printers' Strike of 1836,' *Ontario History*, 59 (1967), 187–96.
2 National Typographical Union, *Proceedings*, 1866, 15–6.
3 George Barnett, 'The Printers: A Study in American Trade Unionism,' *American Economics Association Quarterly*, 3rd series, x (1909), 50.
4 Ethelbert Stewart, 'A documentary history of the early organization of printers,' *Bulletin of the Bureau of Labor*, 61 (November 1905), 849.
6 Cited in Wayne Roberts, 'The Last Artisans: Toronto Printers, 1896–1914,' in Kealey and Warrian (eds.), *Essays in Working Class History* (Toronto 1976).
7 Armstrong, 'Reformer as Capitalist,' 189. See also Zerker, 'History of the T.T.U.,' 38–46.
8 Ibid., 190, and Conner, 'Early Printers Unions.'
9 Armstrong, 'Reformer as Capitalist,' 192–3.
10 Conner, 'Early Printers Unions.'
11 Toronto Typographical Union, *Minutes*, 5 March 1845 (henceforth TTU, *Minutes*).
12 Ibid., 2 July 1845.
13 Hobsbawm, 'Custom, Wages and Work-load,' 347. See also Zerker, 'The Development of Collective Bargaining in the Toronto Printing Industry in the Nineteenth Century,' *Industrial Relations*, 30 (1975), 83–97.
14 TTU, *Minutes*, 2 July 1845.
15 George E. McNeill, *The Labor Movement* (Boston 1887), 185.
16 TTU, *Minutes*, 7 March 1849. The origins of the 'chapel' are obscure. The first usage given by the *Oxford English Dictionary* is 1698 but J. Hagan and C. Fisher, 'Piece Work and Some of Its Consequences in the Printing and Coal

Mining Industries in Australia, 1850–1930,' *Labour History* (Australia), 25 (1973), 19–39, mention that 'Moxon's *Mechanick Exercises* (1683), p. 23 n. refers to the chapel as 'having been established since time out of mind.'

17 *Globe*, 27 June 1888. The extensive historical interests of printers are also evidenced in two early official histories of the TTU: John McVicar, *Origins and Progress of the Typographical Union, 1850–1891* (Lansing Mich. 1891), and George A. Tracey, *History of the Typographical Union* (Indianapolis 1913).

18 *Typographical Journal*, 15 September 1889.

19 ITU, *Proceedings*, 1881, 46. John R. Commons, one of the founders of academic American labour studies, spent his summers while an undergraduate at Oberlin in the 1880s as a typesetter. This experience influenced his understanding of the importance of craft traditions and trade unionism to printers: 'My only rights and liberties in typesetting were created by that little society of printers and had been administered, since the gilds of the Middle Ages by the "father of the chapel."' John R. Commons, *Myself* (Madison 1963), 19.

20 Wright's 'Restriction of Output,' pp. 60–90, is a good general discussion.

21 Ibid., 88–91.

22 NTU, *Proceedings*, 1858, 45–6.

23 ITU, *Proceedings*, 1871, 47.

24 George A. Barnett, 'The Printers,' 296 ff.

25 ITU, *Proceedings*, 1873, 45, and Elizabeth Baker, *Printers and Technology: A History of the Printing Pressmen and Assistants' Union* (New York 1957) 215. See also her 'The Printing Foreman–Union Man: A Historical Sketch,' in *Industrial and Labor Relations Review* (1951), 223–5.

26 *Globe*, 21 July 1884. In Australia the same custom was followed but 'subs' were known as 'grasshands.' Hagan and Fisher, 'Piece Work and Some of Its Consequences,' p. 26.

27 Barnett, 'The Printers,' especially 218–21; the following quotations on 212–13, 320.

28 Ibid., 228–42 and *Typographical Journal*, 15 July 1890.

29 *Royal Commission on the Relations of Labor and Capital*, Ontario Evidence, p. 46.

30 Zerker, 'Development of Collective Bargaining,' 84–8.

31 Zerker, 'George Brown and the Printers' Union,' *Journal of Canadian Studies*, 10, 1 (1975), 47.

32 Barnett, 'The Printers,' 109

33 'The letter 'm' in all early founts occupied the full square of the body of the type, and the letter 'n' half of this area. Printers therefore adopted the 'em' and the 'en' as units of measure.' Hagan and Fisher, 'Piece Work and Some of Its Consequences,' 22 n.

34 A humorous example of the last was the Vancouver 'cap "I" strike' of 1889.

The printers struck against the *World* for two days when management refused to pay for corrections in faulty copy. See George Bartley, *An Outline of History of Typographical Union, no. 226, Vancouver, B.C., 1887–1938* (Vancouver 1938), 8.

35 In an 1872 dictionary of printing, 'fat' was defined as 'Advantage easily obtained. With compositors, light open matter and short or blank pages.' George Barnett, 'The Printers,' 117, n. 7.

36 Barnett, 'The Printers,' 108–42; and Zerker, 'A History of the Toronto Typographical Union,' 1–14. John R. Commons, in *Myself*, (pp. 18–9), recounts how as a young compositor working as a sub, he won the fat in an auction only to have the printers bid him up too high the next time to teach him a lesson.

37 TTU, 'Scale of Prices' in *Minutes*, 17 March 1883.

38 *Royal Commission on the Relations of Labor and Capital*, Ontario Evidence, p. 44.

39 TTU, *Minutes*, 20 December 1890. There were constant struggles over the fat in Australia as well. See Hagan and Fisher, 'Piece Work and Some of Its Consequences,' p. 25.

40 Ibid., 17 March 1883; 6, 20 December 1890; 28 March, 5 December 1891.

41 Baker, *Printers and Technology*, 69. For a discussion of the historical roots of ITU strength and for contemporary twentieth-century examples see S.M. Lipset, M.A. Trow and J.S. Coleman, *Union Democracy: The Internal Politics of the I.T.U.* (Glencoe Ill. 1956), ch. 2.

42 Baker, *Printers and Technology*, 59–60, 69.

43 Ibid., 74.

44 Toronto Printing Pressmen's Union, Local 10, *Minutes*, 8 July to 14 October 1887.

45 Roberts, 'Toronto Printers' and Ross Harkness, *J.E. Atkinson of the Star* (Toronto 1963), 28.

46 ITU, *Minutes*, 2 July 1845.

47 *Globe*, 29 March 1872.

48 Zerker, 'George Brown,' passim; for greater detail on TTU struggles in the 1850s, see Appleton, 'The Sunshine and the Shade,' 103–16. These political themes will be discussed in detail in chs. 8, 10–12.

49 TTU, *Minutes*, 3 June 1882.

50 *Globe*, 21, 23, 30 March 1882.

51 Michael Gordon, 'Irish Immigrant Culture and the Labor Boycott in New York City, 1880–1886' in Richard L. Ehrlich (ed.), *Immigrants in Industrial America, 1850–1920* (Charlottesville, Va. 1977), 111–22. See also Gordon's 'The Labor Boycott in New York City, 1880–1886,' *Labor History*, 16 (1975), 184–229.

52 Barnett, 'The Printers,' 268–70.
53 Ibid., 269.
54 *Globe*, 5 July 1884.
55 TTLC, *Minutes*, 15 August 1884.
56 *Labor Commission*, Ontario Evidence, 36–51.
57 *Globe*, 5, 6, 21, 22 July 1884 and ITU, *Proceedings*, 1885, 1886.
58 *Palladium of Labor* (Hamilton), 19 July 1884.
59 Ibid.
60 TPPU, *Minutes*, 11 December 1885.
61 *Globe*, 8, 11, 15, 16, 19, 22 December 1885. Following quotations are from 4 January 1886, (emphasis in original); 5 January 1886; and 16 July 1888.
62 Ibid., 26, 27 July, 8, 15 August 1888.
63 *Typographical Journal*, 15 September 1889.
64 *Mail*, 17 August 1889.
65 Printing Pressmen, *Minutes*, 11 October 1890.
66 W.B. Prescott to Macdonald, Toronto, 5 May 1890, p. 241968, Macdonald Papers.
67 TTU, *Minutes*, 5 December 1891.
68 Ibid., 5 March 1892. For switch from the boycott to the union label in the ITU see Barnett, 'The Printers,' p. 274.
69 Zerker, 'A History,' ch. 3.
70 For the best discussion of the effects of mechanization on printers see George E. Barnett, 'The Introduction of the Linotype,' *Yale Review* (November 1904), 251–73. A good summary of all the literature on printers and mechanization is Harry Kalber and Carl Schlesinger, *Union Printers and Controlled Automation* (New York 1967), especially ch. 1.
71 ITU, *Proceedings*, 1888, and Barnett, 'The Printers,' 197.
72 ITU, *Proceedings*, 1889. For the struggle in New York, which set the continental pattern see Kalber and Schlesinger, *Union Printers*, ch. 1.
73 ITU, *Proceedings*, 1891.
74 Barnett, 'The Printers,' 132.
75 Wright, 'Restriction of Output,' 36.
76 Ibid.
77 For a similar success in Vancouver see Bartley, *Outline History*, 12.
78 ITU, *Proceedings*, 1893.
79 Wright, 'Restriction of Output,' 38.
80 Zerker, 'A History,' 160–5, 202–7; Harkness, *Atkinson*, 25–6; Barnett, 'The Printers,' ch. 11, and Wright, 'Restriction of Output,' 35–55.
81 For the English response to typesetting machines see Ellic Howe (ed.), *The London Compositor* (London 1947), ch. 19. For an excellent autobiographical

account of an Edwardian compositor, which illustrates many of the themes discussed here, see John Burnett (ed.), *The Annals of Labour: Autobiographies of British Working Class People 1820–1920* (London 1974), 330–40.
82 Wright, 'Restriction of Output,' 37.
83 Barnett, 'The Printers,' 202.
84 Ibid., 124. Gompers was testifying before the Industrial Commission.
85 Stewart, 'Documentary History,' 937.
86 For the subsequent history see Roberts, 'The Last Artisans.'

CHAPTER 7

1 Hector Charlesworth, *Candid Chronicles* (Toronto 1925), especially his Foreword.
2 Martin Robin, *Radical Politics and Canadian Labour, 1880–1930* (Kingston 1968), Introduction, especially pp. 5–6.
3 Pentland, 'Labour and the Development of Industrial Capitalism in Canada,' 259. Recent work by University of Toronto geographers Cecil Houston and William J. Smyth has added greatly to our knowledge of the Orange Order in Ontario. Although differing in emphasis, and despite their disclaimers, in most aspects I find their work compatible with my own interpretation. However, I disagree with their interpretation of the Orangemen's 'garrison mentality,' their dismissal of territoriality as a useful analytic device, and their insistence on the Order's cross-class membership. See especially their 'The Orange Order in Nineteenth-Century Ontario: A Study in Institutional Cultural Transfer' (Department of Geography, University of Toronto, Discussion Paper No. 22, 1977); and 'Toronto, the Belfast of Canada' (unpublished paper).
4 Maureen Wall, 'The Whiteboys,' in T. Desmond Williams, *Secret Societies in Ireland* (Dublin 1973).
5 E.P. Thompson, *The Making of the English Working Class* (London 1968), 470–1.
6 Kevin B. Nowlan, 'Conclusion,' in Williams, *Secret Societies*, 183.
7 J.C. Beckett, *The Anglo-Irish Tradition* (London 1976), 45.
8 Hereward Senior, 'The Genesis of Canadian Orangeism,' *Ontario History*, 60 (1968), 13–4; *Orangeism: The Canadian Phase* (Toronto 1973), ch. 1–2; 'Ogle Gowan,' in *Dictionary of Canadian Biography*, x (Toronto 1972), 309–14.
9 W.B. Kerr, 'When Orange and Green United, 1832–1839: The Alliance of Macdonnell and Gowan,' *Ontario History*, 34 (1942), 34–42.
10 For examples see William Shannon, *The United Empire Minstrel* (Toronto 1852), 42–3; Shannon, *The Dominion Orange Harmonist* (Toronto 1876), 27

and chronology. See also R. McBride, *The Canadian Orange Minstrel for 1860* (London 1860), and *The Canadian Orange Minstrel for 1870: Written for the Purposes of Keeping in Remembrance the Dark Doings and Designs of Popery in This Country* (Toronto 1870). The best description of the Slabtown Affair is provided by J. Lawrence Runnals, *The Irish on the Welland Canal* (St Catharines, 1973). On 12 July 1849 Irish Catholics gathered to prevent the Orangemen from 'walking,' but when the Orangemen failed even to try, the Catholics settled for three cheers – one for the queen, one for the governor, and one for the pope. The Orangemen responded with a volley of shots which left two Catholics dead and four others wounded. For a similar event in Irish history, see H. Senior, *Orangeism in Ireland and Britain, 1795–1836.* (Toronto 1966), 16.

11 For examples, see Loyal Orange Institution of British North America, *Laws, Rules, and Regulations*, Cobourg, 1846, and Belleville, 1850; *Constitution and Laws of the Loyal Orange Institution*, Toronto, 1855.

12 Loyal Orange Institution of British North America (LOIBNA), *Forms to Be Observed in Private Lodges*, Toronto, 1855.

13 For ritual see Hobsbawm, *Primitive Rebels*, 150–74; for Masonic roots see Senior, *Orangeism in Ireland*, 12, and Nowlan, p. 183 in Williams, *Secret Societies*; for actual ritual forms see LOIBNA, *Charges to Be Delivered at the Initiation of Members*, (Toronto 1856); *Forms to Be Observed in Private Lodges* (Toronto 1855); *Orange Ritual* (Belleville 1874); *Forms of the Royal Blue Order* (Toronto 1855); *Ritual of the Blue Order* (Belleville 1864); *Forms of the Royal Blue Order* (Toronto 1869); *Forms of the Purple Order* (Toronto 1855); *Forms of the Royal Arch Purple Mark* (Toronto 1855, 1869); *Forms and Ritual of the Royal Scarlet Order* (Cobourg 1846, 1864); *Ritual of the Royal Scarlet Order* (Toronto 1886).

14 Conrad Arensberg, *The Irish Countryman* (New York 1937), 215–16.

15 LOIBNA, *Charges to be Delivered ... and Services for the Burial of Orangemen, The Dedication of an Orange Lodge, and for the Installation of Officers*, Toronto, 1856.

16 As late as 1969 partisan historians were still claiming that 'in fact the Twelfth in Toronto is second only to that on the field at Finaghy.' M.W. Dewar, John Brown, S.E. Long, *Orangeism: A New Historical Appreciation* (Belfast 1969), 17.

17 Much of it is drawn from Leslie H. Saunders, *The Story of Orangeism* (Toronto 1941). However, Provincial Grand Lodge Proceedings, Toronto Orange Directories, Toronto City Directories, and the Toronto press have also been utilized. The extremely useful work of Cecil Houston and William Smyth,

drawn from archival materials still held by the order, differs generally on the level of a few lodges only, and I have tried to cite their evidence when it is opposed to my own.

18 These figures and those following are from LOIBNA, Provincial Grand Lodge of Canada West, *Proceedings*, Toronto, 1872, 1876, 1880, 1883.

19 Houston and Smyth, 'The Orange Order,' 5, 44–51 but especially 50–1. This useful discussion clarifies some of the bewildering array of numbers used when discussing Orange membership.

20 Pentland, 'Labour and the Development of Industrial Capitalism,' 247 ff. Pentland's work on the order is the most insightful we have, but he makes the error of assuming that 'the typical urban Orangeman was a skilled worker, a craftsman' (p. 257). However, he was quite aware of the Orange Order's predominant working-class membership and its importance. Both these insights have not been picked up by scholars writing after him.

21 The data are from the following sources: *By-laws of Loyal Orange Lodge, No. 328*, Toronto, 1846, 1852, 1856, and 1872. Lodge 137, Treasurers Book, 1889–1907 and Roll Book, 1885– . Lodge 173, Minutes, 1883–1903 and Roll Book, 1883–1896. Lodge 711, Minutes, 1873–1906; Membership and Degree Book, 1890– ; Proposition Book, 1890– ; Roll Book, 1875–1895. The Manuscript Records of Lodges 137, 173 and 711 are all in The Baldwin Room of Metropolitan Toronto Central Library.

22 *By-laws of Loyal Orange Lodge, No. 328*, Toronto, 1872.

23 Minutes, LOL No. 137.

24 Houston and Smyth, 'Toronto, the Belfast of Canada,' 11, 12–13, 14.

25 Ibid., and 'The Orange Order in Nineteenth-Century Ontario,' 6–7.

26 Houston and Smyth, 'Toronto, the Belfast of Canada,' 13.

27 For the opposite argument see Senior, 'Orangeism in Ontario in Politics, 1872–1896,' 136–7 in Donald Swainson, *Oliver Mowat's Ontario* (Toronto 1972). Data on lodge masters were taken from the following sources: Thomas Keyes, *Orange Directory of Western Ontario* (St Catharines 1871); *Second Annual Orange Directory of Lodges, Meetings, Officers, etc. for Toronto* (Toronto 1876). *Toronto Orange Directory, 1878* (Toronto 1878). LOABA, Provincial Grand Lodge of Canada West, *Proceedings*, Toronto, 1888. These lists of masters were then traced in directories for occupational data.

28 The 1878 and 1886 data are from the above sources; the 1871 list of all officers was compiled from the lists appearing in the *Globe* after each lodge election was held.

29 Senior, 'Orangeism in Canadian Politics,' 136–7.

30 For all these functions see Minutes of Lodges 173 and 711. See also Lodge By-laws of the following Toronto lodges: Virgin No. 328, 1846, 1852, 1856, and

1872; Schomberg No. 212, 1882; McKinlay No. 275, 1874; York No. 375, 1866 and 1894; Enniskillen No. 711, 1898; and *Constitution and Laws of the Orange Mutual Benefit Society of Ontario West*, Toronto, 188?.

31 Houston and Smyth, 'Toronto, the Belfast of Canada,' 21.

32 Membership lists for the lodges studied and lists of lodge officers confirm this. See also patronage correspondence in Macdonald Papers, PAC, and *Irish Canadian*, 8 March 1876, 9 October 1884, and 7 May 1885.

33 See especially *Irish Canadian*, 12 November 1885 and 21, 28 August and 11 December 1884.

34 Senior, *Orangeism: The Canadian Phase*, especially ch. 2.

35 LOABNA, *Proceedings of the Grand Lodge*, Toronto, 1856.

36 William Perkins Bull, *From the Boyne to Brampton* (Toronto 1936), 138.

37 *By-laws*, Toronto, 1872.

38 *Constitution and Laws*, Belleville, 1875.

39 Senior, 'The Genesis of Canadian Orangeism,' 27.

40 Sybil E. Baker, 'The Orange and Green,' 789–814 in Dyos and Wolff, *The Victorian City: Images and Reality* (London 1973).

41 The data are taken from a daily reading of the Toronto press for the 25-year period. The best Canadian analysis of Orange-Green conflict is Michael Cross, 'Stony Monday, 1849: The Rebellion Losses Riot in Bytown,' *Ontario History* (1971), 177–90. See also his 'The Shiners War: Social Violence in the Ottawa Valley in the 1830s,' *Canadian Historical Review* (1973), 1–26, for a fine description of pre-industrial Green organization.

42 Natalie Zemon Davis, 'The Rites of Violence: Religious Riot in Sixteenth Century France,' *Past and Present*, 59 (1973), 51–91, and Baker, 'The Orange and the Green,' 790–7.

43 *Globe*, 23 July 1870, and W.B. Kerr, 'The Orange Order in the 1820s' from *The Orange Sentinel* now on microfilm in Toronto Public Library.

44 *Globe*, 13 July 1870, 11 July 1876, 13 July 1877, 13 July 1888; *Mail*, 19 June 1877, 13 July 1877.

45 *Globe*, 30 July 1873, 27 July 1874; *Leader*, 30 July 1873; *Irish Canadian*, 30 July 1873.

46 *Irish Canadian*, 22, 29 March, 5 April 1871; *Globe*, 6, 13 April 1871; 19, 20 March 1872; 19, 22 March 1889; *Telegraph*, 19 March 1872.

47 Senior, *Orangeism in Ireland*, 12.

48 For a discussion of the role of adolescent males in collective violence of a traditional sort, see Davis, 'Rites of Violence'; for specific Orange data on boys, see Baker, 'Orange and Green'; *Globe*, 2, 3, 5, 6, 12, 14, 20, 21 September 1870. See also LOIBNA, Grand Lodge of Canada West, *Proceedings*, Toronto, 1873; Orange Young Britons, Grand Lodge, *Proceedings*, Toronto, 1878.

49 For a detailed discussion of the O'Brien riot see: Desmond Morton, *Mayor Howland* (Toronto 1973), 77–82; Colonel George T. Denison, *The Struggle for Imperial Unity: Recollections and Experiences* (Toronto 1909), 70–6; and *Globe*, 16, 18, 19, 21 May 1887.

50 *Globe*, 12 July 1888, 13 July 1889; *Irish Canadian*, 16 July 1885, 15 July 1886. For the events of 1875 see Martin Galvin, 'Catholic-Protestant Relations in Ontario 1864–1875' (MA thesis, University of Toronto 1962), and Galvin, 'The Jubilee Riots in Toronto,' *Canadian Catholic Historical Association Annual Report* (1959), 93–107. See also E.C. Guillet, *Toronto: Trading Post to Great City* (Toronto 1934), 216–18.

51 For arrests and trials see *Globe*, 27, 28 September; 4, 5, 9, 12 October; 17–21, 28 January 1876.

52 Ibid., 7 August 1875.

53 *Globe*, 19, 20, 22, 27 March 1878; *Mail*, 19, 20 March 1878.

54 Rowland Berthoff, *An Unsettled People* (New York 1971), 274.

55 Kenneth Duncan, 'Irish Famine Immigration and the Social Structure of Canada West,' *Canadian Review of Sociology and Anthropology* (1965), 39 and Davis, 'The Rites of Violence,' 91. For an excellent analysis of the utility of Irish cultural traditions for the emerging labour movement, see Michael A. Gordon, 'Irish Immigrant Culture and the Labor Boycott in New York City, 1880–1886,' *Labor History*, 16 (1975), 184–229.

56 This rather obvious point is added to prevent further misreadings of the kind made by John Smart, 'Archivists, Nationalists and New Leftists – Themes, Sources and Problems in English Canadian Labour History since 1965' (unpublished paper), especially 14–17.

CHAPTER 8

1 Despite the dominance of political history in the Canadian historiographic tradition, there is little to help us enter the realm of working-class politics. Traditional political history has never allowed the unwashed to sully its elegant pages. The biographies of politicians also manage to avoid discussions of those whose votes made their subjects famous and often rich. On this score, however, one should note that J.M.S. Careless, *Brown of the Globe*, 2 vols. (Toronto 1963), is vastly more useful than the hagiographic Donald Creighton, *John A. Macdonald*, 2 vols. (Toronto 1955). Other biographies of little use are Dale Thomson, *Alexander Mackenzie: Clear Grit* (Toronto 1960), and Joseph Schull, *Edward Blake*, 2 vols. (Toronto 1975). At the provincial level there is less. Bruce Hodgins, *John Sandfield Macdonald* (Toronto 1971), is very thin on his years as Ontario premier, and on Mowat we have only the official

biography by C.R.W. Biggar, *Sir Oliver Mowat*, 2 vols. (Toronto 1905), and Margaret Evans 'Oliver Mowat and Ontario, 1872–1896 ' (unpublished PH D thesis, University of Toronto 1967).

Stepping away from traditional political history into labour history we encounter different problems. Most of the literature about workers' politics tends to dismiss it as immature. The most detailed study of this kind is Bernard Ostry's otherwise still useful 'Conservatives, Liberals and Labour in the 1870s,' CHR, 41 (1960), 93–127, and 'Conservatives, Liberals and Labour in the 1880s,' CJEPS, 27 (1961), 141–61. Less useful are Martin Robin, *Radical Politics and Canadian Labour* (Kingston 1968), ch. 1–2, and 'The Working Class and the Transition to Capitalist Democracy in Canada,' *Dalhousie Review*, 47 (1967–68), 326–43. The analyses closest to my own include the pioneering Frank Watt, 'The National Policy, the Workingman, and Proletarian Ideas in Victorian Canada,' CHR, 40 (1959), 1–26; Steven Langdon, *The Emergence of the Canadian Working Class Movement* (Toronto 1975); and Russell Hann, 'Brainworkers and the Knights of Labor: E.E. Sheppard, Phillips Thompson, and the Toronto News, 1883–1887,' in G.S. Kealey and Peter Warrian (eds.), *Essays in Canadian Working Class History* (Toronto 1976), 35–57.

2 Brian Harrison and Patricia Hollis, 'Chartism, Liberalism, and the Life of Robert Lowery,' *English Historical Review*, 82 (1967), 505.

3 For the Irish Catholics see Hereward Senior, *The Fenians and Canada* (Toronto 1978), especially ch. 3.

4 The question of the extent of their vote must be addressed here. The following discussion draws on: John Garner, *The Franchise and Politics in British North America, 1755–1867* (Toronto 1969); Norman Ward, *The Canadian House of Commons: Representation* (Toronto 1950); and Thomas Hodgins, *The Canadian Franchise Act* (Toronto 1886). The year before Confederation, the urban parliamentary franchise in the Canadas had been narrowed to owners and occupants of real property, assessed at an actual value of $600. This was an intentional action, aimed at minimizing the influence of urban labourers. The first federal and provincial elections were held under that franchise. In 1868 John Sandfield Macdonald's Ontario government extended the franchise, a trend which the Mowat government continued until, by 1885, it included nearly all adult males, and in 1888 it included full adult male suffrage. Federally, the story differed. John A. Macdonald continued to use the 1866 Ontario franchise in 1872, but the new Liberal government conducted its elections under 'the contemporaneous provincial franchises.' After much pressure John A. Macdonald was forced to pass a federal franchise in 1885. It was extremely complicated, however, and set higher property requirements for voting than those current in Ontario elections: in cities, owners of properties worth $300 (actual

value), tenants who paid $2 a month or $20 a year rental and had been resident
for at least one year, occupants of property worth $300 and resident for at least
one year, individual wage earners with a $300 annual income, and sons of
owners whose father's property was worth an additional $300 per son gained
the vote. These changes remained in effect until 1898, when the Liberal
government in Ottawa reverted to provincial rules which approached full adult
male suffrage, since, by that date, only Nova Scotia and Quebec had retained a
property suffrage. What all this meant for actual working-class electoral participation remains unclear. Certainly Toronto workers suffered from franchise
limitation, especially in federal elections. The organized labour movement was
the major force behind franchise extension, and the struggle for the vote is a
factor which separates Canadian working-class experience from American.
5 See Appendix III for full Toronto election results.
6 Crook's election was challenged in the courts on the grounds that his canvas-
sers had been a little too liberal in 'treating' voters. Chief Justice Richards
noted that treating was 'according to custom' and in this case was not
sufficiently serious to overthrow the election result. See Thomas Hodgins,
*Reports of the Decisions of the Judges in the Trial of Election Petitions in
Ontario* (Toronto 1883), 70–96.
7 See, for example, Leon Fink, 'Class Consciousness and Class Conflict in the
Gilded Age: The Figure and the Phantom,' *Radical History Review*, I (Winter
1975); also Bryan Palmer, 'Most Uncommon Common Men: Craft and Culture
in Historical Perspective,' *Labour/Le Travailleur*, I (1976), 5–31.
8 Toronto Trades Assembly, *Minutes*, 1871–72 (henceforth TTA, *Minutes*) and
Eugene A. Forsey, 'The Toronto Trades Assembly, 1871–1878,' *Canadian
Labour* (June 1965–December 1966). For the importance of Jessupp see
Montgomery, *Beyond Equality*, 163–4.
9 Accounts include: Donald Creighton, 'George Brown, Sir John Macdonald,
and the "Workingman",' *Canadian Historical Review*, XXIV (December
1943), 362–76; J.M.S. Careless, *Brown of the Globe*, II (Toronto 1963),
288–300; Steven Langdon, 'The Emergence of the Canadian Working Class
Movement, 1845–1875'; Bernard Ostry, 'Conservatives, Liberals and Labour
in the 1870's'; Sally Zerker, 'George Brown and the Printers' Union,' *Journal
of Canadian Studies*, X (1975); Robert Storey, 'Industrialization in Canada:
The Emergence of the Hamilton Working Class, 1850–1870's,' especially ch.
3; and Bryan Palmer, 'Most Uncommon Common Man,' ch. 6.
  A few points should be made about the nine-hours movement in passing: 1)
Toronto was not 'the pacemaker,' as Charles Lipton (*Trade Union Movement
of Canada* [Toronto 1973], 28–9) has claimed; that honour belongs to Hamilton
where James Ryan led the league brilliantly. 2) The movement was broadly

based and province-wide; meetings all over Ontario, in Montreal and Sherbrooke were huge and enthusiastic. 3) The movement had a clear strategy which Toronto printers proceeded to botch. Strikes were to be carefully orchestrated with Hamilton, the pioneer of the movement, leading on 1 May. Toronto, Montreal, and the smaller centres were to wait so that if needed they could lend financial support to their Hamilton brothers and sisters. After anticipated success in Hamilton, Toronto was to go out en masse on 1 June, and Montreal was to follow on 1 July. However, the Toronto Typographical Union impatiently acted against their bosses, which culminated in the late March strike, endangered this overall strategy, and in the long run may even have contributed to its defeat. 4) Finally, the various nine-hour organizations formed the Canadian Labor Protective and Mutual Improvement Association (CLP) in May 1872, the first Canadian national trade-union centre. John Hewitt, partially in his role as corresponding secretary of the CLP, issued the call in September 1873 for the first Canadian Labour Union convention, which has usually been regarded as the first meeting of Canadian workers that transcended both locale and trade. See John Battye, 'The "Nine Hour Pioneers": Genesis of the Canadian Labour Movement,' *Labour/Le Travailleur* 4 (1980), 25–56.

10 *Leader* and *Globe*, 15 February 1872.
11 *The Ontario Workman* (henceforth OW). 22 August 1872.
12 Ibid., 25 July 1872.
13 Ibid., 2 May 1872.
14 Ibid., 25 April 1872.
15 Ibid., 25 July, 12 September 1872.
16 *Globe*, 16 March 1872.
17 *Leader*, 19 February 1872.
18 OW, 11 June 1872. On Stewart see Montgomery, *Beyond Equality*, 249–60. The relationship of Karl Marx to the Ontario Nine-Hour Movement has been described previously. However, the rather complicated explanation that Stanley Ryerson has offered for the appearance of an excerpt from *Capital* in *The Ontario Workman* is not satisfactory. The romantic story of Mark Szalatnay, the Hungarian revolutionary cigarmaker, adds colour to an account of Toronto labour in this period. But there is a more plausible explanation. John Hewitt probably drew it to the attention of J.S. Williams, his friend and editor of *The Workman*, for the identical excerpt had appeared in the November 1871 issue of the *Coopers' Journal*. See Stanley Ryerson, *Unequal Union* 421, 446, and his sketch of Mark Szalatnay in *Dictionary of Canadian Biography*, X, 670–71. For an interesting, but incomplete, account see Phillip Foner, 'Marx's *Capital* in the United States,' *Science and Society*, XXXI (Fall 1967), 461–6.

19 TTA, *Minutes*, 1 December 1871.
20 *Daily Telegraph*, 2 February 1872.
21 *Globe*, 16 February 1872.
22 Careless, *Brown*, II, 289–90.
23 *Leader*, 18 March 1872.
24 *Globe*, 22 March 1872.
25 *Globe*, 20 May 1872.
26 *Globe*, 22 March 1872.
27 *Globe*, 8 April 1872.
28 *Globe*, 17 April 1872.
29 *Globe*, 7 May 1872.
30 *Globe*, 23 March 1872.
31 *Globe*, 20 May 1872.
32 Steven Langdon, 'The Emergence,' 9–10.
33 Paul C. Appleton, 'The Sunshine and the Shade,' 103–16.
34 *Globe*, 7 May 1872.
35 *Globe*, 30 March 1872.
36 This is somewhat confusing since the jury actually acquitted these cordwainers, mainly because they all established strong alibis. For this important case see *Globe*, 9, 13, 15, 26 January 1858.
37 *Globe*, 30 March 1872.
38 *Globe*, 3, 4 April 1872.
39 *Globe*, 17 April 1872.
40 *Globe*, 19 April, 7, 20 May 1872. J.M.S. Careless's interpretation that this was not what Brown had intended and that the master printers had copious evidence of intimidation, coercion, and violence seems questionable: the evidence that was admitted in the two court hearings showed only weak accusations of threatening, and simply established that the TTU had conducted its strike in the customary manner. Indeed, if evidence existed of stone throwing, pistol shooting, and property destruction of the kind that Brown kept hinting at, and that Careless accepts, why would Brown have dropped the case rather than bring it before the fall assize? Macdonald's Trade Unions Act and Criminal Law Amendment Act of 1872 certainly did not make legal the infringements of the law so blackly suggested. The major evidence offered by Edward J. O'Neill, an MPA detective, was that the ITU had interfered with strikebreaking printers on their way to Toronto, hardly the acts of overt violence, intimidation, or coercion so darkly hinted at. *The Ontario Workman's* conclusion that the case 'has been allowed to go by default for want of sufficient evidence' seems plausible. Another intriguing possibility, which seems quite strong given the source, is the version that Edward Blake gave in the 1887 election cam-

paign. Blake claimed that Oliver Mowat 'ordered the abandonment of the prosecution on the 7th November – within seven days of the time he was sworn into office.' As evidence, he cited the prosecuting attorney's return on the case which recommended that prosecution be abandoned. This version is probably true, which suggests yet again the tension between the Blake-Mowat and the Brown-Mackenzie wings of the Liberal party. On this question see: Careless, *Brown*, II, 299–300; *Globe*, 19 April 1872; OW, 21 November 1872; and Edward Blake, *Speeches in the Dominion Election Campaign of 1887* (Toronto 1887), 374–5.

41 In October 1886, at the height of the independent labour campaigns, an anonymous letter appeared in the *Globe* offering the following version of the 1872 events. This 'bit of secret history' was probably authored by D.J. O'Donoghue: 'On the afternoon of the sixth of May Sir John was in his place in the House and word reached him that he was wanted outside the chamber. Two men were there to interview him and Sir John led the way to his private room. They presented to him the case of the workingmen of Toronto whose trial had yet to come off in the Police Court and urged him at once to proceed to repeal the obnoxious statute. Sir John confessed that he had never thought of the matter before; that he had never looked into the statute and didn't know what he could do but asked his interviewers to call again. They called again the evening of the same day with the old statute in their hands and renewed their plea and in the earnestness of their pleading they hinted that the repeal would be a good political move. Sir John saw the force of their argument and the Bill was introduced the following day. One of the men was D.J. O'Donoghue now of this city ... The other was the late Donald Robertson, Secretary at that time of the Trades Council. Both men were Liberals and their only motive in going to Sir John was to procure the repeal of a statute that was being used to the detriment of the working classes. Its repeal was due to the action of those two men both Liberals. Sir John's part was prompted and his object was not to redress a wrong but to seize upon the mistake of a political opponent for his own advantage' (*Globe*, 12 October 1886). No doubt we can ignore the partisan insights into the prime minister's motivations but the rest of the account sounds quite authentic. This may indeed be an accurate secret history of the Trade Unions Act.

42 John A. Macdonald to McInnis, 7 June 1872; Macdonald to Isaac Buchanan, 29 June 1872, Macdonald Papers.

43 John A. Macdonald to T.C. Patteson, 30 March 1872, Patteson Papers.

44 OW, 5 September 1872.

45 For invitation see John Hewitt to Macdonald, 15 June 1872, Macdonald Papers.

46 *Globe*, 8 July 1872.
47 *Globe*, 8, 13 July 1872.
48 *Globe*, 13 July 1872.
49 *Globe*, 17 July 1872.
50 *Globe*, 15 August 1872.
51 TTA, *Minutes*, 19 July 1872.
52 TTA, 5 July 1872.
53 OW, 25 April 1872.
54 OW, 2 May 1872.
55 TTA, *Minutes*, 19 April 1872.
56 TTA, 21 May 1872.
57 OW, 18 July 1872.
58 Macdonald to Isaac Buchanan, 29 July 1872, Macdonald Papers, and Storey, 'Industrialization in Canada,' ch. 3.
59 See *Globe* and OW for campaign reports.
60 *Globe*, 2 August 1872.
61 *Globe*, 18 September 1872.
62 Macdonald to O'Brien, 3 September 1872, Macdonald Papers.
63 Ibid., A.C. Campbell to Macdonald, 4 September and 14 November 1872.
64 OW, 5 September 1872.
65 Williams to Macdonald, 7 July 1873; Macdonald to O'Brien, 10 July 1873, Macdonald Papers.
66 Ibid., Williams to Macdonald, 7 July 1873. See also Williams' report on his trip in OW, 1873. H.B. Witton, Hamilton Tory-Labour MP, seems to have been responsible for Williams' trip. Witton cited this as evidence of service to his class when he failed to get re-elected. See Storey, 'Industrialization in Canada,' ch. 3.
67 Ostry, 'Conservatives, Liberals and Labour.'
68 On the British junta see S. and B. Webb, *The History of Trade Unionism* (London 1919), especially ch. 5 where they coined the term. See also Henry Pelling, *A History of British Trade Unionism* (Hammondsworth 1963), ch. 4. The most penetrating analysis of British working-class politics in this period, however, is still R. Harrison, *Before the Socialists* (London 1965).
69 TTA, *Minutes*, passim.
70 Ibid., 6 September 1872.
71 OW, 5 September 1872.
72 TTA, *Minutes*, 4, 18 October; 15 November 1872.
73 Ibid., 3 January 1873.
74 Ibid., 17 January 1873.
75 For Mowat's labour legislation see the rather uncritical Margaret Evans, 'Oliver Mowat and Ontario,' especially ch. 3.

76 OW, 6 February 1873.

77 William Arnold Martin, 'A Study of Legislation Designed to Foster Industrial Peace in the Common Law Jurisdiction of Canada' (unpublished PH D thesis, University of Toronto 1954), 78–81.

78 Reports of this meeting are drawn from *Globe*, 12, 13 February 1873 and OW, 13 February 1873.

79 OW, 6 March 1873. TTA, *Minutes*, 7 March 1873.

80 See OW, 13, 20, 27 March; 10 July; 13, 20, 27 November 1873.

81 OW, 20 March 1873.

82 OW, 27 March 1873.

83 OW, 20 March, 15 May 1873.

84 TTA, *Minutes*, 21 March 1873.

85 Ibid., 10 April 1873.

86 Ibid., 16 May 1873.

87 Ibid.

88 Ibid., 2, 3, May 1872.

89 Ibid., 16 May, 6 June; 15, 27 August, 5 September 1873.

90 Leslie Wismer (ed.), *Proceedings of the Canadian Labour Union Congresses: 1873–1877* (Montreal 1951), 15–16, 28 (henceforth CLU, *Proceedings*).

91 Ibid., 20.

92 Ibid., 1873–77.

93 Ibid., 1876, 1877.

94 The statistics on Toronto delegates are: 1873, 26 of 45 (58%); 1874, 4 of 15 (27%); 1875, 10 of 18 (56%); 1876, 19 of 23 (83%); 1877, 13 of 18 (72%).

95 CLU, *Proceedings*, 1873, 18.

96 Daphne Simon, 'Master and Servant,' p. 185 in John Saville (ed.), *Democracy and the Labour Movement* (London 1954).

97 OW, 20 March 1873.

98 OW, 27 March 1873.

99 CLU, *Proceedings*, 1873, 27.

100 TTA, *Minutes*, 6 March 1874.

101 Ibid., 3 March 1874. This committee consisted of Williams and Levesley, among others.

102 Ibid., 12 April 1874. See Canada, House of Commons, *Debates*, 11 May 1874 for select committée (henceforth *Debates*).

103 Ibid., 15 May 1874.

104 CLU, *Proceedings*, 1874, 37, 39–40.

105 Canada, Department of Labour, *Trade Union Law in Canada* (Ottawa 1935), 19. This remains the best discussion of early trade-union legal history. More recent accounts include: J.C. Cameron and F.J.L. Young, *The Status of Trade Unions in Canada* (Kingston 1960), and I.M. Christie, *The Liability of Strikers*

in the Law of Tort: A Comprehensive Study of the Law in England and Canada (Kingston 1967).

106 TTA, *Minutes*, 4, 20 November 1874. Levesley and Williams served on the first committee and were joined by McMillan on the second.

107 *Debates*, 11 February 1875, 35.

108 TTA, *Minutes*, 17 February 1875.

109 Ibid., 17 March 1875 and *Globe*, 17 February 1875.

110 TTA, *Minutes*, 17 March 1875.

111 *Debates*, 24 March 1875, pp. 898–899. The account below is taken from pp. 899–903, 903–4, 928, 1035.

112 *Globe*, 15 April 1875 and TTA, *Minutes*, 7, 22 April 1875.

113 *Mail*, 1 May 1875 and *Globe*, 1 May 1875. The events of the case are described with more understanding of its significance in *The Liberal*, 4 May 1875.

114 *Mail*, 6 May 1875.

115 *Mail*, 8 May 1875. This report also noted McNabb's hostility toward Gibbs, whose testimony he attacked as 'twist[ing] the evidence and bring[ing] out so many fine points that he left the impression that there was something hidden behind the scenes.'

116 *Globe*, 10 May 1875.

117 *Globe*, 17, 24 May 1875.

118 *Globe*, 3 June 1875.

119 *Globe*, 4 June 1875.

120 *Globe*, 15, 19 June 1875; *Mail* 21 June 1875.

121 TTA, *Minutes*, 16 June 1875.

122 *Mail*, 21 June 1875.

123 *Mail*, 7 July 1875; *Globe*, 7 July 1875; TTA, *Minutes*, 7 July 1875.

124 TTA, *Minutes*, 15 May, 7, 21 July 1875.

125 Ibid., 21 July 1875.

126 For the British legislation see Daphne Simon in Saville, *Democracy and the Labour Movement*; S. and B. Webb, *The History of Trade Unionism*, ch. 5, especially 275–91; Henry Pelling, *A History of British Trade Unionism*, 73–6; Royden Harrison, *Before the Socialists*, ch. 6; W. Hamish Fraser, *Trade Unions and Society* (London 1974), ch. 8; Henry Pelling, *Popular Politics and Society in Late Victorian Britain* (London 1968), ch. 4; and Paul Smith, *Disraelian Conservatism and Social Reform* (London 1967), ch. 3–5.

127 TTA, *Minutes*, 4 May, 18 August 1875.

128 CLU, *Proceedings*, 1875, pp. 44, 45, 48–9, 51.

129 TTA, *Minutes*, 20 October 1875.

130 Ibid., 2, 17 November 1875.

131 *Debates*, 17 February 1876, 85.

132 TTA, *Minutes*, 1 March 1876.

133 *Debates*, 7 March 1876, 462.

134 Ibid., 463.

135 TTA, *Minutes*, 8, 15 March 1876.

136 *Debates*, 14 March 1876, 625.

137 CLU, *Proceedings*, 63.

138 Ibid., 66.

139 Statistics were also compiled from incomplete reports in the police court columns of the *Globe*, 1869–76. These have the advantage of descriptions of the cases. The annual breakdown for these was: 1869, 13 cases; 1870, 30 cases; 1871, 33 cases; 1872, 23 cases; 1873, 23 cases; 1874, 6 cases; 1875, 7 cases; 1876, 17 cases.

140 For details on moulders and printers, see chapters 5 and 6.

141 TTA, *Minutes*, 31 March 1874.

142 Ibid.

143 CLU, *Proceedings*, 1874, pp. 37, 39–40; 1875, p. 45.

144 TTA, *Minutes*, 17 November 1875; 5, 19 January 1876.

145 CLU, *Proceedings*, 1876, pp. 64, 71–2.

146 *Globe*, 4 September 1876.

147 *Globe*, 7 September 1876.

148 For Mowat's conscious regard for the labour vote see Margaret Evans, 'Oliver Mowat,' ch. 3. For Blake we have only the evidence of his actions as attorney general and later as opposition leader. Joseph Schull, *Edward Blake*, manages not to consider the question at all.

149 *Globe*, 18 September 1876.

150 *Globe*, 2 October 1876. The *Globe* published a response that day but it had clearly lost the dispute.

151 *Globe*, 19 February 1877.

152 TTA, *Minutes*, 21 February 1877. CLU, *Proceedings*, 1877, 80. *Debates*, 7 March 1877, 524–5.

153 *Debates*, 7 March 1877, 525–5.

154 Ibid., 20 March 1877. The data on this attempt to amend the MSA are from pp. 854–74.

155 On the Grand Trunk strike, see Shirley Ayer, 'The Locomotive Engineers' Strike on the Grand Trunk Railway in 1876–77' (MA thesis, McGill University 1961), and Desmond Morton, 'Taking on the Grand Trunk: The Locomotive Engineer Strike of 1876–7,' *Labour*, 2 (1977), 5–34.

156 Party identifications are drawn from C.H. Mackintosh (ed.), *The Canadian Parliamentary Companion*, 1877 (Ottawa 1877).

157 TTA, *Minutes*, 21 March 1877.

158 *Debates*, 27 March 1877, 1010–19.

159 Ibid., 29 March 1877.

160 TTA, *Minutes*, 17 April 1877.

161 For a slightly different interpretation see Morton, 'Taking on the Grand Trunk,' 32–3.

162 C.R.W. Biggar, *Sir Oliver Mowat*, I, 292–301.

163 The proposed scale was one additional vote for between $1,000 and $2,000 assessment; an additional vote for each additional $1,000 up to $5,000; five votes from $5,000 to $10,000; six for $10,000 to $20,000; and, for more than $20,000, seven additional votes; for a grand total of eight. Bethune carefully calculated the effects of his bill. Using as example one Toronto ward, where the franchise was 1,224 tenants, 842 freeholders, and 58 income voters, he estimated that under his system the freeholders would climb to a total of 2000 votes while the others remained constant. See Biggar, *Mowat*, I, 293–301. For similar schemes in the U.S. and a discussion of the class ideology that underrode them, see John G. Sproat, *'The Best Men': Liberal Reformers in the Gilded Age* (New York 1968), especially ch. 9.

164 Biggar, *Mowat*, I, 293–4.

165 For the TTA response see TTA, *Minutes*, 17 January, 7 February 1877. For their protest meeting see *Mail*, 30, 31 January 1877. The magnitude of the attack, however, was evident in the bipartisan support it gained from *The Mail*, which editorialized that 'the poorer classes [had] proved to be careless custodians of the general property' and worried that 'the floating population had long overinfluenced our elections.' Mowat, however, opposed the bill, since in his experience 'class has not been found arrayed against class. The cases are exceptional in which the poor are not divided as well as the rich.' Given these facts, to deny the working-class political access now might lead to class conflict. Moreover, he assured Bethune that 'equal voting has not prevented men from accumulating wealth. On the contrary all the wealth that has been accumulated was obtained under the present system.' Biggar, *Mowat*, I, 295–6. When the bill was reintroduced the following year, the same activities took place. Junta leader Williams condemned the bill as 'pernicious class legislation,' and it was again defeated. See TTA, *Minutes*, 16 January; 6, 9 February 1878; and *Mail*, 13 February 1878.

CHAPTER 9

1 J.C. Cameron and F.J.L. Young, *The Status of Trade Unions in Canada* (Kingston 1960), 26

2 CLU, *Proceedings*, 20–1.

3 Ibid.

4 Ibid.

5 TTA, *Minutes*, 20 October 1875.

6 *The Liberal* was the daily paper established in Toronto by Blake, Mills, and the 'Canada First' side of the party as a challenge to Brown's hegemony.

7 TTA, *Minutes*, 20 February 1878. CLU, *Proceedings*, 1877, 87. For O'Donoghue's career see Appendix III.

8 See Creighton, 'The "Workingman,"' and Ostry, 'Conservatives, Liberals and Labour in the 1870's.'

9 This grouping deserves an intellectual collective biography. Their basic agreements centred on a populist notion of economic development in which the workers too had an important role to play. They broke quickly with 'Canada First,' which they condemned as elitist and imperialist. Their notion of the empire also differed from that of the Canada Firsters. On Canada First see Carl Berger, *The Sense of Power: Studies in the Ideas of Canadian Imperialism, 1867–1914* (Toronto 1970). A useful introduction to the Buchanan group is Palmer, 'Most Uncommon Common Men,' ch. 5.

10 David Montgomery, *Beyond Equality*; Robert Sharkey, *Money, Class and Party* (Baltimore 1959); Irwin Unger, *The Greenback Era* (Princeton 1964); and, most important, the brilliant new work of Lawrence Goodwyn, *Democratic Promises: The Populist Movement in America* (New York 1976), especially ch. 1–3.

11 CLU, *Proceedings*, 1874, 38.

12 David Lee, 'The Dominion General Election of 1878 in Ontario,' *Ontario History*, 51 (1959), 172–90, is one of the few studies available. It shows some sense of the importance of protection but not specifically with reference to working-class votes.

13 Isaac Buchanan to John Maclean, 26 December 1871, Buchanan Papers.

14 Canada, House of Commons, *Journals*, 1872, Appendix I.

15 Buchanan to Maclean, 23 April 1872, Buchanan Papers.

16 Maclean to Buchanan, 16 May 1872, ibid.

17 Thomas Patteson to Alexander Campbell, 19 November 1889, Campbell Papers.

18 On Howland see ch. 1 above.

19 On R.W. Phipps, see his letters to Macdonald, 20 August 1876, 5 August, and 10 October 1878, Macdonald Papers; and his *Free Trade and Protection Considered with Relation to Canadian Interests* (Toronto 1878).

20 On the *National* and for many of my insights about the newspaper world of the late nineteenth century, I am deeply indebted to the work of Russell Hann.

21 I. Buchanan to the editor of the *National*, 2 and 17 April 1875, Buchanan Papers.

22 A.W. Wright to Isaac Buchanan, 5 November 1878, ibid.

23 *The Beehive*, 26 September 1874, March 1875, and December 1875. On its London counterpart see Stephen Coltham, 'The Bee-Hive Newspaper: Its Origins and Early Struggles'; and R. Harrison, 'Professor Beasly and the Working Class Movement,' in Briggs and Saville, *Essays in Labour History* (London 1967). On Edwards himself see his *Centennial Bitters No. 3, An Account of the Imprisonment in Philadelphia of the Editor and Proprietor of the Beehive in 1876* (Philadelphia 1876). This version of one English radical's disenchantment with the American Republic is of some interest. It also explains, in passing, that *The Beehive* commenced with 'the sum of $2 (voluntarily advanced by a journeyman painter in Toronto) [and] an Order from the Ontario government for 10,000 copies ... [to] distribute among the farm labourers of England.' (pp. 15–16).

24 OW, 13, 27 November 1873.

25 Ibid., 4 December 1873.

26 Ibid., 11 December 1873.

27 Ibid. and *Globe*, 15 December 1873 and 16 January 1874.

28 *Sun*, 22 December 1873.

29 *Globe*, 15, 16 December 1873.

30 *National*, 5 November 1875.

31 Creighton, *John A. Macdonald: The Old Chieftain*, ch. 6 and 7.

32 The WLCU is an organization worthy of study in its own right. Apparently founded by Toronto journalist and currency reformer George Brooks it became a centre of Populist Tory activity and launched figures like J. Ick Evans, F.L. Sims, Alfred Boultbee, and Edward Meek on their careers as party hacks. Of all the prominent WLCU leaders, I can identify only one active trade-unionist, W. Ternent. Yet by 1883 it had some 3,000 members in Toronto. It certainly does not fit the image of the British Conservative workingmen as described by Robert McKenzie in *Angels in Marble* (London 1968). Deference, which he views as crucial both in *Angels* and in his earlier *British Political Parties*, is not at all evident in Toronto.

33 For the National Union see Robert McKenzie, *British Political Parties* (Toronto 1955), especially pp. 146–85; and for Conservative workingmen's associations see H.J. Hanham, *Elections and Party Management Politics in the Time of Disraeli and Gladstone* (London 1959), especially ch. v and vi.

34 TTA, *Minutes*, 19 December 1877.

35 Ibid., 5 January 1878.

36 CLU, *Proceedings*, 1877, 87.

37 TTA, *Minutes*, 20 February 1878.

38 *Globe*, 20 May 1878.

39 Ibid., 1 May 1878.

40 *Mail*, 27 October 1877.
41 Buchanan to W.H. Howland, 2 October 1878, Buchanan Papers.
42 For election results see Appendix IV.
43 On Phipp's defection see his letter to Macdonald, 10 October 1878, Macdonald Papers. For his contribution to the campaign see *Mail*, 15, 29 May 1878. See also his *Free Trade and Protection*, the most widely distributed piece of campaign literature in the 1878 election.
44 A.W. Wright to Isaac Buchanan, 5 November 1878, Buchanan Papers.
45 H.E. Smallpiece and A.W. Wright to Macdonald, 3 June 1879; Macdonald to Smallpiece and Wright, 7 June 1879; Smallpiece and Wright to Macdonald, 21 July 1879; and Wright to Macdonald, 11 December 1879; all in Macdonald Papers. H.E. Smallpiece was co-owner of the *National* with Wright.
46 J. Ick Evans to Macdonald, 8 October 1878, Macdonald Papers.
47 Ibid., WLCU to Macdonald and Thomas C. Holwey to Macdonald, 7 October 1878.
48 For details of this controversy see *Mail*, 14, 18, 21 December 1878, and *Globe*, 10, 13, 14, 16, 20, 21 December 1878.
49 For electoral statistics see Appendix IV.
50 *Globe*, 28 January 1879.
51 Ibid., 13 February 1879.
52 Ibid., 7 May 1879.
53 Evans to Macdonald, 13 March 1879, Macdonald Papers.
54 Ibid., 23 January 1879.
55 Alexander Morris to Macdonald, 8 May 1879, Macdonald Papers, warned: 'Things are in a bad state in West Toronto and immediate intervention is necessary. Great outrage has been taken at some of your recent appointments by the active workers in St. Andrews, St. Stephens, and St. Johns ... The disaffection is very serious – I am doing all I can to heal it – but you must help – the trouble has not yet extended to the East.'
56 Alfred Boultbee to Macdonald, 29 September 1879, Macdonald Papers.
57 J. Ick Evans to Macdonald, 28 April 1880, Campbell Papers. The final archival resting place of this letter indicates how seriously the prime minister took the threat. This letter from WLCU leader Evans and many others were forwarded to Tory lieutenant Alexander Campbell, who, since he was on the scene in Toronto, was expected to quell the revolt.
58 WLCU to Macdonald, 4 May 1880, Macdonald Papers.
59 For Buchanan's role see the broadside, 'Proposal of National Currency Reform League of Canada and the Philosophy and Practice of Currency Reform,' Buchanan Papers. For meetings see *Globe*, 29, 30 January; 7, 19 May; 24 September 1879.

60 Buchanan to Wright, 8 November 1879, Buchanan Papers.

61 *Globe*, 24, 30 September; 8, 16, 29 October; 3, 7, 26 November; 17 December 1879. 'The Currency Question' by 'Finance' appeared in six parts on 19, 23, 31 January and 7, 11, 14 February 1880. There is no discussion of monetary reform in the secondary literature except for the very slight Goodwin, *Canadian Economic Thought*, pp. 82–6.

62 *Globe*, 31 October 1879. 'Beaverback' was simply a canadianized version of the American 'Greenback.'

63 *Globe*, 11, 15 June 1880.

64 See, among others: 'An out and out Conservative' to Macdonald, 1 May 1880; J.A. Macdonnell to Macdonald, 6 May 1880; Richard Love to Macdonald, 6 May 1880; all are in Campbell Papers.

65 J. Ick Evans to Macdonald, 7 May 1880, ibid.

66 George B. Boyle to Macdonald, ? June 1880, 10 June 1880, 19 June 1880, 25 June 1880, ibid.

67 T.C. Patteson to Macdonald, 4 June 1880, ibid.

68 George B. Boyle to Macdonald, 1 July 1880, ibid.

69 James Banks to J.B. Robinson, 12 June 1880, ibid.

70 George B. Boyle to Macdonald, 10 June 1880, and B.B. Gardner to Macdonald, 30 June 1880, ibid.

71 J. Ick Evans to Macdonald, 25 June 1880, ibid.

72 George B. Boyle to Macdonald, ibid.

73 *Globe*, 3, 7 July 1880; *Commonwealth*, 29 July 1880.

74 *Globe*, 29 July 1880; *Commonwealth*, 29 July 1880.

75 See *Commonwealth*, 29 July, 5, 26 August 1880.

76 Ibid., 26 August 1880.

77 Ibid., 5 August 1880.

78 Buchanan to ?, 11 August 1880, Buchanan Papers. 'I wish the government would not set up any other candidate in West Toronto where our friend Mr. Wright would easily, I think, beat the opposition candidate.'

79 *Mail*, July and August 1880.

80 *Globe*, 30 July 1880.

81 Ibid., 21 August 1880. Among Wright's nominators were WLCU leaders Evans, Livingstone, and Cheeseworth.

82 Ibid., 24 August 1880.

83 F.D. Barwick to Sir Alexander Campbell, 23 and 31 July 1880, Campbell Papers.

84 Ibid., 24, 26 August 1880. *Commonwealth*, 26 August 1880.

85 *Globe*, 30 August 1880. See Appendix IV.

86 Campbell to Macdonald, 20 August 1880; other letters regarding Tory strategy

in this by-election include: Campbell to Macdonald, 13 August 1880; Boultbee to Macdonald, 14 August 1880; Campbell to Macdonald, 14 August 1880.

87 Buchanan to Wright, 30 August 1880, Buchanan Papers.

88 *Globe*, 5, 30 November, 7 December 1880.

89 *Globe*, 9 December 1880.

90 Buchanan to Captain Wynne, 25 November 1880 and unidentified press clipping, 'The Currency Reform League,' Buchanan Papers.

91 *Globe*, 9 December 1880. Goodwin, *Democratic Promises*, p. 15, provides the following useful summary: 'soft money theory is most easily grasped as a political ideology grounded in a desire of non-bankers to cope with changing commercial power relationships within an industrial society.'

92 J. Ick Evans to Macdonald, 11 January 1881, Macdonald Papers.

93 *Globe*, 10, 14, 28 January 1881.

94 *Globe*, 9 March 1881 and J. Ick Evans to Macdonald, 5 March 1881, Macdonald Papers.

CHAPTER 10

1 See Appendix II.

2 TTU, *Minutes*, 7 May 1881.

3 *Globe*, 11 June 1881. See also Eugene Donavon's account in *Trades Union Advocate*, 4 May 1882.

4 TTU, *Minutes*, 2 October, 6 November 1880. D.J. O'Donoghue's version is in 'History of the Toronto Trades and Labor Council,' *Labor Day Souvenir, 1898* (Toronto 1898): 'Some years prior to this date the Trades Assembly had wearied of its work and had ceased to meet in 'solemn conclave.' But if all those who composed that once useful and active organization were not dead – neither were they sleeping nor idle. On the contrary some of them were very much alive; they saw their opportunity and promptly seized the advantage.'

5 *Globe*, 25 July 1881, and TTLC, *Minutes*, 23 July 1881.

6 TTLC, *Minutes*, 13 August 1881, and *Globe*, 22 August 1881.

7 The discussion in this chapter is limited to organization and to shop-floor struggle. The Knights' political activities will be considered in chapters 11–14.

8 *Globe*, 16 October 1884.

9 George McNeill, *The Labor Movement*, 403.

10 On the telegraphers see DA's 45 circulars of 27 December 1882 and 20 May 1883. See also Telegraphers' Code Book of 20 October 1882. All in Powderly Papers. (Henceforth PP). These are now available on microfilm at the PAC.

11 Eugene Forsey, 'The Telegraphers' Strike of 1883,' *Transactions of the Royal Society of Canada*, IV Series (1971), 245–59.

12 *Globe*, 18 July; 9, 10, 16 August 1883.
13 Organizational data throughout stem from local sources and from the unpublished work of Eugene Forsey. The bulk of material, however, comes from 'The Knights of Labor Data Bank Project' at the University of Rochester. The principal investigators on that project, with which I was involved during my stay at Rochester, were Jonathan Garlock and N.C. Builder. For a detailed description of the project see Jonathan Garlock, 'The Knights of Labor Data Bank,' *Historical Methods Newsletter*, VI (September 1973), 149–60, and his 'A Structural Analysis of the Knights of Labor' (unpublished PH D dissertation, Rochester 1974).
14 *Labor Standard* (New York), 23 December 1877.
15 Ibid.
16 *Globe*, 14 October 1884.
17 *New York Sun*, 29 March 1886, as cited in Richard T. Ely, *The Labor Movement in America* (New York 1886), 78, n. 1.
18 For a short discussion of the 1882 shoe strike, see ch. 3.
19 Daniel J. O'Donoghue (henceforth O'Donoghue) to Terence V. Powderly (henceforth Powderly), 12 February 1884, PP.
20 O'Donoghue to Powderly, 17 February 1887, PP.
21 Ontario, Bureau of Industry, *Report*, 1886, p. 244.
22 Knights of Labor, General Assembly, *Proceedings*, 1886, 1887, 1889 (henceforth *Proceedings*).
23 Ontario, Bureau of Industry, *Report*, 1886, 1887, 1888, 1889.
24 *Palladium of Labor*, 3 July 1886. *Cigar Makers Journal*, July and August 1886. See Palmer, 'Most Uncommon Common Men,' ch. 7.
25 See ch. 11, this vol.
26 John Peebles, Recollections, Hamilton Public Library.
27 George McNeill, *The Labor Movement*, 428.
28 *The Wage Worker*, 8 March 1883.
29 Ibid., 15 March 1883.
30 *World*, 14 October 1886.
31 See ch. 3, this vol.
32 *Globe*, 28 November 1885.
33 Jean Scott, 'The Conditions of Female Labour in Ontario,' *Toronto University Studies in Political Science*, I (1892), 27.
34 See G.S. Kealey, 'Katie McVicar,' *Dictionary of Canadian Biography*, XI, forthcoming; and Knights of Labor, General Assembly, *Decisions of the General Master Workman* (Philadelphia 1890), 43.
35 *Canadian Labor Reformer*, 12 February 1887; *Globe*, 11 February 1889.
36 *Globe*, 21 March 1887.

37 *Canadian Labor Reformer*, 2 April 1887.

38 *Globe*, 21 April 1887.

39 For further information on this very important Knights' leader see Eleanor Flexner, 'Leonora Barry,' *Notable American Women*, I (Cambridge 1971), 101–2. For a useful general discussion see Susan Levine,' ' "The Best Men in the Order": Women in the Knights of Labor,' paper read at Canadian Historical Association, 1978.

40 *Globe*, 13–15 April 1888. *Proceedings*, 1888, Report of General Investigator.

41 *Globe*, 15 April 1889; *Journal of United Labor* (henceforth JUL), May 1889.

42 JUL, 9 May 1889.

43 Ibid.

44 *Globe*, 1 May 1889.

45 J.W. Lainson to Powderly, 5 April 1889, PP.

46 *News*, 4 October 1886.

47 JUL, 25 April 1886. Marie Joussaye later came to Toronto and was one of the organizers of the Working Girls' Union. See *Globe*, 10 January 1893. The poem quoted here was originally published under a pseudonym but it appears in a slightly different version in Marie Joussaye, *Songs the Quinte Sang* (Belleville 1895). For further discussion see Wayne Roberts, ' "Honest Womanhood": Feminism, Femininity and Class Consciousness among Toronto Working Women, 1893–1914' (Toronto 1977).

48 *Knights of Labor Illustrated, 'Adelphon Kruptos.' The Full Illustrated Ritual Including the 'Unwritten Work' and an Historical Sketch of the Order* (Chicago 1886).

49 The similarities in the rituals of the various fraternal societies and labour organizations can perhaps also be illustrated by the fact that one house published not only the *Adelphon Kruptos* but also *Freemasonry Illustrated, Knights Templarism Illustrated*, and *Revised Oddfellowship Illustrated*. All of these are advertised in the back pages of the Cook edition of the *Adelphon Kruptos*. Earlier editions of the *Adelphon* never mention the name of the order, instead substituting asterisks for every reference to the order, to Knights, and even to knightly. See *Adelphon Kruptos*, n.p., n.d., at State Historical Society of Wisconsin.

50 *Knights of Labor Illustrated*, 37. The Wisconsin version varies slightly, suggesting that it is an earlier edition. The new version deletes all references to God, a concession to Catholic Church opposition to the secret work.

51 Ibid., 28.

52 Ibid., 29.

53 Roger Mullen to Powderly, 27 January 1883; Powderly to Roger Mullen, 2 February 1883, PP.

54 *World*, 15 April 1886.
55 *Trade Union Advocate*, 25 February 1883.
56 O'Donoghue to Powderly, 17 February, 4 March 1885, PP.
57 Knights of Labor, Local Assembly no. 2211, Toronto, *Bylaws of Pioneer Assembly* (Toronto 1887).
58 Henry J. Browne, *The Catholic Church and the Knights of Labor* (Washington 1949); and Phillipe Sylvain, 'Les Chevaliers du travail et le Cardinal Taschereau,' *Relations Industrielles* (1973).
59 *Palladium of Labor*, 15 May 1886.
60 On the merger see *Globe*, 15 July; on new CLR see *Typographical Journal*, 15 November 1889.
61 See *Palladium of Labour*, 16 August 1884. For a brilliant analysis of the *News* and its relationship to the labour movement see R.G. Hann, 'Brainworkers and the Knights of Labor: E.E. Sheppard, Phillips Thompson, and the Toronto *News*, 1883–1887,' in Kealey and Warrian, *Essays in Canadian Working Class History* (Toronto 1976), 35–57.
62 O'Donoghue to Powderly, 17 November 1885, PP.
63 These speeches were all duly recorded in the Toronto press.
64 O'Donoghue to Powderly, 9 December 1885, PP.
65 Knights of Labor, *Decisions of the G.M.W.*, 42.
66 *World*, 15 April 1886.
67 O'Donoghue to Powderly, 24 May 1885, 28 March 1888, 31 August 1888, PP.
68 *Statistics as Collected by Head-Light Assembly, No. 4069, K of L, for its Exclusive Use* (St Thomas, Ont., 1885), PP.
69 Thompson, *Politics of Labor* (New York 1887).
70 Forsey, 'Telegraphers' Strike.'
71 For a general history of the Massey Co. which tends to ignore labour relations, see Merrill Dennison, *Harvest Triumphant* (Toronto 1949).
72 For descriptions and reports on these various groups, see *The Triphammer*, February 1885–February 1886 in Massey Archives, Toronto.
73 Robert Ozanne, *A Century of Labor-Management Relations at McCormick and International Harvester* (Madison 1967), especially ch. 1.
74 Sam McNab to Powderly, 4 November 1884; Powderly to Sam McNab, 18 November 1884, PP.
75 Details of strike from *Globe*, 9–16 February 1886; *World*, 9–12 February 1886; *News*, 8–12 February 1886. Details are not totally reliable in Desmond Morton, *Mayor Howland* (Toronto 1973).
76 *Triphammer* estimate, which is higher than the newspapers' counts.
77 Ozanne, *A Century*, ch. 1.
78 *News*, 11 February 1886.

79 *Triphammer*, February 1886.
80 *Globe*, 11 March 1886. For later history of industrial relations at Massey's see Bruce Scott, '"A Place in the Sun": the Industrial Council at Massey-Harris, 1919–1929,' *Labour*, 1 (1976), 158–92.
81 CLR, 13 November 1886; 'Organization of Company, 1887,' clippings file, Vol. I, Massey Archives.
82 O'Donoghue to Powderly, 14 February 1886, PP.
83 There had been previous, abortive discussions of unionization. In June 1881 the men had tried to create a benefit society, claiming they had no grievances with the company. This appeared to be cover for an attempt to organize, for at the end of the month they submitted a petition against new work rules and threatened to strike. Unfortunately there is no indication of how this conflict was resolved. One year later, however, an anonymous street-railway employee wrote a letter, condemning the extremely low wages paid by the company and drawing the public's attention to its high profits. Again a strike was threatened. *Globe*, 15, 22 June 1881, 19 April 1882.
84 *World*, 8 November 1885.
85 O'Donoghue to Powderly, 8, 15, 23, 24 November and 9 December 1885, PP. Also CLR, 15 May 1886.
86 Kealey, *Canada Investigates Industrialism* (Toronto 1973), 103–9; *Rules and Regulations for Drivers and Conductors of the Toronto Street Railway Company, Toronto, 1880*, Baldwin Room, Metropolitan Toronto Central Library.
87 See calendar of Toronto strikes in Appendix II.
88 See Toronto press 10–15 March 1886 for details. Of the various accounts of the street-car strike, by far the best is David Frank, 'Trouble in Toronto: The Street Railway Lockout and Strike, 1886,' unpublished paper. A more recent description by Desmond Morton, *Mayor Howland*, ch. IV, has most facts correct but is far less acute.
89 *News*, 10 March 1886.
90 *News*, 11 March 1886.
91 Ibid.
92 *News*, 10 March 1886.
93 *News*, 11 March 1886, and Morton, *Mayor Howland*, 48.
94 *News*, 12 March 1886.
95 *News*, 12, 13 March 1886; *World*, 13 March 1886.
96 Frank, 'Trouble in Toronto,' 48.
97 See Bryan Palmer, '"Give Us the Road and We Will Run It": The Social and Cultural Matrix of an Emerging Labour Movement,' in Kealey and Warrian, *Essays in Canadian Working Class History*, 106–24.
98 O'Donoghue to Powderly, 13 March 1886, PP.

99 *Globe*, 14 April 1886.

100 *World*, 20 April 1886.

101 Ibid.

102 *Globe*, 10 May to 1886; CLR, 15 May 1886. For details of strike see Toronto press May to June 1886.

103 *World*, 10 May 1886.

104 *News*, 10 May 1886.

105 For an excellent analysis of the origins of the boycott in the u.s. see Michael Gordon, 'Irish Immigrant Culture and the Labor Boycott in New York City, 1880–1886,' *Labor History*, 16 (1975), 184–229. See also the previous discussion in ch. 6, this vol.

106 *World*, 10 May 1886.

107 *News*, 12 May 1886.

108 *World*, 14, 21 May 1886.

109 *News*, 12 May 1886.

110 For examples of arrests and convictions see *News*, 11, 12, 13, 14, 20, 21, 28 May, 3 June 1886; *World*, 12, 13, 14, 15, 17, 18, 19, 21, 31 May 1886.

111 *News*, 12 May 1886.

112 *World*, 14 May 1886.

113 *News*, 11 May 1886.

114 *World*, 14 May 1886.

115 *News*, 19 May 1886.

116 *World*, 19 June 1886.

117 *World*, 21 May 1886.

118 *World*, 22 May 1886.

119 *World*, 6 July 1886. See also *World*, 24, 26, 30 June 1886, and *News*, 18, 22, 23, 24, 26, 29 June; 3, 10 July 1886.

120 It should be added that public support for the takeover and real consideration of public ownership in 1891 were undoubtedly due, at least partially, to these strikes. For details on the public ownership fight see Christopher Armstrong and V. Nelles, *The Revenge of the Methodist Bicycle Company: Sunday Streetcars and Municipal Reform in Toronto 1888–1897* (Toronto 1977).

121 JUL, 13 November 1890.

122 *Globe*, 6 May 1891. The new company organized a company union in 1894 in response to another attempt at unionization. Only in 1899 did the workers finally reorganize as a local of the Amalgamated Association of Street Railway Employees. In 1902 they fought a virulent struggle with the company, which saw the recurrence of the crowd actions of 1886 in the streets of Toronto. This time, Mayor Oliver Howland (W.H.'s brother) had no compunctions about

calling up the militia 'in aid of civil power.' See David Frank, 'Life and Work in Toronto, 1900–1914,' unpublished manuscript, 50–7.

123 For a lively but inadequate account of the Howland campaigns and mayoralty see Morton, *Mayor Howland*. The major problem with Morton's account is that he tends to downplay labour's role in the Howland coalition and to belittle the importance of the Knights in general.

124 Knights of Labor, *Decisions of the G.M.W.*, 25. Rule 123 is interesting on the question of non-worker members: 'The Constitution implies that a capitalist *may* be admitted to membership in the Order of the Knights of Labor, but the Assembly must be the judge as to whether it will admit him or not.' I have discovered no capitalist members of the order in Toronto.

125 George McNeill, *The Labor Movement*, 411.

126 *Proceedings*, 1887, General Executive Board Doc. 130, pp. 1286–7. See also CLR, 12 March and 19 March 1887, and *Globe*, 10 March 1887.

127 *Proceedings*, 1887, GEB, Doc. 131. See also O'Donoghue to Powderly, 29 April 1887, PP. A caution should be added here that I am discussing the order's leadership only. Local militants were far less hesitant to engage in forms of direct action, as the following report suggests: 'Michael O'Hara, foreman of the workroom of the American Watchcase Company on Adelaide St., was charged at Police court by William Hahn, one of the employees, with assault. The complainant told the Magistrate how O'Hara had on Thursday struck him in the face and threatened to shoot him, at the same time drawing a revolver. He said that the row was caused by his refusal to speak to O'Hara. He had been forbidden to do so by his shop union which O'Hara had refused to join when invited to do so by the other men. Another young man, also a member of the union, told how O'Hara had incurred that body's displeasure by discharging an employee and refusing to ally himself with them. The assault was indisputed, and the defendant was fined $2 without costs' (*Globe*, 18 November 1885; *World*, 18 November 1885). One suspects that a Knight (the union was Local 4025) would have faced a far more hostile court if the assault had been reversed.

128 *Globe*, 10, 11 May 1887.

129 *Globe*, 1 June 1887.

130 *World*, 26 February 1887.

131 *Globe*, 1 June, 19 August 1887.

132 JUL, 18 October 1888.

133 See *The Carpenter*, July, August, October 1887. There was even tension among the carpenters within the order. Document 1253 of the 1887 GA *Proceedings* was a request by LA 8235 (Toronto carpenters) to have the DA force

carpenters who were members of mixed locals to join carpenters' trade assemblies. They gave as their reason the fact that trade assemblies worked only nine hours whereas members in the mixed assemblies were working ten. The GEB refused to allow the DA to force the members to join craft assemblies but did rule that members of mixed assemblies had to abide by craft rules.

134 For shoemakers see *Globe*, 15 February 1890. The shoemakers' attempts to make the order strong on the shop floor are clear in the *By-laws of LA2211*, Toronto, 1887. These rules included shop committees who had to report at every meeting. The committees, however, could not take action without the sanctions of both the local and district assemblies.

135 *Labor Advocate*, 1 May, 2 October 1891.

136 *Proceedings*, 1893, General Executive Board Report.

137 Robert Babcock, 'Samuel Gompers and the Berlin Decision of 1902,' in Richard Preston (ed.), *The Influence of the United States on Canadian Development: Eleven Case Studies* (Durham, NC, 1972), 185–204.

138 *The Wage Worker*, 22 March 1883.

139 As late as 1902, when Knights reflected on their own history, they proudly asserted that their attempt to organize all workers was their greatest contribution: 'A Knight of Labor is more than a mere Trade Unionist working for some single trade. He works for the good of all. Machinery will some day teach the Trade Unionist by sad experience that his only salvation lies in the K. of L. form of organization. The locomotive engineer, the "aristocrat of labor,' will be replaced by the ordinary motorman, the printer by the machine, the cigarmaker by the machine cigar, the glass worker by the laborer, and so on.' (Knights of Labor, D.A. 47, *Twenty Year History of ...* [Cleveland, 1902], 75.)

140 Boston *Labor Leader*, 5 February 1887 as cited in Leon Fink, 'Class Conflict in the Gilded Age: The Figure and the Phantom,' *Radical History Review*, 3 (1975), 56–74. See also Fink's excellent 'The Knights of Labor and the Transformation of American Political Culture,' paper read at Canadian Historical Association, 1978.

CHAPTER 11

1 See chapters 3 to 6 and 10, this vol.

2 TTLC, *Minutes*, 15, 29 October, 18 November 1881.

3 Ibid., 2 December 1881. For Lukes' Report see Canada, Parliament, *Sessional Papers*, 1882, IX, no. 42, and *Globe*, 23 February, 15 March 1882.

4 TTLC, *Minutes*, 15 October 1881.

5 Ibid., 28 October, 16, 29 December 1881.

6 Ibid., 6, 20 January 1882, and *Globe*, 18, 20 January 1882.

7 TTLC, *Minutes*, 3 and 17 February 1882, and *Globe*, 31 January 1882.

8 Ibid., 3 March 1882, and *Globe*, 3 March 1882.

9 Ostry, 'Conservatives, Liberals and Labour in the 1880s.'

10 Oakley was both treasurer of the TTLC and a prominent member of the Legislative Committee.

11 *Globe*, 16 March 1882.

12 For this debate see *Mail*, 18, 21 March 1882, and *Globe*, 18, 23, 24 March 1882. For a later exchange regarding shoemakers, see *Globe*, 17 June 1882, and *Mail*, 19 June 1882.

13 The evidence on these dealings is obscure, but see J. Ick Evans to Macdonald, 13 February 1883; 5 March 1883; 19 April 1883; and J.E. Somerville to Macdonald, 5 March 1883, Macdonald Papers. Basically these letters are a debate between two segments of the WLCU for control of the spoils. See also *Globe*, 13 June 1882 and 24 November 1883. For WLCU campaign work see *Mail*, 15 June 1882.

14 For Wright's return to the Tory camp see *Globe*, 13 May 1882. Also A.W. Wright to Macdonald, 10 May 1882, Macdonald Papers.

15 *Mail*, 23 May 1882; TTLC *Minutes*, 19 May 1882; and *Trades Union Advocate*, 25 May 1882.

16 *Globe*, 27 May 1882.

17 TTLC, *Minutes*, 2 June 1882, and *Mail*, 3 June 1882.

18 *Mail*, 5 June. See also *Trades Union Advocate*, 8 June 1882.

19 The president was Thomas Wilson of the ITU. I have no evidence concerning his party affiliation but the ITU tended to be a Tory stronghold and Oakley's point was not denied by the *Mail* in its subsequent response.

20 The committee, in addition to Oakley and Moor, was composed of Aldridge, Beecher, and Donavon (TTLC, *Minutes*, 6 January 1882). The *Mail* employee must have been Donavon, who was a representative of the ITU and also editor of the *Trades Union Advocate*.

21 *Globe*, 12 June 1882. See also *Trades Union Advocate*, 15 June 1882.

22 TTLC, *Minutes*, 16 June 1882. Reports of the meeting are in *Globe*, 17 June; *Mail*, 17 June 1882; and *Trades Union Advocate*, 22 June 1882.

23 *Mail*, 19 June 1882.

24 The series began on 18 May 1882, appearing in nine parts, with the last appearing on 10 June 1882. They were written in two weeks from 10 to 24 May. See *Globe*, 18, 19, 20, 24, 27, 30, 31 May and 5, 10 June 1882.

25 *Globe*, 10 June 1882.

26 *Mail*, 12 June 1882.

27 *Mail*, 14, 15, 20 June 1882. The last of these was a reprint of the two previous stories run on the very eve of the election.

28 Letters were received from Cornwall, Galt, Campbellford, Peterborough, Strathroy, Berlin, Acton, Paris, and Almonte. These appeared in the *Mail*, 12, 17, 19 June 1882.

29 *Mail*, 20 June 1882.

30 For election results see Appendix IV.

31 *Trades Union Advocate*, 25 May 1882.

32 Ibid., 18 May 1882.

33 TTLC, *Minutes*, 16 June 1882, and *Trades Union Advocate*, 22 June 1882.

34 TTLC, *Minutes*, 7 July 1882, and *Trades Union Advocate*, 13 July 1882.

35 TTLC, *Minutes*, 21 July, 4, 18 August 1882, and *Mail*, 19 August 1882.

36 TTLC, *Minutes*, 18 August 1882, and *Mail*, 19 August 1882.

37 *Trades Union Advocate*, 21 September 1882.

38 Ibid., 12 October 1882, and TTLC, *Minutes*, 6, 20 October 1882.

39 Ibid.

40 *Trades Union Advocate*, 16 November 1882.

41 TTLC, *Minutes*, 17 November 1882, and *Trades Union Advocate*, 23 November 1882.

42 *Trades Union Advocate*, 20 November. For an additional instalment in this debate see *Trades Union Advocate*, 28 December 1882.

43 For details of meeting see *Globe*, 30 December 1882, 1 January 1883, and *Trades Union Advocate*, 4 January 1883. For genesis of meeting see TTLC, *Minutes*, 29 December 1882.

44 The result was Boswell 4,296 and Withrow 4,283.

45 *Trades Union Advocate*, 4 January 1883.

46 Ibid. The Hamilton *Labor Union* of 3 February 1883 drew similar conclusions. They advised the old-line parties to avoid anti-labour candidates or pay the price.

47 TTLC, *Minutes*, 15 December 1882.

48 Ibid., 5 January 1883.

49 *Trades Union Advocate*, 11 January 1883. See also 18 January 1883 for more of the same.

50 TTLC, *Minutes*, 19 January 1883.

51 *Trades Union Advocate*, 1 February 1883.

52 TTLC, *Minutes*, 2 February 1883, and *Mail*, 3 February 1883.

53 *Trades Union Advocate*, 8 February 1883; *Globe*, 5 February 1883; and *Mail*, 5 February 1883.

54 *Trades Union Advocate*, 8 February 1883, and *Mail*, 7 February 1883. The results were Carter 25, Moor 16, Pearson, 3, March 0.

55 A. Morris to Macdonald, 15 January 1883, Macdonald Papers.

56 For nominations see *Trades Union Advocate*, 22 February 1883. This Liberal

decision was a reversal, for the *Globe* initially attacked the labour candidates on 7 February 1883.

57 *Globe*, 8 February 1883, and *Trades Union Advocate*, 8 February 1883.

58 *Mail*, 8 February 1883.

59 *Trades Union Advocate*, 1 March 1883. For a different, favourable assessment see *Globe*, 1 March 1883.

60 TTLC, *Minutes*, 16 March 1885.

61 TTLC, *Minutes*, 6 April 1883. For the complicated history of Dominion Factory Bills see Eugene Forsey, 'A Note on the Dominion Factory Bills of the 1880's,' *Canadian Journal of Economics and Political Science*, 13 (1947), 580–3.

62 TTLC, *Minutes*, 20 April 1883. See also Small to Macdonald, 10 April 1883, Macdonald Papers.

63 TTLC, *Minutes*, 18 May 1883.

64 This critique was not unique to O'Donoghue. As we noted earlier, Jury tried to deflate the national policy advocates in the 1878 campaign by pointing out the contradiction in protection for industry but a free market for labour. For inexplicable reasons this issue was dropped in the campaign of 1882, and O'Donoghue returned it to prominence.

65 TTLC, *Minutes*, 1 June 1883.

66 The original idea was Thomas Moor's. See TTLC, *Minutes*, 17 August, 7 September 1883, but the work was done by O'Donoghue's Legislative Committee.

67 *Proceedings of the Canadian Labor Congress Held in Toronto 1883*, Toronto, 1884, passim (henceforth TLC, *Proceedings*).

68 Ibid., 25.

69 Ibid., 24.

70 See ch. 5, this vol. See also Eugene Forsey, 'The Telegraphers' Strike of 1883,' *Transactions of the Royal Society of Canada*, Fourth Series, IX (1971), 245–59.

71 *Circular* [promoting Trades and Labor Congress], 15 November 1883, PP.

72 TLC, *Proceedings*, 1883, 8–9.

73 O'Donoghue to Powderly, 12 February 1884, PP.

74 Ibid. Also see ch. 10, this vol.

75 TTLC, *Minutes*, 18 January, 2, 16 May 1884.

76 Ibid., 21 March 1884.

77 Ibid., 4 April 1884.

78 Ibid., 18 April 1884. It is extremely unfortunate that the TTU *Minutes* are missing for October 1883 to September 1890. There must have been heated debate surrounding O'Donoghue's role in the TTLC.

79 For the carpenters see TTLC, *Minutes*, 18 April 1884; for stonecutters, 2 May 1884; for moulders, 16 May 1884.

80 For the final resolution of this issue see TTLC, *Minutes*, 16 May 1884.

81 O'Donoghue to Powderly, 16 June 1884, PP.

82 Ibid., 12 February 1884.

83 My thanks to Peter Gillis of the Public Archives of Canada for details on O'Donoghue's early political career in Ottawa.

84 For the Bureau of Industry see O'Donoghue to Powderly, 24 May 1885, PP; for the *Globe* see O'Donoghue to Powderly, 17 November 1885, PP.

85 TTLC, *Minutes*, 15 February, 3 October 1884.

86 For alarmed Tory opinion see Williams to Macdonald, 4 August 1884; Clarke to Macdonald, 5 August 1884; Small to Macdonald, 5 August 1884, Macdonald Papers.

87 John Small to Macdonald, 10 April 1883, Macdonald Papers.

88 A.W. Wright to Macdonald, 17 March 1884, ibid.

89 J.S. Williams to Macdonald, 4 August 1884; E.F. Clarke to Macdonald, 5 August 1884; John Small to Macdonald, 5 August 1884, ibid.

90 Alfred Boultbee to Macdonald, 12 September 1884, ibid.

91 John Small to Sir David [Macpherson], 27 December, ibid.

92 John Small to Macdonald, 29 December, 1884, ibid.

93 Alfred Boultbee to Macdonald, 30 December 1884, ibid.

94 Ibid., 6 January 1885.

95 TTLC, *Minutes*, 6, 20 February, 17 April 1885.

96 O'Donoghue to Powderly, 24 May 1885, PP.

97 Ibid., 25 August 1885. The pamphlet is included and is addressed to Henry Broadhurst, Secretary of the TUC Parliamentary Committee.

98 A case illustrative of O'Donoghue's lobbying skills occurred in 1885. The federal government introduced a bill to modify the Consolidated Insurance Act by forcing registration with the government and a $50,000 deposit. The terms of the new bill would have effectively killed the Knights of Labor Insurance Branch and most other Trade Union or Friendly Society schemes. O'Donoghue circulated a petition to all locals, seeking representations to Ottawa to oppose the bill. The TTLC condemned the proposed amendments and O'Donoghue, supported by the Toronto Knights, rushed to Ottawa to lobby. He was accompanied by his old friend, painter John Carter, who on this occasion represented the Sons of England. After meeting with as many MPs as he could, O'Donoghue attended the meeting of the House Committee on Banking and Commerce where he made a half-hour speech explaining the proposed legislation's effect on the Knights and other similar organizations. Tilley, the minister in charge of the bill, agreed to amend it to protect the Knights, explaining that the aim of the bill had never been to eliminate such operations but rather to protect the public against unscrupulous companies.

O'Donoghue, high on this success, assured Powderly that not only had they won a specific victory, but that 'the visit and the opportunity it afforded of laying before that class of people the aims and objects of our Order, will have given it a greater and more favourable publicity than it would otherwise have received in a long time to come.' O'Donoghue recognized that the 'Joint Stock or Line Insurance Companies' were responsible for trying to put their competition out of business, and that aim had led to this bill. Yet O'Donoghue seemed confident throughout that if rational explanations were made, then the government would reverse its position. The lesson he drew was that 'our phenomenal success in defeating the intent of these people in this case, aptly illustrates what may be done even under adverse circumstances when promptness, tact and intelligence are brought into operation conjointly and for a specific purpose.' See TTLC, *Minutes*, 20 February 1885, and O'Donoghue to Powderly, 17 February, 4 March, 24 May 1885, PP.

99 A copy of the cover letter sent with the petitions, dated 31 January 1885, is contained in the Powderly Papers.

100 See TTLC, *Minutes*, 2 January 1885, for the recommendation and 16 January 1885 for the appointment of the first committee.

101 For George visit see *Globe*, 5 August 1884, and *Palladium of Labor*, 5 August 1884. For impact in Toronto see *Globe*, 15 December 1884, for report of a mass meeting regarding tax exemptions.

102 See ch. 6, this vol.

103 See ch. 10, this vol.

104 TTLC, *Minutes*, 4 December 1885.

105 TTLC, *Minutes*, 14 December; *Globe*, 15 December 1885; *World*, 15 December 1885. For ITU blacklist see *Globe*, 8 December 1885.

106 TTLC, *Minutes*, 15 December 1885.

107 *World*, 22 December 1885.

108 *Globe*, 23 December 1885.

109 *Globe*, 24 December 1885.

110 *Globe*, 30 December 1885.

111 TTLC, *Minutes*, 29 December 1885.

112 *Globe*, 4 January 1886.

113 Ibid. See previous discussion in ch. 6, this vol.

114 O'Donoghue to Powderly, 7 January 1886, PP.

115 *Palladium of Labor*, 5 December 1885.

116 For details see chapter 6. See also *World*, 13, 16 March 1886.

117 Piper to Macdonald, 2 February 1886, Macdonald Papers.

118 Ibid., 3 February 1886.

119 O'Donoghue to Powderly, 23 March 1886, PP.

120 Ibid., 29 March 1886.
121 Ibid.
122 *World*, 12 April 1886.

CHAPTER 12

1 *News*, 9 January 1886.
2 Alfred Boultbee to Macdonald, 14 March 1886, Macdonald Papers.
3 Ibid., 19 March 1886.
4 Ibid.
5 O'Donoghue to Powderly, 7 January 1886, PP.
6 Ibid., 24 January 1886.
7 Ibid., 14 February 1886.
8 Ibid., 29 March 1886. For the report of the DA plan see *Globe*, 15 March 1886.
9 A.W. Wright to Macdonald, 9 June 1886, Macdonald Papers.
10 Ibid.
11 TLC, *Proceedings*, 1886, 12.
12 Ibid., 20–2.
13 Ibid., 40.
14 R.J. Kerrigan, in 'The History of the Trades and Labor Congress of Canada,' *One Big Union Bulletin*, 5 November–17 December 1925, argues strongly that the Knights leaders' failure to push this motion cost them dearly. Writing from a revolutionary syndicalist perspective, Kerrigan argued that 'there would have been none of the craft or trade forty years wandering in the Bourgeois wilderness, had not the boss and his henchmen spiked the natural growth of labour organization.' Specifically, he attacked Knights leaders for refusing to fight the Cigar Makers International Union to the finish in 1886. Claiming that the CMIU's blue label was 'more acceptable to the boss,' he regretted that the TLC had not smashed 'on the rocks' of a heatedly debated resolution about which label to recognize: 'Had it not been for the yellow Knights of Labor in the convention with their political axes to grind, there would have probably been no TLC for many years to come; and craft form of organization might have never taken root in Canada.'
15 For a discussion of the genesis, appointments, and ultimate findings of this commission see Greg Kealey (ed.), *Canada Investigates Industrialism* (Toronto 1973), ix–xxvii; F. Harvey, 'Une enquête ouvrière au XIXe siècle: la Commission du travail, 1886–1889,' *RHAF*, 30 (1976), 35–53; F. Harvey, *Revolution industrielle et travailleurs: une enquête sur les rapports entre le capital et la travail au Québec à la fin du 19e siècle* (Montreal 1978).
16 H.E. Clarke to Macdonald, 21 September 1886, Macdonald Papers.

17 Ibid.

18 *Canadian Labor Reformer*, 9 October 1886, and *Palladium of Labor*, 23 October 1886 (reprinted from *Labor Record*). See also H.E. Clarke to Macdonald, 19 October 1886, for Clarke's explanation of his error.

19 TTLC, *Minutes*, 18 December 1886; *Palladium of Labor*, 18 December 1886, reports actions of DA 125.

20 F.D. Barwick to Macdonald, 25 October 1885, Macdonald Papers.

21 A. Morris to Macdonald, 26 October 1886, Macdonald Papers.

22 For genesis of Clarke nomination see Clarke to Macdonald, 8 November 1886, and John Small to Macdonald, 11 November 1886, Macdonald Papers.

23 *World*, 17 November 1886.

24 E.F. Clarke to Macdonald, 29 November 1886, and H.E. Clarke to Macdonald, 1 December 1886, Macdonald Papers.

25 H.E. Clarke to Macdonald, 1 December 1886, Macdonald Papers.

26 *News*, 25 December 1886.

27 *Palladium of Labor* (Toronto), 9 January 1886.

28 TTLC, *Minutes*, 5 November 1886. O'Donoghue was prominent throughout the campaign because of his accusation: 'while he was a member of the Local House, Mr. Meredith, on behalf of Hon. Mr. Cameron, had offered him a portfolio if he would withdrew his support from the Government, whose overthrow was to be brought about by the defection of six other willing representatives' (*World*, 11 November 1886; *News*, 20 November 1886). Needless to say, Tory leader W.R. Meredith termed the whole story 'absolutely and entirely false' (*News*, 27 November 1886; *World*, 24 November 1886). The following day O'Donoghue swore an affidavit which repeated his story with some additional details (*News*, 25 November 1886; *World*, 25 November 1886). There the matter ended. It was an unlikely start to labour's independent campaign.

29 *Globe*, 13 November 1886; *News*, 13 November 1886; *World*, 13 November 1886.

30 Ibid.

31 The number varied in different reports. The *World* claimed 87 but the *News* list of delegates contained only 84 members – 57 Knights and 27 unionists.

32 *Globe*, 1 December 1886. It is possible that the nominations of former junta member Williams and 1882 candidate Carter were mainly honorific. For more detailed accounts see *News*, 1 December 1886, and *World*, 1 December 1886.

33 Ibid.

34 *Globe*, *Mail*, *World*, 7 December 1886; *News*, 6, 7 December 1886.

35 *Mail*, *News*, 7 December 1886.

36 Ibid., 9 December 1886.

37 *News*, 20 December 1886.

38 *Globe, Mail*, 20 December 1886.

39 See *Mail* throughout December 1886. See also Margaret Evans, 'Oliver Mowat,' ch. 5, 175–90.

40 *News*, 13 December 1886.

41 See various reports of meetings, but especially *Mail*, 7, 10 December 1886.

42 *World*, 17 December 1886.

43 *Globe, World*, 18 December 1886. TTLC, *Minutes*, 17 December 1886.

44 *Palladium of Labor* (Hamilton), 18 December 1886; *World*, 11 December 1886.

45 *Canadian Labor Reformer*, 11 December 1886.

46 For examples, see *World*, 14, 16 December 1886.

47 *News*, 14 December 1886.

48 *News*, 16 December 1886.

49 *World*, 3 December 1886.

50 For election results see Appendix IV. Calculations are difficult because of the peculiar electoral arrangements established by the Mowat gerrymander. The results in the text and in the appendix are a rough approximation of the actual percentage of voters. The possibility of plumping and splitting ballots makes precise formulations impossible.

51 *Mail*, 29 December 1886.

52 Ibid.

53 *News*, 29 December 1886.

54 *Canadian Labor Reformer*, 8 January 1887.

55 TTLC, *Minutes*, 2 and 21 January 1887.

56 *World*, 29 December 1886. On GTR strike see ch. 8, this vol.

57 Ibid.

58 *News*, 3 January 1887.

59 *World*, 4 January 1887.

60 For results see *Globe*, 4 January 1887. For the TTLC decision see *Minutes*, 18 December 1886. For a short description of the campaign see Desmond Morton, *Mayor Howland*, ch. V.

61 *Mail*, 4 January 1887.

62 Eugene O'Keefe to Macdonald, 9 February 1887, Macdonald Papers.

63 *The Daily Standard* was published in direct response to the defection of the *Mail* from party ranks. It was under the editorship of Louis Kribs, who had previously worked with E.E. Sheppard and Phillips Thompson at the *News*. Kribs thus knew the Toronto working-class world extremely well, and his paper reflected this. 'Pica,' Kribs' *News* pseudonym, had actively supported the independent labour candidates in the provincial election.

64 *Daily Standard*, 27 January 1887.

65 Ibid.
66 O'Donoghue to Powderly, 10 November 1886, PP.
67 Edward Blake, *Speeches in the Dominion Election Campaign of 1887* (Toronto 1887), 329–50.
68 Ibid., 351–75.
69 *World*, 2 February 1887, and *Mail*, 9 February 1887. A similar motion was passed in West Toronto, not endorsing Sheppard but agreeing not to oppose him. *World*, 3 February 1887.
70 *Canadian Labor Reformer*, 12 February 1887.
71 See Appendix IV for detailed results.
72 *Mail*, 23 February 1887.
73 Ibid. For J.S. Williams see *World*, 25 January 1887.
74 Ibid., 24 February 1887.
75 O'Donoghue to Powderly, 12 January 1887, PP.
76 Ibid., 7 April 1887.

CHAPTER 13

1 *Canadian Labor Reformer*, 26 February 1887.
2 Ibid., 6 March 1887.
3 Ibid.
4 Ibid., 19 March 1887. For that episode see *World*, 20 January 1887.
5 Ibid., 26 March, 2 April 1887.
6 O'Donoghue to Powderly, 7 April 1887, PP.
7 Ibid.
8 Ibid., 29 April 1887.
9 *Journal of United Labor*, 2 September 1887.
10 E. Cannon to Powederly, 12 September 1887, PP.
11 Ibid., 19 September 1887.
12 Ibid., 12 September 1887.
13 Knights of Labor, General Assembly, *Proceedings*, 1887, 1729–30.
14 O'Donoghue to Powderly, 3 October 1887, PP.
15 For LA 2305 see *Journal of United Labor*, 29 October 1887, and Knights of Labor, General Assembly, *Proceedings*, 1888, Document 102, 12. For LA 7025 see Knights, G.A. *Proceedings*, 1887, Document 367, 43.
16 Knights of Labor, General Assembly, *Proceedings*, 1887, p. 1587.
17 Ibid., p. 1819.
18 Ibid., pp. 1729–30, 1822.
19 O'Donoghue to Powderly, 9 November 1887, PP.
20 TTLC, *Minutes*, 14 June 1887.

21 Ibid., 17 June 1887.

22 Ibid., 15 July 1887.

23 Powderly to O'Donoghue, 23 November 1887, PP.

24 O'Donoghue to Powderly, 29 November 1887, PP.

25 Powderly to O'Donoghue, 9 December 1887, PP.

26 O'Donoghue to Powderly, 12 December 1887, PP.

27 John F. Redmond to Powderly, 19 January 1888, PP.

28 W.J. Shaw to Powderly, 24 January 1888, PP.

29 *Globe*, 31 January 1888.

30 Powderly to W.J. Shaw, 27 January 1888, PP.

31 George Collis to Powderly, 4 February 1888, PP.

32 Powderly to George Collis, 14 February 1888, PP.

33 George Collis to Powderly, 20 February 1888, PP.

34 W.J. Shaw to Powderly, 5 March 1888, PP.

35 Knights of Labor, *Report of the Canadian Legislative Committee*, Toronto, 1888, 3.

36 O'Donoghue to Powderly, 28 March 1888, PP.

37 TLC, *Proceedings*, 1887, 12.

38 Ibid., 1888, 10–12, 25.

39 TTLC, *Minutes*, 6 April 1888.

40 Knights, *Report of the Canadian Legislative Committee*, 1888, 4–6, 9–11.

41 Ibid., 3, 6–9, 12–16.

42 TTLC, *Minutes*, 2 December 1887.

43 *Globe*, 28 December 1887.

44 TTLC, *Minutes*, 2 December 1887.

45 Ibid., 20 January 1888.

46 For a more detailed description of this campaign see Morton, *Mayor Howland*, ch. VIII, and Armstrong and Nelles, *The Revenge of the Methodist Bicycle Company*, ch. II. For results see *Globe*, 3 January 1888.

47 For TTU presentation see *Globe*, 16 January 1888.

48 Wright to Powderly, 11 July 1888, and Powderly to Wright, 24 July 1888, PP. For the announcement see *Journal of United Labor*, 16 August 1888 and 20 September 1888.

49 O'Donoghue to Powderly, 9 August 1888, PP.

50 Ibid., 31 August 1888.

51 M. O'Halloran to Powderly, 20 October 1888, PP.

52 O'Donoghue to Powderly, 26 October 1888, PP.

53 Knights of Labor, General Assembly, *Proceedings*, 1888, 74–5.

54 O'Donoghue to Powderly, 28 November 1888, PP.

55 Ibid., 11 December 1888.

56 Ibid., 13 December 1888.

57 For DA 125's support of Jury see R.W. Glockling to Powderly, 14 December 1888, PP.

58 TLC, *Proceedings*, 1888, 10.

59 Ibid., 33.

60 Ibid., 1889, 8–9.

61 TTLC, *Minutes*, 1 March 1889.

62 'Report of the Canadian Legislative Committee' in Knights of Labor, General Assembly, *Proceedings*, 1889, 5–20.

63 For secondary accounts of this Act see Morton, *Mayor Howland*, ch. VII, and Michael Bliss, 'Another Anti-Trust Tradition: Canadian Anti-Combines Policy, 1889–1910,' *Business History Review*, 47 (1973). See also House of Commons, *Debates*, 1888, pp. 1544–5; 1889, pp. 1111–17, 1437–47, 1468, 1689–91; Senate, *Debates*, 1889, pp, 583, 621–2, 631–55.

64 'Report of the Canadian Legislative Committee,' 1889, 10.

65 *Globe*, 23 November 1889.

66 Ibid.

67 TTLC, *Minutes*, 1, 15 March 1889; *Mail*, 4 May 1889.

68 *Globe*, 26 April 1889.

69 *Globe*, 30 April 1889, and *Mail*, 30 April 1889.

70 *Globe*, 28 June 1889.

71 TLC, *Proceedings*, 1889, 24.

72 For Elliot see 'Report of the Legislative Committee,' 1889, and *Globe*, 23 November 1889; for Carey see *Globe*, 22 April 1889. For evidence that Elliot was involved in complicated Tory intrigues, see A.W. Wright to Macdonald, 18 April 1889, Macdonald Papers. In this letter Wright again proposes that the Tories take the *Canadian Labor Reformer* off his hands – for a suitable sum of course. 'This would require the raising of about twelve shares ($1,200). I propose that this should be raised among good reliable men and the stock subscribed in the name of some one or more whose connection with the labor movement is well known and who are in every way trustworthy. (I would suggest Mr. Elliott and Mr. A.B. Ingraham, [sic] M.P.P.) whose names would appear among the incorporators. Each subscriber of stock would of course understand that the paper would continue to be as it has been an honest exponent of the Labour movement and not in any sense a party organ. At the same time it would never be used for the purpose of injuring the Conservative party as its possible successor most assuredly would.'

73 *Mail*, 21 December 1889.

74 Powderly to Robert Glockling, 1 February 1889, PP.

75 Wright to Powderly, 29 January 1889, PP.

76 O'Donoghue to Powderly, 3 August 1889, PP.
77 Powderly to O'Donoghue, 18 September 1889, PP.
78 O'Donoghue to Powderly, 7 October 1889, PP.
79 Powderly to O'Donoghue, 31 October 1889, PP.
80 O'Donoghue to Powderly, 3 November 1889, PP.
81 Powderly to O'Donoghue, 18 December 1889, PP.
82 Powderly to James H. Gilmore, 7 November 1889, PP.
83 Powderly to Wright, 9 November 1889, PP.
84 O'Donoghue to Powderly, 12 December 1889, PP.
85 Powderly to R.R. Elliot, 9 March 1890, PP.
86 Ibid., 28 April 1890.
87 For Elliot's view see 'Report of the Canadian Legislative Committee' in Knights of Labor, *Proceedings*, 1890, 5–6. For TTLC and TLC views see House of Commons, *Debates*, 1890, pp. 4841–2.
88 O'Donoghue to Powderly, 1 April 1891, PP.
89 Powderly to O'Donoghue, 6 April 1891, and Powderly to William Glockling, 7 April 1891, PP.
90 For these episodes see TLC, *Proceedings*, 1890, and R.J. Kerrigan, 'History of the T.L.C.'
91 Thompson, *The Politics of Labor*, 100–1.
92 Ibid., 101.
93 Ibid., 102.
94 Ibid., 104.
95 Ibid., 109.
96 Ibid., 110–11.

CHAPTER 14

1 Another group quite worthy of study, which unfortunately cannot be pursued here, is the Toronto secularists who joined together in a series of organizations in the 1870s and 1880s. They were closely tied to the labour movement through individual members (such as Alfred Jury) and through political groups such as the WLCU. A number of WLCU leaders, including J. Ick Evans and J.I. Livingstone, were prominent freethinkers. The Tory government's insistence on seizing classics by such prominent atheists as Voltaire and Paine led to a very hostile response from the Toronto Secular Society. (On this episode see *Globe*, 10, 11, 13 October; 24 November 1881; James Patton to J. Johnson, 18 October 1881, Macdonald Papers; J. Ick Evans to Macdonald, undated, Macdonald Papers, pp, 144139–45.) In addition, the arrival in Toronto of Charles Watt, the most prominent of Charles Bradlaugh's English supporters,

strengthened free thought. Invited 'to a free thought pastorate' in Toronto in 1886, Watt took over the leadership of the movement, published an important journal, and maintained close ties with the labour movement through his membership in the Knights of Labor. He actually sat as a local representative at the TTLC for a short time. The best works on secularism and its relation to the working class are Warren Sylvester Smith, *The London Heretics* (London 1967) and Edward Royle, *Victorian Infidels* (Manchester 1975).

2 For an excellent description of 'the shadowy political underworld of the Irish in Canada in the 1870s and early 1880s' see D.C. Lyne and Peter M. Toner, 'Fenianism in Canada, 1874–1884,' *Studia Hibernica*, 12 (1972), 27–76.

3 *Globe*, 27 January, 12 February 1881.

4 *Globe*, 2, 8 March 1881.

5 *Globe*, 15, 18 March 1881.

6 *Globe*, 16 May 1881.

7 *Globe*, 30 May 1881.

8 *Globe*, 2, 22 June 1881. See also Henry George, Jr., *The Life of Henry George* (Toronto 1900), 351–2.

9 *Globe*, 5, 6 July 1881.

10 The series ran from 16 November 1881 to 4 January 1882. It is interesting to note that the *Globe* sent Thompson to Ireland at precisely the same time as Patrick Ford of the *Irish World* sent Henry George. The latter event was to have a broader impact, but the two labour reformers reacted to the Irish experience almost identically in 1881.

11 *Globe*, 29, 31 December 1881 and 4 January 1882.

12 George, *The Life of Henry George*, 358–400.

13 For McCormick see his letters in *Irish Canadian*, 8, 15 February, 19 July 22 November 1871, 26 June 1873. On his interest in labour see his letters in *Ontario Workman*, 1872.

14 John McCormick, *The Conditions of Labour and Modern Civilization* (Toronto 1880).

15 Phillips Thompson to Henry George, 23 October 1882, Henry George Papers.

16 Thomas N. Brown, *Irish-American Nationalism* (New York 1966), 117–30.

17 *Globe*, 29 September 1885.

18 Lyne and Toner, 'Fenianism in Canada,' 42–4 and passim.

19 On the George campaign see George, *The Life of ...*, 459–81; Brown, *Irish-American Nationalism*, 146–51; Thomas J. Condon, 'Politics, Reform and the New York City Election of 1886,' *New York Historical Society Quarterly* (1960), 363–93.

20 Eric Foner, 'Class, Ethnicity and Radicalism in the Gilded Age: The Land League and Irish-America,' *Marxist Perspectives*, 2 (1978), 6–55.

21 For the origins of the APS see George, *The Life of ...*, 482–503; Barker, *Henry George*, ch. XVI.

22 *Globe*, 17 May 1887.

23 *Globe*, 6 June 1887.

24 The history of free speech in Queen's Park is worthy of a chapter in itself. With the rise of popular dissent, the issue of speakers in the park became prominent. When only religion had been at issue, there had been little concern, but with the rise of secularism, and later of the single tax, it became an oft debated topic. See *Globe*, 8, 10, 15 July 1878, 2 May 1881, 12 May 1884, 17 May 1887, 30 July, 27 August, 10 September 1888, 1 April 1889, 8 August 1890. Finally in 1891, the city council passed a by-law suppressing free speech in the park, an attempt that led to a series of riots in 1891. See *Globe*, 20, 27, 28 July; 3, 10, 17, 31 August; 7, 14 September 1891. The attempt at narrowing the parameters of permissible debate in the society seems typical of this period which was also witnessing the demise of a vibrant, critical press in Toronto. For further evidence of this process note how easily the press could be bought – literally – for purposes of financial exploitation in the 1890s. This sorry episode is recorded in Armstrong and Nelles, *The Revenge of the Methodist Bicycle Company*, passim.

25 *Globe*, 5, 12 November, 10 December 1887. Lancefield's lecture was published as a pamphlet, *Why I Joined the New Crusade* (Toronto 1888). In it he condemned 'the intensity of competition on every hand [and] the insensate race for wealth' (p. 10). He noted that the poverty of London and New York was also present in Toronto – all caused by 'the private ownership of land' (p. 21).

26 *Globe*, 25, 28 January; 4 February 1888. TTLC, *Minutes*, 2 December 1887, 20 January, 3 February, 19 October 1888.

27 *Globe*, 16 February 1888.

28 *Globe*, 18 June 1888.

29 *Globe*, 3 September, 18 December 1888; *Standard*, 1 September 1888.

30 *Globe*, 5 November 1888; *Standard*, 17, 24 November 1888.

31 *Globe*, 28 December 1888.

32 *Globe*, 29 December 1888.

33 *Globe*, 1, 8 June 1889.

34 *Globe*, 8 August 1889.

35 *Globe*, 15 November 1889; *Standard*, 23 November 1889.

36 See *The Social Reformer*, 1, 16 November 1889, on 'Taxation and Exemption.'

37 For Thompson's European trip see his open letter to the STA in *Globe*, 8 January 1889, and his excellent series on the Scottish crofters' question which parallels his earlier investigation of the Irish land question in *Globe*, 27 October

1888 to 5 January 1889. See also his notebook (in Thompson Papers, PAO) in which he recorded speeches he heard.

38 *Globe*, 22 June 1889.

39 *Globe*, 19 October and 21 December 1889. For a review of the debate in New York, where things were far more heated, see Laurence Gronlund, *Socialism vs. Tax Reform* (New York 1887).

40 TLC, *Proceedings*, 1889, 7.

41 *Globe*, 18 July 1890. To trace the history of the nationalists in Toronto see the reports of their meetings in the *Labor Advocate* and in the *New Nation*, 1891–94.

42 For Bellamy see F.C. Jaher, 'Introduction' to the Greenwood Press reprints of *The Nationalist*, 1889–91 and *New Nation*, 1891–94. Also see the rather dated Arthur E. Morgan, *Edward Bellamy* (New York 1944), especially 245–384.

43 For examples see membership lists in *Globe*, 11 October 1890 and 10 December 1890.

44 TTLC, *Minutes*, 15 August, 3 October, 20 November 1890. The paper was also partially financed by its publisher, The Grip Publishing Co. *Grip* was a humour magazine edited and owned by J.W. Bengough.

45 The *Labor Advocate* was published from 5 December 1890 to 2 October 1891.

46 Thompson, *The Politics of Labor*, 168–73.

47 The following account of the street-railway struggle draws on four studies: John David Bell, 'The Social and Political Thought of the Labor Advocate' (unpublished MA thesis, Queen's University 1975); Dennis Carter-Edwards, 'Toronto in the 1890's: A Decade of Challenge and Response' (unpublished MA thesis, University of British Columbia 1973); Christopher Armstrong and H.V. Nelles, 'The Un-bluing of Toronto and the Revenge of the Methodist Bicycle Company: The Fight over Sunday Street Cars, 1891–1898,' unpublished paper; Armstrong and Nelles, *The Revenge of the Methodist Bicycle Company*.

48 TTLC, *Minutes*, 20 September 1889.

49 Ibid., 21 December 1889.

50 *Globe*, 31 December 1889.

51 For this background see Carter-Edwards, 'Toronto in the 1890's,' 116–30.

52 TTLC, *Minutes*, 17 May 1890.

53 Ibid., 5 July 1890; *Mail*, 7 July 1890.

54 *Mail*, 20 November 1890.

55 Ibid.

56 Ibid., 18 December 1890.

57 *Globe*, 10 December 1890; *Labor Advocate*, 12 December 1890.

58 *Labor Advocate*, 26 December 1890.

59 Ibid.

60 Ibid., 2 January 1891.

61 Ibid., 9 January 1891.

62 Carter-Edwards, 'Toronto in the 1890's,' 121.

63 TTLC, *Minutes*, 2 January 1891; *Labor Advocate*, 9 December 1891.

64 *Labor Advocate*, 30 January 1891.

65 Ibid., 13 March 1891.

66 Ibid., 20 March 1891.

67 Ibid., 8 May 1891; TTLC, *Minutes*, 1 May 1891.

68 *Labor Advocate* and TTLC, *Minutes*, 15 May 1891. See also *Mail*, 16 May 1891.

69 *Labor Advocate*, 22 May 1891.

70 Ibid., 29 May 1891; TTLC, *Minutes*, 5 June 1891.

71 *Labor Advocate*, 5 June 1891; *Globe*, 2 June 1891.

72 *Labor Advocate*, 12 June 1891.

73 Ibid., 25 June 1891; TTLC, *Minutes*, 3 July 1891; *Mail*, 4 July 1891.

74 *Labor Advocate*, 10 July 1891.

75 Ibid., 17 July 1891.

76 TTLC, *Minutes*, 17 July 1891; *Labor Advocate*, 17 and 24 July 1891; *Mail*, 18 July 1891.

77 *Labor Advocate*, 24 July 1891.

78 Ibid., 31 July 1891, and *Mail*, 21, 22 July 1891.

79 *Labor Advocate*, 7 August 1891.

80 TTLC, *Minutes*, 7 August 1891; *Mail*, 8 August 1891; *Labor Advocate*, 14 August 1891.

81 *Labor Advocate*, 21 August 1891; *Globe*, 15, 20 August 1891; *Mail*, 18, 19 August 1891.

82 *Labor Advocate*, 28 August 1891.

83 TTLC, *Minutes*, 21 August 1891; *Mail*, 22 August 1891; *Labor Advocate*, 28 August 1891; *Globe*, 25 August 1891.

84 Ibid.

85 *Labor Advocate*, 28 August 1891.

86 *Labor Advocate*, 28 August and 4 September 1891; *Globe*, 24, 25, 26, 29 August; 1 September 1891; *Mail*, 22, 24, 25, 29 August; 1 September 1891.

87 *Labor Advocate*, 4 September 1891.

88 Ibid.

89 Ibid.

90 *Mail*, 19 September 1891; TTLC, *Minutes*, 18 September 1891; *Labor Advocate*, 25 September 1891.

91 Ibid.

92 TTLC, *Minutes*, 6 December 1891.

93 Compilations from Middleton, *Municipality of Toronto*, Appendix A, p. 808.
94 See Carter-Edwards, 'Toronto in the 1890's,' 126–7; Armstrong and Nelles, 'The Un-bluing of Toronto'; Armstrong and Nelles, *The Revenge*, ch. 8.
95 See H.V. Nelles, *The Politics of Development: Forests, Mines and Hydro-Electric Power in Ontario, 1849–1941* (Toronto 1974), especially chs. 6, 7, and 12.
96 See Carter-Edwards, 'Toronto in the 1890's,' ch. 2; *The Social Reformer*, II, 4, 5, 6 (April–June 1892); A.C. Campbell, 'The Problem of Poverty and Riches' (Toronto 1892); 'Conference on Social Problems' (Toronto 1893); and 'Address to the Churches' (Toronto 1893). The last four items are broadsides. See also ongoing Toronto reports in Henry George's *The Standard* for 1892.
97 Richard Allen, *The Social Passion* (Toronto 1971). For a more recent account see Gene Howard Homel, 'James Simpson and the Origins of Canadian Social Democracy' (PH D thesis, University of Toronto 1978), especially chs. 1–2.
98 R.G. Hann, *Farmers Confront Industrialism* (Toronto 1975).

CHAPTER 15

1 See Craig Heron and Bryan Palmer, 'Through the Prism of the Strike: The Contours and Context of Industrial Conflict in Southern Ontario, 1901–1914,' *Canadian Historical Review*, 58 (1977), 423–58.
2 Montgomery, *Beyond Equality*, 143.
3 Ibid., 144–5.
4 Edward and Eleanor Marx Aveling, *The Working Class Movement in America* (London 1888), 19.
5 Uncle Thomas (S.T. Wood), 'The Regenerators,' *Canadian Magazine*, I (March 1893), 67.

Bibliography

A / MANUSCRIPT COLLECTIONS

Canada, Department of Labour, Ottawa. Vertical Files
Catholic University of America, Washington, DC, Hayes Papers; Powderly Papers
City of Toronto Archives. Toronto Assessment Rolls; Toronto City Council, Minutes
Hamilton Public Library. John Peebles, Recollections
McMaster University, Hamilton. J.S. Bengough Papers
Massey Archives, Toronto. Clipping Files; Massey Account Books
Metropolitan Toronto Central Library. Albert Hall Rental Book; Loyal Orange Lodge, No. 711, Toronto, Minutes, Membership and Degree Book, Proposition Book, and Roll Book; Loyal Orange Lodge, No. 173, Toronto, Minutes and Roll Book; Loyal Orange Lodge, No. 137, Toronto, Treasurer's Book and Roll Book
Public Archives of Canada, Ottawa. George Brown Papers; Isaac Buchanan Papers; H.E. Clarke Papers; Eugene Forsey Papers; W.C. Good Papers; Industrial Census, Manuscript (Toronto 1871); King Papers; Laurier Papers; John A. Macdonald Papers; John O'Donohoe Papers; James Rose Papers; Phillips Thompson Papers; Toronto Musicians' Association, Minute Book; Toronto Printing Pressmen and Assistants' Union, No. 10, Minutes; Toronto Trades Assembly, Minutes; Toronto Trades and Labor Council, Minutes; Toronto Typographical Union, Minutes; A.W. Wright Papers
Public Archives of Ontario, Toronto. Sir Alexander Campbell Papers; Aemilius Irving Papers; T.C. Patteson Papers; Phillips Thompson Papers; Toronto Coffee House Association Ltd. Papers
Trent University Archives, Peterborough. Peterborough Iron Moulders International Union, No. 191, Minutes
University of Toronto. James McArthur Connor Papers

B / NEWSPAPERS

American Workman (Boston)
The Bee Hive (Toronto)
British American Magazine (Toronto), 1863–64
Canadian Illustrated News (Hamilton), 1862–63
Canadian Labor Reformer (Toronto)
Canadian Merchants' Magazine and Commercial Review (Toronto), 1857–59
Canadian Monthly and National Review (Toronto)
The Carpenter (Indianapolis)
Cigar Makers Journal (Washington)
The Commonwealth (Toronto)
Coopers Journal (Cleveland)
Daily Standard (Toronto)
Fincher's Trades Review (Philadelphia)
Globe (Toronto)
Irish Canadian (Toronto)
Iron Molders Journal (Cincinnati)
Journal of the Board of Arts and Manufactures for Upper Canada (Toronto),
    1861–67
Journal of United Labor (Philadelphia)
Labor Advocate (Toronto)
The Labor Leaf (Detroit)
Labor Standard (New York)
Labor Union (Hamilton)
Leader (Toronto)
The Liberal (Toronto)
Machinists and Blacksmiths Journal (Cleveland)
Mackenzie's Weekly Messenger (Toronto), 1853–54
Mail (Toronto)
Monetary Times (Toronto), 1867–72
The National (Toronto)
Nationalist (Boston)
The New Nation (Boston)
News (Toronto)
Northern Journal (Montreal)
Ontario Workman (Toronto)
The Orange Sentinel (Toronto)
Palladium of Labor (Hamilton)
The People's Journal (Hamilton and Toronto)
Shoe and Leather Reporter: Annual, 1888

The Social Reformer (Toronto)
The Socialist (Chicago)
The Standard (New York)
The Sun (Toronto)
Telegram (Toronto)
Telegraph (Toronto)
Trade Union Advocate (Toronto)
The Triphammer (Toronto)
Typographical Journal (Indianapolis)
Workingman's Advocate (Chicago)
The Workingman's Journal (Hamilton)
World (Toronto)

C / PROCEEDINGS

Association for the Promotion of Canadian Industry. *Its Formation, By-Laws, etc.* (Toronto 1866)
Association for the Promotion of Canadian Industry. *Horace Greeley's Labour's Political Economy or the Tariff Question Considered, to which is added the Report of the Public Meeting of Delegates* (Toronto 1858)
Association for the Promotion of Canadian Industry. *Report of the Public Meeting of Delegates ... and Proceedings of the Association ...* (Toronto 1858)
British American League. *Minutes of the Proceedings of a Convention of Delegates* (Kingston 1849)
British American League. *Minutes of the Proceedings of a Convention of Delegates* (Toronto 1849)
Canadian Labour Union. *Proceedings, 1873–1877* (Ottawa 1951)
Central Council of Mechanical Engineers of North America. *Constitution and Rules of Order* (Milwaukee 1878)
Coopers International Union. *Coopers' Ritual* (Cleveland 1870)
Coopers International Union. *Proceedings*
Coopers International Union. Executive Board. *Price List* (Cleveland 1872)
Coopers International Union. Executive Board. *Names and Addresses of all Corresponding Secretaries of all the Unions* (Cleveland 1873)
Dominion Board of Trade. *Proceedings. 1871–79*
International Typographical Union. *Proceedings*
Iron Molders International Union. *Proceedings*
Knights of Labor. *Adlephon Kruptos*. n.p. n.d.
Knights of Labor. General Assembly. *Decisions of the General Master Workman* (Philadelphia 1890)
Knights of Labor. General Assembly. *Proceedings*

Knights of Labor. *Report of the First Annual Session of the Boot and Shoe Workers of the United States and Canada* (Boston 1887)

Knights of Labor. Pioneer Assembly, No 2211, Toronto. *By-Laws* (Toronto 1887)

Knights of Labor. Local Assembly, No 4069. *Statistics as Collected by Head-Light Assembly ... for its Exclusive Use* (St Thomas, Ontario 1885)

Knights of St Crispin. *Ritual of the Order of the Knights of St. Crispin* (Milwaukee 1870)

Knights of St Crispin. International Grand Lodge. *Proceedings*

Knights of St Crispin. London Lodge, No 242. *Constitution, By-Laws, and Rules of Order* (London, Ontario, 1872)

Loyal Orange Institution of British North America. *Charges to be Delivered ... and Services for the Burial of Orangemen, The Dedication of an Orange Lodge, and for the Installation of Officers* (Toronto 1856)

Loyal Orange Institution of British North America. *Charges to be Delivered at the Initiation of Members* (Toronto 1856)

Loyal Orange Institution of British North America. *Constitution and Laws* (Toronto 1855)

Loyal Orange Association of British North America. *Constitution and Laws of the Orange Mutual Benefit Society of Ontario West* (Toronto 188?)

Loyal Orange Institution of British North America. *Forms and Ritual of the Royal Scarlet Order* (Coburg 1846, 1864)

Loyal Orange Institution of British North America. *Forms to be Observed in Private Lodges* (Toronto 1855)

Loyal Orange Institution of British North America. *Ritual of the Blue Order* (Belleville, 1864)

Loyal Orange Institution of British North America. *Forms of the Royal Blue Order* (Toronto 1855, 1869)

Loyal Orange Institution of British North America. *Forms of the Purple Order* (Toronto 1855)

Loyal Orange Institution of British North America. *Forms of the Royal Arch Purple Mark* (Toronto 1855, 1869)

Loyal Orange Institution of British North America. *Laws, Rules and Regulations* (Coburg 1846, Belleville 1850)

Loyal Orange Institution of British North America. *Orange Ritual* (Belleville 1874)

Loyal Orange Institution of British North America. *Ritual of the Royal Scarlet Order* (Toronto, 1886)

Loyal Orange Institution of British North America. *Provincial Grand Lodge of Canada West*. Proceedings

Loyal Orange Lodge, No. 212, Schomberg. *By-Laws* (Toronto 1882)

Loyal Orange Lodge, No. 275, McKinley. *By-Laws* (Toronto 1874)

Loyal Orange Lodge, No. 328, Toronto. *By-Laws* (Toronto 1846, 1852, 1856, and 1872)

Loyal Orange Lodge, No. 375, York. *By-Laws*. (Toronto 1866, 1894)

Loyal Orange Lodge, No. 711, Enniskillen. *By-Laws* (Toronto 1898)

Machinists and Blacksmiths Union, No. 1 of Wisconsin. *By-Laws* (Milwaukee 1876)

Manufacturers' Association of Ontario. *Proceedings of Special Meeting ... 1875* (Toronto 1876)

Orange Young Britons. Grand Lodge. *Proceedings*

St. George's Society. *Reports* (Toronto 1859–)

St. Patrick's Benevolent Society. *Rules* (Toronto 1841)

Toronto Board of Trade. *Reports* (Toronto 1856, 1857, 1861, 1863, 1864, 1865, 1868, 1882, 1884, 1886, 1896, 1904)

Trades and Labor Congress. *Proceedings*

D / BOOKS AND PAMPHLETS BY CONTEMPORARIES

Adam, Graeme M. *Toronto Old and New*. Toronto 1891

Annuaire du Commerce et de l'Industrie de Québec pour 1873. Quebec 1873

Arch, Joseph. *The Story of His Life*. London 1898

Aveling, Edward, and Eleanor Marx. *The Working Class Movement in America*. London 1888

Bartlett, James Herbert. *The Manufacture, Consumption, and Production of Iron, Steel and Coal in the Dominion of Canada*. Montreal 1885

Bellamy, Edward. *Looking Backward*. New York 1960

Bishop, J. Leander. *A History of American Manufactures from 1608–1860*. 3 vols. Philadelphia 1868

Blake, Edward. *Speeches in the Dominion Election Campaign of 1882*. Toronto 1887

Bray, A.J. *Canada under the National Policy*. Montreal 1883

Buchanan, Isaac. *Britain the Country Versus Britain the Empire. Our Financial Distresses – Their Legislative Causes and Cure*. Hamilton 1860

– *The British American Federation, A Necessity. Its Industrial Policy also a Necessity*. Hamilton 1865

– *Le succès des manufactures canadienne est maintenant assuré. Lettre de W. Barber et Frère à Isaac Buchanan, MPP*. Quebec 1860

– *Letters Illustrative of the Present Position of Politics in Canada*. Hamilton 1859

– *A Permanent Patriotic Policy*. n.p. 1860

– *Relations of the Industry of Canada with the Mother Country and the United States*. Montreal 1864

Buchanan, Joseph R. *The Story of a Labor Agitator*. New York 1903

Burgess, Rev. William. *Land, Labor and Liquor: A Chapter in the Political Economy of the Present Day*. Toronto 1887

Business Sketches of Toronto, 1867. Toronto 1867

Campbell, A.C. *The Problem of Poverty and Riches*. Toronto 1892

Chamberlin, Edward Martin. *The Sovereigns of Industry*. Boston 1875

Clark, C.A. *Of Toronto the Good*. Montreal 1898

Clayden, Arthur. *The Revolt of the Field*. London 1874

Conference on Social Problems. Toronto 1894

Denison, Col. George T. *Recollections of a Police Magistrate*. Toronto 1920

– *The Struggle for Imperial Unity: Recollections and Experiences*. Toronto 1909

Dominion National League. *Country before Party*. Hamilton 1878

Douglass, W.A. *Antagonisms in the Social Forces*. Toronto 188[9]

Easton, George. *Travels in America with Special Reference to the Province of Ontario as a Home for Workingmen*. Glasgow 1871

Edwards, David. *Centennial Bitters, No. 3. An Account of the Imprisonment in Philadelphia of the Editor and Proprietor of 'The Beehive.'* Philadelphia 1876

Ely, Richard. *The Labor Movement in America*. New York 1886

Fleming, J.C. *Orangeism and the 12th of July Riots in Montreal*. Montreal 1877

Foran, Martin. *The Other Side: A Social Study Based on Fact*. Washington 1886

Galbraith, Thomas. *Bensalem or the New Economy: A Dialogue for the Industrial Classes on the Financial Question*. New York 1874

– *A New Chapter Added to Political Economy* ... Toronto 1882

– *New Monetary Theory*. Montreal 1863

Galt, Hon. A.T. *Canada 1849 to 1859*. Quebec 1860

George, Henry. *Progress and Poverty*. New York, n.d.

Gowan, Ogle Robert. *An Important Letter on Responsible Government*. Toronto 1839

Gronlund, Laurence. *The Co-operative Commonwealth*. Cambridge, Mass. 1965

– *Socialism vs. Tax Reform: An Answer to Henry George*. New York 1887

Hess, Joseph F. *Out of Darkness and into Light; or, The Story of My Life*. Toronto 1890

Hicks, Obadiah. *Life of Richard Trevellick*. New York 1971

Hilton, Rev. John. *An Address to the Orangemen of Canada*. Port Hope 1859

History of Toronto and the County of York. Toronto 1885

Hodgins, J. George. *The City of Toronto*. Toronto 1870

Hodgins, Thomas. *The Canadian Franchise Act*. Toronto 1886

– *Reports and Decisions of the Judges for the Trials of Election Petitions in Ontario*. Toronto 1883

Home Industries. Canada's National Policy. Protection to Native Products. Development of Field and Factory. Speeches by Leading Members of Parliament. Ottawa 1876

How to Have a Good Time in and about Toronto. Toronto 1885

Hulburt, J.B. *Protection and Free Trade.* Ottawa 1882

Industries of Canada: Historical and Commercial Sketches of Toronto and Environs. Toronto 1886

Jelley, S.M. *The Voice of Labor,* Philadelphia 1888

Johnson, David N. *Sketches of Old Lynn.* Lynn 1880

Johnson, William Wycliffe. *Sketches of the Late Depression.* Montreal 1882

Journeymen Printers of Toronto. *An Address to the Working Classes of Canada.* Toronto 1853

Joussaye, Marie. *Songs the Quinte Sang.* Belleville 1895

Keys, William. *Capital and Labour.* Montreal 1896

Knights of Labor. *Report of the Canadian Legislative Committee.* Toronto 1888

Knights of Labor, D.A. 47. *Twenty Year History of ...* Cleveland 1902

Knights of Labor, D.A. 125. *Report of A.W. Wright ... of the Philadelphia General Assembly.* Toronto 1893

Knights of Labor Illustrated, 'Adelphon Kruptos.' The Full Illustrated Ritual Including the 'Unwritten Work' and an Historical Sketch of the Order. Chicago 1886

[Labor Publishing Co.] *Labor: Its Rights and Wrongs.* Washington 1886

Lancefield, R.T. *Tim and Mrs. Tim: A Story for the 'Club' and 'Society' Men and the New Women.* Toronto 1897

– *Why I Joined the New Crusade: A Plea for the Placing of Taxes and Land Value Only.* Toronto 1888

Leavitt, Lydia. *Bohemian Society.* Toronto 1885

Lepine, A.T. *Explication de la déclaration de principes de l'ordre des chevaliers du travail.* Montreal 1887

Liberal Conservative Association of the City of Toronto. *Constitution.* Toronto 1893

Lindsey, Charles. *The Life and Times of William Lyon Mackenzie.* Toronto 1862

McBride, R. *The Canadian Orange Minstrel for 1860.* London, Ont. 1860

– *The Canadian Orange Minstrel for 1870: Written for the Purposes of Keeping in Remembrance the Dark Doings and Designs of Popery in this Country.* Toronto 1870

McCormick, John. *The Conditions of Labour and Modern Civilization.* Toronto 1880

Macdonald, Sir John A. *Speech to the Workingmen's Liberal Conservative Union of Ottawa and La Cercle Lafontaine.* Ottawa, 1886

Mackenzie, Alexander. *Address to the Toronto Workingmen on the 'National Policy.'* Toronto 1878

KcKeown, H.C. *The Life and Labours of the Most Reverend John Joseph Lynch, D.D.* Toronto 1886

Maclean, John. *The Complete Tariff Hand-Book.* Toronto 1880

– *Protection and Free Trade.* Montreal 1867

McNeill, George, ed. *The Labor Movement.* Boston 1887

McVicar, John. *Origins and Progress of the Typographical Union, 1850–1891.* Lansing, Mich. 1891

Marx, Karl. *Capital.* Vol. 1. London 1976

– *Capital.* 3 vols. Moscow 1967, 1971

Morris, Alexander. *Nova Britannia; or British North America, Its Extent and Future, A Lecture.* Montreal 1858

Mulvany, C. Pelham. *Toronto, Past and Present.* Toronto 1884

Patterson, W.J. *Statements relating to Trade, Navigation, and Mining for …* Montreal 1868, 1871, 1877, 1878

Pearson, William Henry. *Recollections and Records of Toronto of Old.* Toronto 1914

Pennington, Myles. *Railways and Other Ways.* Toronto 1894

Perry, Charles E. *Lectures on Orangeism.* Toronto 1892

Phipps, R.W. *Free Trade or Protection.* Toronto 1878

Powderly, Terence V. *Thirty Years of Labor, 1859–1889.* Columbus 1889

Powderly, T.V., and A.W. Wright, eds. *Labor Day Annual, 1893.* Philadelphia 1893

Referendum Committee. *The Initiative and Referendum: Needed Reforms in Representative Government.* Toronto 1891

Reysh, Tamen. *The Life of 'Doc' Sheppard.* Toronto 1881

Ross, Alexander Milton. *Memoirs of a Reformer, 1832–1892.* Toronto, 1893

– *Recollections and Experiences of an Abolitionist.* Toronto 1875

Scadding, H., and J. Dent. *Toronto: Past and Present.* Toronto 1884

The Secret Revealed; or the Origin and End of Orangeism. Montreal 1872

Shannon, William. *The Dominion Orange Harmonist.* Toronto 1876

– *Narrative of the Proceedings of the Loyal Orangemen of Kingston and Belleville on the 4th, 5th and 6th of September 1860 in Connection with the Visit of H.R.H. The Prince of Wales.* Belleville 1861

– *The United Empire Minstrel.* Toronto 1852

Small, H.B. *The Products and Manufactures of the New Dominion.* Ottawa 1868

Smith, W.H. *Canadian Gazeteer.* Toronto 1846

Sorge, Frederich A. *Labor Movement in the United States: A History of the American Working Class from Colonial Times to 1890.* Edited by Philip S. Foner and Brewster Chamberlin. Wesport, Conn. 1977

Sullivan, Robert Baldwin. *Lecture before the Mechanics Institute, on the 17th November, 1847*. Hamilton 1848

Taylor, C.C. *The Queen's Jubilee and Toronto Called Back from 1887 to 1847*. Toronto 1887

Thompson, Phillips. *The Future Government of Canada*. St Catharines 1864
- *The Labor Reform Songster*. Philadelphia 1892
- *The Politics of Labor*. New York 1887

Thompson, Samuel. *Reminiscences of a Canadian Pioneer for the Last Fifty Years*. Toronto 1884

Timperlake, J. *Illustrated Toronto: Past and Present*. Toronto 1877

Titus, F.E. *The Initiative and Referendum*. Toronto 1891

Toronto in the Camera: A Series of Photographic Views. Toronto 1868

Toronto Street Railway Company. *Rules and Regulations for Drivers and Conductors*. Toronto 1880

Toronto Trades and Labor Council. *Labor Day Souvenir, 1898*. Toronto 1898

Toronto Trades and Labor Council. *Labor Day Souvenir, 1900*. Toronto 1900

Uncle Thomas [S.T. Wood]. 'The Regenerators.' *Canadian Magazine*, 1 1893), 64–7

Union Label League of Toronto. *Labor Day Souvenir, 1896*. Toronto 1896

Waters, Robert. *Career and Conversations of John Swinton*. Chicago 1902

Wingfield, Alexander H. *Poems and Songs*. Hamilton 1873

A Working Man. *Reminiscences of a Stonemason*. London 1908

Young, John. *Letters First Published in the 'Northern Journal' during 1871*. Montreal 1872

E / UNPUBLISHED THESES AND OTHER MANUSCRIPTS

Acheson, Thomas William. 'The Social Origins of Canadian Industrialism: A Study in the Structure of Entrepreneurship.' PH D thesis, University of Toronto 1971

Appleton, Paul C. 'The Sunshine and the Shade: Labour Activism in Central Canada, 1850–1860.' MA thesis, University of Calgary 1974

Armstrong, Christopher, and H.V. Nelles. 'The Un-bluing of Toronto and the Revenge of the Methodist Bicycle Company: The Fight over Sunday Street Cars, 1891–1898.' York University 1973

Armstrong, F.H. 'Toronto in Transition: The Emergence of a City, 1828–1838.' PH D thesis, University of Toronto 1965

Atherton, James J. 'The Department of Labour and Industrial Relations, 1900–1911.' MA thesis, Carleton University 1972

Atkinson, William David. 'Organized Labour and the Laurier Administration: The Fortunes of a Pressure Group.' MA thesis, Carleton University 1958

Ayer, Shirley Ann. 'The Locomotive Engineers' Strike on the Grand Trunk Railway in 1876–1877.' MA thesis, McGill University 1961

Baldwin, Douglas. 'Political and Social Behaviour in Ontario, 1879–1891. A Quantitative Approach.' PH D thesis, York University 1973

Baskerville, Peter. 'Professional vs. Proprietor: Power Distribution in the Railway World of Upper Canada/Ontario, 1850–1881.' Unpublished paper, Canadian Historical Association 1978

Battye, John. 'The "Nine Hour Pioneers": Genesis of the Canadian Labour Movement.' Unpublished paper, Canadian Historical Association 1978

Bell, John David. 'The Social and Political Thought of the *Labor Advocate*.' MA thesis, Queen's University 1975

Berland, Oscar. 'Essay on Content and Significance of the Papers of Terence Vincent Powderly.' Washington 1970

Bleasdale, Ruth. 'Class Conflict on the Canals of Upper Canada in the 1840s.' Unpublished paper, Canadian Historical Association 1978

Bliss, J.W.M. 'A Living Profit: Studies in the Social History of Canadian Business, 1867–1911.' PH D thesis, University of Toronto 1969

Cahan, Jacqueline F. 'Survey of the Political Activities of the Ontario Labour Movement, 1850–1935.' MA thesis, University of Toronto 1945

Carter-Edwards, Dennis. 'Toronto in the 1890s: A Decade of Challenge and Response.' MA thesis, University of British Columbia 1973

Chan, Victor O. 'The Canadian Knights of Labor, with Special Reference to the 1880s.' MA thesis, McGill University 1949

Common, Sarah. 'A History of Business Conditions in Canada, 1870–1890.' MA thesis, Queen's University 1930

Cuneo, Carl. 'First Wave of Montreal Annexationists.' Unpublished paper, McMaster University 1978

– 'The Montreal Annexation Executive.' Unpublished paper, McMaster University 1978

Dawley, Alan. 'The Artisan Response to the Factory System: Lynn, Massachusetts.' PH D thesis, Harvard University 1971

Dyster, Barry. 'Toronto 1840–1860: Making It in a British Protestant Town.' PH D thesis, University of Toronto 1970

Evans, A. Margaret. 'Oliver Mowat and Ontario 1872–1896: A Study in Political Success.' PH D thesis, University of Toronto 1967

Faler, Paul. 'Workingmen, Mechanics and Social Change: Lynn, Massachusetts, 1800–1860.' PH D thesis, University of Wisconsin 1971

Falzone, Vincent Joseph. 'Terence V. Powderly: Mayor and Labor Leader, 1849–1893.' PH D thesis, University of Maryland 1970

Fink, Leon. 'The Knights of Labor and the Transformation of American Political

Culture: The Invigoration of Two-Party Politics.' Unpublished paper, Canadian Historical Association 1978
- 'Workingmen's Democracy: The Knights of Labor in Local Politics, 1886–1896.' PH D thesis, University of Rochester 1977
Forsey, Eugene A. 'The Knights of Labor.' Ottawa 1975
Frank, David. 'Life and Work in Toronto, 1900–1914.' University of Toronto 1972
- 'Trouble in Toronto: The Street Railway Lockout and Strike, 1886.' University of Toronto 1972
Galvin, Martin. 'Catholic-Protestant Relations in Ontario, 1864–1875.' MA thesis, University of Toronto 1962
Garlock, Jonathan. 'A Structural Analysis of the Knights of Labor.' PH D thesis, University of Rochester 1974
Gerrard, D.W. 'The Development of Labour Politics in Ontario between 1880–1923.' Hamilton 1973
Gutman, H.G. 'The Labor Policies of the Large Corporation in the Gilded Age: The Case of the Standard Oil Company.' Stanford University 1966
Hall, John. 'The Gentle Craft: A Narrative of Yankee Shoemakers,' PH D thesis, Columbia University 1953
Homel, Gene Howard. 'James Simpson and the Origins of Canadian Social Democracy.' PH D thesis, University of Toronto 1978
Houston, Cecil, and William J. Smyth. 'Ontario's Orange Landscape.' University of Toronto
- 'The Orange Order and the Expansion of the Frontier in Canada.' University of Toronto 1977
- 'Toronto, the Belfast of Canada.' University of Toronto 1977
Ingram, J. Clarence. 'The Financial Depression of 1873 and Its Effects on Canadian Industry.' MA thesis, Queen's University 1929
Jackson, Andrew. 'Divided Dominion: Class and the Structure of Canadian Federalism from the National Policy to the Great Depression.' University of British Columbia 1978
James, Edward T. 'American Labor and Political Action 1865–1896: The Knights of Labor and Its Predecessors.' PH D thesis, Harvard University 1954
Jones, E.H., and Douglas McCalla. 'Toronto Waterworks, 1840–77: Continuity and Change in Nineteenth Century Toronto Politics.' Trent University 1977
Kleiner, George. 'Capital Accumulation in Canada since Confederation.' MA thesis, McGill University 1937
Langdon, Stephen. 'The Political Economy of Capitalist Transformation, Central Canada from the 1840s to the 1870s.' MA thesis, Carleton University 1972
Levine, Susan. '"The Best Men in the Order," Women in the Knights of Labor.' Canadian Historical Association 1978

Livermore, John Daniel. 'Toward a Union of Hearts: The Early Career of Edward Blake, 1867–1880.' PH D thesis, Queen's University 1975

Lyne, Daniel Calhoun. 'The Irish in the Province of Canada in the Decade Leading to Confederation.' PH D thesis, McGill University 1960

McCalla, Douglas. 'The Buchanan Businesses, 1834–1872: A Study in the Organization and Development of Canadian Trade.' PH D thesis, Oxford University 1972

McGee, Robert F. 'The Toronto Irish Catholic Press and Fenianism, 1863–1866.' MA thesis, University of Ottawa 1969

Martin, William Arnold. 'A Study of Legislation Designed to Foster Industrial Peace in the Common Law Jurisdiction of Canada.' PH D thesis, University of Toronto 1954

Montgomery, David. 'Trade Union Practice and the Origins of Syndicalist Theory in the United States.' Pittsburgh 1970

Mood, W.J.S. 'The Orange Order in Canadian Politics, 1841–1867.' MA thesis, University of Toronto 1950

Morris, James Matthew. 'The Road to Trade Unionism: Organized Labor in Cincinnati to 1893.' PH D thesis, University of Cincinnati 1969

Neidhardt, W.S. 'The Fenian Brotherhood and Southwestern Ontario.' MA thesis, University of Western Ontario 1967

Palmer, Bryan. 'Most Uncommon Common Men: Craft, Culture and Conflict in a Canadian Community, 1860–1914.' PH D thesis, State University of New York at Binghamton 1977

Palmer, Bryan, and Peter Warrian. 'The Great Debate: The Origins of Early Canadian Working Class Thought.' Toronto 1976

Panitch, Leo. 'The Role and Nature of the Canadian State.' Carleton University 1976

Parks, Judith L. 'The Reverend Henry Scadding 1813–1901. An English Victorian in Canada.' MA thesis, University of Guelph 1969

Penner, Norman. 'The Socialist Idea in Canadian Political Thought.' PH D thesis, University of Toronto 1976

Pentland, H.C. 'Labour and the Development of Industrial Capitalism in Canada.' PH D thesis, University of Toronto 1960

Piva, Michael. 'The Decline of the Trade Union Movement in Toronto, 1900–1915.' Canadian Historical Association paper 1975

Pomfret, Richard, 'Capital Formation in Canada, 1870–1900.' Concordia University 1977

Rice, James Richard. 'A History of Organized Labour in St. John, New Brunswick.' MA thesis, University of New Brunswick 1968

Richardson, W.A. 'The Nine Hour Movement in Canada: The 1872 Printers' Strike in Toronto.' University of Toronto 1974

Roberts, Wayne. 'Toronto Metal Workers and the Second Industrial Revolution, 1896–1914.' University of Toronto 1977

Ross, Marc. 'John Swinton, Journalist and Reformer: The Active Years, 1857–1887.' PH D thesis, New York University 1969

Rotenberg, Lori. 'An Analysis of the Ideological Content of the *Ontario Workman*.' University of Toronto 1974

Smart, John. 'Archivists, Nationalists and New Leftists – Themes, Sources and Problems in English Canadian Labour History since 1965.' Ottawa 1977

Spencer, Stephen. 'Municipal Triumvirate: Politics, Services, and Economy in Late Nineteenth Century Toronto.' University of Western Ontario 1973

Storey, Robert. 'Industrialization in Canada: The Emergence of the Hamilton Working Class, 1850–1870s.' MA thesis, Dalhousie University 1975

Thomson, Ross. 'The Origin of Modern Industry in the United States: The Mechanization of Shoe and Sewing Machine Production.' PH D thesis, Yale University 1976

Watt, F.W. 'Radicalism in English Canadian Literature since Confederation.' PH D thesis, University of Toronto 1957

White, Graham. 'Social Change and Political Stability in Ontario: Electoral Forces, 1867–1977,' PH D thesis, McMaster University 1979

Williams, C.B. 'Canadian-American Trade Union Relations: A Case Study of the Development of Bi-national Unionism.' PH D thesis, Cornell University 1964

Williams, Glen. 'The National Policy and Import Substitution Industrialization.' Paper presented at CPSA meetings 1978

Zerker, Sally Friedberg. 'A History of the Toronto Typographical Union.' PH D thesis, University of Toronto 1972

Index